The Kennedy Assassination
and the
American Public

Social Communication in Crisis

The Kennedy Assassination
and the
American Public

Social Communication in Crisis

Bradley S. Greenberg

Edwin B. Parker

Editors

1965
Stanford University Press
Stanford, California

Stanford University Press
Stanford, California
© 1965 by the Board of Trustees of the
Leland Stanford Junior University
Printed in the United States of America
L.C. 65-15755

Preface

With the words "All I have I would have given gladly not to be standing here today," Lyndon Johnson began his first speech as President to a joint session of Congress on November 27, 1963. In this spirit we and the contributors wish this book might never have been possible.

Given that history does not rescind itself but remains to be recorded, these pages record. They were written principally by social scientists from across the country, who felt the same sorrow and grief at the tragedy that everyone felt. But their second response was, as scientists, to come to know and understand how their fellowmen reacted to such a tragedy. Some have said that to conduct such research was irreverent, that those who conducted it could not have felt the anguish felt by more sensitive men. This is simply not true. Many of the researchers whose work appears in these pages told us that it was impossible for them to be emotionally detached from their research and its social context. Rather, their anguish was continued by the repeated contact with their data. They kept at it only because they believed that science must deal with tragic incidents as well as less distressing ones. Similarly, the mass media professionals who contributed to this volume were under considerable emotional stress both during their long, busy hours that weekend and as they recalled the events later. Instead of dwelling on their emotional reactions, they have provided factual accounts of how the news was reported.

Here, then, is a compilation of responses. The introduction summarizes how the mass media reported the news, and how people generally learned and responded to that news. The papers in Part I describe the tasks of the mass media as perceived by those responsible for performing them as well as by scholars and researchers. The papers in Part II describe how the public received the news and how they subsequently used mass media and interpersonal communication channels. Part III, dealing with the wide range of public reactions, has three sections. The first contains general surveys of public response, the second surveys of children's and students' responses, and the third studies of changes in response over time. Part IV is concerned with political behavior and political beliefs in response to the assassination. A final chapter summarizes the social research findings.

The contributors—sociologists, psychologists, social psychologists, political scientists, communication researchers, and mass media professionals—worked closely and at length with us in preparing original manuscripts and often in extensive editing toward a more integrated set of papers. For all their efforts we are most grateful. We did not attempt to exhaust the extant research. Rather, we attempted to portray comprehensively the responses of the mass media and the American public, selecting the best research available and commissioning descriptive papers in a few areas where little or no research had been done.

The genesis of this volume warrants a brief description. From a meeting in Washington on November 24, 1963, described in the Sheatsley and Feldman article, stemmed the national survey of the public's response, as well as several local surveys. One participant at that meeting, Robert Bower, director of the Bureau of Social Research, Inc., Washington, D.C., began to assemble a list of social scientists who had done research on the assassination. This list was the seed from which this volume grew. Correspondence with those on the list, and with many others who became part of a larger list, revealed a desire that the research be assembled in a single volume. Such a volume promised to be more meaningful than the normal isolated publication of results in a dozen or more professional journals.

Financial support came principally from the Institute for Communication Research at Stanford University and from the Department of Communication at Michigan State University. The Stanford Institute's director, Wilbur Schramm, consistently encouraged this work and made available the resources required for its completion. When one of us changed institutions midway through the preparation of the book, the facilities of the Department of Communication at Michigan State University were graciously and liberally added to our resources. Recompense has not been a motive of the dozens of persons who have either directly or peripherally helped prepare this volume. All royalty payments normally provided for authors and editors are being paid by the publisher directly to the Kennedy Memorial Library in the names of those who contributed manuscripts for this volume. In a similar spirit, the one previously published article in this volume was made available by the *Public Opinion Quarterly* without its usual fee.

Many others deserve thanks for their contributions to this volume, including Gracie Barron, Brenda Cook, Linda Miller, Shirley Sherman, and Cynthia Stabb, who supervised the necessary secretarial chores. Thanks are due to Clifford Weigle for his helpful critical reading of part of the manuscript. We also wish to thank several persons who contributed manuscripts for this volume, but whose papers could not be printed. Space limitations made it necessary for us to choose from a large number of manuscripts. Some excellent manuscripts were omitted because they had already been published, some because they would have duplicated ideas or material in other manuscripts, some because deadline pressures did not allow time for revision to fit the volume's planned editorial organization, and some doubtless because of our fallible judgment about what would provide a coherent collection of papers. In recognition of their contributions, the following names will be included in the list of those contributing royalty payments to the Kennedy Memorial Library: R. Bruce W. Anderson, Thomas J. Banta, Samuel G. Blackman, Waldo W. Burchard, Ronald Glassman, Oliver E. Graebner, Lawrence Laurent, Harold Mendelsohn, Harry E. Moore, Alice E. Moriarty, Lois B. Murphy, Karl J. Nestvold, Marie Smith, Arthur R. Stevens.

These comments are being written on Sunday morning, November 22, 1964. Today's drum roll will be heard at a football game on television. Today's riderless horse will be a team mascot. Yet the incredible tragedy is as vivid and real as on the Friday morning a year ago. There is the awe, the anger, the sorrow, the whole emotional drain all over again. This book is dedicated to the thought with which President Johnson followed the quotation that begins this preface:

"Today John Fitzgerald Kennedy lives on in the immortal words that he left behind. He lives on in the minds and memories of mankind. He lives on in the hearts of his countrymen."

B. S. G.

E. B. P.

November 22, 1964

Contents

Contributors

LEE F. ANDERSON (Audience Perceptions of Radio and Television Objectivity) is Assistant Professor of Political Science, Northwestern University.

JAMES D. BARBER (Peer-Group Discussion and Recovery from the Kennedy Assassination) is Assistant Professor of Political Science at Yale University.

CHARLES M. BONJEAN (Reactions to the Assassination in Dallas) is Assistant Professor of Sociology at the University of Texas.

NORMAN M. BRADBURN (Public Apathy and Public Grief) is Assistant Professor of Behavioral Sciences, Graduate School of Business, and a Senior Study Director at the National Opinion Research Center, University of Chicago.

JAMES S. COLEMAN (Changes in Belief in the Weeks Following the Assassination) is Professor in the Department of Social Relations at the Johns Hopkins University.

J. DAVID COLFAX (The Fate of Due Process in a Time of Crisis) is Assistant Professor in the Department of Sociology and Anthropology at the University of Connecticut.

JACOB J. FELDMAN (A National Survey of Public Reactions and Behavior *and* Public Apathy and Public Grief), Director of Research for the National Opinion Research Center, University of Chicago, at the time the articles were written, is now Senior Research Associate, Department of Biostatistics, School of Public Health, Harvard University.

NORMA FESHBACH (Personality and Political Values: A Study of Reactions to Two Accused Assassins) is Mrs. Seymour Feshbach, and Assistant Professor in the School of Education at the University of California, Los Angeles.

SEYMOUR FESHBACH (Personality and Political Values: A Study of Reactions to Two Accused Assassins) is Professor of Psychology at the University of California, Los Angeles.

S. THOMAS FRIEDMAN (Attitudinal Strategies in American Undergraduates' Interpretations of the Assassination) is Assistant Professor in the Department of Educational Psychology at the University of Texas.

BRADLEY S. GREENBERG (Diffusion of News About the Kennedy Assassination, Newspaper Content on the Assassination Weekend, _and_ Social Research on the Assassination), co-editor of this volume, is Assistant Professor of Communication, Michigan State University.

FRED I. GREENSTEIN (College Students' Reactions) is Associate Professor in the Department of Government, Wesleyan University.

RICHARD J. HILL (Reactions to the Assassination in Dallas) is Professor of Sociology at Purdue University.

SIDNEY HOLLANDER, JR. (Changes in Belief in the Weeks Following the Assassination) is President of Hollander Associates, Baltimore.

CHRISTOPHER J. HURN (Grief and Rededication) is a Research Associate in the Center for Metropolitan Studies at Northwestern University.

GERALD D. HURSH (Television's Functions on the Assassination Weekend) is Director of Social Issues Research, Inc., Minneapolis.

LEWIS LIPSITZ (The Fate of Due Process in a Time of Crisis) is Assistant Professor of Political Science at the University of North Carolina.

RUTH LEEDS LOVE (The Business of Television and the Black Weekend) is Research Associate at the Bureau of Applied Social Research, Columbia University.

ELMER W. LOWER (A Television Network Gathers the News) is President of News, Special Events, and Public Affairs for the American Broadcasting Company.

HARRY W. MARTIN (Reactions to the Assassination in Dallas) is Assistant Professor of Sociology at Southwestern Medical School in Dallas.

MARK MESSER (Grief and Rededication) is a Research Associate in the Center for Metropolitan Studies at Northwestern University.

MONROE MILLER (Immediate and Subsequent Reactions in Manhattan) is Instructor in Psychology at Southern Connecticut State College, New Haven.

WILLIAM A. MINDAK (Television's Functions on the Assassination Weekend) is Associate Professor of Journalism, University of Minnesota.

EMERSON MORAN (Audience Perceptions of Radio and Television Objectivity) is a journalism student at Northwestern University.

EDWIN B. PARKER (Newspaper Content on the Assassination Weekend *and* Social Research on the Assassination), co-editor of this volume, is Associate Professor of Communication at Stanford University.

TOM PETTIT (The Television Story in Dallas) is a staff news reporter for the National Broadcasting Company.

JOHN PIERCE-JONES (Attitudinal Strategies in American Undergraduates' Interpretations of the Assassination) is Professor of Educational Psychology at the University of Texas.

WILLIAM L. RIVERS (The Press and the Assassination) is Associate Professor of Communication at Stanford University.

HARRISON E. SALISBURY (The Editor's View in New York) is Assistant Managing Editor of the *New York Times*.

WILBUR SCHRAMM (Communication in Crisis) is Janet M. Peck Professor of International Communication and Director of the Institute for Communication Research at Stanford University.

DAVID O. SEARS (Effects of the Assassination on Political Partisanship) is Assistant Professor of Psychology at the University of California, Los Angeles.

PAUL B. SHEATSLEY (A National Survey of Public Reactions and Behavior) is Director of the Survey Research Service of the National Opinion Research Center, University of Chicago.

ROBERTA S. SIGEL (Television and the Reactions of Schoolchildren to the Assassination) is Associate Professor of Political Science at Wayne State University.

NANCY S. SPITZER (Diffusion of News of the Kennedy and Oswald Deaths) is the wife of Stephan P. Spitzer.

STEPHAN P. SPITZER (Diffusion of News of the Kennedy and Oswald Deaths) is Assistant Professor of Sociology at the State University of Iowa.

SIDNEY VERBA (The Kennedy Assassination and the Nature of Political Commitment) is Professor of Political Science at Stanford University.

TOM WICKER (That Day in Dallas) is chief of the Washington Bureau of the *New York Times*.

ROGER ZIMMERMAN (Immediate and Subsequent Reactions in Manhattan) is a graduate student at the New School for Social Research, New York.

The Kennedy Assassination
and the
American Public

Social Communication in Crisis

Wilbur Schramm

Communication in Crisis

The title of this paper may be misleading, because it appears to reify communication. Communication, of course, has no life of its own. It is something people do. It is a—perhaps *the*—fundamental process of society. The chief reason for studying it is to find out more about people and their societies. This book, therefore, is primarily about *people*, rather than communication, in crisis.

Yet because communication is one of the most common behaviors of man, and because in a crisis those who are responsible for information are deeply and powerfully involved, it is often possible in a time of crisis to see the social institutions and uses of communication in sharp outline and clear perspective. This is how one studies communication, not as a thing in itself, but rather as a window on man and society, which in turn throws light on the acts and organizations of communicating.

The articles in this book, then, are about the reaction of the American people to the critical and shocking events beginning with the assassination of President John F. Kennedy, and, in particular, how the flow of information through society helped shape that reaction.

The crisis

The uniqueness of the happenings of November 22, 1963, and the days following has been often remarked. Yet it remains to say just what makes them unique. It was, of course, not the first assassination of an American President. Many people still alive remember the shock of McKinley's assassination in 1901, and a few must recall Garfield's twenty years earlier. A very few may still remember Lincoln's in 1865. Nor was the reaction to Mr. Kennedy's murder the first national outpouring of sorrow over the death of a chief executive within memory of a large proportion of Americans. The memory of Franklin D. Roosevelt's death, in 1945, is still fresh in the minds of most Americans over 25, and, as newspaper accounts and the few available studies show, many of the reactions at that time were much like those of November 1963.[1]

The unique quality of the events we are talking about arose from their surrounding circumstances. For one thing, the man struck down was an extraordinarily young and vital President, who, together with his beautiful wife and attractive children, had become well known in an unusually personal and intimate way through the mass media. Franklin Roosevelt had been struck down in the fullness of years and accomplishment. His loss, to a greater degree than John Kennedy's, must have been that of a father surrogate. Kennedy must have seemed less a father figure than a leader figure, and his loss focused attention, unconfused by the venerability of age or the psychological complications of father imagery, on what a *leader* means to Americans.

In the course of a nationwide survey during the week following the assassination, over 1,300 respondents were asked what other experiences they were reminded of by their feelings when they heard the news about President Kennedy. The majority said they "could not recall any other times in their lives" when they had the same sort of feelings. Of those who could think of similar feelings, most mentioned the death of someone near and dear to them, about 8 per cent mentioned Pearl Harbor, and about one-fourth named the death of Franklin Roosevelt (Sheatsley and Feldman, p. 154).

The events in Dallas clearly had some of the impact of both Pearl Harbor and the death of Roosevelt, and yet the fact that so few people mentioned the resemblance shows that there were basic differences. Like Pearl Harbor, Dallas came suddenly, shockingly, unexpectedly; and it too bore a threat to national security and a blow to national pride, although less than Pearl Harbor. But Dallas was personified and focused on an individual in a way that Pearl Harbor was not. It was something we had done to ourselves rather than something done to us by a foreign enemy, and the disturbed ex-Marine and the impulsive nightclub owner

---

[1] H. Orlansky, "Reactions to the Death of President Roosevelt," *Journal of Social Psychology* (1947), *26*, 236–66; D. E. Johannsen, "Reactions to the Death of President Roosevelt," *Journal of Abnormal and Social Psychology* (1946), *41*, 218–22.

offered no such broad target for hatred as the foreign aggressor who dropped bombs on Hawaii. There were no immediate channels for working off one's grief and anger on November 22. After Pearl Harbor one could seek one's place, civilian or military, in the war effort; there was much to be done, and in general everyone knew what it was. But after November 22—well, one could think it over by oneself, or say a prayer, or try to talk out one's feelings, or watch television. This is doubtless a reason for the rather compulsive attention to television: not only was it therapeutic, it also provided something to do when no one knew just what to do.

News of the death of President Roosevelt, like news of the death of President Kennedy, caused deep grief, mass anxiety, and widespread rumors. In 1945 it was widely reported that Fiorello LaGuardia and Jack Benny had also died; in 1963 it was reported widely that Lyndon Johnson had suffered another heart attack and that John McCormack had been slain.[2] But the death of Roosevelt had not been as completely unexpected as that of Kennedy. FDR's loss of weight, his weariness and grayness, had not been entirely hidden from the public. John Kennedy, on the other hand, was the epitome of youth, health, and vigor. When people talked about his future, they were more likely to wonder what he would do when he retired from the presidency in his early fifties than to wonder whether he would survive that long. John Kennedy was a life and immortality symbol; the destruction of that symbol by violence was all the more shocking. Violence was missing from the story of Roosevelt's demise; as it must to all men, death came to him. But John Kennedy was jerked away from health, from a young family, from leadership, by a senseless act of violence.

It is of considerable importance that these events should have occurred in the full bloom of the Age of Television. President Kennedy's loss was the first loss of a national leader reported in any such detail on the picture tubes of a nation. President Harding's death, in 1923, came at the very beginning of the Age of Radio; both information and transportation were so slow that the impact was diffused. Roosevelt's death came when radio was well developed, but amidst the great distractions of war news and national preoccupation with wartime duties and casualty lists. The Kennedy story, however, was carried into more than 90 per cent of American homes by television so quickly that over

[2] *Ibid.*

half of all Americans apparently heard the news before the President was pronounced dead, only 30 minutes after the shooting, and so fully that millions of Americans actually saw Oswald killed and heard the shot as soon as it echoed through the basement of the Dallas courthouse. Immediacy was one striking quality of the information flow during those days of crisis; another was the pervasiveness of it. For all practical purposes there was no other news story in America during those four days, and all the mass media concentrated on telling it. There were times during those days when *a majority of all Americans* were apparently looking at the same events and hearing the same words from their television sets—participating together, at least to that extent, in a great national event. Nothing like this on such a scale had ever occurred before. And if anything of significance connected with these events was not seen or heard at the instant it occurred, it was sure to be seen or heard or read shortly thereafter by almost everyone who could see, hear, or read. Never before, it is safe to say, has such a large proportion of the American people been able to feel so instantly and closely, for three and a half days, a part of events and deeds of great national significance.

These events were unique also because they represented the first such loss of a national leader that social scientists were ready to study. There was little or no social science in Lincoln's time, and the accounts by Sandburg and others can only suggest the opportunities that were missed to study social dynamics on that occasion. A few studies were made of reactions to Roosevelt's death, but the scholars who made them lamented that more data could not be gathered at the time. In 1963, however, social scientists were better able to seize opportunities. A series of studies of disasters had been made.[3] These had established the pattern of being able to go into the field on short notice. Survey research centers had interviewers available, and were prepared to draw samples and construct questionnaires quickly. Communication research had been considerably developed at enclaves of various kinds within a number of universities. When scholars recovered from the shock of the first news on November 22, many of them realized that this was a chapter in national history that should be studied, and they set plans in motion to collect information while it was still fresh. This was not a ghoulish act; rather it was

[3] For a summary, see A. H. Barton *et al., Social Organization Under Stress: A Sociological Review of Disaster Studies* (Washington, D.C.: National Academy of Sciences—National Research Council, 1963).

an effort to contribute to the understanding of great national events, and through them to the better understanding of a national society.

A surprising amount of research was planned and conducted in the week following November 22. A national sample survey and at least 15 local studies were in the field within that time. Other studies were made later. This book represents by no means all of this research, although the editors have tried to represent the most interesting parts of it. Undoubtedly no unexpected event in our history has ever been so fully studied at the time it happened.

These studies confirm that the Kennedy story provided a stimulus more like the Roosevelt than the Pearl Harbor story, but with added overtones of violence and irony, and with full and vivid television coverage. Television, more than any of the other media, during the preceding years must have made Americans feel that they knew the Kennedys very well. To the American people the event was clearly a signal for grief and national mourning for a man who was as close at hand as the picture tube but still not close enough for people to do the usual things they do about the death of a loved person. In this respect, too, television found itself playing an unusual part in the lives of its viewers.

There is relatively little previous scholarship about such an event. We have mentioned the series of studies on disaster. There are also studies of persons under stress.[4] There has been some attention to the behavior of personal bereavement and to the clinical nature of grief.[5] But these are only tangentially related to what happened on November 22, 1963, and the days following. That remains in most respects a unique event, in our scholarship as in our history, and the papers in this volume are therefore plowing new fields.

The part communication plays in crisis

When a crisis interrupts the slow, ongoing rhythms of communication —scanning the environment, disposing of the day-to-day needs and problems of the system, filing away and sharing the increment of experience—the rate of information flow is enormously increased. A message signals the emergency. Information rushes to and from the point

[4] For example, see I. L. Janis, *Air War and Emotional Stress* (New York, 1951).
[5] For example, E. Lindemann, "Symptomatology and Management of Acute Grief," *American Journal of Psychiatry* (1948), *101*, 141–48, and G. L. Engel, "Is Grief a Disease?" *Psychosomatic Medicine* (1961), *23*, 18–23.

of crisis, which becomes a new focus of attention as the system strives
to adjust to the problem.

This is the case regardless of the size of system. A message that unusual heat is being felt on a finger will alert a human system to move
the finger, check the situation visually if possible, take steps to repair
the damage, and so forth. A message that one member of a group is de-
viating will interrupt the usual humdrum communication of the group
for a great flow of persuasion to the deviant until he is restored to loyal
membership or the cause is seen to be hopeless. So in Dallas on November 22 the reporters, broadcasters, photographers, and their equipment
were operating routinely until 12:30. They were providing routine coverage of a chief executive. Then came the bulletin that roused the men
and facilities of communication to such efforts that it was many days
before information from Dallas and the coverage of the American chief
executive could again be called routine.

The National Research Council's studies of disaster identified five
stages in society's response to crisis. These are (1) the pre-disaster
period, (2) the period of detection and communication of a specific
threat, (3) the period of immediate, relatively unorganized response,
(4) the period of organized social response, and (5) the long-run post-
disaster period when the society is restored to equilibrium and the "permanent" effects of the disaster have been incorporated into it.[6] Each of
these periods has its own kind of communication to meet its special
needs. The pattern, however, fits great disasters and accidents better
than it fits the events that concern us here. There is no warning of an
assassination, as there is of a tornado, and thus no period in which people
can prepare, physically or psychologically, to meet the threat. There is
no widespread need for physical help or relief, as in most disasters. Indeed, one of the characteristics of the events of November 22–25 was
that there were no organized activities for most people to take part in;
the widespread response to the suggestion that the slain policeman's
wife, and later Mrs. Oswald, needed money, may have been an indication that organized social actions in time of crisis are themselves therapeutic. Another difference between the Kennedy assassination and most
of the crises studied for the National Research Council was that in November of 1963 there was no widespread destruction of the sort on
which the analysts of disaster-research base hypotheses relating the

[6] See Barton *et al.*, pp. 14–15.

amount of communication to the amount of destruction seen. Except for the three dead men in Dallas, the casualties of the events we are considering were psychological and political.

Systems theory would describe the response to crisis as a sudden imbalance in the system, followed by emergency steps to restore balance, and then a gradual restoration of normal functioning around whatever new balance is achieved.[7] This comes closer to describing what seems to have happened in the case of the Kennedy assassination. We can identify three periods. First came the time when the news had to be told. Then followed a period when society staggered under the blow but struggled to restore equilibrium—the shocked response of ordinary men and women, the shocked but disciplined response of officials striving to maintain law, order, and government. And finally came a period of social reintegration: the government closed ranks around a new chief, and the people overcame their shock, expiated their grief, and returned to old responsibilities in a new situation.

Each of these periods, as we have suggested, made its own special demands for communication. At 12:30 on November 22 the machinery of newsgathering was suddenly jarred out of its routine. The first staccato bulletin from Dallas was followed by a veritable ocean of telephoned news, wire copy, radio, television, and film, until all sides of the monstrous events had been filled in, and the chief actors had moved or been moved elsewhere.

This roused two great waves of communication in response. About one of these we know relatively little, and probably shall continue to know little until the autobiographies and the "now it can be told" articles begin to appear. This was the great and urgent flow of administrative communication, beginning in front of the Texas School Book Depository and the Parkland Hospital, and speedily involving the local and national police agencies, the White House, and Congress as officialdom took the actions required to protect the new President, bring the murderers to justice, and arrange a farewell to the leader and an orderly transition of leadership. The Warren report has told us a little of what went on during that time, and it is possible to piece together other bits. For example, there was for a time a question whether the killing of the President was an isolated act or was part of a conspiracy that might

[7] For example, L. Bertalanffy, "General Systems Theory: A Critical Review," *Yearbook of the Society for General Systems Research* (1962), 7, 1–22, and K. E. Boulding, *The Image* (Ann Arbor, Mich., 1956).

strike other leaders in an effort to take over the government. Unlikely as it may seem, still this was a possibility that had to be recognized and guarded against.

About the other wave of response to the crisis news, however, we know a great deal. This was the great ground swell of grief aroused in the American people and to some extent in people of other countries. There were incredulous questions, as we know; there was anger, but less of it than one might have expected; there was a certain amount of anxiety and withdrawal, and a considerable feeling of need to "talk it over." There was apparently a compulsive need to glue oneself to television and thus vicariously take part in the events and the farewells. About this response of nonofficial America we know a great deal, and what we know is documented by the articles in this volume.

After the news of the crisis and the shocked official and unofficial responses, there was the longer period of reintegration, when society closed ranks again, resolved most of its doubts and questions, worked out its grief, and returned more or less to normal. Much of this, but by no means all, was accomplished by the end of the day when John Kennedy was laid to rest in Arlington. Some of the scars lingered. The enormous sale of the memorial books and pictures, and of the Warren Commission report nearly a year later, testifies to how long the memories and the questions have lingered.

Three periods, three different demands on communication. Throughout all three periods, but most urgently at first and diminishing with time, was the demand for facts, for swift and full answers to the questions the nation was asking: Exactly what had happened in Dallas? How had it happened? Who had done it? Was he caught? Did they know he had done it? Was the Vice-President all right? Had he been sworn in? And so forth. That was the first demand—for facts. The second was for interpretation. This demand increased after the first shock, and it was still high enough to sell upwards of a million copies of the Warren report. How could it have happened? Why did he do it? Can we be sure of his guilt? What will this event mean for us all? These were the kinds of questions for which American society began to demand answers as soon as the first harsh news was absorbed. The demand for this kind of information was greatest in the third period, the period of reintegration; the demand for facts and bulletins was greatest in the first period, when the events were just becoming known. There was still another demand, which was perhaps highest in the second response period. This was the need to shake off the shock of the news, to talk or be talked to, to draw strength and reassurance from the groups and individuals one values, and to do something, even if it were no more than watching the television, to express one's grief. In other words, communication was called on for a kind of therapy, as it had been also for facts and meanings.

In all these uses of communication, mass and interpersonal uses were intertwined. The first news came by mass media, but half the people heard it first by word of mouth. Therapeutic communication was as likely to come from "talking it over" with one's friends or family, as from watching the President's funeral on television. Interpretive communication was more likely to come from the media, but there were many amateur interpreters, and some surrendered their amateur status and began to lecture on the subject. Nevertheless, one of the things that distinguished the kind of communication in this crisis, as we have tried to point out, was the extraordinary amount of mass media coverage. The fact that the transition was so orderly and reintegration was accomplished so quickly must be credited in no small degree to the efficiency and amount of media attention. The very fact that so little, apparently, was kept from the people of this country, that the channels of information were so constantly open, that representatives of the public were on the scene to report by press and broadcast, must have helped greatly to reduce the anxiety that would have been fed by a more secretive policy or less full coverage. The fact that most of the people of a nation felt that they could join together, even through television, in memorial services to a fallen leader must have helped greatly to expiate the grief and speed social reintegration. For these reasons, and because it is easier to assemble hard facts on the content and performance of mass media than on the content and uses of interpersonal communication, we shall emphasize the media in the remainder of this paper.

What the media did

The networks abandoned entertainment programs and commercials, and devoted themselves to the big story from Friday noon through Monday evening. Many of the smaller and independent stations did not abandon their usual programming after the first day; they had neither the program resources nor the financial security to do so.[8] But the networks

[8] K. J. Nestvold, "Oregon Radio-TV Response to the Kennedy Assassination," *Journal of Broadcasting* (1964), *8*, 141–46.

and network stations concentrated on the great story and its background. The newspapers covered it in extenso, and the wire services moved hundreds of thousands of words on it. From Friday noon until Monday evening, this was the story.

There has been a great deal of study of the content of mass media, but relatively little study of what happens between a news event and its appearance in the media. This is what fascinates us about the handling of a great story like the events in Dallas. How was it covered? How were the decisions made about what people to talk to, what questions to ask, what pictures to take? What concepts of public interest governed the choice of details? What standards of evidence determined when a report should be incorporated into the news? What is the difference between news coverage policies for press and for broadcast? Matters like these obviously determine what kind of lens the news media use to show us the world, but we know less than we should like to about them.[9] It is therefore interesting and revealing to read the accounts by professionals in this volume describing how they covered the Kennedy story.

Anyone who believes that the coverage of a crisis is a routine and straightforward job should ponder over Part I of this book. Despite the size of the news corps accompanying the President, there were simply not enough professionals at the right places to cover the confused story for the number of bureaus, services, and networks represented. Those who could send in more men did so. In the broadcasting networks, as Lower says (p. 68), every member of the news department and many members of other departments worked constantly for the better part of four days. Wicker (p. 35) reported something that newspaper men ten years ago might not have admitted, that they often found television helpful: it gave them another pair of eyes where they could not be in person.

During the first hours the problem was to bring order out of confusion. Conflicting reports and wild rumors circulated. The new President

---

[9] There have been a few research studies in this area. Examples are M. Charnley's not very reassuring "A Study of Newspaper Accuracy," *Journalism Quarterly* (1935), *12*, 349–401; a study by G. E. Lang and K. Lang of the MacArthur parade in Chicago, "The Unique Perspective of Television: A Pilot Study," *American Sociological Review* (1953), *18*, 3–12, which demonstrates that television can convey an impression of an event that is quite different from what is seen by those present; and W. Breed's "The Newspaperman, News, and Society" (Ph.D. dissertation, Columbia University, 1952), which studies how policy is made and communicated in the city room. These are samples from a scant literature.

was going to be sworn in when he returned to Washington—or while he was still in Dallas. (Actually it was on the plane before it left the Dallas airport.) The gun was a Mauser; it was an Italian make; it was several other kinds. *Two* heads had been seen at the window from which the assassin's bullets were reported to have come. Some of the shots were thought to have come from an overpass rather than the building. Oswald had been seen with Ruby. Oswald had been heard to say this and that. These and potentially more serious reports (for example, about the assassin's relation to foreign countries and to political groups in this country) were spoken as gospel truth and offered to reporters.

Consequently, a reporter on the Dallas story was from the very first up against one of the classical problems of journalism: What constitutes evidence? When does a report have enough support to justify passing it along? The newspapers and wire services passed on some rumors with sources duly noted—a "buyer beware" technique that never has much to say for it, and still less in a delicate situation like that surrounding Dallas. The television reporters found, Love says (p. 82), that "though rumors can be reported as rumors in a newspaper, to do so on television is much more difficult." In a sense television journalism grew up in Dallas, for never before had it faced such a story with so much of the responsibility for telling it. As a result of this experience journalists will come to understand better the differences between television and newspaper coverage of news. One thing that became clear, to quote Love again (p. 85), is that "all the news that's fit to print is not necessarily fit to be seen." For example, there was the question of whether the amateur movie containing pictures of the President actually being struck by the bullets should be shown on television. Apparently the networks decided against it, although *Life* later published a sequence of still pictures from the same film. Love said the picture would have been used if available on November 22, but later it would have seemed "too horrible" on television.

If the first problem was simply to get reporters where the news was breaking, and the second was to sort out the confused welter of evidence, half-truths, and rumors, a third was to provide enough background, enough news in depth, so that people could understand and evaluate what was happening. Here again Dallas suggested one of the fundamental differences between television and print journalism. Pettit expressed it this way: "Live television is peculiarly ill-equipped for investigative reporting. It shows only what is there" (p. 64). Therefore television was at its best in transporting the viewer to the scenes of news —the memorial events in Washington, the return of the new President to the capital, the news conferences, the unforgettable scenes of the dead President's wife and children, and the terrible scenes in the Dallas police headquarters. To fill in between events like these, the networks depended for a while on street interviews until they could prepare documentaries and memorial programs. With the newspapers, however, it was quite different. To see how at least one paper viewed its investigative responsibilities, one has only to read Salisbury's description in this volume. He describes the working approach of the *New York Times* to an event of this type. The newspaper's first responsibility is to provide an "intimate, detailed, accurate chronology of events," an account that would "enable the reader to pick his way fairly well through fact, fiction, and rumor" (p. 38). But the *Times* did not propose to stop with that. It dug into the story with all the men it could assign, and, as a matter of fact, investigated many of the questions later given to the Warren Commission. The list of studies programmed by the *Times* that appears on p. 39 of this volume will give many readers a new concept of how some newspapers view their public responsibilities. The *Times* actually found itself going over the same ground as the FBI and the Warren Commission, and kept up its private plowing of this ground until early in 1964.

In Dallas, then, reporters were covering a story that was a mystery from the first minute, and that was doomed to remain in part a mystery forever because of the shooting of the chief suspect. They were operating amidst great confusion and under the shadow of high emotion. Furthermore, they remained competitive on most of the coverage. This situation gave rise to some of the darker hours, as well as some of the most remarkable accomplishments, of news coverage in Dallas.

More than anything else, the newsmen have been criticized for what happened in the Dallas police headquarters. The worst that can be said about the news representatives in this respect is that they *share* responsibilities with Dallas police and officials for the confusion, for the statements in advance of trial about Oswald's guilt, and for the final public showing of Oswald that exposed him to Ruby's gun. Apparently nothing was done by the Dallas officials to systematize their contacts with newsmen or cameramen. There was no place through which news could be funneled. News conferences were held on the run, and police officers appeared to have no compunction about giving a frank interview whenever asked. Officials said things in these interviews that would surely have been ruled prejudicial if the case had ever come to trial. Some of this conduct on the part of the Dallas officers is explained by a document reprinted in the report of the Warren Commission. This is a general order of the Dallas Police Department that puts on the policemen "a responsibility to lend active assistance" to the press, and forbids an officer to "improperly attempt to interfere with the news media representative. . . . Such activity . . . is regarded by the press as an infringement of rights and the Department shares this view." So far as this goes it is all right, but the directive might well have defined proper "active assistance" and improper "interference." The lack of any well-understood limit of this kind set the stage for the drama of confusion played out on the third floor of the police headquarters, where officers sought to interrogate Oswald, as Oscar MacKenzie says drily in *The New Statesman*, "in the intervals between public appearances."[10]

Margaret Mead once wrote of the disastrous consequences that occurred when young people of two cultures were brought together during wartime, those of one culture having learned that it is the girl's responsibility to say no, the others that it is the boy's responsibility.[11] Something like that was happening at Dallas. Newsmen were taught to be aggressive and to go as far as they could in covering a story, expecting officials to draw the limits necessary to protect the persons and rights of accused criminals. The Dallas police, one can imagine from the general order, had been taught to be permissive with newsmen and perhaps to expect them to exercise due restraint in criminal cases. Needless to say, there were special reasons on those days for newsmen to be especially aggressive and for Dallas officials to be especially permissive. But the cultural misunderstanding that occurred demonstrated the need for a clearer understanding of limits and responsibilities in this area, perhaps not a written code of conduct but at least a set of agreed-upon principles. As Rivers says in his paper in this volume (p. 51), what happened in the Dallas police headquarters calls for serious discussion of the "area of uncertainty" about what are a reporter's rights, privileges, and duties in covering a criminal case, and especially a very important criminal

[10] Oscar MacKenzie, "Attention Must Be Paid," *New Statesman* (1964), *68*, 475–76.
[11] Margaret Mead, "Some Cultural Approaches to Communication Problems," in L. Bryson, ed., *The Communication of Ideas* (New York, 1948).

case like this one. The Kennedy story was not the first one to bring these problems to light, but it throws a pitiless glare on them.[12]

How was the news circulated?

There are some remarkable figures in the Nielsen report on television viewing for November 22–25.[13] During these days the average home in the Nielsen sample had a television receiver tuned to the Kennedy report for a total of 31.6 hours. During that time, Nielsen estimates, approximately 166 million Americans in over 51 million homes were tuned at some time to the Kennedy program, and in one-sixth of those homes people had their television on the big story for more than 11 hours per day! These figures are supported by the NORC survey (pp. 149–77), for which people estimated that they spent, on the average, 8 hours Friday, 10 Saturday, 8 Sunday, and 8 Monday watching television or listening to the radio.[14]

Undoubtedly no event like this, where so many Americans have concentrated vision and hearing on the same story at the same time for so long a period, has ever occurred before. It is difficult from existing records to estimate the amount of listening to and viewing of the Roosevelt story, but at that time radio and newspapers carried the burden of news diffusion and there was no such concentration on one story as there was in November of 1963.[15] A very rough estimate suggests that for an average family the television viewing of the Kennedy story was greater than the radio listening to the Roosevelt story by a factor of perhaps 5 to 8 times.

One result of the enormous flow of information on the events in Dallas, and the extraordinary public attention to this information, was that there was apparently in this case no hard core of know-nothings. It is a rule of thumb in survey research that 10 to 20 per cent of a national sample will probably be unaware of almost any news event. But 99.8 per

---

[12] Public reaction was in general quite favorable to the coverage of the story, particularly to its speed and ampleness, and to the three and a half days of television. The chief criticism was professional rather than general, and referred to the sort of things I have been talking about. Some idea of the public criticism can be gained from the reports in this volume by Mindak and Hursh and by Anderson and Moran.

[13] A. C. Neilsen Co., "TV Responses to the Death of the President" (New York, 1963).

[14] However, Nielsen found Monday—the day of the funeral—the day of heaviest television viewing.

[15] A telegraphic poll taken after Roosevelt's funeral indicated that about 88 per cent of American adults had listened to the radio at *some* time during the three days following the President's death. This NORC poll is cited by Sheatsley and Feldman (p. 159).

cent of the NORC national sample reported having heard the news by 6
P.M. on Friday—five and a half hours after the President was shot. Furthermore, the news traveled with almost unbelievable swiftness. Two-
thirds of the people seem to have heard it within half an hour, even before the President's death was announced. Table 1 gives comparable figures for four of the studies made at the time.

TABLE 1

| | Proportion of people who heard news within | | | |
Sample[a]	15 min.	30 min.	45 min.	60 min.
National		68%		
Dallas 67%	67%	84	89%	93%
San Jose, Calif. 42	42	62	81	90
Iowa City, Iowa		70		91

[a] The national sample is reported on in this volume by Sheatsley and Feldman; the San Jose
sample by Greenberg; and the Iowa City sample by Spitzer and Spitzer. The report on diffusion
in Dallas is in R. J. Hill and C. M. Bonjean, "News Diffusion: A Test of the Regularity Hypothesis," *Journalism Quarterly* (1964), *41*, 336–42.

There are no entirely comparable figures from earlier events in this
class. A sample of students attending one college at the time of Roosevelt's death showed that 83 per cent of them heard the news within 30
minutes and 93 per cent within an hour, but these young people were
living in close contact in dormitories.[16] Eleven hours elapsed before 90
per cent of a university faculty community heard of the death of Senator Taft, and 14 hours before 90 per cent of the eventual knowers in a
housing project heard it.[17] Samples of the general public on previous occasions have usually returned much lower figures than those obtained in
1963, although it must be noted that these earlier stories have not had
the news value of the Kennedy story. For example, 26 per cent of the
persons in two samples in different parts of the country reported that
they had heard of Eisenhower's stroke within an hour of the time the
news became available, 43 per cent knew of the first Explorer satellite
within an hour, and only 6 per cent had heard of the voting of statehood
for Alaska within an hour.[18]

How was the news heard? The studies are in general agreement: a

[16] D. C. Miller, "A Research Note on Mass Communications," *American Sociological
Review* (1945), *10*, 691–94.
[17] O. M. Larsen and R. J. Hill, "Mass Media and Interpersonal Communication in the
Diffusion of a News Event," *American Sociological Review* (1954), *19*, 426–33.
[18] P. Deutschmann and W. Danielson, "Diffusion of Knowledge of the Major News
Story," *Journalism Quarterly* (1960), *37*, 345–55.

little less than half heard by television or radio; a little over half heard from another person, either face to face or by telephone. Table 2 gives comparative figures from the same four studies just reported upon. Here again we have no strictly comparable figures from the past. The telegraphic survey at the time of Roosevelt's death indicated that 47 per cent of people had learned the news from radio or the press, 53 per cent from interpersonal sources. Of the college students in dormitories studied by Miller, 88 per cent reported they had heard the news from another student.

TABLE 2

| Sample | First source of news | | | |
	TV	Radio	Personal	Newspaper
National	47% (TV + radio)		49%	4%
Dallas	26	17%	57	
San Jose	20	28	50	
Iowa City	19	25	55	

Table 3 gives figures for lesser stories. These figures suggest a pattern as to how fast and by what means a news story reaches the public. The two chief variables would seem to be news value and the time of day when the story breaks. Greenberg was able to show that when a story has narrow interest so that it receives little or no mass media treatment, it is likely that more people who hear about it will hear from other persons.[19] When news value is perceived to be sufficient that the mass media generally carry the story, then, other things being equal, the greater the news value, the more the story is passed on by word of mouth and therefore the higher the proportion of persons who hear it from interpersonal sources. Thus, if the neighbor's child has measles, that news is likely to be heard, if at all, by word of mouth. If Alaska is voted statehood, that news may be passed around a great deal by word of mouth in Alaska but will be heard mostly by mass media in the rest of the country. Stories like the death of Taft, the launching of the first American satellite, President Eisenhower's stroke, and his decision to seek a second term are of generally higher news value and therefore more likely to be passed on by word of mouth. We find that about three times as many people heard about these

[19] Bradley S. Greenberg, "Person-to-Person Communication in the Diffusion of News Events," *Journalism Quarterly* (1964), *41*, 489–94.

TABLE 3

Event[a]	First source of news			
	TV	Radio	Newspaper	Personal
Launching of Explorer I, 1958 . . .	41%	23%	18%	18%
Eisenhower's stroke, 1957	38	32	12	18
Alaska statehood, 1958	29	27	38	6
Eisenhower decides to seek second term, 1956	14	39	27	20
Taft's death, 1953	15	49	11	26

[a] The source for the first three of these events is Deutschmann and Danielson. The source for the fourth is W. Danielson, "Eisenhower's February Decision: A Study of News Impact," *Journalism Quarterly* (1956), *33*, 433–41. The source for the fifth is Larsen and Hill.

stories from interpersonal sources as heard from such sources about the vote on Alaska, but still about four out of five persons heard these news stories first from the mass media. But when we have a story of the highest news value, like the assassination of a President, we find that as many as half the population hear the news from other persons rather than the media. Thus Greenberg found a J-curve when he plotted the proportion of people aware of various news events against the proportion who heard of them from interpersonal sources:

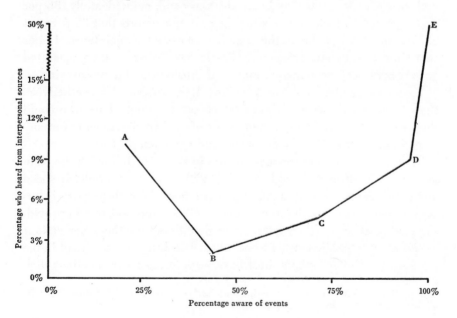

But the time of day makes some difference too. If an important story breaks during hours when many people are at work, then radio and interpersonal channels will handle most of the diffusion for them. If it breaks in the evening, then television will carry more of the diffusion for them. The Kennedy story broke just after noon for the eastern half of the country, just before noon for the western. Exactly half of the NORC sample reported they had heard the news at home, 29 per cent had heard at work, and 21 per cent had heard while shopping, having lunch, or doing something else neither at home nor at work. For the people at home, television and telephone calls were important; for the people at work, radio and interpersonal messages; for the others, a variety of media and interpersonal channels. But both the paramount interest of the news and the fact that it broke in midday contributed to an enormous amount of passing it on and talking about it. Members of the Iowa City sample reported having told the news on the average to between five and six people each. The later news of Oswald's slaying was passed on to an average of three persons. This does not mean, of course, that each of these messages went to someone who had not heard the news; in many cases the conversation must have started, "Have you heard . . .?" Thirty-seven per cent of the national sample reported that they phoned or visited someone else after they heard the news and, coincidentally, 38 per cent reported that someone visited them. Banta reports that 35 per cent of his Denver sample heard the news from a casual acquaintance, 11 per cent from a complete stranger![20] Clearly the Kennedy story generated an enormous and uncommon amount of interpersonal news-carrying.

But when the news had once been heard, interpersonally or otherwise, then there was a rush to radio or television. Five out of six who could drop what they were doing turned to one of the broadcast media for confirmation or further details (Sheatsley and Feldman, p. 154).

Thus we can say that the mass media in the crisis following the Kennedy assassination delivered the news with almost unparalleled speed and thoroughness, and stimulated interpersonal channels to carry it further. We can also note that the media filled an important role in providing confirmation, further details, and doubtless sometimes correction; apparently the public trusted what it heard on broadcasts or read in the newspapers. But the media must have been filling more functions than

[20] T. J. Banta, "The Kennedy Assassination: Early Thoughts and Emotions," *Public Opinion Quarterly* (1964), *28*, 216–24.

these; otherwise, how should we explain the enormous allocation of time to television in the four days of the crisis? To understand better what use was being made of communication in those long hours of viewing between Friday noon and Monday night, let us look more closely at the general reaction of the public to the events.

The public reaction and the function of communication

Beyond passing the news on, and rushing to TV or radio, how did people react? Obviously there was a very deep, a very widespread emotional response. Less than half the people in the national sample could continue their usual activities (Sheatsley and Feldman, p. 154). Some felt the need to be with persons they knew or loved; they hurried home or telephoned or visited friends or relatives. Others wanted to be by themselves; the more they admired the President, the more they felt this need.[21] Television, under differing circumstances, might meet either of these needs; it could be either a solitary or a group activity.

Miller and Zimmerman (p. 272) describe the strange atmosphere in New York City on the afternoon of the slaying. It was a sort of "frantic quiet." The usual tumult and noise of New York were missing. Fewer people than usual were hurrying somewhere. There was an uncommon willingness to stop and talk. People gathered around newsstands or radios, surrounded people with portable transistor sets. There was no hesitation about discussing one's feelings with anyone who wished to talk.

The most general pattern of personal response was at first shock and disbelief. Some merely sought to check the news; some wilfully denied it. As Orlansky reported newsdealers saying of their customers after Roosevelt's death, "They don't wanna believe it," so Greenstein (p. 223) reported respondents saying after Kennedy's, "It can't happen here!"[22]

That first shocked response was succeeded by a developing awareness of the loss, along with feelings of sorrow, sadness, shame, and anger. These feelings rolled over the nation in an immense tide. The most common reactions were to be sorry for Mrs. Kennedy and the children, sorry that a vital young man should be killed at the height of his powers, ashamed that such a thing could happen in our country, sad at the loss of someone well-known and dear, and angry that someone could have

---

[21] According to Sheatsley and Feldman (p. 154), 51 per cent of Negroes said that they had wanted to be by themselves, but only 28 per cent of Southern whites so reported.
[22] Orlansky, pp. 240ff.

done such a deed. These responses were very generally reported. Less often reported, but still mentioned by nearly half the national sample, was worry over how the President's death would affect the political situation. For some Americans these feelings were followed by physical symptoms such as weeping, tenseness, sleeplessness, fatigue, or loss of appetite (Sheatsley and Feldman, pp. 159–60). This was the second stage.

There followed a gradual recovery and return to a normal emotional state. Mindak and Hursh report that their sample in Minneapolis was "normal" again by Monday (p. 140). Both the national sample and the Dallas sample reported that the majority of physical symptoms had departed after four days.[23] By that time also, anger and anxiety were less, the worst of the grief was over, and there were indications of rededication on the part of some people. Hurn and Messer report that about a third of their Chicago sample felt they should personally rededicate themselves by becoming more tolerant (p. 340), and Sears demonstrated that people became less partisan immediately after the events in Dallas (p. 325). In general, there was a social reintegration covering over the scars of the sad weekend. That was the third stage.

Several things can be pointed out about this personal and public response. For one thing it was primarily grief rather than anxiety. The physical symptoms we have listed are typical of grief and bereavement. Anxiety has a different set of symptoms.[24] Bradburn and Feldman (pp. 273–86) were able to document this by comparing two groups of respondents, who were interviewed in October and again after the assassination. One of these was a Negro sample in Detroit, the other a mostly white sample in a suburb of Washington. Between the first interview and the second, grief symptoms rose markedly in both samples, but anxiety symptoms rose only in the Negro sample, where people must have felt more personally threatened by events. And the pattern of reaction in general was typical of mourning—shock and intense sorrow, which was poured out or worked out, permitting the individual to return after a fairly short time to normal patterns of behavior, often with a sense of rededication or moral obligation.

Another observation during those days was the relative scarcity of po-

23 Sheatsley and Feldman, p. 160; Bonjean, Hill, and Martin, p. 185.
24 Engel, pp. 18ff.

litical anxiety and reactions built around fear of a political conspiracy. Concern over who the assassin was and whether he would be apprehended was evident from the first, and about four out of five named an immediate suspect. About one out of four at once suspected a Communist, a Castroite, or a leftist of some other kind; about half that many thought of a segregationist or another right-wing person. But as time passed these suspicions became markedly less; and in particular there was relatively little anxiety lest a foreign group or a conspiring political group be active in the situation (see Miller and Zimmerman, Coleman and Hollander). If Americans had been fearful about the succession of a new President, most of them soon lost these fears. If many of them had first rejected the idea that "one man could do what Oswald did," most of them apparently became sufficiently satisfied with the explanation so that the alternatives did not worry or arouse them.

In the third place, it is worth noting, as do Verba (p. 357) and Hurn and Messer (p. 346), that this crisis was integrative rather than disintegrative for the United States. Unlike most of the world's crises in which a change of chief executive is occasioned by violence, the events of November 22–25 brought Americans together rather than driving them apart. They closed ranks around the new President. Partisanship on a national political level was abandoned during a month of mourning, and, as Sears was able to show, partisanship was reduced on a private and personal level also. If the reaction of the Chicago sample was typical, many Americans were thinking in December of 1963 about their obligation to practice brotherhood, tolerance, and other integrative behavior.

Now why should responses to President Kennedy's assassination and related events have taken these forms? Why should they have been so largely grief rather than anxiety, so relatively lacking in fear of a political conspiracy, and so largely integrative rather than divisive? Why should it have been Europe rather than the United States that kept alive, during the subsequent year, the suspicions of threatening conspiracy? Why was the period of recovery so relatively short, although the grief was manifestly so deep?

There are no simple answers to questions like these. One answer lies in the American people's faith in their national institutions, including the succession to the Presidency and the rule of law. Another is the firm and responsible actions of the new Chief Executive and his government. One out of many others is, as Coleman and Hollander say (p. 268), that the events following the assassination remind us of "the different courses public opinion can take and of our meager knowledge of the dynamics."

But an important part of the answer to such questions must lie in the performance and use of mass communication during the four days. It was extremely important to a shocked public to have such a large and continuing flow of information on the matter that concerned them. Incomplete and grudging information at a time of crisis breeds suspicion and rumor. Able press representatives have always known this. Thus when President Eisenhower had his heart attack, James Hagerty had the President's doctor explain the illness and the prognosis to newsmen and to the television audience; as a result fears and doubts were allayed, people took the illness in stride, and ground was laid for public confidence in the President's ability to carry on his duties and ultimately to serve a second term. The flow of news from Dallas also did something like this. As much as we may regret some of the things that happened in the Dallas police headquarters, still if it were not for the aggressive news coverage by the media and the frankness of officials we should probably have had greater anxiety and a slower integration.

The swift, full coverage undoubtedly grounded many rumors before they could circulate. By speaking so fully and frankly of Oswald and the events in which he was involved, the media helped to reduce fears of a conspiracy and prepare people to believe the theory that a lone, disturbed man had done it. Demonstrating that the Presidential succession was working smoothly, that the government was going forward in firm hands, helped reduce fears and recriminations. For a student of communication, one of the most important deductions from the events of late November 1963 is that Americans trust their free press and their free broadcasting system. In this case it must be said that these did not fail the American people in any important way. The people got the full news, they got it fast, and they got it, with a very few exceptions, accurately.

The function of the news coverage of the Kennedy crisis is thus fairly clear. We understand less well what was happening during those long hours when so many tens of millions watched the television set. Many people have remarked about the compulsive quality of this viewing.

Greenstein (p. 232) documents some of it in his transcriptions of discussion groups:

Subject$_1$. I don't know why we sit here and watch it.
S$_2$. I stayed right up until the network went off.
S$_3$. I don't know. It's just something like this creates . . . kind of like a vacuum in your head of all the things you're used to and you just have to fill it up.
S$_4$. I kept waiting for something that would make me feel more hopeful or feel better about it. It never came, of course, but you're tied to the TV set in hopes that it would.
S$_5$. After the TV went off last night, I thought about . . . why I had spent the whole day and it struck me that I was waiting for somebody to explain why this happened.

These viewers didn't know why they had viewed so long but realized they were doing it to fill a gap, looking for explanation, reassurance, perhaps for something they could not readily articulate. The explanation they were seeking must have been more than a surface one. They were probably seeking, whether they knew it or not, a kind of philosophical explanation for the irony of the loss of a young, admired, and beloved leader, a reconciliation of this event with their ideals of justice and fairness, and an opportunity to get rid of their weight of grief. And as we have said before, they were probably watching because they did not know just what else under the circumstances to do.

This is speculation, of course. Certain things we can say in a less speculative vein about the long listening to television. We can note what was coming to them through the picture tube. In addition to the flow of spot news, they were watching and hearing national leaders, being reminded of national history and the rituals and laws of the national government, reviewing the career of the dead President, seeing the norms and mores of American life exemplified for them by people they admired. In other words they were being *reassured* that the nation, and in particular the presidency, was continuing as they wanted it to, and they were being reminded of a *pattern of conduct* expected of them as Americans.

In the second place they were being shown symbols and events—the flag-draped casket, the young widow and the children, the terrible slow drumbeat of the funeral march—that gave them an opportunity to experience a real catharsis of grief if they wanted to. Aristotle used the word catharsis to describe the aesthetic effect of Greek drama in purging impure and excessive emotions. It has become a bit old-fashioned to talk about catharsis in this sense, and yet this is what introspection tells us must have been happening before many of those television sets. The viewers were purging themselves of their burden of grief and anger by going through acts of mourning, much as they might have done for a family bereavement. They were weeping, secretly or openly, over the sights of the national tragedy. They were participating as much as they could in memorial events. They were going to a funeral.

And they were doing these things *together*! The enormous, the unequaled focus of attention that occurred around the television sets of America during the crisis, and especially on the day of the funeral, when audience measurements in New York found more than 90 per cent of sets tuned at one time to the funeral procession—this concentration of attention deserves more thought than it has been given. How many of the viewers actually felt that they were sitting in a congregation of 150 million Americans, we do not know. Many of them apparently had a sense of participating in a national act. This focus of attention, as Coleman and Hollander have pointed out (p. 255), contained the potential for great national action. If a suitable object for great national anger had emerged from the news of the crisis, it is conceivable that a mass uprising might have occurred. But the very fullness of the news won confidence in it, and developments cut the ground out from under any belief that a nationally dangerous conspiracy was involved. Instead, the focus on the presidency reasserted America's deep commitment to that institution and to the rule of law and order.

The experiences of 150 million Americans before their television sets during the dark weekend, then, were a sharing of common information, a reassertion of national norms, and a national act of mourning, which must have been for many viewers a catharsis of grief. When the experience is seen in this way, it is somewhat easier to understand why the experience was so largely grief rather than anxiety, why Americans closed the book on an anxiety over conspiracy more quickly than Europeans did, and why the recovery after the weekend of grief came so comparatively soon, came with elements of rededication and reintegration rather than divisiveness and disquiet. To sum up, it appears that the essential elements in this response were the enormous flow of news and the enormous focus of attention on television sets that at times could have been described as a truly national act involving most of a major nation's citizens.

There has been a great deal of theorizing about the difference between the conditions under which the mass media have a significant effect
directly on the public, and the conditions under which their effect has to
be mediated by opinion leaders or other interpersonal carriers. Undoubtedly the interpersonal channels of information and influence were working from November 22 through November 25 as at other times, and we
have already noted that the news of the two murders was passed along
from person to person with phenomenal speed. But the general rush to
radio or television as soon as the news was heard, and the enormous concentration on the mass media, especially television, during the next three
days, lead us to think that a two-step flow was not the major factor in the
effects we have been describing. Many Americans, of course, watched
television in family groups during those days, but the significant fact is
that such large numbers were watching: they were not told secondhand;
they came themselves with their sadness, their questioning, to witness
the dramatic events on the picture tube. Television during those four
days was a communication event somewhat like the Kennedy-Nixon debates, in that both events brought very large numbers of people into direct contact with the developments and persons to which they expected
to react. And like the changes in estimation of the candidates and voting
intention that took place after the first debate, so the individual catharsis, the laying of doubts to rest, and the reinforcement of American
norms that took place in audiences after the President's assassination
appear to be examples of the powerful direct effects of which the mass
media, under favorable conditions, are capable.

Part I

The Response and Performance of the Mass Media

Tom Wicker

That Day in Dallas

I think I was in the first press bus. But I can't be sure. Pete Lisagor of the *Chicago Daily News* says he knows he was in the first press bus and he describes things that went on aboard it that didn't happen on the bus I was in. But I still think I was in the first press bus.

I cite that minor confusion as an example of the way it was in Dallas early in the afternoon of November 22. At first no one knew what happened or how or where, much less why. Gradually bits and pieces began to fall together, and within two hours a reasonably coherent version of the story began to be possible. Even now, however, I know no reporter who was there who has a clear and orderly picture of that surrealistic afternoon; it is still a matter of bits and pieces thrown hastily into something like a whole.

It began for most reporters when the central fact of it was over. As our press bus eased at motorcade speed down an incline toward an underpass, there was a little confusion in the sparse crowds that at that point had been standing at the curb to see the President of the United States pass. As we came out of the underpass, I saw a motorcycle policeman drive over the curb, across an open area, and up a railroad bank for a few feet, where he dismounted and started scrambling up the bank.

Jim Mathis of the *Advance* (Newhouse) syndicate went to the front of our bus and looked ahead to where the President's car was supposed to be, perhaps ten cars ahead of us. He hurried back to his seat. "The President's car just sped off," he said. "Really gunned away." (How could Mathis have seen that if there had been another bus in front of

This report is reprinted, with minor modifications, from *Times Talk*, the *New York Times* house organ, December, 1963.

us?) But that could have happened if someone had thrown a tomato at the President. The press bus at its stately pace rolled on to the Trade Mart, where the President was to speak. Fortunately it was only a few minutes away.

At the Trade Mart, rumor was sweeping the hundreds of Texans already eating their lunch. It was the only rumor that I had ever seen; it was moving across that crowd like a wind over a wheat field. A man eating a grapefruit seized my arm as I passed.

"Has the President been shot?" he asked.

"I don't think so," I said. "But something happened."

With the other reporters—I suppose 35 of them—I went on through the huge hall to the upstairs press room. We were hardly there when Marianne Means of Hearst Headline Service hung up a telephone, ran to a group of us, and said, "The President's been shot. He's at Parkland Hospital."

One thing I learned that day; I suppose I already knew it but that day made it plain. A reporter must trust his instinct. When Miss Means said those eight words—I never learned who told her—I knew absolutely they were true. Everyone did. We ran for the press bus. Again a man seized my arm—an official-looking man. "No running in here," he said sternly. I pulled free and ran on. Doug Kiker of the *Herald-Tribune* barreled head-on into a waiter carrying a plate of potatoes. Waiter and potatoes flew about the room. Kiker ran on. He was in his first week with the *Trib* and on his first Presidential trip.

I barely got aboard a moving press bus. Bob Pierrepoint of CBS was aboard, and he said that he now recalled having heard something that could have been shots or firecrackers or motorcycle backfire. We talked anxiously, unbelieving, afraid.

Fortunately again, it was only a few minutes to Parkland Hospital. There at its emergency entrance stood the President's car, the top up, a bucket of bloody water beside it. Automatically, I took down its license number: GG300 District of Columbia.

The first eyewitness description came from Senator Ralph Yarborough, who had been riding in the third car of the motorcade with Vice-President and Mrs. Johnson. Senator Yarborough is an East Texan, that is to say, a Southerner, a man of quick emotion and old-fashioned rhetoric. "Gentlemen," he said, pale, shaken, near tears, "it is a deed of horror."

The details he gave us were good and, as it later proved, mostly accurate. But he would not describe to us how the President looked being wheeled into the hospital except to say that he was "gravely wounded." We could not doubt, then, that it was serious.

I had chosen that day to be without a notebook. I took notes on the back of my mimeographed schedule of the two-day tour of Texas we had been so near to concluding. Today I cannot read many of the notes; on November 22 they were as clear as 60-point type.

A local television reporter, Mel Crouch, told us he had seen a rifle being withdrawn from the corner fifth- or sixth-floor window of the Texas School Book Depository. Instinct again—Crouch sounded right, positive, though none of us knew him. We believed it and it was right.

Mac Kilduff, an assistant White House press secretary in charge of the press on that trip, and who was to acquit himself well that day, came out of the hospital. We gathered round and he told us the President was alive. It wasn't true, we later learned, but Mac thought it was true at that time and he didn't mislead us about a possible recovery. His whole demeanor made plain what was likely to happen. He also told us, as Senator Yarborough had, that Gov. John Connally of Texas had been shot too.

Kilduff promised more details in five minutes and went back into the hospital. We were barred. Word came to us secondhand—I don't remember exactly how—from Bob Clark of ABC, one of the men who had been riding in the press pool car near the President's, that the President had been lying face down in Mrs. Kennedy's lap when the car arrived at Parkland. No signs of life.

That is what I mean by instinct. That day a reporter had none of the ordinary means or time to check and double-check matters given as fact. He had to go on what he knew of people he talked to, on what he knew of human reaction, on what two isolated "facts" added up to, above all on what he felt in his bones. I knew Clark and respected him. I took his report at face value, even at second hand. It turned out to be true. In a crisis, if a reporter can't trust his instinct for truth, he can't trust anything.

When Wayne Hawks of the White House staff appeared and said that a press room had been set up in a hospital classroom at the left rear of the building, the group of reporters began struggling across the lawn in that direction. I lingered to ask a motorcycle policeman if he had heard anything on his radio about the pursuit or capture of the assassin. He hadn't, and I followed the other reporters.

As I was passing the open convertible in which Vice-President and Mrs. Johnson and Senator Yarborough had been riding in the motorcade, a voice boomed from its radio: "The President of the United States is dead. I repeat—it has just been announced that the President of the United States is dead."

There was no authority, no word of who had announced it. But—instinct again—I believed it instantly. It sounded true. I knew it was true. I stood still a moment, then began running.

Ordinarily I couldn't jump a tennis net if I'd just beaten Gonzales. That day, carrying a briefcase and a typewriter, I jumped a chain fence looping around the drive, not even breaking stride. Hugh Sidey of *Time*, a close friend of the President, was walking slowly ahead of me.

"Hugh," I said, "the President's dead. Just announced on the radio. I don't know who announced it but it sounded official to me."

Sidey stopped, looked at me, looked at the ground. I couldn't talk about it. I couldn't think about it. I couldn't do anything but run on to the press room. Then I told the others what I had heard.

Sidey, I learned a few minutes later, stood where he was a minute. Then he saw two Catholic priests. He spoke to them. Yes, they told him, the President was dead. They had administered the last rites. Sidey went on to the press room and spread that word too.

Throughout the day every reporter on the scene seemed to me to do his best to help everyone else. Information came only in bits and pieces. Each man who picked up a bit or a piece passed it on. I know no one who held anything out. Nobody thought about an exclusive; it didn't seem important.

After perhaps ten minutes when we milled around in the press room— my instinct was to find the new President but no one knew where he was—Kilduff appeared red-eyed, barely in control of himself. In that hushed classroom he made the official, the unbelievable announcement. The President was dead of a gunshot wound in the brain. Lyndon Johnson was safe, in the protective custody of the Secret Service. He would be sworn in as soon as possible. Kilduff, composed as a man could be in those circumstances, promised more details when he could get them, then left.

The search for phones began. Jack Gertz, the AT&T man traveling with us, was frantically moving them by the dozen into the hospital, but few were ready yet. I wandered down the hall, found a doctor's office, walked in, and told him I had to use his phone. He got up without a word and left. I battled the hospital switchboard for five minutes and finally got a line to New York—Hal Faber on the other end, with Harrison Salisbury on an extension.

They knew what had happened, I said. The death had been confirmed. I proposed to write one long story as quickly as I could, throwing in everything I could learn. On the desk they could cut it up as they needed —throwing part into other stories, putting other facts into mine. But I would file a straight narrative without worrying about their editing needs.

Reporters always fuss at editors and always will. But Salisbury and Faber are good men to talk to in a crisis. They knew what they were doing and realized my problems. I may fuss at them again sometime but after that day my heart won't be in it. Quickly, clearly, they told me to go ahead, gave me the moved-up deadlines, told me of plans already made to get other reporters into Dallas, but made it plain they would be hours in arriving. Salisbury told me to use the phone and take no chances on a wire circuit being jammed or going wrong. Stop reporting and start writing in time to meet the deadline, he said. Pay anyone $50 if necessary to dictate for you.

The whole conversation probably took three minutes. Then I hung up, thinking of all there was to know, all there was I didn't know. I wandered down a corridor and ran into Sidey and Chuck Roberts of *Newsweek*. They'd seen a hearse pulling up at the emergency entrance and we figured they were about to move the body.

We made our way to the hearse—a Secret Service agent who knew us helped us through suspicious Dallas police lines—and the driver said his instructions were to take the body to the airport. That confirmed our hunch, but gave me, at least, another wrong one. Mr. Johnson, I declared, would fly to Washington with the body and be sworn in there.

We posted ourselves inconspicuously near the emergency entrance. Within minutes, they brought the body out in a bronze coffin. A number of White House staff people, stunned, silent, stumbling along as if dazed, walked with it. Mrs. Kennedy walked by the coffin, her hand on it, her head down, her hat gone, her dress and stockings spattered. She got into the hearse with the coffin. The staff men crowded into cars and followed. That was just about the only eyewitness matter that I got with my own eyes that entire afternoon.

Roberts commandeered a seat in a police car and followed, promising to "fill" Sidey and me as necessary. We made the same promise to him and went back to the press room. There we received an account from Julian Reed, a staff assistant, of Mrs. John Connally's recollection of the shooting. Most of his recital was helpful, and it established the important fact of who was sitting in which seat in the President's car at the time of the shooting.

The doctors who had treated the President came in after Mr. Reed. They gave us copious detail, particularly as to the efforts they had made to resuscitate the President. They were less explicit about the wounds, explaining that the body had been in their hands only a short time and that they had had little time to examine it closely. They conceded they were unsure of the time of death and had arbitrarily put it at 1 P.M., CST. Much of their information, as it developed later, was erroneous. Subsequent reports made it pretty clear that Mr. Kennedy was probably killed instantly. His body, as a physical mechanism, however, continued to flicker an occasional pulse and heartbeat. No doubt this justified the doctors' first account. There also was the question of national security and Mr. Johnson's swearing-in. Perhaps too there was a question about the Roman Catholic rites. In any case, until a later doctors' statement about 9 P.M. that night, the account we got at the hospital was official.

The doctors had hardly left before Hawks came in and told us Mr. Johnson would be sworn in immediately at the airport. We dashed for the press buses, still parked outside. Many a campaign had taught me something about press buses and I ran a little harder, got there first, and went to the wide rear seat. That is the best place on a bus to open up a typewriter and get some work done. On the short trip to the airport, I got about 500 words on paper, leaving a blank space for the hour of Mr. Johnson's swearing-in and putting down the mistaken assumption that it would take place somewhere in the terminal. As we arrived at a back gate to the airport, we could see Air Force One, the Presidential jet, screaming down the runway and into the air.

Sid Davis of Westinghouse Broadcasting, one of the few reporters who had been present for the swearing-in, had been left behind. Roberts, who had guessed right in going to the airport when he did, had been there too and was aboard the Presidential plane on the way to Washington. Davis climbed on the back of a shiny new car that was parked near where our bus halted. I hate to think what happened to its trunk deck. He and Roberts, true to his promise, had put together a magnificent pool report on the swearing-in. Davis read it off, answered questions, and gave a picture that so far as I know was complete and accurate.

I said to Kiker of the *Trib*: "We'd better go write. There'll be phones in the terminal." He agreed. Bob Manning, an ice-cool member of the White House transportation staff, agreed to get our bags off the press plane, which would return to Washington as soon as possible, and put them in a nearby telephone booth. Kiker and I ran a half-mile to the terminal, cutting through a baggage-handling room to get there. I went immediately to a phone booth and dictated my 500-word lead, correcting it as I read, embellishing it too. Before I hung up, I got Salisbury and asked him to cut into my story whatever the wires were filing on the assassin. There was no time left to chase down the Dallas police and find out those details on my own.

Dallas Love Field has a mezzanine that runs down one side of its main waiting room and is equipped with writing desks for travelers. I took one and went to work. My recollection is that it was then about 5 P.M., New York time. I would write two pages, run down the stairs and across the waiting room, grab a phone, and dictate. Miraculously I never had to wait for a phone booth or to get a line through. Dictating each take, I would throw in items I hadn't written, sometimes whole paragraphs. It must have been tough on the dictating room crew.

Once while in the booth dictating I looked up and found twitching above me the imposing mustache of Gladwin Hill. He was the first *Times* man in and had found me right off; I was seldom more glad to see anyone. We conferred quickly and he took off for the police station; it was a tremendous load off my mind to have that angle covered and out of my hands.

I was half through, maybe more, when I heard myself paged. It turned out to be Kiker, who had been separated from me and was working in the El Dorado room, a bottle club in the terminal. My mezzanine was quieter and a better place to work, but he had a TV going for him, so I moved in too.

The TV helped in one important respect. I took down from it an eyewitness account of one Charles Drehm, who had been waving at the President when he was shot. Instinct again—Drehm sounded positive, right, sure of what he said, and his report was the first real indication that the President was probably shot twice.

Shortly after 7 P.M., New York time, I finished. So did Kiker. Simultaneously we thought of our bags out in that remote phone booth. We ran for a taxi and urged an unwilling driver out along the dark runway. As we found the place, with some difficulty, an American Airlines man was walking off with the bags. He was going to ship them off to the White House, having seen the tags on them. A minute later and we'd have been stuck in Dallas without even a toothbrush.

Kiker and I went to the *Dallas News*. The work wasn't done; I filed a number of inserts later that night, wrote a separate story on the building from which the assassin had fired, tried to get other *Times* reporters on useful angles as they drifted in. But when I left the airport, I knew the worst of it was over. The story was filed on time, good or bad, complete or incomplete, and any reporter knows how that feels. They couldn't say I missed the deadline.

It was a long taxi ride to the *Dallas News*. We were hungry, not having eaten since an early breakfast. It was then that I remembered John F. Kennedy's obituary. Last June, Hal Faber had sent it to me for updating. On November 22 it was still lying on my desk in Washington, not updated, not rewritten, a monument to the incredibility of that afternoon in Dallas.

The Editor's View in New York

The bulletin announcing that President Kennedy had been shot in Dallas was received in the *New York Times* offices at 229 W. 43rd Street at approximately 1:40 P.M., EST, Friday, November 22. The first decisions made by the editors were not philosophical. They were logistic. We had to get more men to the scene—and fast.

Except in unusual circumstances only one *Times* correspondent travels with the President. The Texas trip was routine. Tom Wicker, the *Times* White House man, was alone on the assignment. In fact, but for a last-minute change of mind, a second-string substitute would have been in Dallas. The *Times* maintains no bureau in Texas. Thus Mr. Wicker was alone on the scene when Mr. Kennedy was shot.

The *Times* by principle and by habit considers itself a "newspaper of record." That is, it consciously seeks to present all of the facts required by a public-spirited citizen to formulate an intelligent opinion. Clearly the shooting of the President would require an extraordinary record— detailed, accurate, clear, complete.

Before any other decisions were made, the first urgent matter was to get reinforcements to the scene. By 2 P.M., EST, four *Times* men had been contacted in various parts of the country and directed to Dallas. They were Gladwin Hill in Los Angeles, Joe Loftus on assignment in St. Louis, Don Janson on assignment in Omaha, and John Herbers on assignment in Albany, Ga. By the time the President's death was officially reported a few minutes after 2 P.M., five more correspondents had been assigned to proceed to Dallas. They were Fendall Yerxa, the *Times* bureau manager in Washington, who happened to be in New York

City, Fred Powledge of the New York staff, Ned Kenworthy and Marjorie Hunter of the Washington staff, and James Reston, Washington correspondent of the *Times*, who was in Winston-Salem, N.C. When it was learned about 3 P.M. that the plane carrying President Johnson and President Kennedy's body was returning to Washington, D.C., the instructions to Kenworthy, Hunter, and Reston were canceled.

Meanwhile, in both Washington and New York, a large staff was being designated for coverage assignments. In New York, for example, the assignment sheet for the evening of November 22 shows at least 32 correspondents assigned to the Kennedy story. The entire working staff in Washington, about 20 persons, not counting those assigned to the story outside the capital, was drafted for the task. So was the network of 10 regional correspondents, each of whom was assigned to special tasks in his own geographical area. The principal foreign bureaus—London, Moscow, Paris, Rome, Bonn, Tokyo, Hong Kong, and the United Nations staff—were also committed to the Kennedy story. About half the available editing staff in New York was concentrated to handle the assassination material.

The reason I stress logistics is that without the commitment of a large reportorial and editing staff the *Times* could not have undertaken the coverage responsibilities that it assumed. First we had to get the men into the field and provide editors to handle their copy. Only then could we give form to the concept we had in mind. From almost the first moment the working approach of the editors was this:

The assassination is an event of unparalleled magnitude. It has occurred in a setting that is certain to stimulate passionate suspicion, political repercussions, and, quite possibly, serious international reactions. Thus the initial responsibility of the *Times* is to provide an intimate, detailed, accurate chronology of events. As clues, suspicions, and allegations arise, each must be investigated with care. The *Times* record must be one that will enable the reader to pick his way, fairly well, through fact, fiction, and rumor. If it does not provide all the answers, at least it will provide a framework on which reasonable hypotheses can be erected. The *Times* must report not only the facts, but also the theories that others evolve about those facts.

Thus the first instructions given to Mr. Wicker when he telephoned in at 2:30 P.M. were to write a simple, chronological account that would incorporate every detail that he observed, every fact that he had ascertained, and as much physical description as possible, to enable the reader to visualize the action and locale. Because it would be two, three, or four hours before other members of the *Times* staff could reach Dallas, it seemed likely that Mr. Wicker's story would be the only major dispatch from the scene written by a *Times* staff man in the first editions. Also since Mr. Wicker was the only *Times* man present when the President was killed, his narrative would have special historic value. The *Times* would also present narrative accounts by other reporters who were with the President at the time of the shooting.

It should be said here that throughout that weekend the editors of the *Times* tried consciously to apply standards of historic judgment to their treatment of a complex, swiftly shifting story. They sought to provide a record for history and for historians. Thus when Lee Harvey Oswald was arrested sometime between 3 and 4 P.M., EST, November 22, and charged with being the assassin, when he was identified as a "Marxist," a member of the Fair Play for Cuba Committee, and a one-time defector to Moscow, the following efforts were begun: an attempt to put together every possible item about Oswald's personal history; an examination of the Fair Play for Cuba Committee, its activities, and its personalities; a careful study of Marxist and Leninist attitudes toward individual terrorism; a study of the philosophy and motivation of other assassins, both American and foreign; an examination of extremists, of their organizations active in the South, and of other recent assassinations and acts of terrorism committed by such groups.

Because a possible political motivation of the assassin might have international repercussions, instructions were sent to correspondents in Moscow and other Communist countries to watch reactions closely and report them promptly. A special watch on Cuban and Chinese reactions was ordered. A specialist in Soviet affairs provided an analysis of the Kennedy-Khrushchev relationship and the status of Soviet-American affairs.

All this material was designed to provide the reader with a background against which to assess the credibility of Oswald's motivation. It was not presumed that authoritative evidence could be presented about Oswald in a matter of hours. But it was thought essential in view of the possible portentous involvements that extraordinary efforts be made to flesh out this background as fully as possible.

There were four possibilities presented by Oswald's arrest: First, that he was innocent and had no connection with the case. Second, that he had committed the act on his own—that it was a deed of a probably deranged individual. Third, that he was the agent of a Communist conspiracy directed from either within or without the United States. Fourth, that he was the agent of a right-wing conspiratorial group. The *Times* coverage of the assassination from the earliest moment was designed to engage all of these possibilities.

Because of lack of manpower at the scene in Dallas until reinforcements arrived on Friday evening, most of the background material for the first assassination paper (on Saturday) was provided by staff men in New York. There were two notable stories from Dallas. One was Mr. Wicker's painstaking minute-by-minute reconstruction of the scene during and after the firing of the shot. The other gave the details on Oswald's arrest and background that were made public by police and other official sources in the first confusing hours after the President had been killed. These two articles were to provide a base line for all future reports about Mr. Kennedy's last day. Many of the anachronisms that would later be cited as examples of conflicts in testimony, or as evidence that officials were seeking to frame Oswald or cover up some kind of conspiracy, were to stem from minor errors and inaccuracies that in reality were the mere fruit of haste by overworked, excited reporters or by minor officials suddenly cast into the national spotlight and inadequately prepared by temperament or training to present a sober and unprejudiced record.

In retrospect the errors do not seem large. In an ordinary case they would not have mattered. But this was no ordinary case. The death of a President of the United States under dramatic and mysterious circumstances was involved. The record would be scrutinized time and time again. Even typographical errors would ultimately loom as potent clues.

With these two straightforward, largely chronological accounts, the *Times* was able to present in the Saturday paper two notable examples of special reporting that helped readers put events into some perspective. One was an analysis by Claude Sitton of the recent growth in the South of various terrorist organizations that had employed violence and assassination locally. The article made clear that though there was no connection between Oswald and such organizations, the techniques which he allegedly had employed were not unfamiliar in the area. The other was the first of a series of remarkable reports by Peter Kihss, a veteran *Times* correspondent, that started the task of sketching in the personal background and history of Oswald.

Kihss's first article outlined most of the essential details of Oswald's life that were to be fleshed out in the days to come. Many of the events during his defection to the Soviet Union were noted; so were his interest in Marxism, his flirtations with the Fair Play for Cuba Committee and the Castroites, his itinerant nature, his querulous and contentious personality, his career as a U.S. Marine, his difficulties in supporting his family, his difficulties in school, and his apparent lack of close friends and connections.

The next day's reporting began where the first day's left off. On this day and for many subsequent days the first task of the editors in New York was to check every bit of published material in the *Times*, the other New York papers, the Texas papers, and the wire services for discrepancies and hitherto unreported angles. This checklist, composed with the demands of the skeptics and the future researchers consciously in mind, was the starting point of each day's reporting.

This painstaking effort continued for well over a month after the assassination and was discontinued only when the field for effective reporting had been to all practical purposes foreclosed by the FBI. As a routine procedure, the FBI sought to persuade each person whom it questioned not to give information to any other person and particularly not to newspapermen.

Thus the paper of Sunday, November 24, went over for a second time and in great detail the sequence of events reported by the police that led to the capture of Oswald. Specific corrections were made of errors in previous stories. For example, the assassination weapon, described the previous day as a German Mauser, was now correctly identified as an Italian-made 1938 Carcano. Oswald's personality was further illuminated through a lengthy interview with Mr. and Mrs. Michael R. Paine, who had been close friends of Mrs. Oswald. A beginning was made at sketching a biography of Marina, Oswald's Russian wife. More details about Oswald's background, such as his angry letters to Gov. John J. Connally of Texas (when Mr. Connally was Secretary of the Navy), were uncovered. And an expert medical analysis of the President's fatal wound based on the best reconstruction of its nature obtainable up to that point was written by Dr. Howard A. Rusk.

On Sunday, November 24, the whole case took a spectacular turn with the killing of Oswald by Jack Ruby, the Dallas nightclub operator. It was recognized that the killing of Oswald by Ruby opened up a series of new and difficult questions: Was there a connection between Oswald and Ruby? Was Oswald shot to cover up the connections that he had with other conspirators? Were the Dallas authorities in some manner involved in the case? Did Ruby act on his own? Or was Ruby connected with right-wing or left-wing conspirators or with the Dallas police? The questions were new, but the task of the *Times* as conceived by its editors did not change.

Thus the paper of Monday, November 25, began by reporting every ascertainable detail about the physical circumstances of Oswald's killing by Ruby. Reporters from Dallas to Chicago searched for facts about Ruby's background that might indicate political orientation, motivation, or connection with Oswald.

But even more important for the historical record, 48 hours of intensive investigation were providing a firm and certain context for the many facets of the assassination. A remarkable piece of investigative reporting by Peter Kihss had drawn together an extremely detailed report about Oswald from the cradle through his brief adulthood. The essentials of his life in New Orleans, in the Bronx, in Fort Worth, in the Marine Corps, in Russia, and in Texas after his return had been reconstructed. Another reporter went over once again the detailed record that the police had compiled to indicate that Oswald was indeed the assassin. Another reporter was able for the first time to present in some depth a portrait of Marina and to answer many questions bearing on possible conspiratorial connections between Oswald and the Russians. An arms specialist was able to present substantial evidence about the weapon used by Oswald. Another reporter, casting back over the philosophical differences between Karl Marx and various revolutionary terrorists, was able to present the assassination in a historical context.

Only 48 hours after the President's death and less than 12 hours after the death of the man who almost certainly killed him, the work of the *Times* staff had begun to establish consistency among the facts about the two murders. This consistency first appeared in the background of Oswald. Every effort to establish close relationships or connections between Oswald and others petered out. Every person who had known him in the Marine Corps, in public school, in Russia, on the job in Dallas, or in

Fort Worth had the same report: a surly, difficult man with few associations, and these of a fleeting nature.

Almost immediately rumors started about connections between Ruby and Oswald. Each was checked and failed to be substantiated. Ruby's background was investigated with the same care, not only in Dallas but in Chicago and San Francisco, where he had lived. Here too was consistency. His life had followed a pattern of existence on the fringe of the underworld, in the world of nightclubs, gangsters, and petty rackets, but there was nothing to link him to political activity of any consequence, nothing to show that his path had ever crossed Oswald's.

Two pieces of brilliant postulative reporting in the next two weeks strengthened this picture. It was postulated that a man such as Oswald would be a lone public library reader, a patron of public facilities near his home. A check of the branch library nearest his rooming house in New Orleans supported the hypothesis. His reading list was as much recreational (light detective fiction) and anti-Communist as leftist, and was singularly devoid of genuinely dialectical works.

When it became known that Oswald had visited Mexico in an effort to obtain a visa for Cuba and Russia, it was postulated that he must have met and conferred with individuals in Mexico City. If he were indeed an agent for a foreign power, it seemed logical that the contacts would have been made there. However, a painstaking bit of detective work by Peter Kihss in Mexico City produced a picture which fitted the pattern of lonely behavior. He located not only the hotel where Oswald stayed but also the restaurant where he ate his meals. In both places he had been alone. Most of his brief time in Mexico City had been passed in movie houses. No sign of contacts or human associations turned up.

Each time a sequence was checked out and produced this kind of pattern, the stronger the probability grew that the reporters were obtaining a genuine, unsimulated picture of the man who was believed to have killed the President. However, throughout the active period of inquiry into the President's death, the possibility was held open that despite the accumulating mass of evidence there was in fact some plot, conspiracy, or network tying all the disparate elements together. It was conceded by the editors of the *Times* that it was not possible to prove that a plot did not exist. But it was demonstrated that none of the evidence produced by the *Times*, or produced by anyone else and examined by the *Times*, supported the plot or conspiracy theory.

As time went on, hypotheses were constructed based on supposed discrepancies in reports about the actual shooting—conflicts in the number of bullets, conflicts in police officers' statements about fingerprints and palm prints, conflicts in the angle of the shots, in the time required to fire the gun, etc. Each of these conflicts was examined. None proved consequential. Most of them arose from hasty or inexact statements made in the early hours after the assassination. Some arose because of difficulty in interpreting photographic evidence. One such "clue" was a photo that showed a man standing in the doorway of the Texas School Book Depository at the moment the President was shot. The man looked like Oswald. However, careful comparison of this photo with pictures of Oswald clearly revealed differences in facial characteristics and in clothing (both wore sports shirts open at the neck but the pattern differed), and a check of Depository employees revealed the identity of the man in the doorway; he was not Oswald.

Active investigation of the case by the *Times* continued until about January 1, 1964. It was then brought virtually to a close because every lead and clue that the editors could obtain had been investigated to the limits of the correspondents' ability. Correspondents in Switzerland had investigated the Albert Schweitzer College (actually a small fellowship institution), which Oswald once had indicated interest in attending. In Japan a *Times* man had talked to all the Marines who remembered serving with Oswald there. His Marine mates in California had been tracked down. His teachers, social workers, and psychiatrists in New York were interviewed. His relatives in four southern states were traced. His correspondence with the Fair Play for Cuba Committee and the Communist Party as well as that with his mother was examined.

There were a few areas that could not be checked. Permission could not be obtained from Soviet authorities to visit Minsk, where Oswald had worked, nor could the Soviet report on Oswald be obtained from the State Department. The FBI continued to hold Marina Oswald incommunicado for a long time, so that much of her story was inaccessible. Oswald's brother, Robert, consistently refused to talk to reporters. The Dallas Police Department would not make available much of the actual ballistics data on the shooting that was needed to resolve precisely what happened to each bullet fired. Certain other bits of police evidence were sealed off.

It seemed apparent, however, that there was little likelihood that this evidence or any other evidence the Warren Commission would submit would materially change the fundamentals established in the *Times* reporting. And in any event, the editors had achieved their purpose: to present a detailed, objective, and inclusive record against which all future official versions and unofficial rumors might be evaluated and confirmed or disproved.

Edwin B. Parker and Bradley S. Greenberg

Newspaper Content on the Assassination Weekend

Newspapers, like the other mass media, concentrated on bringing the people all the news about the assassination, discussions of its implications, and background information that might help them understand it. But exactly what did people get? What did the newspapers look like on the assassination weekend? How did the coverage differ from normal coverage? How much space was allocated to advertising and to other news?

To answer such questions, we systematically analyzed the contents of 26 U.S. newspapers.[1] The papers were selected, primarily on the basis of availability, from cities of varying sizes all over the United States. They are not a probability sample of U.S. newspapers, although they intuitively appear to provide a reasonable cross section. They include evening papers for Friday, Saturday, and Monday, morning papers for Saturday, Monday, and Tuesday, and Sunday editions of both morning and evening papers.[2] Since we wish to compare the contents of these papers with

[1] The authors wish to thank Stanford graduate students Joseph Marfuggi and Richard Farr, who did much of the tabulating for this article, and Fred I. Greenstein of Wesleyan University, who provided several of the newspapers.

[2] The evening papers were: *The Bay City Times* (Bay City, Michigan), *The Commercial Mail* (Columbia City, Indiana; Saturday only), *Columbia City Post* (Columbia City, Indiana; Friday and Monday only), *The Denver Post*, *The Jamestown Sun* (Jamestown, North Dakota), *The Milwaukee Journal*, *Newport Daily News* (Newport, Rhode Island), *The Pratt Daily Tribune* (Pratt, Kansas), *St. Louis Post-Dispatch*, *Shreveport Journal* (Shreveport, Louisiana), and *Evening Journal* (Wilmington, Delaware; Friday only). The morning newspapers were: *Atlanta Constitution*, *The Sun* (Baltimore, Maryland), *Chicago Tribune*, *The Plain Dealer* (Cleveland, Ohio), *The Dallas Morning News*, *Duluth News-Tribune* (Duluth, Minnesota), *Great Falls Tribune* (Great Falls, Mon-

the contents of papers for a similar period, we also analyzed 10 Saturday morning papers, 6 Sunday papers, and 6 Monday morning papers from the same weekend of the previous year, November 23–26, 1962.[3]

Newspapers on the assassination weekend devoted about half their available news space to assassination news. Table 1 presents the allocation of space in 26 newspapers. Only 13 per cent of the news space of the Friday afternoon papers was used for assassination material; the event occurred too late in the day to allow remaking of much more of the papers. By Saturday morning, 52 per cent of the news space was given over to assassination material, and the average for the rest of the weekend was between 45 and 54 per cent. Assassination coverage was classified into three broad categories: the events themselves, including biographies of the principals; discussion of effects, including people's reactions at home and abroad; and background material, including discussion of the Secret Service, the presidential succession, previous assassinations, and the funeral ceremony. What space was available on Friday was used almost exclusively for material on the events themselves and for Kennedy's obituary. By Saturday morning, papers were able to include more information on effects and background. The proportion of space devoted to events decreased from a high of 31 per cent of news space Saturday morning to a low of 17 per cent Tuesday morning. Space used for discussion of effects and background material climbed to highs of 20 and 17 per cent, respectively, by Tuesday morning. There was little change during the weekend in the amount of miscellaneous material, such as comics, bridge columns, and recipes. The amount of space used for local, state, and other national news dropped sharply between Friday and Saturday, and then retained the Saturday level through Tuesday.

---

tana), *Los Angeles Times, New York Herald-Tribune, The New York Times, The Oregonian* (Portland, Oregon), *San Francisco Chronicle, Seattle Post-Intelligencer, The Washington Post,* and *Wilmington Morning News* (Wilmington, Delaware). The 16 Sunday papers were those listed above except for the following: *Atlanta Constitution, Duluth News-Tribune, The Jamestown Sun, Newport Daily News, The Pratt Daily Tribune, Shreveport Journal,* and *Wilmington Morning News.*

[3] The Sunday papers for which the 1962 and 1963 coverage was compared were: *Baltimore Sun, Denver Post, New York Herald-Tribune, Portland Oregonian, St. Louis Post-Dispatch,* and *San Francisco Chronicle.* The Monday papers for the 1962–63 comparison were: *Atlanta Constitution, Chicago Tribune, Los Angeles Times, Seattle Post-Intelligencer,* and *Washington Post.* All of these except the *Denver Post* and the *St. Louis Post-Dispatch* were included in the Saturday comparison.

TABLE 1

News Space Used for Types of News

Newspapers	Assassination news			Other news				
	Event	Effects	Back-ground	Local	State	Na-tional	For-eign	Misc.
Friday evening (1,865)ᵃ	11%	2%	0%	32%	10%	24%	4%	17%
Saturday morning (3,634) . . .	31	18	3	14	3	7	4	20
Saturday evening (1,716) . . .	29	19	4	17	4	10	1	16
Sunday (4,062)	23	18	4	17	6	12	6	14
Monday morning (3,222). . . .	24	14	12	16	3	11	3	17
Monday evening (2,000)	19	14	13	15	6	13	2	18
Tuesday morning (3,301) . . .	17	20	17	15	3	8	4	16

ᵃ Figures in parentheses show average available space in column inches for the 26 newspapers on the assassination weekend.

Table 2 compares the allocation of news space in 12 papers for three days of the assassination weekend and of the weekend of the year before. To make room for assassination news, all other categories of news were given a smaller percentage of the total space than in the year before. The greatest change was the reduction by about two-thirds in the percentage of space devoted to other national news. There was less change in the percentage devoted to miscellaneous material than to any other type.

The use of news space devoted to assassination coverage differed from normal news coverage chiefly in that a greater percentage of the space was devoted to pictures. Analysis of the same 12 papers showed that

TABLE 2

Distribution of News Space by Type of News

Type of news	Saturday morning papers		Sunday papers		Monday morning papers	
	1962 (2,885)ᵃ	1963 (4,102)	1962 (3,303)	1963 (4,043)	1962 (2,790)	1963 (3,772)
Assassination	—	52%	—	44%	—	48%
Other:						
Local	29	14	26	17	33	18
State	7	3	12	6	5	3
National	21	6	30	13	25	10
Foreign	10	4	13	6	14	3
Miscellaneous	33	21	19	14	23	18

ᵃ Figures in parentheses show the average space in column inches that was available for news in the 12 papers analyzed.

35 per cent of the assassination coverage on Saturday morning was pictorial, compared with 16 per cent of the non-assassination news and 19 per cent of the news space on the comparable Saturday in 1962. On Monday morning 36 per cent of the assassination coverage was pictorial, compared with 17 per cent of the non-assassination news and 16 per cent of the news space in the previous year. On Sunday, a traditional day for news pictures, and a day on which few new assassination photographs were available, 26 per cent of the assassination coverage was pictorial, compared with 22 per cent of the non-assassination news and 21 per cent of the news in the comparable Sunday papers in 1962. Even in an age of television, newspapers still place considerable emphasis on broad pictorial coverage of major news events.

Table 3 compares the amount of newspaper advertising space on the assassination weekend with that on the comparable weekend of the previous year. There was considerably more advertising, in both column inches and percentage of total space, on November 23, 1963, than on the comparable Saturday the year before. Although some newspapers canceled advertising to free more space for news, there is little evidence of it here.[4] On Sunday and Monday the amount of advertising, whether measured in column inches or as per cent of total, was considerably less than the year before. The advertising space in the Sunday papers was reduced from 63 to 40 per cent, and in the Monday papers from 65 to 50 per cent. The fact that stores were closed Monday, November 25, for the national day of mourning undoubtedly contributed to the reduction in advertising space. These average figures conceal considerable variability. For example, the percentage of total space devoted to advertising on Monday ranged from a low of 39 per cent for the *New York Times* to a high of 61 per cent for the *Washington Post*. In the same papers the year before, it ranged from 59 per cent in the *Atlanta Constitution* to 74 per cent in the *Chicago Tribune*.

The amount of advertising in newspapers contrasted sharply with the general cancellation of commercials in the broadcast media. In a study of the reactions of the broadcast media in Oregon, Nestvold found that only one-third of the AM radio stations canceled all advertising, one-fifth canceled about three-fourths of their advertising, and so forth, down to about one-fifth that canceled less than half of their commercials. He also found that cancellation was a function of market size and

4 See *The Bulletin* of the American Society of Newspaper Editors, No. 471 (1964), p. 3.

TABLE 3

Allocation of Newspaper Space

Newspapers for the last weekend of November in 1962 and in 1963	Average space in column inches		Per cent of space	
	1962	1963	1962	1963
Saturday morning ($n = 10$)				
Total advertising	2,200	4,061	43%	50%
Memorial advertising	—	33	—	0.4
All other	2,885	4,102	57	50
Sunday ($n = 6$)				
Total advertising	5,687	2,726	63	40
Memorial advertising	—	302	—	4
All other	3,303	4,042	37	60
Monday morning ($n = 6$)				
Total advertising	5,261	3,699	65	50
Memorial advertising	—	555	—	7
All other	2,790	3,772	35	50

network affiliation; i.e., large stations and network-affiliated stations were more likely to follow the lead of the television industry and to cancel more.[5]

While broadcast media canceled both advertising and entertainment material to devote their entire programming to news coverage of the assassination, newspapers did not make such drastic changes. More nonadvertising space was available than in the year before, and about half of this space was devoted to assassination coverage. Reductions in advertising, which presumably resulted primarily from advertiser cancellation and nonplacement, apparently reduced the total size of the newspaper more than they increased the amount of nonadvertising space. For example, Sunday papers were reduced from about 9,000 column inches in 1962 to less than 7,000 column inches, while nonadvertising space increased by about 700 column inches. Space was made available for assassination coverage not so much by cancellation of advertising and entertainment material such as comics, as by the reduction of space devoted to other news. Presentation of advertising and entertainment material that might have appeared in bad taste on broadcast media may not have seemed out of place in newspapers. The reader can decide how much and what to read in the newspapers, but the viewer does not have the same control over broadcast media exposure.

[5] Karl J. Nestvold, "Oregon Radio-TV Response to the Kennedy Assassination," *Journal of Broadcasting* (1964) , *8*, 141–46.

William L. Rivers

The Press and the Assassination

The reports of President Kennedy's assassination and its aftermath were swift, lengthy, appropriately couched in grief and boxed in black, and the various journals of the news business made it clear during the following weeks that the press was proud of them. The chronicle of reporters' actions and the advertisements acclaiming them in *Editor & Publisher*—the Associated Press bought two pages, United Press International bought four—were highly self-congratulatory. The analyses of press performance in *The Masthead* and in *The Bulletin* of the American Society of Newspaper Editors were similarly positive. Although W.S. Harrison of the *Toledo Blade* charged in *The Masthead* that the press must share in the blame for the murder of Lee Oswald, such questioning voices were muted. Other, louder voices in the same issue held that the Dallas police were responsible: they should not have given in to the demands, primarily from television, that Oswald be transferred publicly from jail to jail. And although television may have emerged from Dallas with honor for having given up millions to broadcast nothing but unsponsored news for nearly four days, Earl Johnson consoled the newspaper world in the *UPI Reporter* by pointing out that TV's sacrifice was more apparent than real: some sponsors paid for their broadcast time anyway, and others simply rescheduled commercials for a later date.

There seemed to be little change even when, months later, the Warren Commission report criticized the mass media for swamping Dallas in reporters. The report quoted one FBI agent as likening conditions at the police station to "Grand Central Station at rush hour," and pointed out that newsmen in the mass may influence events almost as decisively as they cover them. The Commission called on the press to develop a code of ethics and practices embracing crime and court proceedings. This was a sobering indictment. Miles Wolff, President of the American Society of Newspaper Editors, called together newspaper and broadcasting representatives to discuss it. The group was concerned enough to select a five-man steering committee to study the Warren Commission recommendations, but made it clear that the sense of the meeting was not at all apologetic: "Within forty-eight hours, the print and electronic media reported the Dallas Story so accurately and completely that the Warren Commission, in ten months and with unlimited resources, did not alter the basic outlines of what the media had reported." All in all, if the assassination coverage was not a journalistic triumph but a chaotic encounter of the unprepared with the unforeseen, the press is not saying so.

Much of the self-congratulation seems deserved. The press associations and many metropolitan newspapers and mass magazines put platoons of editors and reporters on every aspect of the story everywhere without regard to cost. Some newspapers canceled columns of scheduled advertising to make room for sidebars to the assassination story. With only hours to go before their weekend deadlines, the news magazines were transformed. *U.S. News & World Report* junked its deadline along with many pages that were ready for printing, produced twenty new pages, and remade the entire issue. *Newsweek* produced twenty-five new pages. *Time* added seventeen pages, including a cover story on President Johnson. It was all worthwhile; not even hugely increased press runs could satisfy the demand. (In the first real test of the print media *versus* total news on television, the record indicates that electronic journalism is never likely to make newspapers and magazines obsolete.) In Dallas, the *Times-Herald* sold eighty thousand copies more than its daily norm. The first issue of *Life* after the assassination was quickly depleted; single copies were selling for as much as ten dollars in San Francisco.

Some of the individual reporting performances were remarkable. Tom Wicker of the *New York Times* stitched together a lengthy report that was at once a crisp news story, a detailed chronicle, and a stark revelation of mood and atmosphere. Merriman Smith of United Press International, who won the Pulitzer Prize for his work in Dallas that day, proved himself capable of distinguishing between the moving and the maudlin in a time of tragedy by writing an almost clinical account of what he heard and saw:

The President was face down on the back seat. Mrs. Kennedy made a cradle of her arms around the President's head and bent over him as if she were whispering to him.

Gov. Connally was on his back on the floor of the car, his head and shoulders resting in the arms of his wife, Nellie, who kept shaking her head and shaking with dry sobs. Blood oozed from the front of the Governor's suit. I could not see the President's wound. But I could see blood spattered around the interior of the rear seat and a dark stain spreading down the right side of the President's dark gray suit.

And yet there is much more to say about press performance during the assassination period that is far less positive. And if nothing like a solution to the problem of crisis reporting emerges from saying it, it may nonetheless suggest some of the questions that might have accompanied the self-appreciation.

The story of the press and the assassination actually began several hours before a shot was fired. Early on the morning of November 22, the issue of *Editor & Publisher* dated November 23 came off the press carrying a curious article. Headlined "The S.S. Ruffians," it was a reporter's protest that the Secret Service is overprotective in guarding the President—and the writer's acidity creates the suspicion that the use of "S.S." was not so much designed to save space as to suggest an unpleasant analogy with Hitler's crack troops. The reporter, Thomas Del Vecchio, wrote as a veteran of 24 years of interviewing dignitaries who arrived at airports. His complaint was that reporters were often excluded from the groups that greeted President Kennedy at Idlewild:

How come? What's happened here?

It's all in the name of security.

Now where does the problem of security end and the problem of a controlled press kept from access to the news begin?

There is no question that the press and the Secret Service have reached that point and beyond.

On top of all this is the rudeness and ruffian manner a good many of these agents assume toward the press under the guise of security.

They often act as though newsmen were not Americans and did not have a record almost as impressive as theirs for respect for their President and his security.

Just where do the rights under the First Amendment end and the assumed and overriding rights of the Secret Service take complete charge?

There was much more in the same outraged tone. Predictably, the article provoked a strong reaction. One reader's reproving letter to the editor of the magazine pointed out that even aside from the assassination Del Vecchio's article was bitter, petty, subjective, and poor journalism. Editor Robert U. Brown responded with a column entitled "Hindsight Criticism," holding, "If such articles have to be written with some intuition as to whether the President might not be alive tomorrow because of an assassin's bullet, there would be very little criticism." It was a predictable rejoinder, and perhaps a persuasive one, but it dealt not at all with the central question: Was Del Vecchio right? Brown might have decided this easily by pondering a related question: Would he have published the article after the assassination?

It would have been a curious article had there been no assassination. Despite charges that the Kennedy Administration "managed the news," the President's own relations with the press were open to the point of porosity. Never in history had so many reporters been so free to talk with the President and explore the presidency. In sharp contrast to his predecessor (who preferred the company of businessmen to journalists and preferred reading Luke Short to Walter Lippmann), Mr. Kennedy fostered such warm relations with many Washington correspondents that his press secretary once complained amiably that the comings and goings of reporters were creating a traffic problem in White House corridors.

Del Vecchio's article is chiefly notable for showing that some spokesmen for the press, not content with continuing dialogues with the President in Washington or with frequent confrontations elsewhere, demand unlimited access wherever the President touches ground. The President is not to be a public servant but public property. That this is something more than one peeved reporter's view is suggested by the fact that *Editor & Publisher*, which echoes the opinions and yearnings of a good many newspapers, chose to make "The S.S. Ruffians" its lead article. Copies of the issue were flown to Miami for distribution at an Inter-American Press Association meeting on November 22. Presumably, some editors and publishers were reading the article when they learned of the assassination.

The two issues of the *Dallas Morning News* that appeared immediately before the assassination are similarly interesting. Much has been made of the full-page advertisement purchased by the "American Fact-finding Committee" in the issue of November 22. Headed "Welcome Mr.

Kennedy," the advertisement posed questions like, *"Why* have you scrapped the Monroe Doctrine in favor of the Spirit of Moscow?" and *"Why* have you ordered or permitted your brother Bobby, the Attorney General, to go soft on Communists. . . ?" Incredibly, Robert U. Brown of *Editor & Publisher* undertook, in a column entitled "More Hindsight," to defend the *News.* " In the first place," he wrote, "it was not a 'hate' ad. It was a political advertisement. . . ." Then, in a defense for which few editors and publishers will thank him, Brown held that not one of the questions in the advertisement "hasn't been asked in one form or another on the editorial page of some American newspaper."

The editors of the *News* have answered critics by pointing to the sweetly phrased editorial with which they greeted the President. One editorial could hardly change the image of a paper whose publisher, E. M. "Ted" Dealey, had become a national figure of sorts in 1961 by charging at a White House luncheon that Kennedy and his administration were "weak sisters." Dealey had interrupted the President to say that the nation needs a man on horseback, but "you are riding Caroline's tricycle." However, the most provocative aspect of Dealey's paper during Kennedy's tour of Texas was neither the advertisement nor the editorial but the news columns. The day before the President arrived, the top of the front page was covered almost five inches deep across seven columns with a story epitomized by the headline "JFK Visit Ires San Antonio Liberals." Three columns at the bottom were given over to "Rain Seen in Dallas During JFK Visit"—a "weather story" in the conventional sense only until it reached the third paragraph, where the reporter slid smoothly into the real subject with "political skies should remain dark" and went predictably on from there.

The *News* of the following morning, the day Kennedy was to arrive, was a strange celebration of a Presidential visit. The lead story on the front page ran across two columns that extended from the top almost to the bottom of the page. Headed in huge type across seven columns "Storm of Political Controversy Swirls Around Kennedy Visit," it was built largely on Senator Ralph Yarborough's complaint that Governor John Connally had not invited Yarborough to a reception at the Governor's Mansion. Nearly four columns at the bottom of the page were covered with a story headed "Yarborough Snubs LBJ." All eight columns at the top of page 12 were four inches deep with "President's Visit Seen Widening Democratic Split."

One cannot know the extent to which the *News*, always passionate, excites the passions of Dallas. But surely Walter Lippmann is correct in contending that Dallas is the very atmosphere of violence and that it is only incidental that Lee Oswald turned left while those Dallasites who assaulted Lyndon Johnson and his wife in 1960 and those who hit and spat upon Adlai Stevenson a month before the assassination turned right. "The common characteristic of all of them," Walter Lippmann wrote, "was their alienation, the loss of their ties, the rupture of the community." On the morning that this analysis was published, Jack Ruby killed Lee Oswald. One could hardly ask for stronger confirmation.

But one can commend these issues of the *News* to those who study conflict as it is promoted in the press. And one can venture that the *News* and similar papers, so many of them so noticeably devoted to seeking out political conflict, should consider the possibility that they are manufacturing it as well.

As for the coverage of the assassination, the problem for the reporter may be suggested by the fact that the most recent precedent was more than six decades in the past. The President is shot. The natural movement is toward him; this much is certain. But, the President is dead— bewilderment reigns. Does the reporter stay near the body to glean the details of death? Or does he try to attach himself to the police who seek the assassin? Or does he attempt to divine the next movements of the new President and move with him? And whatever his decision, what should be his manner, what are his rights and privileges, what is the priority of information in tragedy's hierarchy of values?

Above all, where in the midst of chaos does the reporter find incontrovertible fact? This is the most important question, for one who reviews the journalistic record of the assassination period can recognize the inevitable difficulties, award many high marks for enterprise and diligence, and yet be left with the inescapable conclusion that the press reported many more facts than there actually were.

Item: The rifle was found by a window on the second floor of the Texas School Book Depository. Or it was found in the fifth-floor staircase. Or it was hidden behind boxes and cases on the second floor. Ultimately, all reports agreed that it had been found on the sixth floor.

Item: The rifle was first reported to be a .30-caliber Enfield. Then it was a 7.65mm Mauser. But it was also an Army or Japanese rifle of .25 caliber. Finally, it became an Italian-made 6.5mm rifle with a telescopic sight.

Item: There were three shots. But some reports mentioned four bullets: one found on the floor of the President's car, one found in the President's stretcher, a third removed from Governor Connally's left thigh, and a fourth removed from the President's body. There was even one report of a fifth bullet found in the grass near the side of the street where the President was hit. Finally, there was general agreement that there were only three bullets.

So far, the mistakes seem to be of no great moment—small discrepancies fairly quickly resolved. But when these conflicting reports were coupled with some of the more mystifying details, the pivotal importance of absolute accuracy became evident:

Item: The first reports of the President's wounds described "a bullet in the throat, just below the Adam's apple" and "a massive, gaping wound in the back and on the right side of the head." The position of the President's car at the time of the shooting, seventy-five to one hundred yards beyond the Texas School Book Depository, explains the head wound. But how can one account for the bullet in the throat?

Item: The shots were fired between 12:30 and 12:31 P.M., Dallas time. It was reported at first that Oswald dashed into the house at Oak Cliff where he was renting a room "at about 12:45 P.M." Between the time of the assassination and the time of his arrival at the rooming house, Oswald reportedly (1) hid the rifle, (2) made his way from the sixth floor to the second floor of the building, (3) bought and sipped a Coke (lingering long enough to be seen by the building manager and a policeman), (4) walked four blocks to Lamar Street and boarded a bus, (5) descended from the bus and hailed a taxi, and (6) rode four miles to Oak Cliff. How did he accomplish all this in fourteen minutes?

Item: Oswald was only an average marksman in the Marines. Yet gun experts who were meeting in Maryland at the time of the assassination held that, considering the rifle, the distance, the angle, and the movement of the President's car, "the assassin was either an exceptional marksman or fantastically lucky in placing his shots." The Olympic champion marksman, Hubert Hammerer, said upon being interviewed in Vienna that *one* shot could have been made under the conditions described, but he considered it unlikely that anyone could have triggered three accurate shots within five seconds with a bolt-action rifle. How did Lee Oswald do it?

All this is the stuff of conspiracy theories. Given a mass of conflicting and mystifying detail about the actions of an accused assassin, it is natural to seek an easier explanation. One is that Oswald was not the assassin—except that so many of his actions were suspicious. Another is that he had an accomplice—"No one remembered for sure seeing Ruby between 12:15 and 12:45," one press report ran—and the mind leaps to the desired assumption. Small wonder that the Warren Commission's findings are unlikely ever to receive anything approaching total belief.

It is a curious fact that the most involved of the conspiracy theories sprang from those who are usually the sniffiest about press reports, the academicians. Some of them know that the press goes to the authorities for quotations on matters of moment. Deep down, they are likely to suspect authority more than they suspect the press. Thus it was that a political scientist and a historian, Jack Minnis and Staughton Lynd, wrote "Seeds of Doubt," which appeared in *The New Republic*.

"Seeds of Doubt" was by far the most remarkable article to appear during the assassination period. Without ever actually saying that someone was suppressing information and rearranging evidence, Minnis and Lynd seemed to be saying nothing else. Their article was a catalogue of conflicting press reports from the time of the first news up to mid-December, and broadly hinted that the authorities were making changes as they went along in order to bring inconvenient facts into line with indisputable evidence. The tone was typified by the section dealing with the speed of the President's car:

All early accounts of the assassination put the speed of the President's limousine at about 25 miles per hour, but now it has slowed to 15 miles per hour (*Life*, November 29), "no more than half the 25 miles per hour first estimated by authorities" (*Newsweek*, December 9), and 12 miles per hour (*U.S. News & World Report*, December 9). The latter magazine comments: "If President Kennedy's car had been moving even 20 miles per hour, the experts say, it might have made the lead time too difficult a problem for the sniper."

Assessing the Minnis-Lynd article and an accompanying sidebar that speculated about the throat wound and the whereabouts of Jack Ruby at the time of the assassination, one horrified reader commented,

"What can it all mean, except the insinuation that Oswald and Ruby *were* connected and that Oswald's death was part of a mysterious conspiracy in which both were engaged and which the authorities are trying to hush up?"

As it turned out, the structure of the Minnis-Lynd thesis came crashing down only a few days after the article appeared. The President's throat wound, it was finally determined, had not been caused by the entry of a bullet but by the exit of a fragment. Oswald had not made his trip in fourteen minutes but in thirty, having arrived in Oak Cliff at about 1:00. The exceptional marksmanship is perhaps best explained by Gertrude Himmelfarb: "But why . . . assume that each of the shots found its intended mark? It would appear that not three out of three but one out of three achieved its purpose (the first inflicting no serious injury and the second hitting Governor Connally). To know how extraordinarily successful or lucky an assassin is, one would have to know how often he was unsuccessful or unlucky." As if to confirm this diagnosis, it was later reported that Oswald had earlier shot at General Edwin Walker.

In the end, one must conclude that the press performed in *its* best tradition. The *news* of the assassination was made up almost entirely of authoritative reports. After all, reporters did not say that a bullet entered the President's throat; they quoted Drs. Malcolm Perry and Kemp Clark of the Parkland Memorial Hospital in Dallas. The Dallas police first identified the rifle as a .30-caliber Enfield and a 7.65mm Mauser. A Secret Service man said he thought the weapon was a .25-caliber Army or Japanese rifle. The housekeeper at the Oak Cliff rooming house said that Oswald had come dashing in at about 12:45. And so on.

But the central question is whether the best tradition of the press is good enough. To blame a quoted authority is not a defense of the press but an explanation of two errors: the authority's for making a mistake and the press's for publishing it. The lesson of Dallas is actually an old one in responsible journalism: reporting is not democratic to the point that everything posing as fact has equal status.

It must be said immediately that some errors were inevitable. Governor Connally says that the car had just made the turn at Elm and Houston Streets when the firing began. Mrs. Connally says that the car was near-

ing the underpass—220 yards from the turn. Both cannot be right—
in fact, the consensus indicates that both were wrong—but where can a
reporter find better authorities than those who were in the car at the
time?

Putting aside the discrepancies that are never likely to be resolved,
one must ask whether the press was too eager to satisfy the hunger for
detail and to beat the competition. It is one thing to report certainties
such as that the President has been shot and is dead, and quite another
to quote a seeming authority—the nearest Secret Service man, a flus-
tered housekeeper—whose speculations breed suspicion. Is satisfying
the public desire for a story adequate reason for rounding it out with
supposition? Is it possible that the proud Age of Instant Communication
sparks competition that debases journalism? These are questions, in
any case, that might be debated at the next meeting of the American
Society of Newspaper Editors.

The Television Story in Dallas

The first bulletins about the shooting in Dallas began to arrive at NBC News headquarters in Burbank, California, just after 10:30 A.M., PST. It was my job to read them on the air for West Coast NBC stations, which at that hour normally receive programs from the Burbank control point.

Long afterward I learned that at the same moment NBC News correspondent Robert MacNeil, who had been covering President Kennedy's Texas trip, was on the telephone from Dallas to NBC News headquarters in New York, beginning a series of firsthand reports on the shooting of President Kennedy. MacNeil had jumped off the White House press bus in the Dallas motorcade at the first sound of gunfire. NBC News cameraman David Weigman also left the motorcade briefly to film the scenes of spectators throwing themselves on the ground, of police officers running with drawn guns, and of the building known as the Texas School Book Depository.

I was sitting in Studio 6 at Burbank, continuing to read the AP and UPI bulletins as they came in. This went on for about twenty minutes, until control of the entire NBC network was assumed by New York news headquarters. It had been an unnerving experience, because the truth of the news had been as difficult to grasp in the reading as it must have been in the hearing.

The task of continuing and expanding the news coverage overrode emotion. NBC at first planned to send a chartered Boeing 707 jet with newsmen and technicians from New York to Dallas, but that flight was diverted to Washington after President Johnson returned there. In Dallas the burden of coverage fell on correspondent MacNeil, reporter

Charles Murphy of NBC-affiliated station WBAP-TV in Fort Worth, and, later on, a contingent from the West Coast.

Few of us had time to pack. Almost as soon as I left the studio in Burbank, I was ordered to depart for Dallas with two film crews, news editor Don Roberts, and producer-director Frederic Rheinstein. Other news agencies sent personnel from their West Coast bureaus. Most of us were aboard American Airlines Flight 20, which arrived in Dallas little more than four hours after President Kennedy was shot. NBC White House correspondent Sander Vanocur, cutting short a vacation, was also on that flight, which continued on to Washington from Dallas. As we flew toward Dallas, he remarked that he had great faith in the power of the presidency, and that an orderly continuation of government under Lyndon Johnson was assured. Later that night Vanocur was on the air from the White House, making a similar observation.

It was a long flight. For more than two hours we were almost out of touch with the flow of events, except for piecemeal radio dispatches received in the cockpit and relayed to the passengers over the public-address system by the pilot or by one of the newsmen who were allowed to monitor the radio.

All the while, of course, coverage in Dallas was continuing. NBC's resident cameraman in Dallas, Maurice Levy, had assumed the task of coordinating the efforts of other cameramen and supervising the editing and airing of the first films. Correspondent MacNeil completed his reports from Dallas, including a broadcast from Parkland Memorial Hospital just after the death of President Kennedy was confirmed. MacNeil joined Murphy in handling studio telecasts from WBAP-TV.

Late on Friday, after Oswald had been captured, live television coverage was extended to the Dallas city jail. Telephone companies had improvised circuits for all three networks to handle the massive demands for telecasts from Dallas. One hastily arranged hookup led from Dallas through Fort Worth, Los Angeles, San Francisco, Denver, Oklahoma City, Chicago, and Buffalo, and then into NBC headquarters in midtown Manhattan.

It was almost dusk when our flight landed at Love Field in Dallas. News editor Roberts and producer-director Rheinstein took over our temporary headquarters at WBAP-TV. By telephone to NBC News in New York, they coordinated the flow of telecasts from Texas into the network coverage. Roberts supervised preparation of film and videotape materials. Rheinstein and several WBAP-TV directors supervised the actual telecasts. Roberts also handled assignments of correspondents and film crews, a job complicated by the fact that WBAP-TV is located in Fort Worth and the news was happening in Dallas. It was the only television origination point available to NBC, whereas the other networks have affiliates in Dallas proper.

My assignment was to cover Dallas police headquarters with the assistance of several film crews. NBC did not have a functioning, live mobile unit there until Saturday morning. The engine of the WBAP-TV unit had burned out in an earlier rush to drive it to Parkland Hospital. Rheinstein later hired a wrecking truck to tow it from place to place.

It was night when I arrived at Dallas police headquarters and went to the third-floor administrative offices. At that moment, Lee Harvey Oswald was being led through a milling, shouting crowd of reporters and photographers. He was saying, "They're holding me because I was in the Soviet Union. The police won't let me have representation." Flashbulbs went off. Battery-powered floodlights glared. Microphones were thrust about like electronic bayonets. The eye of the live television camera peered into the confusion and transmitted the first images of Oswald, wearing a grubby white T-shirt and that strange . . . sneer? Smirk? Insane smile? Television viewers probably saw and heard more than the reporters in that mass-media gauntlet which Oswald was forced through to get to the interrogation room of the Dallas Homicide Bureau.

In that throng it was difficult for any reporter to sort out who was who. But for the television reporters the problem was compounded by the need for simultaneous transmission. What was recorded by microphones and cameras (either film or live) would go on the air without much editing. What transpired in the hallway was broadcast without much opportunity for evaluation. And the television reporter could not move about freely, since his own movement was limited by the length of his microphone cable.

It was obvious that the police had no systematic method for disseminating information. A number of police officials made statements, but these did not add up to a full explanation of events. Thus there was inadequate explanation of the rifle that was carried aloft for all to see, of the coffee can filled with wax that was carried through the corridor after Oswald was given the paraffin test for powder burns, or of the card with Oswald's newly obtained fingerprints that was displayed. Television

showed these events without full explanation because full explanation
was not available. Television showed what was happening; it conveyed
the confusion of the moment.

Just before midnight on Friday, Chief Jesse Curry announced that
Oswald, already charged with the murder of police officer J. D. Tippit,
would also be charged with the murder of President Kennedy. Just after
midnight, Oswald was paraded into the police lineup room to be exhibited for photographs. On television, the viewer could see a hundred
or more reporters and photographers taking every available seat in the
room, some standing on tables, and Oswald entering, surrounded by reporters, photographers, cameras, and microphones. Oswald said he first
heard about being charged with the President's death when a reporter
told him in the hallway outside. Oswald's voice was barely audible in the
room. But it was heard on television, and most reporters got their quotes
from the audio engineers.

On Saturday the absence of an orderly public-information process was
made more conspicuous. The Night Superintendent of Police went on
national television to report that Oswald had spent Friday night in his
cell. District Attorney Henry Wade went before the cameras to state that
he would seek the electric chair for Oswald, and that there already was
adequate evidence to convict and to get the death penalty. Chief Curry
held a running interview in his office. Reporters and cameras would move
out into the hallway every time Oswald was moved from his cell on the
fourth floor to homicide headquarters on the third floor.

People who came to police headquarters that day could not evade the
television cameras. They recorded the arrival of Oswald's mother, wife,
and two small children. Marina Oswald, seeking some measure of privacy, was heard to say, "Leave me alone. Leave me alone." But no one
was left alone, because, in the absence of a coherent and full police account of the assassination, reporters were left on their own to fill in the
missing pieces.

Live television is peculiarly ill-equipped for investigative reporting.
While live cameras were reporting the comings and goings at police
headquarters Saturday, correspondent MacNeil and a film crew were
reconstructing the events of Friday by talking to the very people who
later gave their stories to the Warren Commission. But live television remained essentially limited to whatever comments the officials cared to
make. Most of those comments implied or stated that Oswald was guilty.

District Attorney Wade said Oswald had refused to take a lie-detector test. Homicide Captain J. W. "Will" Fritz called it a "cinch" case.

Thus, every public utterance, and there were many, necessarily had to be qualified by the reporter. Oswald had to be referred to as "the alleged killer" or "the accused killer." Repeated use of such terms may have inadvertently contributed to the notion that Oswald was the wrong man. He himself was heard to say on television, "I'm only a patsy." Incomplete information about the assassination, speculation about a possible conspiracy of unknown magnitude, and thoughts that the supposedly real killer might still be at large all contributed to an ominous atmosphere in Dallas.

On Sunday morning, when Oswald was to be transferred from the city jail to the county jail, there were disconcerting reports that death threats against Oswald had been received during the night by the FBI and the Dallas police. Extraordinary security precautions were in effect when I arrived at police headquarters. The basement where Oswald was to leave the jail had been searched. It was guarded by policemen with rifles. Everything was ready to whisk Oswald through the basement and into an unmarked squad car for the trip to the county jail. Live cameras were ready and set up in the basement.

Shortly after 11 A.M., I was standing with a microphone, relaying the information I had about plans to move Oswald. I was to tell the control room in New York when I had him in sight. That would be the cue to switch to Dallas. One police officer, to whom I shall long be grateful, urged me to stand on the north wall rather than the south wall of the jail entrance. Had I remained in the first spot, I would have been in the direct line of fire.

Oswald was brought down. He walked through a basement office. I said to the control room, "Let me have it," meaning, "Put me on the air." They did. I was looking directly into Oswald's face. Within seconds he had been shot. He crumpled to the pavement. I kept on talking as well as I could. There was unbelievable confusion and excitement. Some detectives drew guns. I looked for a place to hide, expecting more gunfire. There was no place to hide, and fortunately there was no more shooting. There was little that I could do except move around with the microphone and pick up bits and pieces of information. At the time there was an inescapable feeling that what was happening could not be happening. But it was. Oswald was dragged inside, then carried back out for the futile ambulance trip to Parkland Hospital. There had been a man with a gun who was subdued and taken into custody. Viewers who saw the events as they happened, and on the videotape playback a few minutes later, saw more than I did. Although I was just a few feet from Oswald, I did not see the actual firing of the shot.

And when other reporters were free to go inside police headquarters to get more information, I still was tied to the live microphone. Reporters on the inside obtained the name of the gunman, and it went out over the wire services before I learned it. A producer in New York relayed the information to me through the director and then through the stage manager, who was standing near our camera to give cues. I had great difficulty in getting the name correctly. At first I gave it as "Jack Lobee." Then they corrected me: "Jack Ruby, Dallas nightclub operator." I gave it just before signing off.

People who watched the events in Dallas on television probably saw more than those of us who were there. Television almost always permits people to see things more perceptively than they could if they actually were at the scene of an event, because cameras and microphones create an extension of the senses. When events are happening in several places, television coverage permits the viewer, in effect, to be in more than one place at the same time. People who spent many hours at their television sets had a more comprehensive account of what was happening than the individual correspondents, who were isolated while covering individual threads of the story.

Elmer W. Lower

A Television Network Gathers the News

In covering the assassination of President Kennedy and the resulting events, every member of the ABC news department and many members of other departments worked almost constantly for the better part of four days. Every camera and every piece of electronic equipment was pressed into service.

One problem in getting organized during those first minutes after the bulletin came through was that most of the news executives were at lunch. I was in the swimming pool at the New York Athletic Club when I received word of the tragedy by telephone.

Jesse Zousmer, who had joined ABC only ten days before as TV news director, set up operation of the main news studio. He rapidly gave orders to a large crew whose members didn't even know who he was. He got many curious glances, but no one questioned his authority or refused to do what he said.

ABC was the first network that switched directly to Dallas, where our affiliate WFAA-TV started reporting from the scene of the luncheon President Kennedy was to have addressed. While our affiliate gathered those early facts and reported them to the nation, we in the New York office were able to plan our next moves. Camera crews and correspondents, videotape facilities and live remote vans, writers, film editors, and news executives had to be dispatched to Dallas. As WFAA was feeding the network, our Washington bureau was also getting organized to report on the reaction to the assassination in the nation's capital.

It was during this breather that we finished setting up our main news studio, "TV 11," as our central video control in New York. The studio from which the first live reports were made had only one camera and was inadequate for sustained broadcasting. We lost time and efficiency in being forced to change studios in the early minutes of broadcasting. Not having a central TV news set to use both as control center and as an on-the-air studio proved to be a big handicap. We set up a control center on the seventh floor of our main building on West 66th Street. The operational studio was in the basement of another building on West 67th Street. Trying to work at a point so removed from the studio, still keep abreast of things, and give timely instructions to the staff was difficult.

At a meeting on Friday evening, we decided to suspend all regular programming and all commercials until after the funeral. It was then that we realized what an enormous job was ahead of us. The first reaction of our staff people was the same as that of any citizen: shocked disbelief. Being in the news business, we had to quickly shake off this feeling, this personal involvement, and get on with the task of reporting the story. I think that the very nature of the story we were reporting made our news department a more cohesive unit.

Many people pressed themselves beyond normal endurance levels, skipping sleep and grabbing sandwiches on the run. Bill Seamans, who became executive producer of our convention and election coverage, spent the first 36 hours of the weekend in the control room of "TV 11." He was finally forced to take a break when his eyes became so irritated from lack of sleep that he couldn't force them open all the way. He left the studio squinting. The engineering department did some extraordinary things that weekend, producing equipment on short notice and quickly moving it to Washington or Dallas as it was needed.

Some people who weren't even on the staff yet went to work ahead of schedule. Bill Downs started with the Washington staff two weeks earlier than planned. Tom Wolf, now executive producer of "ABC Scope," volunteered his services while his contract was still being negotiated and while he still had free-lance commitments. He produced an excellent film biography of the new President for us and then continued on the staff after the weekend was over. This forced him to complete his previous obligation to another network while under contract to us. This type of moonlighting is usually frowned upon, but in this case it was completely understandable.

During the weekend, the network absorbed the entire news staff of our New York City stations WABC-TV and WABC-Radio. Zousmer observed later that we had overlooked a vast reserve of experienced newsmen during our coverage. Newsmen at our larger affiliates, such as those in Chicago, Detroit, and San Francisco, could have been put on temporary network duty to relieve the burden on network newsmen. During that period, ABC-TV became a network devoted exclusively to news, and for the first time the news department took over and ran the network.

Other departments at ABC gave the news department splendid co-operation. The sports department volunteered equipment which had originally been scheduled for coverage of sporting events that weekend. The programming department chipped in by arranging for suitable memorial programs such as concerts and tributes from members of the performing arts. These helped bridge the long gaps between news developments.

The combination of Howard K. Smith and Edward P. Morgan as ABC's team of political commentators developed that weekend, some-what by accident. When the assassination took place, Smith was flying back to New York from Cairo, where he had taped an interview with President Nasser. He heard about the assassination in the cockpit of a jet through a radio call from Zousmer. When he got to New York, he went directly on the air. He had already gone 18 hours without sleep. I asked him what he thought he could do, and he replied, "If you let me go back to Washington and get a night's sleep, I'll do anything you say." That was Friday night. He reported for work at 6 A.M. Saturday in the Washington studio.

When the first bulletin came over, Morgan was having lunch at a Latin American embassy in Washington with Senator Hubert Humphrey and a White House staff aide, Fred Dutton. All three rushed back to the White House, from where Morgan relayed the first official confir-mation that President Kennedy had been killed. He gathered more in-formation at the White House before heading for our news studios in downtown Washington. He went directly on the air, live, to report on the stunned reaction at the White House and on the preparations that were already under way to transfer power to President Johnson. He drew on his personal recollections and on telephone calls from other close friends of the President to maintain a steady flow of fresh material that kept us, at a time when we were committed to open programming, from having to repeat ourselves.

At first our Washington bureau manager, Bob Fleming, alternated Smith and Morgan so that one could rest while the other was on the air. Then, naturally enough, they engaged one another in conversation on the air, and a new team of commentators was born.

Since the assassination was felt as such a personal tragedy by so many people, it was a very delicate subject for newscasting. It presented us with many tough decisions, which had to be made under the pressures of time and of network competition.

On Sunday we had one bad break, which eventually presented me with a pair of difficult decisions. We did not have a live camera on the scene when Oswald was shot. I did not know it at the time, but we had only one live mobile unit to cover the event and it had been assigned to cover Oswald's arrival at the county jail. The rationale for that decision was that if anyone was going to take a shot at Oswald, he would try at the county jail end, where the prisoner would have to walk in the open for fifteen feet.

After this, we quite naturally wanted to recover our losses. When our film of the shooting was processed, we found that the film was taken at a better angle than the previous videotape reports and the principals were more clearly defined. But by the time we got the film, the procession from the White House to the Capitol had begun, and we decided it would have been improper to break in and put the film on the air.

While the late President's body was lying in state and our cameras in Washington were trained on the bier and on the mourners passing by, we received the word that Oswald had died. I called our Washington remote to arrange a method of relaying this vital information to our viewers. I had Washington switch from the view of the bier to a shot in the driveway outside. Then we superimposed the words "Oswald is dead" over a ten-second view of President Johnson's car arriving. In this way we fulfilled our primary obligation of reporting the major news without going beyond the bounds of good taste.

A photograph that was supposed to show Oswald standing in the doorway of the Texas School Book Depository at the time the assassination was taking place also presented a tough decision. If it really were Oswald, then he could not have been the assassin. The fuzzy figure in the greatly enlarged photo bore a striking resemblance to Oswald. The facial features, the hairline, and the clothes were very much like Oswald's. The question was whether to use this picture, which appeared to prove that Oswald was not the assassin, and thereby to create a sensation. We decided against using the picture immediately. Instead we informed the FBI about it. The FBI checked out the photo and determined conclusively that the man in the picture was not Oswald, but another employee of the school book depository building. We never did use the picture.

Clearly the keen news competition among the three TV networks did not disappear entirely during the weekend, but it was more subdued than usual. Cooperation was greater than it had ever been in the industry's history. The pool coverage of events in Washington was an example of cooperation among the rival networks in the public interest.

John Casserly, our Rome bureau manager at the time, was able to get a rare, exclusive statement from Pope Paul VI; to get the statement, Casserly and his crew had to rush to the papal apartment in the Vatican in the middle of the night on ten minutes' notice. With this journalistic coup on film, we had to decide whether to ship it to New York on the first available jet or to wait until the communications satellite, Relay, was in position to carry the statement direct to New York. The latter course would automatically make the ABC film the common property of the three networks. I made my final decision in the spirit of cooperation that had been pledged by a news executive at another network. The interview was sent by Relay and was used by all networks. On Sunday, I called that same news executive to request a similar favor: the videotape of the Oswald shooting. He agreed at first, then later backed off. He threatened legal action if ABC used the tape on the basis of his original agreement to cooperate. For me, that was the one sour note in the coverage of the assassination, as far as the industry was concerned.

The industry did contribute greatly to the maintenance of stability during those trying days. The entire industry showed that it could conduct itself responsibly under unprecedented circumstances, that while it was keeping on top of the news, it could still be conscious of the sensibilities of a nation that was stunned, shocked, and distressed. I intended ABC news coverage to be sensitive and completely responsible, without broadcasting a lot of vague rumors at such a critical time. I think we accomplished our goal of providing competitive news coverage while maintaining standards of good taste.

Television held this nation together for four days, keeping people informed by a steady flow of news, and showing them vividly that President Johnson had taken command of the situation and that the transfer of power had taken place smoothly. That may seem like an overstatement, now that the event itself is so far removed. At the time, however, a great many responsible people felt that television was a cohesive force in our national life. I don't mean, of course, that subversive elements were ready to take over the government, but that people did feel terribly uncertain and shocked that something like this could happen in America. The steady flow of news gave a sense of confidence.

Ruth Leeds Love

The Business of Television and the Black Weekend

The television audience and the output of television have received considerable attention from audience studies like those undertaken by the Bureau of Applied Social Research and from content analysis projects like those undertaken by Kurt and Gladys Lang.[1] But no systematic study has to my knowledge been undertaken of the organizational structure of the industry. At present, anyone who is interested in the industry must turn to journalistic accounts like Opotowsky's *The Big Picture,* to college texts on broadcasting, or to "advice to the public" books like *Television and the Public Interest,* the contents of which are not as awesome as the title.[2]

Following the President's assassination, the Bureau of Applied Social Research, Columbia University, and the Morse Communication Research Center, Brandeis University, had an opportunity to embark on a study of the industry, specifically, to investigate the behavior of television news people during November 22–25.[3] Between December 5

Portions of this paper were presented at the annual meeting of the American Association for Public Opinion Research, Excelsior Springs, Missouri, May 1964.

1 Gary A. Steiner, *The People Look at Television* (New York, 1963). Kurt Lang and Gladys Engel Lang, "The Unique Perspective of Television and its Effect," *American Sociological Review* (1953), *18,* 3–12 and "The Inferential Structure of Political Communications," *Public Opinion Quarterly* (1955), *19,* 168–83.

2 Stan Opotowsky, *The Big Picture* (New York, 1962). A. W. Bluem, J. F. Cox, and Gene McPherson, *Television and the Public Interest* (New York, 1961).

3 The project committee, headed by Louis Cowan and Paul Lazarsfeld, included Allen Barton, Herta Herzog, Patricia Kendall, and Clara Shapiro. David Elesh and Louise Johnson assisted with the coordination of interviews in New York. Miss Johnson and Gene Levine interviewed the people in Dallas, Texas. Herbert Gans, Albert Gollin, and Grace Malakoff conducted interviews in Washington, D.C. Interviews in New York were conducted by David Elesh, Faye Ennis, Jack Ferguson, Herbert Gans, Margit Johannson,

and January 8, 90 interviews were conducted: 36 at NBC News, 30 at ABC News, and 21 among radio, television, and newspaper people in Dallas, plus several persons in New York and Dallas on the AP and UPI staffs. The interviewers worked with a flexible, open-ended schedule, spending an average of two hours with each respondent.

From these interviews we obtained a fairly comprehensive picture of how the network news departments operate, how they organize the coverage of an unanticipated, complex, national event, and how the norms and values of the news department influence the coverage. The broadcasters described their personal and professional reactions to the news of the assassination, their perceptions of the audience, and the problems they encountered during three-and-one-half days of continuous coverage. This paper presents only some of the findings, focusing primarily on a few of the norms and values that guide the broadcasters.

On November 26, following the national day of mourning, the nation resumed its business. The business of the television critics was to evaluate the way television had covered the presidential assassination and funeral.[4] In general, the critics agreed that television had come of age during these four days. Words like "honor" and "heroic" were applied to the coverage. Television was praised for its exercise of taste and its display of public responsibility, which are generally said to be lacking at other times. The more sophisticated critics observed that such comprehensive coverage was feasible only because the advertising revenues that support "the wasteland" also support news coverage.[5] But the full logical implications of such an observation were lost amid the laurels on the printed page.

Possibly it was not so much that television rose to heroic heights to meet the occasion but that the occasion rose to the heights that television is more or less prepared to attain in this decade. One NBC respondent said:

Louise Johnson, Patricia Kendall, Gene Levine, Rolf Meyersohn, Julian Nixon, Hubert O'Gorman, Adele Seltzer, Mary Simmel, Vivian Vallier, Hannah Wartenberg, and David Wilder. The Bureau of Applied Social Research, Columbia University, and The Morse Communication Research Center, Brandeis University, administered the project.

[4] See, for example, Jack Gould, "TV: A Chapter of Honor," *New York Times* (November 26, 1963), and John Marshall Cuno, "In Time of Crisis Wasteland Bloomed," *Christian Science Monitor* (December 2, 1963).

[5] See, for example, Jack Gould, "TV Risked Profits in Kennedy Shows," *New York Times* (December 1, 1963), and his column in the theater section for the same day.

In terms of taste, of course, it's what you leave out—assuming that anything is technically possible . . . if what had happened on November 22, 1963, had happened on November 22, 1953, aside from technical matters, it wouldn't have been handled in the same way. We wouldn't have been as impressed with our power then.

Thus, for reasons of style, taste, and technology, the coverage of a similar event ten years ago would have been quite different. Yet it is likely the critics would have heaped praise on television in 1953 just as they did in 1963. Critics seem to think in terms of the here and now, contrasting today with yesterday but never with a more remote past. It seems that none of today's critics cited the fact that radio performed heroically on D day in 1944. A few compared the length of the continuous coverage on the black weekend with the length of the continuous coverage following FDR's death, but the comparison was only used as a ploy to bestow accolades. Nor was it mentioned that radio intended to perform heroically on V-E and V-J days but produced only anticlimactic coverage. The general praise of the Kennedy coverage masks the emergence of a tradition for the electronic coverage of overwhelmingly significant national events.

The specific praise is also misleading. The networks were lauded for their "unselfishness" in pooling the funeral coverage. The praise again masks a norm, that of pooling when the story takes on vast proportions. The first eyewitness accounts of the D-day landings were pooled and carried simultaneously by all networks.

Like the unassuming persons who participate in community disaster work but do not perceive themselves as heroes, some of the respondents did not see themselves as having done anything heroic. Several NBC respondents even objected vehemently to the critics' superlatives as indicating a lack of understanding of the business of television. The respondent said:

The Kennedy thing—there was a lot of turning on the camera. When the . . . thing was over, divorcing all false modesty . . . it was terribly successful. In responding to the outpouring of reaction, my reaction was: yes, and that's what the viewer deserved, what he's entitled to. I've spent ten years as a TV producer and eight years before that as a newspaper man. . . . Why shouldn't I be able to report on the most significant and important story of our time? So this is my reaction now to the kudos on the Kennedy thing: thanks a lot, but people are entitled to it. . . . The Kennedy program was not that much better than our normal programming. Huntley-Brinkley, Cronkite—every night they are almost as distinguished as the Kennedy thing. . . . We've been mature for a long time, and it shows.

ABC also did not perceive itself as having done anything heroic, but it appears to have accepted the critics' praise as an indicator of the blooming of its news department. The ABC staff is largely new, compared with the staff at NBC. At the time of the assassination, one executive had been there only four months, and another had been there two weeks. A few quotes from various ABC executives will help explain ABC's situation.

Great human events, this is what we are born . . . to cover; things as they are happening is TV's great forte. . . . We are the third network and are at a disadvantage. . . . The concern now is to build the news department. . . . The budget has gone from 2 to 18 million in 2½ years. . . . [As a result of the assassination coverage] now they can't say we are not around. . . . Our correspondents are top men and they proved it.

My feeling is that we did a tremendous job on a story that I wish hadn't happened. But in the whole history of the operations at ABC they've never done anything this well. . . . We don't have a terribly good plant at ABC, especially communications . . . but I've been promised that this will be taken care of.

I think a year from now that the organization here would have been different. . . . We have tremendous physical limitations, especially for remote, live news coverage, and these will be improved. They were going to be anyway, but I think this speeds the process.

Television was engaged in business and not heroics on the black weekend, and the business of that weekend did have both unusual and usual aspects. The business of television was unusual in that the network's program department, which handles the entertainment and commercial aspects of the industry, was virtually unemployed, while the news department, which handles the news and public service aspects of the industry, was intensely overemployed. Business was unusual in that technical facilities were heavily taxed. In practical terms, this meant there was a built-in demand for cooperation between the networks. Since the norm of reciprocity can be expected to operate in the future as well as in the present, it is advantageous to cooperate. Business was unusual in that commentators broadcasted without scripts, chains of command were ignored or short-circuited, and channels of communication were abbreviated. Business was unusual in that it was toned with high emotion and was carried out with a great sense of public responsibility. Business was unusual in that the planning process and the implementation process were virtually one. And finally, business was unusual in that the public saw for 71 hours the output of a network department that it can normally view only for an hour or so each day.

But business was as usual in that the news department was covering a story via film, live telecasting, and commentary. Business was as usual in that virtually everyone carried out his normal duties. There was relatively little pinch-hitting. Business was as usual in that the news division had a bank of accumulated experience to guide its responses to what proved to be a national tragedy. And finally, business was as usual in that the norms and values of the news profession were in force more or less in the same way as they are at any other time. It is this last aspect of "business as usual" that will be elaborated here.

Because the norms of news organizations demand that the President be covered at all times and that one anticipate or "second guess" when and where news might occur, it was virtually chance that only the citizens near the school book depository witnessed Kennedy's assassination. The norm that requires constant presidential coverage was expressed at both ABC and NBC. An ABC executive relates:

On the previous night, the director called me at home and said that the Washington correspondent had to go to the studio to narrate over a film for the six o'clock show. This was in Houston, and the correspondent was supposed to be covering a banquet for Kennedy. I said "So?" He said, "That would leave Kennedy uncovered." I said, "That's ridiculous. What would happen if the President got shot?" "I gotcha," he says. You've got to have a local man cover for you. That's my stock phrase in cases like this. You got to use the impossible in cases like this, otherwise they don't get it. So I said get a local. I don't care what a man wants to do . . . you've got to be covered. It's strictly *pro forma*.

And a Southwest-based NBC respondent said:

I was with Truman every minute everywhere he went during the '48 campaign. . . . You sense these things as you are covering. You work closely with the Secret Service, and the routine of covering a President is always that the guy is going to get killed. . . . When you cover a President as a photographer, you have three networks and two wire-service photographers usually in a convertible right ahead of the President. . . . When you drive into a square or a crowd, you look around at the tops of buildings first and then you shoot a picture of the President. It is a normal feeling, and that is the reason you cover him 24 hours . . . because he is going to be shot. This is where you have all the conflict with the Salingers who say, "Why not cut it off?" You can't because they can't tell you when. And if he isn't going to get shot, he is going to pick up a baby. . . . Who is interested in what the President does 24 hours a day? But you are interested when he gets shot.

This norm about always covering the President, and the respondent's sensitivity to the mood of Dallas, led him to anticipate that something might happen during the presidential visit to the city. He kept the New York network office informed of hostile activities in Dallas and of the city's campaign urging good behavior on the part of the citizenry during the President's visit. He suggested that a film story could be built around these events. The New York office gave him permission for it, and the film was aired on the Friday morning news program. As one network executive phrased it, "This was prophetic."

The network, acting on wire-service information and tips from the White House, as well as the reports of its Southwest man, doubled the usual presidential coverage strength for the Dallas visit. The same respondent said, "Normally we would just come with a Presidential cameraman who travels with him—the man out of the White House and one other crew. But this time we had quite a few scattered over the Dallas area. And then we missed [the assassination] by one block."

This laconic comment on the miss is echoed with different feelings in a short post-assassination article written for *Byline* by an ABC commentator, who said, "The know-how and technical facilities that have developed . . . made it possible for television to mount its coverage of the assassination story with no advance preparations . . . and to show the nation every significant event in Dallas and Washington, except (fortunately, I think) the very assassination itself."

These statements indicate that, insofar as the broadcasters are oriented to news, they would have liked to have been able to televise the assassination itself. But since they were also concerned with the impact of the coverage on the audience and with standards of taste, possibly they were, after the fact, somewhat relieved not to have been able to televise the assassination.

Although NBC missed the assassination by one block despite doubling its coverage strength, anticipatory judgment and plentiful facilities enabled the network to televise Ruby's shooting of Oswald. One NBC producer said:

One executive had a premonition, he made sure we were adequately covered in Dallas. He felt something serious might happen, and we had very carefully planned that half-hour to go to Dallas at the time Oswald was brought out. We had cameras at both jails to cover it. All details were planned . . . the New York anchorman would switch to Dallas. Dallas said "give it to me" just as the doors opened. It was not luck, this was well-planned coverage.

And the executive explains his premonition in this way:

They kept talking about the fact of all the precautions, the armored car, the fact that feelings were strong in Dallas, it doesn't take much reportorial instinct that maybe you better go down. . . . Did I expect Oswald to be shot? No. . . . The cameras had already been set up for hours, we'd been down there before, but there wasn't enough happening to stay with it until when it became obvious they were ready to move him.

While the New York NBC people attributed the first live telecast of a murder to foresight and planning, a reporter from the NBC affiliate in Fort Worth stated that the local station had cameras set up only at the county jail. NBC had network cameras at the city jail because of

. . . the foresightedness of the NBC correspondent. . . . I was badly mistaken. I didn't think anything would happen, but I could conceive of some incident at the county [jail] because there was a big mob there. . . . The reason I was at the county for the Oswald transfer was that had he got there I would have had the opportunity to talk to him. . . . The police case would have been made, otherwise he wouldn't have been transferred. . . . Frequently the police don't want you to talk to the prisoner until they have made their case . . . [When] he is simply a prisoner of the Sheriff you can talk to him.

The local reporter's comments indicate that no two persons have quite the same "nose for news." The acuity of a person's news nose is probably a function of both his experience and his sensitivity to the environment. Recruitment policies make it likely that more persons with an acute sense for news will be found the higher one goes in the news hierarchy. For this and other reasons the networks rush their own people to the scene instead of relying solely on the coverage abilities of the local affiliate station. In fact, the news staff of an affiliate station appears to be a recruiting and proving ground for the network news staff. One NBC correspondent came to the network as a result of his coverage of a Southern bus boycott for a local station.

Returning to the coverage of the Oswald murder, ABC was unable to have live television cameras at the city jail and so obtained only film footage of the homicide. ABC had three mobile units in the local area. One of them was at the county jail, and the other two were being used to cover church services that Sunday morning. The network had decided to cover a Baptist church service in Fort Worth (Baptist because of President Johnson's religious affiliation) so that Sunday morning viewers would not tire of coverage that showed only the viewing of the President's casket in the Rotunda and preparations for Oswald's transfer. The local ABC station, independently and possibly for some of the same reasons, elected to cover a Methodist church service in Dallas. Only after the decisions and commitments had been made did it become quite evident that this would leave ABC with only one mobile unit to cover Oswald's transfer. As one ABC executive put it, "Here is a real case of crossed wires. We should have checked with them beforehand, but nobody thought of it." And apparently the commitments were irreversible, although several members of the ABC affiliate later said they thought the network was just being stubborn about not withdrawing from the Baptist service.

Left with one mobile unit, the network people in Dallas and the affiliate station people had to decide how it could be deployed most advantageously. It was felt that this would be a crucial decision. The atmosphere in which the decision was made gave rise to premonitions that something would happen. An ABC producer said:

It was in the air. Somebody was going to get him and everyone knew it. There was no blood lust. . . . Someone called a psychiatrist he knew and asked him if Oswald was to be shot where would it happen? He said near the scene of the actual assassination—the county jail. . . . Also there are wide open spaces, not like the underground passages in the city jail.

Acting on the opinion of the psychiatrist, ABC placed its remaining mobile unit at the county jail and two film cameras in the city jail.

While NBC quietly appreciated its live coverage scoop, ABC was quite frustrated at having recorded the event only on film. ABC soothed its feelings by pointing out that its films of the shooting were of top quality. One ABC executive told us:

We did have two film cameras at the city jail. . . . But if I could do it over, I think I would have had the producer yell louder to me about getting more equipment. Funny thing, though, when people talk to me about the show, missing Oswald is not what people mention. . . . It's my feeling that most people outside the trade don't place much emphasis on this business of getting the Oswald shooting live.

The last comment is illuminating, for it suggests that at least some news values and norms have no meaning for the consumers of news. If certain news values and norms are irrelevant for the consumers, one must ask what functions they serve for the producers of news. An NBC manager's reaction to the fact that CBS aired the bulletin announcing that shots were fired at the President six minutes before NBC did, is revealing:

CBS was on *long* before we were with the bulletin. They beat us by six minutes. One reason [why it is important] is tradition. It's traditional in journalism not to get scooped. Then there's the belief that if you're first and stay ahead, the audience in due time will learn this and learn to depend on you. The competitive edge is broadened. Then there's a negative reason. If you're second there's a potential morale problem among the staff. Look: it's just a lot of nonsense . . . being scooped. If you asked the first 100 people on the street who was first last Friday . . . most would say NBC. Our image is such that they expected it of us . . . if they know which is NBC.

Here, clearly, some careful audience research might help the broadcasters assess what norms and values are deemed important by the consumers. These men are saying that television news has taken over at least some journalism values without questioning their relevance for television. Furthermore, a mythology has developed to justify them, like that surrounding the scoop. And two executives, each from a different network, question the validity of the mythology, i.e., that scoops contribute to the image of the network and are important to the public.

Another ABC executive said, in more general terms:

There has never been any leadership in TV news and particularly in encouraging the best effort from the staff and giving them goals. Instead what we've had is a hodgepodge of newspaper values. . . . These values have made

TV news an ordinary reporting thing. We've got to develop TV news into TV news and get rid of a lot of false values. Too many think that TV news is just sound with pictures, and that's where we get bogged down.

Newspaper values have not been taken over completely, because the nature of electronic journalism has forced some modifications. Several executives explained that the greater impact of television makes a certain kind of caution much more imperative than it is for newspapers. Though rumors can be reported as rumors in a newspaper, to do so on television is much more difficult, for it is too easy for the audience to mishear. Also, since information can be aired much more quickly than it can be printed, such *bon mots* as "Wait for the sweet sacrament of confirmation," or "Get it fast, but wait for verification," are very important norms in the television news organization. Thus an NBC executive said that bulletins of plane crashes are not aired until the flight number and other details have been obtained and verified so as not to alarm more people than absolutely necessary. This policy appears to be adhered to whether or not the competition airs an incomplete bulletin. A similar kind of caution was used in announcing the President's death. Although much information was coming in, NBC withheld any death reports until the priests made their statement. CBS, on the other hand, according to its logs, began relaying unconfirmed reports of the President's death about fifteen minutes before the priests made their statement. NBC was well aware of the fact that CBS had "the President dead," but chose to wait. ABC showed similar caution, waiting until there was official word of the death instead of using the word of informed sources.

The timeliness of news and the appropriateness of presenting it, as well as whether it is a scoop, take on different meanings in the context of television. An ABC executive, quoted earlier, explained that the Oswald homicide films were processed and ready to be shown an hour after the shooting. Showing them as soon as they were ready would have meant interrupting the ceremonies at the Rotunda. The executive said, "I didn't think that was the place to inject a film of Oswald's murder. So we held that film for three hours; we finally worked it in on a switch to Dallas for a recap." Since ABC had voice reports of the murder at the city jail at the time it happened, there was no urgency to show the films of the event. Hence considerations of taste guided the decision not to air the films immediately.

The problematic and often unclear relationship between news values and canons of taste was quite in evidence when the respondents were asked to discuss the assassination film shot by a garment manufacturer and purchased by *Life*. Both ABC and NBC had an opportunity to bid on the film, but neither network desired to do so. The same ABC executive explained:

We had a high council of war on the *Life* film. . . . We sent two men around to view it in Dallas. I talked to them on the phone. The man who works for the ABC affiliate said to me, "I recommend that you don't even bid on it. It's too dramatic; I don't think it is the thing for home television." Our network man in Dallas got on the phone and said, "It's the greatest news film I've ever seen, but I think it would be in bad taste to show it." So we never even bid on it.

The executive was asked why it would have been in bad taste to show the shooting of the President when the network had already shown the film of the Oswald shooting. "That's a good question. . . . You would have to see the film. . . . I understand you can see the President's head snap as the bullet hit him and the blood spurt right out of his temple. It's far too strong stuff to put in the home." Another ABC executive, in response to the question, "Would you have used the *Life* film if you had been a producer?" said:

No. We took a look at the *Life* film, and by the time we got them we had other pictures, and we thought they were too brutal and enough had been shown. I don't know if I had gotten them immediately, though. . . . I would have to take into account when they were available. I might have used some of it instead of stills. The whole gory mess, I don't know; it was news.

The standards of taste change, then, relative to the news value of the item and the network's need to obtain pictures for broadcasting. When the coverage of such an item is live, however, it takes on a different dimension. An NBC producer, when asked, "What were your feelings about getting the Oswald shooting direct?" replied:

I thought it was great. Not the same feelings of taste as having the President shot; it wasn't gory. Even if the [Oswald] shooting had been gory, I would have stayed with it. I think if we had been live, I'd have stayed with the President too; when it's live, you have no control and the judgments differ because of that.

In effect, the producer has little editorial control with live coverage. Had cameras been trained on the President at the moment of assassination, the producer would have been faced with a judgment only after the fact, for he sees what the viewer is seeing, and at the same time, if the coverage is live. If something happens that he wishes to leave out, the producer can switch to another camera. Even so, events—like a man being shot—that happen virtually instantaneously still appear on the home screen at the same time that they appear in the television control room and so cannot be deleted.

But when editorial control can be exercised, news values do give way to taste in certain instances. Another NBC producer said, "We probably would have used some of the *Life* film as stills if we had had it. We have used film of people being killed before, in Viet Nam." He goes on to explain that Oswald's death turned out to be a very clean one.

If it hadn't been a clean death, we'd have been in terrible trouble. The kids would have seen it and we would have gotten letters; the adults would have blamed it on TV. About the *Life* film, it wasn't the fact that it was JFK but . . . the inside of a man's brain being outside that was so awful.

Newspapers are not faced with this type of problem because they do not report an event simultaneously with its occurrence. The wire-service respondents supplied examples of deleted material—parts of quotations that contained blood and gore.

In short, the American public beyond Dallas did not witness the assassination of the President simply because the television cameras had not been set up in the fateful block and because film of the event was not available until some time later, when its news value had changed to historical value. Since the networks were using all material that was related directly to the assassination, it is quite likely that they would have used at least an edited version of the *Life* film had it been available on Friday.

The broadcasters had their own after-the-fact discussion of this matter at a conference of the Radio and Television News Directors Association held February 29, 1964. The news directors of the three affiliated television stations in Dallas and Fort Worth agreed that they would have used the assassination material if it had been available immediately. The NBC affiliate director said, "I think all of us would have put it on the air if we had had it, preceded by a statement of what it contained. I don't see how you could have film like that and not use it." He also said that he would have sent the assassination material to New York on a closed-circuit line in order to let the network decide how to use it. Clearly, the decision to air something as violent as the President's assassination is not an easy one to make. Part of the difficulty of making such a decision might stem from the lack of a well-defined standard that takes both news values and canons of taste into account. The broadcasters might have been stimulated to develop such a standard if the assassination had been covered by live television cameras.

There is one more example of how standards of taste and standards of news are juggled in an attempt to come up with timely, accurate, and yet tasteful coverage. An NBC director recounts a problem that emerged in the control room where the incoming feeds could be viewed.

We went to the Washington Cathedral for a memorial service. When you do a thing like that you can get trapped. There were interesting things happening at the White House; but sometimes you get trapped because whether you can pull out of a church service is a matter of taste. The minister kept talking and talking and the picture at the White House kept getting better and better, and we decided to switch. I remember that the man in charge of special events—mostly religious programming—walked by. We asked him if he thought it would be all right to switch, and he said yes.

Another way of handling the problem would have been to tape the scene at the White House and broadcast it once the minister had finished speaking. But this would have been coverage after the fact rather than live coverage, and live coverage, particularly of national events, is valued more highly by the broadcasters than taped or filmed coverage. And it is the live, continuous coverage of a set of related events happening in different places that makes the relationship between news values and canons of taste problematic.

All the news that's fit to print is not necessarily fit to be seen. And although all the news can be printed at the same time, it cannot be seen at the same time. It is within these constraints that television broadcasters make decisions about news and taste based on experience, pragmatism, and the intuitive knowledge that comes with membership in one's culture.

The direction that such decisions take and the concern that is exercised over them probably are determined in large measure by the nature of the events being covered. Thus, the live coverage of the Glenn parade in Washington was interrupted to show the scene of an airplane crash at Idlewild. On the other hand, during the black weekend the networks reported virtually no news that was not related to the assassination and the funeral. The norms and values that guide the news departments, then, are flexible and adaptable to the needs of the occasion. Business as usual means the ability to grasp what is suitable in a particular situation, given the general values of news and taste.

Part II

The Public Finds Out:
The Use of the Channels of Communication

Bradley S. Greenberg

Diffusion of News About the Kennedy Assassination

The murder of President Kennedy concentrated all channels of communication—both mass media and person-to-person—on a single incident at the same time. Generally, both kinds of communication channel are used to prepare for anticipated major news events; the media organize special staffs, and people talk of forthcoming events. The initial or critical information about such events is typically presented first by the mass media to the public, and then moves into interpersonal channels. For unanticipated events as well, the mass media have been repeatedly shown to be the first source of information for as many as nine out of ten adults, with interpersonal communication slower and less pervasive.[1] This predominance of the mass media in transmitting information contrasts with the finding that interpersonal contacts are of primary importance in transmitting opinions.[2]

This paper describes what, when, where, and how people first found out about the assassination, and how they passed the information along. Comparisons between this study and other studies of the diffusion of news—of anticipated and unanticipated events, both major and minor—may be expected to increase our understanding of how news is diffused.

---

[1] Paul J. Deutschmann and Wayne A. Danielson, "Diffusion of Knowledge of the Major News Story," *Journalism Quarterly* (1960), *37*, 345–55; Wayne Danielson, "Eisenhower's February Decision: A Study of News Impact," *Journalism Quarterly* (1956), *33*, 433–41; Otto N. Larsen and Richard J. Hill, "Mass Media and Interpersonal Communications in the Diffusion of a News Event," *American Sociological Review* (1954), *19*, 426–33; *Satellites, Science, and the Public* (Ann Arbor, Michigan: Survey Research Center, University of Michigan, 1959), 57 pp.

[2] Elihu Katz and Paul F. Lazarsfeld, *Personal Influence* (Glencoe, Illinois, 1955).

Telephone interviews were conducted over a four-day period with adults in San Jose, California (population about 200,000) within 10 days after the assassination. Respondents were randomly selected from telephone listings for the city. Of the 560 sample telephone numbers in service, 419 (75 per cent) yielded completed interviews, 65 (12 per cent) refused, and 76 (13 per cent) did not answer after an interviewer had called at least twice at different times of different days. Interviewers alternated between sexes in choosing respondents; if the first call was to a female, the second was to a male. Our sample contained almost the same distributions for age, sex, marital status, and occupation as were found for the area in the 1960 census.

The first news. Respondents were asked whether the first news they heard was that the President had been shot, announced at approximately 10:30 A.M., PST, or that the President was dead, announced at approximately 11:30 A.M., PST. (The official time of death was later set at 11 A.M., PST, but the actual announcement by the media occurred between 11 and 11:30 A.M.) Those who heard of the shooting before the death announcement were questioned separately about each event. The 88 per cent of the respondents ($n = 367$) who heard of the shooting before the death announcement were classified as Early Knowers (EK); the remaining 12 per cent ($n = 52$), whose first knowledge of the events was after the death announcement, were labeled Late Knowers (LK).

Rate of diffusion. The high percentage of Early Knowers shows how fast the news of the assassination was disseminated—nine out of ten knew of the events within 60 minutes after the first announcement. However, this classification partly masks the real speed of the diffusion. Among EK, 42 per cent heard of the shooting within the first 15 minutes, and more than 70 per cent were informed within 30 minutes. Ninety per cent of the EK, or 79 per cent of the entire sample, heard the news within 45 minutes of the earliest announcement. One-third of the LK first heard of the events within 15 minutes after the announcement that the President was dead. Seventy per cent of the LK had heard of the death within 45 minutes. Across the entire sample, almost everyone heard quite quickly what had happened; the last person informed heard the news about 1:30 P.M., three hours after the event.

Location. The Early Knowers and the Late Knowers tended to be in different places when they first heard the news, the EK when they heard of the shooting, and the LK when they heard of the President's death.

Thirty-eight per cent of the *EK*, but only 19 per cent of the *LK*, were at work ($p < .005$); 21 per cent of the *EK* and 34 per cent of the *LK* were "out someplace," e.g., shopping, visiting, in a car ($p < .02$); the remainder of each group were home at the time. A larger percentage of *EK* than of *LK* were at work, with access to other persons or to a radio; a smaller percentage were "out."

Source of first information. Respondents were asked how they first found out the President had been shot and/or how they first found out the President was dead. No respondent reported first reading about the events in his newspaper—all were informed by the broadcast media or by other persons. Figure 1 shows the distribution of the sources of first information.

One-half the *EK* were first informed by other persons—10 per cent by phone, and 40 per cent in face-to-face meetings. Their reaction was to use the mass media to confirm what they had heard and to obtain new information; 84 per cent of the *EK* reported that they heard of the death on the radio or on television. Two-thirds of the *LK* were informed first by other persons. Their reaction was also to get to a radio or television set quickly for additional information. For both groups, the broadcast media were secondary in the flow of information at the outset of the day's events. For the *EK*, broadcast media were the predominant sources for news of Kennedy's death, but radio told more of the *EK* than television did ($p < .05$).

This high level of interpersonal activity contrasts with the findings of previous diffusion studies, which indicated that the mass media were better at disseminating news of major events. Yet there are degrees of major events, at least in terms of audience attention. In another study, I examined the role of interpersonal communication in the diffusion of news about 18 different events.[3] Audience awareness of the events ranged from 14 to 100 per cent. I expected that interpersonal communication, as the first source of news, would rank higher for news that many or few people knew about than for news that an intermediate number knew about. The data supported this expectation. Similarly, the Kennedy assassination data suggest that news of immense importance is more likely to be disseminated by person-to-person contacts than less important news. (At the other extreme, news of importance to relatively few

[3] Bradley S. Greenberg, "Person-to-Person Communication in the Diffusion of News Events," *Journalism Quarterly* (1964), *41*, 489–94.

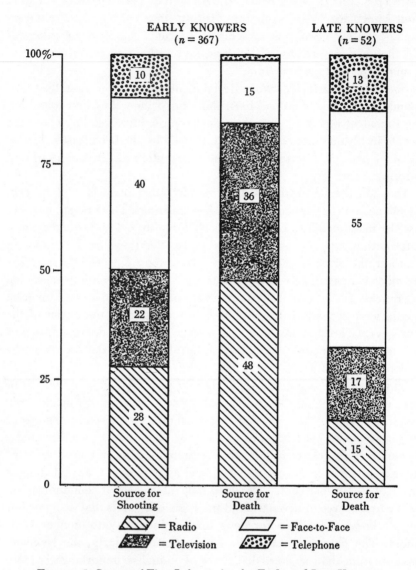

FIGURE 1. Source of First Information for Early and Late Knowers.

TABLE 1

Rate of Diffusion by Media

Time news was first heard (minutes after 10:30 A.M.) and number hearing it at that time	How news was first heard			
	Face-to-face	Radio	TV	Telephone
0–5 min. ($n = 87$)	29%[a]	32%	28%	11%
6–15 min. ($n = 36$)	27	28	39	6
16–30 min. ($n = 87$)	45	33	11	10
31–45 min. ($n = 23$)	57	30	4	9
46–60 min. ($n = 30$)	47	27	20	7
Over 60 min. ($n = 76$)	46	20	22	12
Average diffusion by medium . .	40	28	21	10

[a] Read "Of the 87 respondents who first heard the news in this time period, 29 per cent heard it face-to-face." All rows sum to 100 per cent.

people may be selectively perceived by those who consider it important and passed along by interpersonal channels to others with similar interests.) Given an event of the proportions of the Kennedy assassination, all stops were pulled out, all communication systems were activated.

Diffusion by media. In addition to examining the general diffusion by all media, we also compared the rates of diffusion of the various media. Since the first person in this sample to hear of the assassination had heard of it from radio or television, we expected that the majority who heard the news very early would have heard it from the mass media rather than interpersonal channels. The results of this analysis are in Table 1.

Face-to-face communication was the predominant mode of finding out about the assassination, but was considerably less active during the first 15 minutes than it was some moments later. Interpersonal channels reached their peak of activity during the second half-hour. In contrast, television was busiest for that first 15-minute period; during those minutes, it informed a far larger proportion of people than it did in any one time period thereafter. Radio maintained a fairly constant rate of diffusion during all the time segments, never varying far from the average proportion of the population it informed. Similarly, the telephone informed close to its average of 10 per cent of the respondents during each time period.

Table 2 shows two important findings: (1) Radio did not diffuse the news as fast as television during the first 15 minutes, but exceeded television (and the other sources as well) for the rest of the first hour, prob-

TABLE 2

Cumulative Diffusion Rate of Each of the Media

| Time in minutes after 10:30 A.M. | How news was first heard and number who heard that way | | | |
	Face-to-face (n = 136)	Radio (n = 97)	TV (n = 72)	Telephone (n = 34)
5 min.	18%[a]	29%	33%	30%
15 min.	25	39	53	36
30 min.	54	69	67	62
45 min.	64	76	68	68
60 min.	74	84	76	74
Over 60 min. . . .	100	100	100	100

[a] Read "Of the 136 people who first heard the news from another person face-to-face, 18 per cent heard it in the first five minutes."

ably because the later stages of diffusion occurred during the lunch hour; at that time radios were presumably turned on by some workers who had not previously heard the news. (2) Diffusion of the first news by telephone more closely approximated the diffusion rate of radio and television for the first half-hour than that of face-to-face communication. Those who were learning over the telephone were doing so almost as rapidly as those listening to radio or watching television—and all three groups were hearing sooner than those who eventually found out from others. For really critical events, the telephone may well be the individual's broadcasting facility.

Location and first source. Whether other persons or the mass media were the first of information obviously depended to some degree on where the respondents were. Table 3 presents the first source of information in terms of where the respondents were when they first heard the news.

These data further clarify how information about both the shooting and the death was diffused. Two-thirds of the *EK* who heard about the shooting at home were informed by the mass media, mainly television. Of those at work, 75 per cent were initially informed by other persons; for those "out," personal contacts and the mass media were almost equally active. As indicated earlier, the *EK* with access to broadcast media turned them on. At home, television was heavily favored; at work and "out," radio was more accessible. Among all the *LK*, regardless of location, other persons were the major first source of information.

First personal sources. Respondents who first heard the news from another person were asked to identify the informant as either spouse, other relative, friend or neighbor, co-worker, or stranger. This information is tabulated against location when first hearing the news in Table 4.

Location and source were highly correlated. Those at home learned primarily from relatives, neighbors, or friends; persons working heard from co-workers; those "out" someplace were informed for the most part by strangers. The magnitude of the event activated what would normally be a little-used interpersonal channel for those at work or "out"—talking with strangers. Apparently, for all concerned, proximity was the overriding factor in informing others.

Those who were informed first by another person were compared with those informed first by the mass media in terms of sex, marital status, age, and occupation. Among the men, 62 per cent said their source was another person; 44 per cent of the women said theirs was another person $(p < .001)$. The principal sources for the men, of course, were co-workers. Exactly 50 per cent of both the married and unmarried respondents first learned from other people. Fifty-four per cent of those under 50, and 42 per cent of those 50 or older, heard first from others $(p < .10)$. Finally, those in higher occupational categories—the professionals (70 per cent), proprietors and managers (56 per cent), and the clerical, sales, and technical people (59 per cent)—were more likely to hear from other persons $(p < .02)$ than those in lower occupational categories (44 per cent). The most likely interpretation of this difference is that professionals are more routinely in contact with other people than are people in lower occupations.

First persons told. Respondents were also asked to state whom they had first chosen to tell the news to (or discuss it with) after hearing it

TABLE 3

Where News Was Heard and Media

First Source of News	Early Knowers						Late Knowers		
	News of Shooting			News of Death			News of Death		
	Home[a] ($n = 147$)	Work ($n = 136$)	Out ($n = 78$)	Home ($n = 159$)	Work ($n = 131$)	Out ($n = 74$)	Home ($n = 24$)	Work ($n = 9$)	Out ($n = 17$)
Radio . . .	22%[a]	22%	49%	25%	63%	66%	13%	22%	20%
TV	44	3	9	69	3	18	33	0	13
Personal . .	34	75	42	6	34	16	54	78	67

[a] Read "Of the 147 people who were at home when they heard of the shooting, 22 per cent first heard of it from radio."

TABLE 4

Person Learned From and Location

Person learned from	Location		
	Home $(n = 60)$	Work $(n = 96)$	"Out" $(n = 36)$
Spouse	12%	3%	3%
Other relative	35	2	6
Friend or neighbor	49	2	27
Co-worker	3	77	0
Stranger	1	16	64

themselves. As might be expected, these choices were highly correlated with where the respondents were at the time (see Table 5). Two-thirds of the people at home spoke first to a member of their family. Workers (72 per cent) spoke initially with co-workers. Greater variety is found among those who were "out" someplace, cut off from their normal interpersonal channels. Strangers, friends or neighbors, and spouses were equally likely to be told the news. Who was around to be told or could be reached by phone clearly had a lot to do with who was told.

Content. We also asked whether respondents had been the first to tell anyone the news. In all, 36 per cent reported that they had. Interestingly enough, when we separate the respondents into those who first learned from the mass media and those who first learned from other persons, we find that equal proportions (37 and 39 per cent, respectively) first told the news to at least one other person. Once again we are struck by the pervasiveness and speed of interpersonal channels.

Scope of interpersonal communication. People talked to a great many other people on Friday. Only 2 per cent of this sample reported talking with no one at all about the assassination; one-third of the respondents reported conversations with 15 or more people. Frequency of conversations was checked against the available demographic characteristics of the respondents. The most frequent talkers—those who reported having 20 or more separate conversations with as many different people—were identified as: 36 per cent of the men and 17 per cent of the women $(p < .001)$; 37 per cent of those in their twenties, 24 per cent of those in their thirties, 22 per cent of those in their forties, and 15 per cent of those who were 50 or older $(p < .01)$; and 33 per cent of the professionals, 34 per cent of those in technical and clerical occupations, 18 per cent of the managers, 23 per cent of the skilled workers, and 11 per cent of the retired and unemployed ($p < .05$). Marital status did not differentiate the frequent talkers from the infrequent.

Those who first heard the news from another person were more likely to discuss the assassination with a large number of other persons; 31 per cent of those whose first source of information was another person reported 20 or more conversations, whereas only 17 per cent of those whose source was radio or television reported that amount of talking ($p < .001$). This relationship remains the same even after controlling both for sex and for all three locations. For example, among the men who first heard from another person, 39 per cent reported 20 or more subsequent conversations; among men who learned the news from radio or television, 27 per cent reported that many conversations. Among the women who first heard the news from another, 22 per cent cited 20 or more conversations; of women who learned the news from radio or television, only 12 per cent recalled having had that many conversations. This suggests that access to other persons may be not only a matter of physical location, but also, to some degree, a matter of "social location." That is, some people seem to be able to locate themselves in, or perhaps create, a social situation in which interpersonal communication is more likely, regardless of physical location. Further research could well be devoted to study of the role in the news diffusion process played by such people, who are presumably both more receptive to communication and more talkative than others.

This study differs from previous studies of the diffusion process in several particulars. First, there is the *event* itself. Not since V-J day has there been a comparable spontaneous reaction to a single event. An event of this magnitude leads to different patterns of response from an event of lesser magnitude. Its study yields valuable insights about in-

TABLE 5

First Person Told and Location

First person told	Location		
	Home ($n = 161$)	Work ($n = 153$)	"Out" ($n = 92$)
Spouse	38%	15%	26%
Other relative	30	6	16
Friend or neighbor	11	1	23
Co-worker	16	72	8
Stranger	5	6	27

dividual reactions to perceived stress or crisis. Here the communication aspects of these reactions have been explored. Second, there is the single focus of all *channels* of communication. Previous studies have had to accommodate competing events, messages, and channels. In such studies the news inevitably failed to reach some people. In the present case, one can imagine no class of persons who did not know of the assassination by the evening of the day it occurred. This monopoly of all the channels of communication maximized the chance for diffusion to occur. Third, there is the *time* element involved. Earlier studies, including those on the more general diffusion of influence or of innovation, have been concerned with events that took place over hours or weeks or even longer.[4] Word of the assassination spread in a matter of minutes to virtually all the population.

In this rapid flow of information about the day's events, interpersonal communication was far more important than previous studies would have predicted. It was posited that interpersonal communication is most prominent, relative to the mass media, in transmitting information about events that are of interest to practically everyone or to practically no one. When the news has universal interest, the public has a more general "need to know," and a corresponding desire to generate or participate in social discourse about the news. When the news reflects very special interests, the "need to know" is quite narrow in scope. Among persons with those special interests, however, the information presumably is worth passing on to others with similar interests, who may well have missed hearing about it because little attention was paid to it by the mass media. In the middle comes news that will interest perhaps one-half to two-thirds of the potential audience. The bulk of the news is of this intermediate type, according to most readership studies.[5] It is read, seen, or heard, perhaps remembered for a while, but rarely transmitted further. Such news, whatever its intrinsic importance, does not greatly activate interpersonal channels. It is, in effect, consumed.

[4] Katz and Lazarsfeld, *Personal Influence*. See also Elihu Katz, "The Two-Step Flow of Communication: An Up-to-date Report on a Hypothesis," *Public Opinion Quarterly* (1957), *21*, 61–78; Everett M. Rogers, *Diffusion of Innovations* (New York, 1962); Elihu Katz, Martin L. Levin, and Herbert Hamilton, "Traditions of Research on the Diffusion of Innovation," *American Sociological Review* (1963), *28*, 237–52.

[5] R. Nafziger, "Newspapers and Their Readers" (Minneapolis: Research Division, University of Minnesota School of Journalism, 1948–49, mimeo.); Wilbur Schramm and David M. White, "Age, Education, Economic Status: Factors in Newspaper Reading," *Journalism Quarterly* (1949), *26*, 149–59.

Stephan P. Spitzer and Nancy S. Spitzer

Diffusion of News of Kennedy and Oswald Deaths

During the last decade sociologists have become increasingly interested in the process of diffusion, since the communication structure of a society is an integral part of its social organization. One direction that this interest has taken is toward investigation of the flow of information about important news events.[1]

Upon the death of President Roosevelt in 1945, Miller conducted one of the first studies of the diffusion of a major news story. In 1954 Larsen and Hill investigated the impact of the death of Senator Taft. Danielson conducted a panel study of reactions to President Eisenhower's 1956 decision to run for reelection. Shortly thereafter, Deutschmann and Danielson gathered information on four additional news stories (Eisenhower's heart attack, the launching of Explorer I and Sputnik, and Alaskan statehood) and attempted to describe apparent regularities and differences in the diffusion process. As a result of these and other related investigations, a series of findings describing the diffusion process has been accumulated.[2] This study investigates the flow of information that followed the assassination of President Kennedy and the murder of Lee Oswald.

Knowledge about the diffusion of news events is in its formative stage. Research on the mechanisms regulating the flow and uses of information

[1] The authors are grateful to the following students, without whose assistance in interviewing the study could not have been accomplished: Norman K. Denzin, Erwen W. Graber, Kathryn H. Hauser, Donald G. Moore, James H. Parker, Kathleen A. Peterson, Margaret Rutherford, Beverly A. Scott, and Janet A. Spading.
[2] Delbert C. Miller, "A Research Note on Mass Communication," *American Sociological Review* (1945), *10*, 691–94; Otto N. Larsen and Richard J. Hill, "Mass Media and Interpersonal Communication in the Diffusion of a News Event," *American Sociological*

remains necessary, for the following reasons. First, since the importance of the earlier events studied varied markedly, it is quite difficult to reach valid generalizations about the diffusion process. Second, owing to the continuing "communications explosion," people's habits may have changed since the earlier studies were conducted. Third, the earlier investigators were forced to spend many hours in developing research designs and measurement techniques before going into the field. They also had to allow sufficient time for the news they wanted to focus on to travel through the social structure. Waiting for the news to spread was most necessary for events with only moderate impact. The price of this delayed action was most likely an increase in the number of forgotten or distorted details. Fourth, although the many research methods used have a common core, they have tended to obfuscate the mechanisms of social diffusion. Not until recently have criteria for diffusion studies been established. Few investigations contain all the elements of a diffusion study as defined by Katz: the *temporal* spread of an *item* over specified *channels* of communication through some delimited *social structure*.[3]

The Kennedy and Oswald deaths provided an opportunity to test the universality of previous findings, as well as to describe the characteristics of the diffusion process in these two specific cases.

Sample and method

Because there were earlier investigations of major news events, it was possible to borrow from their methodology. The study was designed, the questionnaire was constructed and printed, and the interviewers

Review (1954), *19*, 426–33; Wayne A. Danielson, "Eisenhower's February Decision: A Study of News Impact," *Journalism Quarterly* (1956), *33*, 433–41; Paul J. Deutschmann and Wayne A. Danielson, "Diffusion of Knowledge of the Major News Story," *Journalism Quarterly* (1960), *37*, 345–55. See also Nahum Z. Medalia and Otto N. Larsen, "Diffusion and Belief in a Collective Delusion: The Seattle Windshield-Pitting Epidemic," *American Sociological Review* (1958), *23*, 180–86; Elihu Katz and Paul F. Lazarsfeld, *Personal Influence* (Glencoe, Ill., 1955); Elihu Katz, "The Two-Step Flow of Communication: An Up-To-Date Report on a Hypothesis," *Public Opinion Quarterly* (1957), *21*, 61–78; Georg Karlsson, *Social Mechanisms* (Glencoe, Ill., 1958), 18–55; Everett M. Rogers, *Diffusion of Innovations* (New York, 1962); Elihu Katz, "Communication Research and the Image of Society: Convergence of Two Traditions," *American Journal of Sociology* (1960), *55*, 435–40; Elihu Katz, Martin L. Levin, and Herbert Hamilton, "Traditions of Research on the Diffusion of Innovation," *American Sociological Review* (1963), *28*, 237–52.
[3] Elihu Katz and Martin L. Levin, "Traditions of Research on the Diffusion of Innovation," paper read at the American Sociological Association meeting, Chicago, September 1959.

B.4413

were trained within three hours after Kennedy was shot. The inter-viewers contacted the first respondents in the Kennedy sample three and one-half hours after the first news report. They contacted the first respondents in the Oswald sample half an hour after the first news.

The respondents were asked: (1) whether they knew of the event; (2) how they had heard of it, and in what order they turned to the differ-ent sources of information (if the respondent reported hearing from another person, he was asked to state his social relationship to the per-son); (3) where they were when they heard the news; (4) whether they had told other persons (if the respondent said he had told another person, he was asked to state how many persons he had told and his social relationship to each). Several open-ended questions were asked to check the validity of the respondent's statement that he knew about the event. The age, sex, and occupation of the respondent and the time of the interview were also recorded.

The interviews took place in Iowa City, a university town of 35,000, and in the surrounding semi-rural area. Interviewing teams were sent to six sections of the town and surrounding area with instructions to go from household to household and to interview the adult or teen-ager who answered the door. The median values of the homes in these areas range roughly from upper-middle to lower-lower class, and represent a reasonably adequate cross-section of the community. All interviews were completed within ten hours after the shooting of the President and within seven hours after the shooting of Oswald. The refusal rate for both samples was about six per cent.

Of the 151 persons interviewed in the Kennedy sample, 69 were male and 82 were female. The mean age was 33 for males and 40 for females, with a range of 15 to 76 for males and 13 to 88 for females. All but one of the respondents were Caucasian. Of the 131 persons in the Oswald sample, the 50 males ranged in age from 18 to 79 with a mean of 37, while the 81 females ranged in age from 13 to 82 with a mean of 40. All were Caucasian.

Results

Extent of news diffusion. Unlike previous diffusion studies, which were based on interviews collected days after the events, this investiga-tion attempted to measure the hourly spread of knowledge by inter-

TABLE 1

Rate of News Diffusion After the Shootings

	Per Cent Who Learned During Each Half-Hour				
Event	1st half-hour	2nd half-hour	3rd half-hour	4th half-hour	5th half-hour to 10th hour
Kennedy ($n = 151$)	70%	21%	3%	2%	5%
Oswald ($n = 123$)	57	24	8	6	5

viewing almost simultaneously with the diffusion of the message. Eighty-two per cent of the Oswald sample interviewed during the first hour after the shooting knew of the event. The proportion informed during subsequent hours continued to rise; all persons interviewed during the fourth and later hours had heard of the slaying. All respondents in the Kennedy sample had heard the news before interviewing began.

The extent of knowledge found by this study contrasts with earlier findings, in which diffusion of knowledge was typically less complete. Miller found that all respondents were aware of Roosevelt's death. Deutschmann and Danielson found 100 per cent knowledge in only one of seven samples drawn to study the diffusion of four news stories.[4] The remaining six samples showed that knowledge ran 88 per cent for Sputnik, 89 and 90 per cent for Alaskan statehood, 93 per cent for Explorer I in two different samples, and 95 per cent for Eisenhower's stroke. Danielson found 96 per cent knowledge of Eisenhower's decision to seek reelection. Larsen and Hill found knowledge of Taft's death among 88 per cent of a faculty community and 93 per cent of a laboring-class community. Bogart's study of diffusion of a local event found that 27 per cent of persons with less than high school education and 77 per cent of persons with some college were aware of the event.[5] An additional study reported by Deutschmann and Danielson on knowledge of the Sputnik story in Chile showed that 95 per cent were informed.

Time of learning the news. That respondents knew about the event by the time they were interviewed does not indicate how soon the news of the shootings reached them. Table 1 shows the percentage of knowers

[4] The one sample was in Palo Alto, California, about Explorer I.
[5] Leo Bogart, "The Spread of News on a Local Event: A Case History," *Public Opinion Quarterly* (1950), *14*, 769–72.

in the Kennedy and Oswald samples who learned of the events during each half-hour interval after the first reports. The majority of both samples heard the news during the first half-hour after the shootings. The percentages of persons who learned during subsequent intervals declined regularly. The major difference between the two samples is that more of the Kennedy sample than of the Oswald sample heard the news during the first half-hour after the shooting ($p < .05$). This difference can be partly attributed to greater interpersonal communication of the news of the Kennedy assassination to persons not in contact with mass media sources, as will be shown in the following analysis.

The flow of information found by this study was somewhat slower than the diffusion of the news of Roosevelt's death in the student sample, but faster than the diffusion of the news of Taft's death in the general population. Ninety-four per cent of the knowers in Miller's sample had learned of Roosevelt's death by the end of the first hour; 91 per cent and 81 per cent of the knowers had learned of the Kennedy and Oswald deaths, respectively, by the end of the first hour. By the end of the second hour, the Roosevelt news had reached 99 per cent of Miller's sample, and 96 per cent and 95 per cent of the Kennedy and Oswald samples, respectively. The news of Taft's death took 11 hours to reach 90 per cent of the eventual knowers in a faculty community and 14 hours in a laboring-class community.[6]

Comparisons between investigations of rates of flow must be made with caution, since earlier studies are based on information collected 18 hours to four days after the initial news reports. Miller, for example, found that 21 of 139 respondents recalled hearing the news before the initial report.

Initial source of the news. Table 2 shows the percentage of persons who learned of the events from each of the various media. Interpersonal channels were the single most important source of the news in the Kennedy sample. Television was the most important source of the news in the Oswald sample. Fifty-five per cent of the informed respondents in the Kennedy sample and 29 per cent of the informed respondents in the Oswald sample reported other persons as their first source of the news ($p < .01$). Radio was the source of the first news about equally for both samples, but television was more frequently the source for the Oswald sample. The 50 per cent of the Oswald sample who said television was

[6] Larsen and Hill.

TABLE 2

Per Cent Who Learned From Each of the Media

Medium	Kennedy ($n = 151$)	Oswald ($n = 123$)
Radio	25%	21%
Television	19	50
Newspaper	0	0
Interpersonal	55	29
Other[a]	1	0

[a] Commercial wired music system or public address system.

their initial source is significantly greater than the 19 per cent of the Kennedy sample who said so ($p < .01$).

The Kennedy sample showed that interpersonal channels were the source of the first news more than in previous diffusion studies. Almost all recent diffusion studies have shown that the mass media, especially radio and television, are more instrumental than are interpersonal networks in disseminating major news. Of the investigations reviewed thus far, only Miller found other persons to be the most frequent source of the first news. The event studied by Miller, like this the death of a President, gave results that closely resemble our findings on first news sources. Miller's findings suggest, but do not establish, that the degree to which interpersonal networks are activated depends on the importance of the event. Since most of his college-student respondents did not have immediate access to the mass media, they could only learn by word of mouth. The three other stories about statesmen, the death of Taft, the illness of Eisenhower, and Eisenhower's decision to seek reelection, were not as sensational as the President's shooting, and showed less extensive interpersonal communication. In short, the evidence of all these investigations suggests that readiness to engage in interpersonal communication increases with the magnitude of the event.[7]

The findings from the Oswald sample indicate that television was more important than it was in most earlier news-diffusion studies. Television was the initial source of the news for only 14 per cent of the knowers interviewed after Eisenhower's 1956 decision to seek reelection. Somewhat greater television usage was found by Deutschmann and

[7] Gordon W. Allport and Leo Postman, *The Psychology of Rumor* (New York, 1947). See also Stanley Schachter and Harvey Burdick, "A Field Experiment in Rumor Transmission and Distortion," *Journal of Abnormal and Social Psychology* (1955), *50*, 363–71.

Danielson in their 1957–58 studies of four news stories; learning from television ranged from 20 to 38 per cent. The increase in television viewing may be partially attributed to the increase in television sets owned (radio was usually the main source of first news in studies before 1957) and to the consequent change in patterns of media usage.[8] However, it also seems likely that the heavier usage of television in the Oswald sample resulted from *sensitization to the mass media* because of the assassination. That is, so many persons learned of or saw the shooting of Oswald on television because they had turned to television to follow the drama that was begun by the shooting of the President.

TABLE 3

Location at Time of First Hearing About Each Event

Location	Kennedy (n = 151)	Oswald (n = 123)
Home	56%	82%
Work	22	2
Campus	13	1
Church	0	3
Other	9	11

Place and time of learning, and media usage. Table 3 shows that most of the knowers in both samples were at home when they heard the news. However, more of the Oswald sample (82 per cent) than of the Kennedy sample (56 per cent) were home when they learned the news ($p < .01$). The next most frequent location of hearing for the Kennedy sample was work (22 per cent), but for the Oswald sample it was "other," which indicates that 11 per cent of the Oswald sample were out visiting, in automobiles, in restaurants, etc.

These location differences most likely resulted from the fact that more people could be home on a Sunday and stayed home to watch the compelling televised events. If the news had not broken during the lunch hour on Friday, an even smaller proportion of the Kennedy sample would have been at home.

Were there any specific places that increased or decreased the time it took to hear the news? Table 4 shows the time and place at which

[8] There was one television set per 3,800 United States homes in 1946. Now nine out of ten homes in America have at least one set. See Otto N. Larsen, "Innovators and Early Adopters of Television," *Sociological Inquiry* (1962), *32*, 16–33.

TABLE 4

Diffusion Rate for Each Location and Event

	Time Interval			
Location	1st half-hour	2nd half-hour	3rd half-hour	4th half-hour to 10th hour
Kennedy:				
Home (n = 84) 80%		8%	1%	11%
Work (n = 33) 67		24	6	3
Campus (n = 20) 20		75	5	0
Other (n = 14) 86		14	0	0
Oswald:				
Home (n = 101) 57		22	9	12
Other (n = 22) 54		32	5	9

persons heard the news. Persons in the Kennedy sample tended to hear the news within half an hour of its occurrence if they were at home, work, or some other place. Persons on the campus most frequently heard the news during the second half-hour after the initial report, usually from people returning from lunch.

Table 5 relates the types of media through which respondents learned the news to their locations. Those in the Kennedy sample who heard at home most frequently heard the news from another person. Those in the Oswald sample who heard at home most frequently received the news from television. Persons at work, on campus, or in other places heard most frequently from other persons.

Our findings on *location* when the news was heard agree with Deutschmann and Danielson, who found that people were most likely to receive

TABLE 5

Knowledge of Each Event for Each of the Media and Location

	Medium				
Location	Radio	Television	News-paper	Inter-personal	Other
Kennedy:					
Home (n = 84) 30%		30%	0%	40%	0%
Work (n = 33) 24		6	0	67	3
Campus (n = 20) 0		0	0	100	0
Other (n = 14) 36		7	0	50	7
Oswald:					
Home (n = 101) 19		57	0	24	
Other (n = 22) 27		18	0	55	

news in their homes. However, our results on place of hearing and source of news differ in one respect from previous findings. Deutschmann and Danielson found that people at home were most likely to hear from television, while people at work were most likely to hear from other people. The high rate at which people at home learned of the Kennedy assassination from other people suggests that the assassination activated person-to-person channels of communication that are dormant for all but highly unusual events.

Supplementary sources of information. Previous studies of how news travels have indicated that people tend to use more than one source of information in trying to verify, reinforce, or supplement their initial knowledge. The reports by Deutschmann and Danielson and by Danielson showed that 89 per cent or more of their respondents consulted supplementary sources. Larsen and Hill found that 59 and 34 per cent of two samples consulted additional sources. Bogart reported that 23 per cent of his sample received information from more than one source. In this investigation, 82 per cent of the Kennedy and 47 per cent of the Oswald sample consulted supplementary sources ($p < .01$).

TABLE 6

Supplementary Media Choices for Each Event

Medium	Kennedy ($n = 213$)	Oswald ($n = 67$)
Mass Media Combined	66%	69%
Radio	27	21
Television	29	48
Newspaper	10	0
Interpersonal	34	31

The way people use the various media to get more information during the early hours following major news events seems to differ from the way they use them after several days have passed. Table 6 shows how the mass media, taken singly and in combination, compared to interpersonal channels as supplementary sources of information. There were 213 consultations of supplementary news sources by the 151 persons in the Kennedy sample; supplementary sources were consulted 67 times by the 123 knowers in the Oswald sample. The mass media were mentioned as supplementary sources about twice as often as personal sources in both samples. Interpersonal supplementary sources were more frequently used than any other medium in the Kennedy sample. Television was the most frequent supplementary source in the Oswald sample. These data differ from those of previous studies, in which the most frequently reported supplementary source was the newspaper.[9]

Respondents in both samples who received the news from other people were more likely to consult additional sources than those who received the news from the mass media. In the Kennedy sample 96 per cent of those who learned from other people consulted additional sources, but only 65 per cent of those who learned from the mass media consulted supplementary sources ($p < .01$). In the Oswald sample, 72 per cent of those who learned from other people consulted supplementary sources, but only 37 per cent of those who learned from the mass media consulted supplementary sources ($p < .01$).

Influences on interpersonal communication. In the Kennedy sample, 64 per cent of the respondents reported starting conversations with other persons about the event. Only 38 per cent of the Oswald sample told other people ($p < .01$). These percentages are somewhat lower than those reported in previous studies. Bogart found that 70 per cent of high-school graduates and 42 per cent of people with less education told other people about a community event. Larsen and Hill reported that 85 per cent of their faculty community and 80 per cent of their laboring-class community talked with others about Taft's death. Deutschmann and Danielson indicated that 66 per cent of their respondents talked with other people about various events.

Not only was there a greater percentage of respondents who told other people in the Kennedy sample than in the Oswald sample, but there was also a significant difference in the mean number of persons told. The tellers in the Kennedy sample told an average of 5.59 persons, but the tellers in the Oswald sample told an average of only 3.00 persons ($p < .01$). The average number of persons told equaled (in the Oswald sample) and surpassed (in the Kennedy sample) what Larsen and Hill found to be the median number of persons spoken to about Taft's death, which was approximately three persons.

Since interviewing took place within ten hours of each shooting, the number of conversations had surely not reached its maximum. Many respondents said that the interviewer was the first person with whom they had spoken about the event. The earlier studies had been conducted after

[9] Deutschmann and Danielson; Danielson; Larsen and Hill.

the diffusion process had been under way much longer, which provided more time for conversations. Furthermore, the figures may also reflect the wording of the earlier questions about interpersonal communication. The question in our study asked the respondent to focus on initiated communication, i.e., persons told, rather than to report all conversations about the events. Earlier studies recorded all reported conversations.

On the assumption that a person is more interested in talking about something if he thinks his audience has not heard about it, it would be expected that respondents who heard the news very soon after the shootings would be more likely to pass the information along than respondents who heard about it at a later time.[10] The Kennedy and Oswald samples were therefore divided into "Early Knowers" (heard within one half-hour) and "Late Knowers" (heard after one half-hour). The Early Knowers in the Kennedy sample were more likely to tell other people than the Late Knowers; 70 per cent of the Early Knowers, but only 52 per cent of the Late Knowers, transmitted the information ($p < .05$). In the Oswald sample only a slightly greater proportion of Early Knowers (44 per cent) than Late Knowers (32 per cent) told other people ($p < .10$). It is likely that the Early Knowers in the Oswald sample were less prone to tell others, because they assumed that almost everyone had been watching television.

TABLE 7

Relation to Person Who Was Source for Initial and Supplementary News

	Kennedy		Oswald	
Person	Initial ($n = 83$)	Supplementary ($n = 72$)	Initial ($n = 36$)	Supplementary ($n = 21$)
Relative	15%	18%	28%	14%
Friend	42	42	56	67
Acquaintance	29	26	8	5
Stranger	13	6	8	5
Other	1	8	0	10

Social relationships and message reception. Table 7 shows the relationship to the respondents of the persons who were the sources of the news. Friends were the most frequent initial as well as supplementary

---

[10] Newcomb makes the point that under most conditions, people do not transmit information to persons known to have it already. See Theodore M. Newcomb, "The Study of Consensus," in Robert K. Merton, Leonard Broom, and Leonard S. Cottrell, Jr., eds., *Sociology Today* (New York, 1959), p. 280.

sources in both samples. The second most important personal sources in the Kennedy sample were acquaintances. However, relatives were the second most important sources in the Oswald sample. Strangers were the least probable as supplementary sources, although receiving the news from a stranger was somewhat more common in the Kennedy sample. Selectivity in choosing an audience for the Kennedy news may have been lowered because family networks were less closely integrated on a working day, and because people told whoever was available.

Social relationships and message transmission. Forty per cent of the tellings in the Kennedy sample were to friends, 28 per cent to relatives, 28 per cent to acquaintances, and 4 per cent to strangers. In the Oswald sample, 47 per cent of the tellings were to relatives, 36 per cent to friends, 11 per cent to acquaintances, and 5 per cent to strangers. Comparing the two samples, we find that intrafamily communication was less pronounced in the Kennedy sample ($p < .05$). The percentage of tellings to friends was not significantly different in the two samples. The two samples differed significantly, however, in the percentage of tellings to acquaintances ($p < .01$). The operation of family communication networks, as demonstrated in other investigations, was most evident in the Oswald sample.[11]

Summary and conclusion

The Hyman and Sheatsley hypothesis that some persons remain uninformed no matter how available the information, has been borne out by previous diffusion studies.[12] However, psychological barriers such as selective exposure, selective perception, or physical isolation were not powerful enough to screen out awareness of the events of November 22 and 24. If a hard core of know-nothings existed in the community studied, we were unable to find them.

This study showed that all respondents had heard the news four hours after the events; most heard within one half-hour. The most frequent initial source of the Kennedy news was another person; television was the most frequent initial source in the case of Oswald. Most of the respondents who learned the news by word of mouth heard it from

[11] Larsen and Hill; also Melvin L. DeFleur and Otto N. Larsen, *The Flow of Information* (New York, 1954).
[12] Herbert H. Hyman and Paul B. Sheatsley, "Some Reasons Why Information Campaigns Fail," *Public Opinion Quarterly* (1947), *11*, 413–23.

friends. Persons were most likely to be home when they first heard the news; they were most likely to learn the news about Kennedy from a person but to learn the Oswald news from television. Most knowers consulted supplementary sources, especially if they first heard the news through interpersonal channels. The mass media in general were the most important supplementary news sources for the Kennedy news, but no specific one of them was consulted more frequently than other persons. For the Oswald sample, the mass media were used more frequently than other people as supplementary sources; television was the most important single source. Respondents were more likely to relay the news about Kennedy than the news about Oswald. The news that Kennedy had been shot was relayed most frequently to friends, that Oswald had been shot to relatives; persons who learned during the first half-hour were more likely to relay the news than persons who learned later.

Obviously, the magnitude of an event affects the amount of diffusion. An event as significant as the shooting of the President would be expected to stimulate much communication. That event activated interpersonal communication networks, which quickly relayed the news to people not then in contact with the mass media. Since the murder of Oswald was presumably less significant, one might expect people to talk less about it. People learned of the Oswald murder primarily because they were part of a large, attentive, mass media audience, and only secondarily as a result of interpersonal communication. Had the shooting of Oswald taken place, say, several days after the President's funeral, when the mass media coverage was less intense, then the diffusion of news would probably have been much slower. This suggests that the extent and rate of diffusion of news depend not only on the relevance of the event but also on when it occurs in relation to other events.

James D. Barber

Peer Group Discussion and Recovery from the Kennedy Assassination

Well, when I first heard, my husband ran back in and he said, "You know, Mary,"—he was on his way to work—he says, "You know, the President has been shot." I said, "Oh, turn the television on, quick, quick." We turned the television on and . . . I felt terrible, just awful, so I said to myself, "Well, he'll be all right, he'll be all right. I know he'll be all right." And then a few minutes later here it came, he's dead. Well, then I just went all to pieces and said, "Well, he will not die in vain," and I cried. That's how I felt.

It is all there: the sense of shock and horror, the immediate turning to television, the hope against hope, and the tears. Mary expresses in these sentences thoughts and feelings that were shared by the whole national community as the news of the President's murder spread. Over the following weekend the nation engaged in concerted mourning, spending hour after hour watching and listening to television. The rapid recovery, the sense of continuity and confidence that promptly reasserted itself, can be largely attributed to the networks' decision to broadcast nothing but programs related to the President's death. This provided the public with a sustained opportunity to participate, vicariously but intensely, in the experience and expression of grief. The contrast with the slow and incomplete recovery following Lincoln's assassination is clear.[1]

The communal character of this experience went beyond membership in a national audience. Many people were at work when the news came;

---

[1] On the mourning process, see Otto Fenichel, *The Psychoanalytic Theory of Neurosis* (New York, 1945), pp. 395–96, and Jules Vuillemin, *Essai sur la signification de la mort* (Paris, 1948), pp. 147–52. On the reactions to the Lincoln assassination, see Carl Sandburg, *Abraham Lincoln* (New York, 1939) vol. 4, chaps. 74–76, and Theodore Roscoe, *The Web of Conspiracy* (Englewood Cliffs, N.J., 1959).

they learned of the assassination from fellow workers, and their immediate reactions were expressed in a group setting.[2] Many felt the need to be with relatives or friends, or at least to telephone them. A nurse who was at home when the news came told me, "I saw my neighbor from across the street and she came over and we kind of sat and talked. It seemed good to have someone to talk it over with." People watched television in small and large groups, and talked to one another about their reactions as the story unfolded.[3] And in the days following, families, neighbors, and friends sought explanations and meanings in informal conversations.

The content of these conversations is important for understanding the public's reaction. Survey data on individual responses can tell us which of the many themes from the media were retained by the public. But communication in natural groups provides significant, additional information. Group members consciously or unconsciously select certain themes to tell those with whom they have continuing, close relationships. These themes encounter reinforcement or resistance in the group setting. Interpersonal influence processes come into play, shaping a collective interpretation that fits the particular needs of the group. Over time, these group-formulated and group-supported interpretations tend to override or replace idiosyncratic individual ones. They become part of the group myth, the collection of common opinions to which the members generally conform.[4]

In an attempt to get at the dynamics of this process, I tape-recorded conversations among eight groups at their places of work or recreation. These sessions, averaging about thirty minutes each, took place on Monday after the funeral and on Tuesday morning. With one exception, the people in the groups were of equal job and social status; a fire chief was the only superior present (although not participating) in any group. The groups were: four male cooks, six female kitchen helpers, four truck

[2] See Bradley S. Greenberg, "Diffusion of News of the Kennedy Assassination," *Public Opinion Quarterly* (1964), *28*, 227–31.
[3] On group viewing of the Kennedy-Nixon debates, see Richard F. Carter, "Some Effects of the Debates," in Sidney Kraus, ed., *The Great Debates* (Bloomington, Indiana, 1962), p. 254.
[4] On "the social validation of meanings," see Tamotsu Shibutani, *Society and Personality* (Englewood Cliffs, N.J., 1961), pp. 108–18. On "group absorbents of media radiation," see V. O. Key, Jr., *Public Opinion and American Democracy* (New York, 1961), pp. 366–69. Cf. S. M. Lipset, "Opinion Formation in a Crisis Situation," *Public Opinion Quarterly* (1953), *17*, 20–46; Elihu Katz, "The Two-Step Flow of Communication: An Up-to-date Report on a Hypothesis," *Public Opinion Quarterly* (1957), *21*, 61–78; A. Paul Hare, *Handbook of Small Group Research* (New York, 1962), chap. 2.

drivers, eight female laundry workers (but two had to leave during the session), four firemen, six nurses in a Catholic hospital, four members of a service club, shortly before their weekly meeting, and four young men, between about 19 and 21 years old, in a pool hall. All but the last two groups were recorded at their places of work.

I posed four broad questions:

Now that you have had a chance to think about this whole set of events, what do you think its meaning will be? What is the significance of it?
How did you learn about it and what was your immediate reaction?
Who or what do you feel is really responsible for this?
What is it going to mean for relations among various groups in this country such as Negroes and whites, Catholics and Protestants, Republicans and Democrats?

The respondents were encouraged to develop their answers in their own way; additional questions were posed when necessary to keep the conversation going. The group members appeared to be responding to one another at least as much as to me, developing side conversations and reacting to themes others introduced.

Analysis of these data suggested a focus on the social recovery from the shock of the assassination. The transcripts show the intensity and character of identifications with the President that were shared by the group, and also the ways in which a variety of socially pathological interpretations of his murder were corrected or modified in the course of the group discussion. The severity of psychological disturbance can be traced to the strength of the links these persons had developed, perhaps largely latently, with President Kennedy. In turn the shock set the stage for the emergence of personal fears and anxieties in the form of certain new political perspectives, which, if they had been allowed to spread and deepen, might well have resulted in considerable damage to the stability and rationality of the political system. That such themes were expressed and that groups could draw on resources of confidence and reason to check them are significant facts for the maintenance of central democratic values.

Shared links to the President

Examination of the transcripts reveals a number of sources for the common feeling that the loss was personal, linked in a variety of ways with the respondents' own lives and fortunes. The most frequently mentioned type of linkage was familial. Here two dimensions stand out: an awareness of the President in a family role like that of the respondent, and a sense that he was a model performer in that role, one to be imitated by all Americans. A nurse said, "I think he was a good father. . . . I think many of us identified ourselves as being a family like that." A woman laundry worker said, "He really cared for his family. He was a husband to all his family as well as . . . President of the United States." The "father image" inherited from the Eisenhower presidency appears to be only one aspect of the response to Kennedy. In his middle forties, he could be perceived from several angles. Thus a cook with a young family said, "It's really a big loss. And my youngest boy, whose name is John too, says, 'I wonder who is going to take care of little John' . . . It's still going to be tough to get used to the idea, because I know, I have a couple of kids myself and it kind of makes me wonder, well, suppose the same thing happened to me?" A college boy in the pool hall saw the President as "a typical American, like a family man. You think of your family, if your father got killed, it would be just as important to you as it was to Kennedy's family."

The many family roles in which Kennedy was known—son, husband, father, and brother—permitted a wide range of familial identifications. In this sense many respondents appear to have felt that they were like Kennedy or a member of his immediate family. They felt they knew how those near him must have thought and felt and acted, by extrapolation from their own similar family experiences.

Other comments stressed the President's family life as an example to be imitated. For instance, in the following passage an elderly kitchen helper invoked this ideal:

If a man and woman stick together like those two people, I think it's not necessary to live like this—one hate the other. Just example from them— the people got to realize we got a man and a wife in the White House. They're supposed to follow that too. They'll be no argument, they'll be no this nor nothin'—just pleasant life for everybody. But nobody think about that. They think to be mean to one another. But if they watch that family, wherever they went or wherever they go to trip, to pleasure—everybody likes them.

Here the link to the President's family does not depend directly on a consciousness of similarity, but on an ego ideal, one that may have been brought into many a family argument. Thus identification, both in the sense of likeness and in the sense of a model, is evident as a personal linkage.

Identification with President Kennedy as a Catholic and as a religiously devoted person was evident in several responses, but presented a special problem. One pool-hall boy, asked if he had had similar feelings before, said, "The nearest I came to it was when Pope John died." A nurse in a Catholic hospital stressed the President's religious devotion, and introduced the difficulty others also had to deal with: "I felt that he stood up for his religious rights as well. He went to Mass and behaved as he should, and yet I don't feel that he let it interfere at all with his State duties." Two respondents, one Catholic and the other probably a Protestant, illustrate clearly the conflict some felt regarding Kennedy's religious image. The Catholic, an Italian kitchen helper, said, "On the Catholic part—was not interfere with his duty at the White House. Catholic, you know—it was first with him the Catholic religion, but he was keepin' aside to the duty of the White House. Religion come after, for the family and the kids." The Protestant, a young Negro woman working in a laundry, said:

At first, people were against President Kennedy because he were a Catholic. But he was so good and so everyone has shown a feeling and expressed their feeling toward [him]. Everyone, mostly, I've talked with about how they feel about Kennedy, you don't hear them say, "Well, he was a Catholic and I don't like him because he was a Catholic." They are very upset just about the shock of his death, that he was such a wonderful man. But his religion, regardless, if he is a good man, what type of religion that he like . . . it's just only one God.

It appears that Kennedy's expressed position on his religious convictions and their relation to his official duties got through to these two people. Both are able to maintain a relatively elaborate identification with the President as a Catholic and, more generally, as a religious man, while agreeing with his church-state position. For the first respondent, the dissonance is resolved by compartmentalization: Kennedy's religion was for Sunday and his family, and was kept separate from his White House work. The second respondent manages the problem by referring it to a higher unity: the President's belief in the one God of all. The fact that a religious identification can be maintained in the face of considerable complexity testifies to its strength and significance.

A third set of personal linkages can be classified as characterological. Some of the respondents commented on specific virtues of the President that were of particular significance to their groups. For example, one of the Negro laundry workers explained, "He's not a man that, when you talk, he look in the other direction. He look right toward you just as though you were in the audience, like you to me." A young man in the pool hall mentioned Kennedy's youthful look, and a nurse, on duty Monday night after the funeral, pointed to his hard work: "He worked way into the late hours of the night on government matters and things like that, and he was always a diligent worker. . . . It seems everybody made him their ideal." And the service club members, several of whom disagreed with the President's policies, seemed to admire him for courageous adherence to principle:

R_1: Well, if courage makes a man great and if understanding makes men great, he'll be great if he's measured in those terms. He certainly had courage, there's no question of that.
R_2: He certainly had the courage of his convictions.

These comments suggest that people tended to evaluate the President's character in terms of values most salient for their particular groups. Underlying the generally favorable reaction to Kennedy as a good man, selected characteristics were stressed in special ways.

Respondents identified with President Kennedy partly because they liked his policies. Of special significance were what they perceived as actions that benefited them and as his steadfast control of threatening forces. Both the laundry workers and the kitchen ladies, for whom the matter was of direct import, commented enthusiastically that the President raised the minimum wage, that he was "trying to do something for the working people," and that he "fixed it so that unemployed people have jobs." Here the rewards seem direct and personal; they are perceived as flowing from the President's own efforts. The laundry workers developed similar themes about care for the needy:

R_1: I think President Kennedy was more for the colored people than any other president.
R_2: Yeah, yeah, that's right. Because he wanted the two of them to be alike— am I right or wrong?
R_1: He wanted us to have equal rights.
R_3: That's right, he did.
R_1: He tried to have them integrated.
R_3: Together, to get along.

The image of the President as a "benevolent leader" who mediated practical and emotional help is evident in these comments.[5] Respondents also stressed Kennedy's steadfast pursuit of international stability, holding Castro and Khrushchev in line without risking war. A fireman who was critical of Kennedy nevertheless called his stand on Cuba "probably the greatest thing that he did during his three years in office." A cook explained, "Well, one thing . . . I liked about him, he didn't mix his words. He didn't say one thing and do another. . . . take like this Castro deal—I mean, he really stood up and he didn't back down for nothin'. Very strong character." A kitchen helper emphasized Kennedy's maintenance of the balance of power:

He keep Khrushchev level: "I'll level with you and you level with me," he says. "Don't go any further step because I'll catch you. I don't go any further step because you going to catch me, so let's stay level." When you don't talk, you shoot the gun and that's bad.

These responses appear to delineate the two major dimensions of presidential policy, dimensions against which the public measures other presidents. He is appreciated for making life easier at home and safer abroad. These policies are seen as springing from his personal characteristics: he is at once kind and strong.

Reviewing these responses, one is impressed first by the variety of identifications that can be developed; there is nothing here reflecting a uniform public response imprinted by exposure to a single source of information. Rather, the identifications people have with the President are those that fit their own particular life situations and that are strengthened by being shared with friends and co-workers. Furthermore, the main ones appear to be related to some of the deepest dimensions of human experience: the family, religion, character, and basic needs for sustenance and protection. Had the President been perceived as just another distant public official, it is doubtful that so many would have reacted so intensely to his death. The evidence suggests that the profound sense of bewilderment and grief was one result of the sudden shattering of personal bonds with an important ego ideal.

[5] Fred I. Greenstein, "The Benevolent Leader: Children's Images of Political Authority," *American Political Science Review* (1960), *54*, 934–43, and his *Children and Politics* (forthcoming, Yale University Press, 1965).

The need for an interpretation

In the aftermath of the assassination, people sought to "make sense" of what might have been considered an absurd accident. Once the reality could no longer be escaped, it had to be worked into some acceptable interpretation. The respondents were concerned with three primary problems of interpretation. First, they wanted an explanation, an understanding of the causes of the President's murder. A laundry worker struggled with this problem as follows:

The only thing you heard about is, why did this guy kill him? Why were they not for him to be the President of the United States as long as he could be or until the Lord has taken his life away? Why would a man have to take his life away? I mean, I think that what everyone are really concerned about. At least me, myself, I like to be knowin' why. And now that they have killed him, he can't say why.

Second, they wanted meaning, some positive, significant implication for the good. Like Mary, the kitchen worker whose reactions I quoted at the beginning, a truck driver "would like to think his death was not in vain —I hope, certainly I hope it wasn't." Third, people wanted reassurance, a prediction that somehow or other the nation would come through without severe harm. One of the pool-hall boys showed this concern when he said:

I think if it has any political affiliations or anything like that, that's the thing most people are afraid to even think about. If it is true, then we are in for an awful shock very soon, because they got to the point where it came out in the open that a president was shot for political reasons—then something's going to happen very soon.

Six of the eight groups carried on this search for interpretations. The two deviant groups—the service club members and the laundry workers— illustrate blocks in the group recovery process.

Perhaps the least healthy response to the assassination would have been no response. People needed to grieve, to share their grief with others, and to work out some acceptable set of feelings about the situation.[6] In the service club group there was very little emotional expres-

---

[6] See Lewis Wender, "The Dynamics of Group Psychotherapy and its Application," in Max Rosenbaum and Milton M. Berger, eds., *Group Psychotherapy and Group Function* (New York, 1963), pp. 211–17. On the obstacles to healthy grieving in Western culture, see Robert N. Wilson, "Disaster and Mental Health," in George W. Baker and Dwight W. Chapman, eds., *Man and Society in Disaster* (New York, 1962), p. 127.

sion. They discussed the details of the two murders and the television coverage. Only near the end, and then tentatively, did any positive feeling toward the President emerge. Their tendency to avoid emotional expression may have left them with unresolved tensions. For such groups, recovery was likely to be slower.[7]

The laundry workers let their feelings flow freely, but there was very little thematic development in their discussion. The pattern was assertion and agreement; almost any interpretation went unchallenged. The killer should be cremated; a gang, possibly the Mafia, was responsible; Ruby was Oswald's confederate, etc. What seemed to be accomplished here was catharsis but no correction. The group atmosphere encouraged unfettered expression of whatever came to mind. No one opposed or criticized another's idea. Interpretations spilled out one after another. There was no attempt to develop a coherent group position.[8]

In the other groups, one finds both expression and constraint, the development of some relatively consistent and reasoned interpretations. These more common conversations show how several somewhat dangerous themes met corrective responses.

Dangerous tendencies

When the news came, "I felt like I'd been struck by a thunderbolt," said one man; "I felt sick at my stomach," said another. Close on the heels of shock and disbelief came fundamental emotions that had to be managed in some way by individuals and groups. The ways they managed them, the interpretations they developed, in many cases had implications which could have led to widespread demands for political policy changes detrimental to democratic order.

In the first place, the violent surprise of the assassination, which was so quickly followed by another murder, engendered fear that something had gone fundamentally wrong and that the normal restraints on violence had broken down.[9] A nurse expressed this fear of contagious vio-

---

[7] Research on the reactions of middle-class Americans generally would probably reveal less emotional expression than for working-class ones. See David Krech, Richard S. Crutchfield, and Egerton L. Ballachey, *Individual in Society* (New York, 1962), pp. 374–75.

[8] On the persistence of conspiracy theories after the assassination, see the article by Paul B. Sheatsley and Jacob J. Feldman in this volume. On the spread of "fear-justifying" rumors among those distant from a disaster, see Leon Festinger, *A Theory of Cognitive Dissonance* (Stanford, Calif., 1957), pp. 236–43.

[9] On the death of another as a threat to the self, see George A. Kelly, *The Psychology of Personal Constructs* (New York, 1955), vol. I, pp. 489ff.

lence when she said, "I think it shows the emotional state of mind of people of this day. They go into a frenzy and a state of frustration. It just seems that anything could happen really, the way they react." The "killing and frenzy," she felt, "could go on until it's all the way back up here." A pool-hall boy thought that "something's going to happen very soon," and explained:

Well, I think something else will come out in the open like that . . . couldn't say mass assassination, but some sort of mass demonstration where the same thing will happen in key positions all over the United States. That's what I'm worried about. If someone could master-plan something like that where high people in positions of authority all over the United States could be assassinated at the same time or captured at the same time . . . it could be just as easy to overthrow this government as any other government.

A cook expressed similar concerns: "I mean, it puts a lot in your mind to think, because they have someone like that can actually get at a president. I mean, it's hard to tell just what is what in times coming. 'Cause anything can happen." The dangerous implications of such feelings are hinted at by a truck driver's comment that "something has to be done so a thing like this should never, ever happen again." Fears of violence, a breakdown of confidence in the safety and stability of the system, might have resulted in demands for extraordinary preventative measures, demands, for example, that the president be confined behind armed guards or that mass demonstrations be outlawed. At a somewhat deeper level, fear of this kind probably works to inhibit public acceptance of innovation and experimentation in politics. There is a sense that only the tried and true are safe. And since fear often causes withdrawal from the threatening situation, it might lead people to turn away from active political participation, to escape from an arena of action that had become dangerous.

Another frequently expressed emotion, derived in part from those fears, was hostility, especially toward Oswald and others thought to share the responsibility. A truck driver suggested a classic punishment: "They should let him loose in the country and don't let anyone do anything to him. Just let him walk around with that guilt. That's my feeling. Just let him walk around knowing that he shot the President." The pool-hall boys reported their immediate desire was to "string him up," or subject him to "medieval torture or something along that line." A kitchen helper felt that "it's too good to give him the electric chair . . . too quick to die like that. They have to make him suffer, royal." One is reminded here of the interviews shortly after Oswald's murder with some Dallas citizens, who were mainly glad about the revenge. The threat to democratic order in such sentiments is obvious: a breakdown in standards of justice, a willingness to make the kind of exception that can weaken and eventually destroy the rule.

But some responses indicated hostility reaching beyond the individual murderer. Some revealed a suspicion that a gang of some sort was really responsible. A truck driver saw a tangle of conspiracy surrounding Oswald and Ruby:

I think the man that shot Oswald ... was hired by someone ... because I don't think he'd give his life that freely, just run up and shoot him in front of everyone. .... He couldn't possibly get away so he was either forced to do it or he was threatened. They'd probably kill his family if he didn't.

The next comment reluctantly attributed blame to Southern segregationists: "I don't like to make a statement like that, but there was a lot of ill feeling in the South due to the fact that Kennedy's civil rights program was something they didn't care for." In the cooks' conversation several groups were mentioned:

R_1: We have a lot of Communists in this country. We have it in all walks of life.
R_2: These people who are against civil rights. ... There could be a lot of groups that would just say, well, "He stepped on our toes."
R_1: You have right-wingers. You have left-wingers. You have everything in this country. I mean, you have them in all walks of life. .... You have Communism. I mean, it's been in the papers for years and years. There are doctors, lawyers—you even have professors ...

The variety of available targets for blame, and uncertainty about which of them might be really responsible, dampened the force of these responses. The political harm inherent in such sentiments is, however, evident: the threat of breakdown in the sense of political community, an unwillingness to tolerate dissent or to enter into negotiations with the supposedly guilty ones. The destructive crosscurrents of group blame and guilt that followed Lincoln's assassination are reflected in these comments, albeit in considerably milder form.

A third strong response, already illustrated in quotations above, was the wave of adulation for President Kennedy. Paradoxically, these feelings might well have disrupted the people's ability to judge their political leaders rationally. Some of those who were most enthusiastic about Kennedy as President and person found it difficult to accept the idea that Lyndon Johnson could carry on effectively. One kitchen lady said, "Mr. Johnson will never be the man Mr. Kennedy was . . . he isn't capable enough in any way." "The greatest President," "another Lincoln," "a hero who died for his people," would be extremely difficult to follow on the national stage until other, calmer standards were brought to bear.

Thus imbedded in the healthy expressions of feeling after the assassination were certain themes that, had they not been brought out into the open and dealt with effectively, might have spread and interfered significantly with the maintenance of national confidence, devotion to fair procedures, and adherence to rational standards of political evaluation. How were these problems resolved in the conversations of ordinary citizens?

Group response

Perhaps one of the healthiest responses in the group discussions was willingness to withhold judgment until the social recovery process had run its course.[10] Although the respondents were ready to express their feelings and opinions, they did not fasten irrevocably onto interpretations in the immediate aftermath. A cook wanted to wait "until the smoke clears" before he decided what the impact would be; a nurse was glad there will be "a full investigation" because "the case is not closed" regarding Oswald; a fireman said, "We'll have to wait and see just how well we can bring about the transition of power." These groups kept their thoughts tentative, exploring possible implications without committing themselves to any. The conspiracy theories, the predictions of more violence, the doubts about Johnson's abilities, most often met a wait-and-see attitude that left the door open for later correction.

The most frequent type of response to fears that violence would spread throughout the country or lead to the overthrow of the government was to isolate the threat by concentrating on detailed events.[11] This is clear, for example, in the reactions to a nurse who repeatedly generalized the

[10] See James E. Dittes, "Impulsive Closure as Reaction to Failure-Induced Threat," *Journal of Abnormal and Social Psychology* (1961), *63*, 562–69.
[11] On "morselizing and contextualizing" in political perceptions, see Robert E. Lane, *Political Ideology* (New York, 1962), pp. 350–53.

dangers, predicting outbreaks of "emotional frenzy." The comment that immediately followed her first suggestion that "anything could happen" moved at once from the general to the particulars of Oswald's murder: "The police had arrested the suspected murderer. . . ." The fearful nurse picked this up in her next comment: "I studied the television picture of Ruby, the man who shot Oswald. Well, if you notice the expression on Oswald's face. . . ." After some group discussion of the Dallas police, she reiterated her concern that "there could have been a lot more killing and frenzy," but receiving no encouragement for this theme, she joined in the discussion of details: "I think the greatest reaction was people saying there was no top there on the car." Some minutes later, she tried again, referring to a general "emotional crisis," but the response she got discussed Oswald as "emotionally unstable." At last she dropped the contagious violence theme and ended the discussion on a positive note: "I think of the good Kennedy will leave with the people rather than anything else." Tendencies to exaggerate the scope and intensity of danger were averted by a continual returning to the scene of the crime. The implications were isolated and restricted to the particular situation.

A second response to fear was to perceive the threat as normal, as a risk that is necessary and has been borne before without disrupting the whole society. The pool-hall boy who feared that "hate has traveled into politics and it's traveled into everything, every field of life," met this reaction from the next commentator:

Well, as far as it happening, I don't think it has that much to do with this country. I mean that's been around since Caesar was assassinated. . . . It's still the same basic thing that goes on in every country, but it just happened to strike us with the President getting killed. . . . people are getting killed every day, people are getting beat up, skulls bashed in, but its shock was really because it's someone who was at the pinnacle of the highest office you could get in the country—it happened to him.

The cooks developed this theme as follows:

R_1: All I can say is it's a crying shame that you can't control something like that . . . but you can't over-protect anybody, and you can't let the President go out for a walk and turn out an entire regiment to protect the man. . . . There's always a person like this in the world that will try something like that.

R_2: There's always someone trying to gain recognition through one way or the other.

R_3: There's not a President we've had who hasn't had it tried after him.

The invocation of the historical context and of similar crimes was a re-
minder that nothing fundamentally new has happened, that the danger
was to be expected and therefore should be taken in stride. As one cook
put it: "I don't think there will be any drastic changes. There may be
some changes, because it's an ever-changing world to begin with, let's
face it. We don't know what's goin' to happen next week. I don't think
they'll be any big changes, though."

Many respondents felt that, far from generating more conflict, the assassination would either soon be forgotten or teach people tolerance.
The latter theme was especially prevalent, and was typified by a fireman's remark that "it will make people more patriotic and give them a
better approach to the problems of the country. There won't be so much
hate spoken and things like that. It will draw the country closer. Maybe
. . . it could be a good lesson." Less frequently expressed was the idea
that attention to the assassination would be short-lived, as when a truck
driver said that within a few weeks "they'll be watching the Giants play
on Sunday and I think they'll have forgotten—not entirely yet and
maybe not in two weeks, but certainly in several months, I think it will
be all over."

The result of these responses to expressions of fear was to leave them
without much social support and to turn attention elsewhere. Of the several themes taken up in the discussions, the contagious violence theme
was the one most rapidly interpreted away.

As we have seen, the impulse to punish the President's killer was
strong and was shared by many respondents. But in almost every case it
immediately encountered assertions that the law should take its course.
For example, in the truck driver's discussion, the respondent (R_1) who
thought that Oswald should have been left to wander the earth like Cain
met this immediate response:

R_2: The law should take justice, that's all. Justice should be dealt out to him
by the law and nobody else, and if the law is death, he should get death.
Whatever the law of the country is, he should get.
R_1: In my feeling, death's too quick.
R_2: It shouldn't be taken into the hands of any individual or anything. What-
ever the laws of the country are, that's what we have to abide by.
R_3: I agree. He's right. He should get a fair trial, and that's it.

The pool-hall boys worked this out in similar fashion, differentiating
more clearly between their feelings and their recommendations:

R$_1$: Just a regular punishment is enough and sufficient unless you're a sadist and want to see the man—well most of the people *want* to see the man tortured and pay for this deed he has done. But the same punishment as anybody else should pay; just because [Kennedy was] a high official doesn't mean he should be rendered any worse punishment than a regular person that has killed a man, which is the same thing—a man is a man, no matter what position he holds and no matter how he dies.

R$_2$: He should get just the regular justice, because actually he just committed an act of murder. As he just said, this is not a federal offense; he should just have been given a regular trial.

R$_1$: That's the *right* thing to do, but that's not the reaction I had.

More succinctly, a kitchen lady replied to the suggestion that Oswald be made to "suffer, royal," "This is America. We don't do that here."

Attempts to blame the assassination on groups or forces beyond Oswald got responses that maintained the right to dissent. Few felt any sympathy for the Communists, hoodlums, or segregationists seen dimly in the background, but most felt that their rights to exist and to have their say should be protected. The cooks, for example, after elaborating on various possibly guilty parties, proceeded in this way:

R$_1$: Let's face it—everybody's an individual in their own rights. That's why you have all these different groups. Ah, in this country . . . it is a free country where you could have them.

R$_2$: There are always going to be some, what do you say, hullabaloo or name-calling or mud-slinging between the different masses. It has to be, because otherwise it wouldn't be a democracy if it wasn't. We each have our own rights to say what we want, and what I think about him or what he thinks about me.

Or, as a fireman explained,

Well, I think Oswald represents the lunatic left—definite left-wing as opposed to representing the right-wing. There will be, I think, certain pressures and probably some proposed legislation on curbing the activities of these groups, such as Fair Play for Cuba. But I personally don't think that there should be any curbs on it. This is a nation that is based on people being able to express their opinions whatever they are.

To these invocations of democratic ideology, most groups added another dimension: the assassin as mentally ill. Oswald was pictured, not as a moral leper to be scourged, but as "emotionally disturbed" (by a nurse), "an unstable individual" (by a fireman), "mentally sick" (by a truck driver), "a deranged person" (by a pool-hall boy). In several cases, there were long discussions of Oswald's background, full of details picked up from television, offered as explanations for his crime. The emphasis here was on understanding the killer's motives rather than on stereotyping him as essentially evil and thus more readily available as a target for aggression. Explanation substitutes for blame. As the discussions moved past reports of initial reactions, Oswald began to emerge as a person more deserving of psychotherapy than of torture.[12]

In the early phases of these discussions, when the respondents' whole attention was devoted to the slain President, Kennedy was described in extremely positive terms, as a man of exceptional character and a President of heroic proportions. These feelings were not amended in the conversations; the affection was as strong at the end as at the beginning. But as these people turned their thoughts to the future, they slowly shifted their frame of reference from the man to his policies, and the latter were evaluated in a more balanced way. The truck drivers supply an example. Two of them expressed strong feelings of appreciation for President Kennedy as one who "loved the people of the world, because after all his job, that he took upon himself, he really didn't need"; he was "for the poor as well as the rich . . . a second Lincoln." The next respondent said, with some hesitation, that he was not "a supporter of Kennedy or Roosevelt and I . . . still haven't changed my views on Roosevelt or would I change them, I doubt very much, on Kennedy. I don't think he accomplished much in his short period of time in office." A third member then picked up the argument and developed a synthesis:

I think he tried to do a good job where he could. I think he was partial in some ways. In some ways I think he was . . . a good man for trying to bring a better understanding among the colored and white in this country. I still uphold him for his admiration of President Eisenhower, and I like to say this, . . .

at which point he began a discussion of Kennedy's efforts to close the missile gap, his fostering of science, and so on. Similarly the firemen got into a long conversation about medicare, federal aid to education, civil

---

[12] For evidence that this was the most frequent characterizationn of the suspected assassin, see Thomas J. Banta, "The Kennedy Assassination: Early Thoughts and Emotions," *Public Opinion Quarterly* (1964), *28*, 220.

rights, and tax reduction; in this area there was little hesitation about criticizing particular details of the Kennedy program. The transition was made from an emotional reaction of respect and affection for the President as a person to reasoning about his policy recommendations. The hero was still there, but he could be wrong.

Initial feelings that Lyndon Johnson could not possibly match President Kennedy's stature give way to the idea that Johnson is different but adequate to the role. A cook who felt that President Kennedy was "dynamic" and that Johnson "will never get reelected . . . I don't think he has the energy, to begin with," was answered as follows:

I think President Kennedy was a very great man. His whole life, his background, and everything showed it. But, now you take Johnson, from what I've read about him . . . in the newsreel when he traveled around and has been close to the President . . . that man has . . . been second to nobody in all his climb to political power. And he has always been a man to stand on his own two feet in a more definite way, where President Kennedy was more energetic and . . . commanded respect because of his dignity and the way he was, while Johnson, in his way of coming up to it . . . he had a bull-like way of forcin' it on 'em. And, in a way [laugh] it almost amounted to the same thing in how he used pressure. And, like I say, as far as political, I don't think too many people would push Mr. Johnson around either. I think he'd be a pretty firm man too. . . . In political procedures his tactics might be a little different but if they achieve the same end, it's the same end. . . . It's what you think a man can do.

When one of the kitchen helpers said that Johnson "will never be the man Mr. Kennedy was," that "he isn't capable in any way," her Negro friend replied:

R_1: Well, he's an intelligent man too, been in politics for years.
R_2: I guess he knows. He knows a lot, too.
R_3: He can't be fooled. He can't be fooled by anybody in the United States because he knows the government situation from the foot up. He knows it. He knows the crisis we're in. Some young President like President Kennedy, coming in from the North, ah, he studied wide in Europe, he knows about European countries and things, but to know the bitter hatred in the South, he did not know it.

And an Italian added that Johnson has traveled "all over the world to see what's going on" and "he know the same as much as President Kennedy know."

Finally, there was a focus on continuities in government. A truck driver thought that Johnson or whoever else would be elected in 1964 would "reap the benefits of what's been done in the Kennedy administration." He felt that "it's the science that's behind this government that makes a president able to talk strong or not be able to talk strong." A fireman stressed the fact that "we're committed to a foreign policy that's supposedly the ideas of several people and Johnson [cannot] really deviate radically from our policy as it is now." Another mentioned that the presidency is still in the hands of the same party. Others referred to the carry-over of the cabinet.

Turning from admiration to calm evaluation was difficult for these people. But they did recover their balance. A cook summed up their feelings, "History is going to keep going on, whether we like it or not. The government's going to keep going on. . . . Things will have to fall into place as they have in the past."

The main outlines of the group recovery process that emerges from these data can be summarized as follows:

1. Certain personal links to the President, particularly familial, religious, characterological, and political, were expressed in ways salient to the group and were reinforced by social support from peers.

2. When these strong links were broken, respondents felt the need for interpretations, particularly explanation, meaning, and prediction, that would palliate the disturbance. They sought these interpretations in group conversations.

3. Strong emotional reactions to the assassination, particularly fear, hostility, and adulation, were expressed to others. This was a healthy catharsis in the group setting, but it also had potentially pathological implications of breakdowns in important political orientations.

4. These dangerous tendencies were corrected by the process of group discussion. Of particular interest are the specific mechanisms by which socially healthier interpretations counteracted and replaced the less healthy ones.

By the time these conversations were completed the day after the funeral, processes of social recovery were already well advanced. People had expressed their feelings and reestablished their political equilibrium. They concluded that the country would go on, that no radical changes were called for, and that the basics of democracy still held true. Their ability to roll with the punch of the assassination had revealed for the moment some strong, shared resources that support democracy in the face of crisis.

William A. Mindak and Gerald D. Hursh

Television's Functions
on the Assassination Weekend

This is a report of how residents of a large midwestern city reacted to the assassination and on the role that television, in particular, played in influencing those reactions. Findings are from tape-recorded "depth" interviews with 48 adult residents of Minneapolis during the week after the assassination. The sample was provided by the Communication Research Division of the School of Journalism, University of Minnesota, and was randomly selected from areas in the city of Minneapolis.[1] It yielded a reasonably good cross section, although there were frequent difficulties in getting emotionally spent residents to submit to an interview. The sample breakdown is presented in Table 1.

Initial reactions to the news

The assassination created an ambiguous, unstructured situation that was outside normal experience. It was necessary to probe beyond the mere "echoing" of media commentary in the attempt to reconstruct spontaneous reactions to the news. Without exception, the accounts revealed one or more of the classic responses to a threatened crisis, e.g., psychological evasion, irrational behavior, expressions of fear:[2]

I just got cold and started to shake. I couldn't do anything. I just sat there numb. Then when the announcer said, "The President is dead. We will now observe a moment of silence," I started to cry. I couldn't help it; I just felt all sort of sick inside.

---

[1] This study was financed by a grant from the Graduate School of the University of Minnesota and was conducted with the assistance of Gale R. Hursh and people in the Communication Research Division of the School of Journalism.

[2] Ralph H. Turner and Lewis M. Killian, *Collective Behavior* (Englewood Cliffs, New Jersey, 1957), chap. 2.

I felt very insecure, like something was there that was sturdy and steady, and all of a sudden it just wasn't there anymore. Like my hopes ... not exactly my hopes, but my security was gone.

Frequently more than one initial reaction was recalled. Two-thirds could not immediately comprehend the reality of the President's murder. They expressed disbelief, and were defensively shocked, stunned, or dazed. About 20 per cent of the respondents had felt stupefied, and had dulled recollections of their initial behavior. Another 20 per cent recalled an immediate and deep sense of sorrow for the Kennedy family and for Kennedy himself. Other reactions were: a sense of personal loss, deep hurt, anguish (15 per cent); outbreaks of crying, swearing, shouting (15 per cent); fear, nervousness, insecurity (10 per cent); random, nonconstructive behavior or wandering (8 per cent); and seeking religious comfort in prayer (6 per cent).

Behavior in crises frequently includes the gathering of crowds and a heightened susceptibility to rumor which might be the result of a need to define ambiguous situations. Along with the first reports of the assassination, half the sample heard rumors that the Vice President had been stricken or shot, that Mrs. Kennedy had been shot, or that a Secret Service man had been shot or had shot the President, as well as rumors

TABLE 1

Distribution of respondents by five demographic variables ($n = 48$)

Sex:	Men	48%
	Women	52
Age:	18–29	21
	30–49	56
	50+	23
Education:	0–8 years	19
	9–12 years	31
	1–2 years college	23
	3+ years college	27
Religion:	Protestant	52
	Catholic	31
	Jewish	10
	Other	2
	No affiliation	4
Political Party:	Democrat	48
	Republican	35
	Independent	17

about the identity of the assassin, the arrests of different suspects, a Communist conspiracy, and attempts on the lives of other top government and military leaders. Within the week, all had heard at least one of these rumors.

Although the assassination created some conditions that might have led to collective disorder, there was no widespread hysteria. From the despondency and vulnerability on Friday to the relative equanimity and guarded optimism on Monday, television seemed to play a significant role in setting the mood of the community.

Reactions to the media

Within one hour, 90 per cent of the respondents knew of the assassination.[3] Forty-eight per cent heard by telephone or face-to-face, and 42 per cent from the broadcast media (television, 23 per cent; radio, 19 per cent). However, within that hour 80 per cent of the sample became part of the radio-television audience. All of those informed personally turned to radio or television unless neither was available, as for some who were at work. Wherever television was accessible, radio listeners switched to it anticipating "better" coverage, but TV viewers did not switch to radio.

In sudden disruptions of the environment, people tend to look to other people for information that will reduce anxiety by verifying their knowledge. But in this case, almost all of those who heard about the assassination from another person did not believe the news until they had confirmed it themselves by hearing it from radio or television.

I didn't really trust the person, because I usually don't trust something like that until I hear it at least on the radio or television.

One of my co-workers told me that the President had been shot in Dallas. . . . I just didn't believe it. I didn't think it would be a joke, if it would it would be a cruel joke, but I didn't believe it. Somebody said there was a radio out in the hall, so we walked out there and caught it on the radio then.

In the few instances where another person was believed, the belief was the cumulative result of several conversations in situations where no

[3] For similar, more definitive findings see the paper by Sheatsley and Feldman in this volume.

media were available. Those who first heard the news directly from radio or television all believed it without needing further confirmation.

Over three-fourths of the respondents started face-to-face or telephone conversations within minutes after they first heard the news. Nearly all of these "talkers" were informed personally or by the radio. Only one person informed by television started a conversation.

A. C. Nielsen's figures show that 96 per cent of U.S. home television sets were tuned to the assassination coverage for an average of 32 hours over the four-day period.[4] At least 70 per cent of the Minneapolis respondents described themselves as so preoccupied with television they might have been glued to the television set for the entire period:

When the station signed off, we signed off. . . . All day Saturday and Sunday I don't remember doing a thing. I didn't get dressed, I didn't make the beds, I didn't do anything. Monday we watched all day and cried all day.

We had the television going until there was no more TV, until we went to sleep; and we have three TV's here so wherever I went, from room to room, I was able to hear it.

On the average, respondents watched television 6.8 hours each day, with the lightest viewing on Friday, an average of 6.2 hours, and the heaviest viewing on Monday, an average of 7.5 hours. Typically, people watched television for slightly more than 27 hours during this period.

Regardless of when people turned to television on Friday, over half showed no channel discrimination at first. These respondents stopped the dial at the first station carrying the news, turned the set on at whatever channel it was set for, or came in on the viewing of someone else. Later, when they knew there would be continuous coverage, and after they had tried some channel-switching for more "up-to-date reports," most respondents established a viewing routine for the weekend. This meant they spent most of their time with the channel they "regularly" preferred for day-to-day news. However, neither habit nor familiar faces and format could sustain loyalty to a single channel throughout the weekend. When the coverage became repetitive or the content less stimulating, three-fourths of the respondents routinely switched channels, but they eventually returned to their usual station.

[4] *Broadcasting* (Feb. 3, 1964), p. 54.

People volunteered essentially the same reasons for watching ABC, CBS, or NBC; all three networks were accorded "best reception," "most interesting personalities," "best commentary," "most up-to-date news," etc. The network credited with the "best" presentation was merely the one the respondents usually watched the news on. Evaluations, in effect, were based on previous viewing experiences. When asked specifically to rate the networks in terms of news quantity, timeliness, accuracy, commentary, balance, and the like, respondents consistently rated CBS and NBC above ABC, but anywhere from one-fourth to two-thirds of the respondents on each rating regarded the coverage of all networks as "all about the same."

About half the respondents were reluctant to judge other media, since they spent so much time with television. Nine out of every ten respondents depended on television for the "most news coverage." About two-thirds of the sample rated TV first on having the "most complete news coverage," the "fairest, most accurate coverage," and the "most meaningful reports." On supplying the "best local news coverage," less than half rated TV first, while one-fourth rated radio first and one-fifth chose newspapers; the rest did not recall local news coverage during the four days.

Radio's principal advantage was its portability, both as the first source of information and later as a supplementary source whenever people were away from television. Newspapers were used for detailed "catch-up" reading or were saved as permanent records.

The reasons people spent much time watching television are to be found in the uniqueness of the coverage. Neither radio nor newspapers could match television's facility for realism and psychological proximity. Television created an extraordinarily deep sense of participation in the flow of events, as these comments, representative of about three-fourths of the sample, indicate:

It seems to be more personal when you see something happening on TV, than just listening about it. I had the feeling that for once in my life I was watching history being made, and what would be in the history books in the future. I was right there when it happened.

It brought you there as if you were one of the close spectators—closer than had you been on the street watching what was taking place. Each time it took you into the rotunda you felt as if you were one of the people passing in review.

As 42 per cent of the sample commented, television attained a clarity and definitiveness previously unparalleled in public affairs reporting:

If it weren't for TV I don't think I would have known about it. I mean I could have listened to the radio and read the paper, but I don't think I would have had as much of an understanding of the whole situation.

Just as things happened, they were right there, bringing everything to you at the moment. It was better than being there; you could see more than you could if you were there, I'm sure.

I don't know how you could beat watching it and drawing your own conclusions. You couldn't possibly in print describe more thoroughly to me what I saw. . . . I don't think anyone [could] give me the same mental picture as having seen it.

Everyone praised some aspect of television's performance. Nearly three-fifths of the respondents said television had done nothing "poorly" in reporting the events surrounding the assassination. The most frequent commendations were on the mobility of the news teams and the vantage points of the cameras at the Rotunda, the Dallas jail, and the funeral (69 per cent), the speed with which networks organized the news flow (46 per cent), the "one picture is worth a thousand words" vividness of the televised accounts (38 per cent), and the "good taste, dignity, and restraint" of the commentators (27 per cent).

Television alone was lauded for the "great public service" it performed. Although much advertising revenue was lost by the other media, about one-fifth of respondents were impressed only by the "sacrifice" made by the TV networks in canceling their commercial programs.

Television may have done its job altogether too well for some people. Once acclimated to television's ability to be "on the spot everywhere," about one-fourth of the respondents seemed to expect almost too much. Beneath their sorrow for Kennedy and admiration for television, their comments revealed dissatisfaction because the camera could neither expose every intrigue nor control the sequence of episodes. It was as though they were reviewing a commercial drama, in that they exhibited mild pique or frustration when the "program" was not to their liking:

I would like to have seen more of the first of it, when he was shot. They should have had a camera on that motorcade, I should think.

They could have started the murder scene [sooner], the shooting of Oswald. It looked too fakey to be real. If you had a play . . . usually it [the murder] would be acted out better.

The parade itself was quite long. It took a lot of time and patience, but I suppose that is what you have to have. You wondered if they'd ever get to the cemetery.

Roughly a third of those interviewed would have preferred to have less of the Oswald shooting, "the incessant lines" at the Rotunda, the foreign visitors' reception, the interviews with Jack Ruby's friends, and the "excessive number" of memorial services. Just about half the respondents were critical of the repetition, network duplication, programming disorganization, news lags, and commentators who "mouthed words" to fill time. Mitigating much of this criticism, however, was some understanding of the many difficulties imposed by the suddenness and the nature of the event being reported. The most severe criticism came from the 27 per cent who were angered by the "insensitive invasion" of Mrs. Kennedy's privacy, and from the 31 per cent who were indignant over television's contribution to the murder of Lee Oswald.

In recounting the specific moments most prominent in their minds, 21 per cent mentioned the assassination itself. The "unforgettable" episodes of the weekend typically were among those seen on television: the Oswald shooting; the crowds passing in silent review of the casket; Mrs. Kennedy kneeling to kiss the American flag; John Kennedy, Jr., saluting his father's casket; the funeral cortege; and the impressive solemnity of the graveside ceremony.

Social functions commonly attributed to the media include enforcement of social norms, conferral of status, and narcotization of action.[5] That television variously performed each of these functions was evident in the respondents' comments about their feelings and behavior during the weekend. After the assassination, television most conspicuously contributed to the enforcement and affirmation of social norms and values. Faith in the future of the country, belief in the form and continuity of the government, these are the cornerstones of the American value system.

---

[5] Paul F. Lazarsfeld and Robert K. Merton, "Mass Communication, Popular Taste, and Organized Social Action," in Wilbur Schramm, ed., *Mass Communications* (Urbana, Illinois, 1960), pp. 492–512.

Allied to these values are canonization of the presidency, esteem for dignity and courage, and reverence for the dead. The comments of 92 per cent of those interviewed show that television reawakened these values for them. Television furnished undeniable evidence of the continuing vitality of the American government.

I think by the use of the documentary and its "Let's look ahead with confidence" they [TV] were able to at least remind a person of the many things they subconsciously knew, and again would lift up your spirits. I think they had a great deal of control over the emotions of the viewing public.

Certainly it was the historic significance of the events and the people, and not television, that raised from obscurity such men as Oswald and Ruby. On the other hand, critics in the American Civil Liberties Union and the American Bar Association have speculated about how much the national television exposure might have jeopardized Oswald's "opportunity to receive a fair trial" and how much it might have influenced Jack Ruby's decision to "avenge" the assassination.[6] If applied here, "status conferral" is simple notoriety.

It was the unique position and personal deportment of Lyndon Johnson and Jacqueline Kennedy, and again not television, that thrust them into prominence. But the "inspirational courage" with which Mrs. Kennedy was seen to endure her grief elevated her stature in the eyes of many respondents. ("How brave Jackie had been. . . 'Jackie,' we talk like she's our sister.") That television contributed directly to the "status" of President Johnson was evident in the speed with which over half the respondents accepted his qualifications. Personal documentaries and background stories appeared almost immediately, and in a matter of hours he moved from the relative limbo of the vice-presidency to the status of a "capable" successor to Kennedy.

One consequence of the flood of information from television and the other media was that it narcotized rather than incited action, action that might have been antisocial. Lazarsfeld and Merton term this the "narcotizing dysfunction" of the media, on the assumption "that it is not in the interest of a modern, complex society to have large masses of the population politically apathetic and inert. . . . [The public mistakes]

[6] *Broadcasting* (Dec. 9, 1963), p. 70.

knowing about the problems of the day for *doing* something about them."[7]

After the assassination, this narcotization seemed to have essentially positive attributes, if one goes by the comments of 40 per cent of the respondents. The absence of extreme behavior seemed in part due to the ease with which people could tell from television how much they might be threatened.

We thanked God we had TV every minute ... I think it actually made us feel better, if we could have felt better, because we knew exactly what was happening. We didn't have to wonder, you know: Why? How?

It did more than satisfy my curiosity ... I could see it. I knew what was happening and I could believe it. It only made you more depressed, but it helped you realize things were OK and got it out of your system.

In this respect, television helped assuage people's fears by providing believable standards of judgment. Indeed, four days of being "glued to the set" left more than half the respondents not only reassured, but "drained," "wrung out," and "exhausted."

So poignantly did television accentuate the pain of the assassination, yet at the same time immobilize the impulse to act, that normal social and introspective outlets were generally ignored. ("He didn't express himself emotionally ... but you could tell it really bothered him.") For two-thirds of the sample, the thirst for information got them much more than they could deal with and so helped create depression.

It just got to the point that I couldn't take it anymore; it was too depressing. When I had TV on too long, then I got depressed.

I was just too depressed to watch it. It made me cry, and I just couldn't stand it.

Television was also dysfunctional in that its continuous and repetitive coverage, monotonous story treatment, and personalization of events forced people to seek diversion. By Saturday night nearly 60 per cent of the respondents initiated some unplanned activity simply to escape the discomfort of the prolonged viewing. The Nielsen figures show an

[7] Lazarsfeld and Merton, pp. 501–2.

inordinate number of sets turned on. Yet there is evidence that viewing was not as continuous as people reported. Although we can accept
at face value the cumulative hours of viewing reported, it would seem
that the gravity of the crisis and the vividness of the television experience left a somewhat inaccurate impression of constant vigilance. Contradictory statements from the viewers themselves indicate this may be
the case. ("We couldn't take it anymore, so we went out. I think that
was everybody's idea, because every place we went sure was crowded.")

At no time, however, did any of those interviewed—including the
diversion seekers—successfully detach themselves from television. The
anxiety underlying the impression of compulsive viewing was a fear of
"being in the dark" and "not knowing what was going on," which was
reported by 38 per cent of the sample. No matter how shocked, depressed, or vulnerable people felt ("If it could happen to him, it could
happen to anyone"), some five out of every six persons interviewed recalled being drawn back to the television set.

I walked around the block because I felt if I didn't I was going to scream . . .
I thought I could get away from it for awhile, but it was like a magnet.

This son of mine did leave the television because he said it was getting him.
He was too depressed from listening, and . . . he got to the point where he
didn't want to watch it. And yet it sort of drew him, you know, to come back.

Crises that society is unprepared to handle routinely produce behavioral extremes, either apathy or hysteria. In such a traumatic situation, the wrong kind of information may intensify agitation and precipitate violence. A person in such a situation, who generally tries to
reduce his anxiety, looks for supportive information and therefore often
achieves a state of exaggerated suggestibility. Although this is merely a
conjecture, it seems very probable that the magnetic attraction that television had for the respondents served as a catalyst to speed up adjustment to the finality of the President's death and to renew faith in the
future.

In this study we found that the people, who on Friday exhibited emotional reactions that usually precede collective disorder, appear to have
acquired after the funeral a more realistic appraisal of the assassination's implications for the future of the country. If one can speculate

on the basis of this small sample, it seems the reversal in mood and in perspective was aided considerably by the presence of television. Although people were reassured of the stability of the government and inspired by the conduct of the Kennedy family, they experienced a restless urgency for release from television and "this mounting depression." By Monday, three-fourths of the respondents said they were finding comfort in the realization that the nation would go on much as before.

I felt more secure—like everything was still going on the same, we have a new President. A great man was lost, but I felt more realistic.

I felt awful bad on Monday night, but at the same time I felt pretty good that we had a new President and the country was going the way it was going before and it would keep on going.

For most of the respondents, the realization that only one life, not a nation, had been lost was not enough to free them from the depression of the weekend. In seeking relief, they experienced vague feelings of guilt about wanting relief. So earnest was this conflict that perhaps only a very dramatic and appropriate event could have resolved it satisfactorily. For these people, specifically, the nationally televised funeral provided a properly dignified and ceremonious conclusion for the emotions of the weekend.

I remember feeling like a tragic weekend was over, and it was kind of a relief. It seemed like a new week started new life for a lot of people.

Friday night it was a feeling of [being] shocked almost to the point of disbelief. And by Monday night there was more a feeling of peace and the end of it all, the funeral having taken place.

By Monday night peace, relief, security, and optimism seemed to prevail, but many respondents said they still found it hard to believe that the assassination of a President of the United States actually had occurred.

There was still an air of unreality about everything, as well as depression. It was something of such great significance, not just the loss of one person, but the symbolic office of the presidency.

I don't know what you would call it. I imagine you were still hoping it was all wrong, that there had been some mistake made.

Conclusions

In the uncertainty caused by the assassination crisis, television was an important source of information that alleviated some of the anxiety to test reality beyond the living room. It structured and clarified the extent of personal threat by providing believable standards of judgment. It was a catalyst for people's emotions, since it induced a deep sense of personal participation in the flow of events. It gave timely reassurance by showing the existence and continuity of cherished institutions and values. It reinforced social prescriptions for correct behavior by showing the exemplary conduct of the nation's leaders. It encouraged almost immediate faith in the new President by rapidly emphasizing his experience and capabilities. And it helped to narcotize behavior that might have been dangerous by exhausting the need for action.

Lee F. Anderson and Emerson Moran

Audience Perceptions of Radio and Television Objectivity

Our purpose in doing this study was to try to answer three questions: How fair or objective did the public think the mass media coverage of the assassination was? What kinds of bias or distortion were perceived? How were perceptions of bias or distortion related to political orientations?

We obtained our data from questionnaires that were filled out by high-school and college students and their parents during the week after the assassination. The sample was the same sample from the Chicago area that is used in the Hurn-Messer paper later in this volume. Answers to the question "Do you think the radio and television broadcasts have slanted the reporting of this event in an attempt to mold public opinion?" were classified as "slanted," "somewhat slanted," or "not slanted."

Of the 1,825 respondents in the sample, 66 per cent said that the coverage was "not slanted." Another 22 per cent said that the coverage was "somewhat slanted." Eight per cent said that the coverage was "slanted." The remaining respondents did not answer. These results show that the majority of the sample thought the media were fair and objective in their reporting. The minority that disagreed was asked to describe the biases perceived. Although many different kinds of bias were described, we were able to group most of them into seven categories. The four major ones are listed and discussed below.

Slanted in a pro-Kennedy direction. These were charges that the media were in some way overly favorable to the late President. Typical responses in this category were that the media "attempted to force a similarity to Lincoln and his times," were "slanted toward late President," were "distorted to make Kennedy a great man," and "made Kennedy seem like a martyr." This category included 43 per cent of the 508 perceptions of bias.

Slanted against Oswald. These were charges that the media had been less than equitable or responsible in reporting the Oswald events. Responses typical of this category were, "Oswald's guilt assumed quickly," "immediately seemed to convict Oswald," and "TV trial of assassin and assassin's murderer." This category, the second largest, included 14 per cent of the responses.

Generally manipulative. These were charges that the media attempted to mold public opinion in some broad or general way. Responses that illustrate this category were: "slanted to make all feel patriotic," "slanted to assure public everything was all right," and "slanted to be sure that world understood that Americans truly grieved." Eleven per cent were in this category.

Overdramatized the event. These were charges that the media had overdramatized or overrated the event's importance or had infused it with excess emotion. The reporters were "too emotional," they "made it more significant than it was," and the media "made a Hollywood production out of it." This category included 10 per cent of the responses.

The three remaining categories were for charges that the reporting was slanted toward Johnson (7 per cent), had some "leftist" slant (3 per cent), or had a rightwing slant (2 per cent). Eleven per cent of the descriptions did not fit into any of these seven categories.

Most of the criticism of the coverage was heavily political. Klapper observes that selective perception operates in audience response just as it does in other areas of social behavior. "The existing opinions and interests of people . . . have been shown profoundly to influence their behavior vis-à-vis mass communications. . . ."[1] In order to find out why the perceptions were so politically oriented, we first assumed that it must be political attitudes that predisposed a respondent toward either perceiving or not perceiving distortion in the coverage of the assassination. We suspected that the two attitudes that would be most responsible for such a predisposition would be the respondent's party identifi-

[1] Joseph T. Klapper, *The Effects of Mass Communication* (New York, 1961).

cation and his opinion of Kennedy. We therefore set up a hypothetical model of influence in which these two attitudes were assumed to be related but still separable. Each would contribute independently to perception of bias, as in the following diagram:

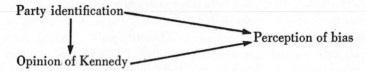

The importance of partisanship in shaping people's perceptions of the political world has been thoroughly documented. Although an event of the magnitude of the Kennedy assassination may be expected to depress the influence of partisanship, it seems doubtful that its effects on perception would be entirely erased. Even in death the President is a partisan leader as well as the chief of state and a national symbol. Hence our hypothesis was, specifically, that Republicans would be more likely than Democrats to see distortion in the reporting of the Democratic President's slaying. Eight hundred and seventy-seven respondents identified themselves as either Democrats or Independents leaning Democratic. Seven hundred and twenty respondents said they were either Republicans or Independents leaning Republican. Of these two groups, 28 and 35 per cent, respectively, thought the coverage was either "slanted" or "somewhat slanted" ($p < .01$).

We also predicted that the intensity of the respondent's partisanship would influence his perception of the coverage. That is, the more intensely he identified with the Democratic Party, the less likely he would be to perceive bias, and conversely, the more intensely he identified with the Republican Party, the more likely he would be to perceive bias. The results of this analysis are given in Table 1.

Our prediction is partly supported by the data. Among the Democrats, perception of bias decreases as intensity of commitment increases. Among the Republicans, the relationship is much less consistent. We expected that "strong Republicans" would perceive a great deal of bias, but we certainly did not expect that "moderate Republicans" would perceive less bias than "Independents leaning Democratic." The data do not reveal a simple relationship between intensity of partisanship and perception of bias, except between the strong and moderate members of each party. Furthermore, the difference between the most partisan

TABLE 1

Party Identification and Perception of Bias

Party identification	Per cent perceiving coverage as "slanted" and "somewhat slanted"
Strong Democrat ($n = 203$)	23%
Moderate Democrat ($n = 357$)	27
Independent leaning Democratic ($n = 310$)	32
Independent ($n = 143$)	34
Independent leaning Republican ($n = 191$)	38
Moderate Republican ($n = 332$)	30
Strong Republican ($n = 196$)	42

Republicans and the most partisan Democrats is substantially greater than the average Democrat-Republican difference of seven per cent.

We included three questions that we hoped would help us find out what relationship there was between the respondent's predisposition to perceive bias and his opinion of Kennedy. One was "Before the assassination, how well did you feel President Kennedy was doing his job as President?" We expected that the higher the respondent's estimation of Kennedy's performance was, the less likely he would be to perceive the coverage as distorted. The relevant data, given in Table 2, confirm this hypothesis.

Respondents were asked whether they had been involved in arguments about the Kennedy administration and, if so, whether they had supported or opposed the administration. We expected that the more opposed a person had been to administration positions, the more likely he would be to perceive bias. The subsample in this analysis included 1,332 respondents. Of those who were "always for," "usually for," "usually against," and "always against" the administration, 22, 35, 39, and 60 per cent, respectively, perceived some bias in the media coverage. Consistently, perception of bias increased as opposition to the Kennedy administration increased.

The third question was asked of those who reported that they had seen the President in person ($n = 333$). We asked, "Were you as impressed as you expected to be when you saw President Kennedy?" We expected that the less impressed a person had been, the more likely he was to think the coverage was distorted. Thirty per cent of the respondents who reported that they were more impressed than they had ex-

TABLE 2

Estimation of Kennedy as President and Perception of Bias

Respondents who thought Kennedy performed:	Per cent who perceived coverage as "slanted" or "somewhat slanted"
As well as any outstanding President ($n = 456$)	25%
Very well ($n = 494$)	27
Moderately well ($n = 533$)	36
Not very well ($n = 127$)	51
Poorly ($n = 24$)	67

pected to be perceived some bias in the coverage; 40 per cent of those who were only as impressed as they expected to be perceived some bias; and 55 per cent of those who were less impressed than they expected to be perceived some bias. The findings supported our expectation.

We had assumed that partisanship would be the prime influence on the respondents' opinions of the late President, although not the sole one. We then assumed that partisanship and opinion of Kennedy would independently affect perception of bias in the radio and television coverage. Partisanship and opinion of Kennedy are positively related ($r = .45$), but nearly 80 per cent of the variance in opinions about Kennedy is not accounted for by partisanship.[2] Thus the first of the assumptions proved to be correct. The correlation between party identification and perception of bias is .43. Opinion of Kennedy alone predicts perception of bias much better ($r = .74$). The multiple correlation of both party identification and opinion of Kennedy ($R = .75$) does not predict significantly better than opinion of Kennedy alone. Thus, the second assumption was not supported.

In this sample of the mass media, no simple and direct relationship was found between party identification *per se* and perception of bias in the media's coverage of the event. The influence of partisanship was mediated by opinion of Kennedy. In contrast to our first influence model, the data suggest the following sequence of relationships:

Party identification ⟶ Opinion of Kennedy ⟶ Perception of bias

Party identification partly conditioned opinion of Kennedy. Opinion of Kennedy in turn conditioned perception of bias in the media's coverage.

[2] For all four of these correlations, $p < .001$.

Part III

The Public Reactions:
Attitudes and Behavior in the Aftermath

Paul B. Sheatsley and Jacob J. Feldman

A National Survey on Public Reactions and Behavior

The assassin's bullet that so abruptly ended the life of John F. Kennedy created a public event unique in the lives of contemporary Americans. The networks of mass communication and personal contacts spread the news with a speed that was in all likelihood unprecedented, and, instantaneously, public attention turned away from everyday personal concerns to the details and meaning of the awesome event. Probably never before were the sentiments of the American public engaged so deeply by a happening on the political scene.

The unique character of the event derived in part from its sudden swiftness and in part from the personality of the man who was killed. Other events in recent times had some of the same elements, but not in the same combination. Attempts had been made upon the lives of Presidents Truman and Roosevelt, but the last actual assassination had been more than sixty years ago, long before most current adults were born. Almost twenty years ago, within the memory of most of the public, President Roosevelt had died in office, but the Kennedy assassination was qualitatively different in two major respects: Roosevelt died of natural causes, whereas Kennedy was murdered; and Roosevelt, in his fourth term of office, was in his sixties, whereas Kennedy, in his first term and not yet fifty years of age, was the very image of youthful energy and vigor. Among contemporary public events, perhaps the closest parallel to the assassination, in its suddenness and its impact upon the population, was the unexpected Japanese attack on Pearl Harbor, which precipitated

U.S. entry into World War II, but that attack lacked the personal element that attended the unbelievable killing of the nation's President.

As unique as the assassination was, it nevertheless provided an opportunity to learn something about more normal phenomena.[1] For instance, we know surprisingly little about the meaning of the presidency to the American public. Many studies have been made of voting behavior with respect to that office, yet we haven't much idea of just what it is that people feel they are electing. Just as a newspaper strike enabled Berelson to gain considerable insight into the functions served by newspapers during normal times, the death of a chief of state can reveal a great deal about the sentiments that normally surround the incumbent of that office.[2]

A survey of reactions to the assassination could also contribute to our knowledge of bereavement. Although mourning and grief have been studied intensively in highly select populations, they have not previously been investigated epidemiologically over a broad population. Admittedly, there might be little correspondence between the emotional patterns elicited by the murder of a President and those elicited by an unequivocally personal loss like the death of a loved one. Still, this was clearly a good chance to learn at least a little about the variation between different segments of the population in the symptomatology experienced in response to more or less the same stressful situation.

Here was an opportunity, then, to collect a body of data with both immediate and long-term significance. None of the other major events of our time had been subjected to detailed investigation; no comprehensive study of reactions to President Roosevelt's death or the attack on Pearl Harbor had been made.[3] Our obligation to the historian of the

---

[1] This investigation was supported by a small grant from the Political Behavior Committee of the Social Science Research Council and from research funds of the Survey Research Center, a division of NORC. It is reprinted, with minor modifications, from *Public Opinon Quarterly* (1964), *28*, 189–215.

[2] Bernard Berelson, "What 'Missing the Newspaper' Means," in Paul Lazarsfeld and Frank Stanton, eds., *Communications Research, 1948–49* (New York, 1949).

[3] Several studies of reactions to Roosevelt's death were published, but they were all based on data that were far from systematically collected. In fact, Orlansky, in his analysis of press reports concerning public reactions to the event, expressed considerable regret that more systematic data had not been collected. Among the discussions on Roosevelt's death were: Sebastian de Grazia, "A Note on the Psychological Position of the Chief Executive," *Psychiatry* (1945), *7*, 267–72; Dorothea E. Johannsen, "Reactions to the Death of President Roosevelt," *The Journal of Abnormal and Social Psychology* (1946), *41*, 218–

future would not be fulfilled unless we acted. Consequently, when a meeting was called in Washington by social scientists of similar opinions, the National Opinion Research Center (NORC) was quick to respond.[4] Peter H. Rossi, NORC Director, attended this meeting on Sunday, November 24, and a series of studies was planned, one of which was to be national in scope. He returned to Chicago Sunday evening with a preliminary draft of a questionnaire. Although at the time there was no firm prospect of financing the study, it was decided to go ahead in any case. Hopefully, financial support would be obtained somehow later on.

To capture the mood and engagement of the American public in all its immediacy, it was necessary to start our field work as quickly as possible. NORC staff members volunteered their services to work around the clock to set the machinery of a national sample study in motion. The capability to carry out rapidly a "flash" study is a characteristic of a national survey organization such as NORC. A nationwide corps of trained and experienced interviewers is available; national samples are already drawn and ready for use; and printing and duplicating facilities are on the premises. Perhaps most important is the cadre of professional study directors with years of experience and encyclopedic memories. With the preliminary questionnaire at hand, a team of four study directors worked through Sunday night on a final round of questionnaire construction. New questions about the assassination were invented, and old files searched for past questions that might now have value for trend purposes. By early Monday morning an acceptable draft had been completed. Meanwhile, the Field Department spent Sunday night and Monday morning alerting interviewers around the country by means of telephone and telegraph.

To avoid the delay caused by callbacks on designated respondents who are not available on the first call, a modified probability sample was

---

22; Kurt H. Wolff, "A Partial Analysis of Student Reaction to President Roosevelt's Death," *The Journal of Social Psychology* (1947), *26*, 35–53; Harold Orlansky, "Reactions to the Death of President Roosevelt," *The Journal of Social Psychology* (1947), *26*, 235–66; Sebastian de Grazia, *The Political Community* (Chicago, 1948) pp. 112–15. A forerunner of these studies dealt with the death of George V; it was W. R. D. Fairbairn, "The Effect of a King's Death Upon Patients Undergoing Analysis," *The International Journal of Psychoanalysis* (1936), *27*, 278–84.

4 The meeting was called by Dr. Leonard Duhl of the National Institutes of Health, acting primarily in his private capacity as a social scientist, and was attended by Henry Riecken, Leonard Soskin, Marc Fried, Robert Bower, Eric Lindeman, Robert Leopold, and Ivor Wayne.

used, of the type known as "block sample." Interviewers were directed
to randomly chosen blocks or rural segments, given a prescribed route,
and instructed to call at every dwelling unit to try to fill age-sex quotas.
To ensure an adequate number of working women, the female quota
was divided between housewives and employed women. Sampling materials for this type of assignment were already available from past surveys,
and these were made ready by the Sampling Department by Monday
noon. Following a final conference on the questionnaire at 10 o'clock
Monday morning, that document was turned over to typists, and work
began on drafting instructions for the interviewers. Copies of our final
questionnaire were sent to other participants in the Sunday conference
in Washington, for use in modified form in their own sub-studies.
Materials were completed by early afternoon, and, thanks to the work
of many volunteers who gave up the holiday occasioned by the President's funeral, all assignments were in the mail at O'Hare Airport by
2:45 Tuesday morning. In spite of the fact that no interviews were
attempted on Thursday, Thanksgiving Day, 97 per cent of the 1,384
interviews were completed by Saturday, November 30.

What follows is a summary of the major findings, together with a
limited analysis based on the reactions of five population groups: (1)
Negroes, (2) Northern whites who "preferred" Kennedy in the 1960
election, (3) other Northern whites, (4) Southern whites who "preferred" Kennedy in 1960, and (5) other Southern whites.[5]

How the news spread, and first reactions

The President was shot at 12:30 P.M. CST, on Friday; he was pronounced dead at 1 o'clock. By that time 68 per cent, or two out of every
three adult Americans, had heard the news. Within another hour,
an additional 24 per cent learned of the assassination, so that in less than
two hours, it appears, 92 per cent of the public was aware of the event.

---

[5] Admittedly, retrospective "preference" for Kennedy in the 1960 election is not the same
as feeling positively toward him and his program in 1963, but, since we obviously lack
any measure of the attitudes of these respondents immediately before the assassination, it
is probably the best measure available to us. It correlates well with respondents' current
ratings of Kennedy's stature as President. More people now claim to have favored him
in 1960 than actually voted for him, but this is a common phenomenon in public opinion
surveys. Though he was elected by little over 50 per cent of the popular vote, 59 per cent
in a June 1963 NORC survey said they favored him in 1960, and in the current study 65
per cent claimed him as their 1960 preference.

By 6 P.M. the penetration had reached 99.8 per cent.[6] (Two of the 1,384 respondents told interviewers they did not hear of the assassination until the following day.) This abnormally fast and deep penetration of the news is probably without parallel in the past, although we have no comparable data concerning Pearl Harbor or the death of Roosevelt.[7] Certainly, the fact that two-thirds of the public were reached in one hour, nine out of ten in two hours, and almost everybody in less than four hours contrasts sharply with findings by Gallup and others that only rarely are more than 80 per cent of the population *ever* aware of any given personality or event.[8]

About half the people (47 per cent) received word of the assassination by means of radio or television, the other half (49 per cent) through telephone calls or personal messages. (Four per cent first learned from newspapers or other sources.) Here we do have comparable data from a telegraphic survey that NORC conducted immediately after the death of President Roosevelt in 1945, and the results are remarkably similar. At that time, 47 per cent of the public first heard of the event through radio or the press, while 53 per cent heard from other people. Half the adult population (50 per cent) were at home when they first got news of Kennedy's assassination, 29 per cent were at work, and the remainder were outside shopping, having lunch, driving, or elsewhere. Only a third (32 per cent) were alone when they first heard the news; all the others

[6] Respondents were asked, "When did you first hear of the assassination of President Kennedy? (About what time of day was it?)" and all replies were converted into Central Standard Time.

[7] A 1945 paper by Miller reports that 91 per cent of 143 students at Kent State University heard about the death of Roosevelt within half an hour of the first news flash (Delbert C. Miller, "A Research Note on Mass Communication," *American Sociological Review*, 1945, *10*, 692). In contrast, Larsen and Hill, studying diffusion of the news of the death of Senator Robert A. Taft, found that eleven hours had elapsed before 90 per cent of a university faculty community heard of the event, and fourteen hours before 90 per cent of the eventual knowers among residents of a low-rent housing project heard of it (Otto N. Larsen and Richard J. Hill, "Mass Media and Interpersonal Communication in the Diffusion of a News Event," *American Sociological Review*, 1954, *19*, 429). The homogeneous and geographically limited nature of these samples and the obviously lesser impact of the death of Senator Taft rule out any comparisons with our findings.

[8] A Gallup release dated December 15, 1963, notes a survey by the Gallup affiliate in Greece, which found that "Just 24 hours after the assassination, 99 per cent of Athenians were found to be aware of the tragic occurrence—a remarkably high awareness score when compared, for example, with the fact that one-fourth of the people of that city were unable to identify Premier Charles de Gaulle of France just a few days before his arrival in Athens."

were with someone, generally family members at home, or co-workers on the job or at lunch.

Some measure of the impact of the event upon the public may be gathered from the fact that the majority (54 per cent) said they did not continue their usual activities after they heard the news; and of those who did, most said they found it more difficult. Only 19 per cent reported that they were able to carry on "pretty much as usual." Of those who dropped what they were doing, five out of six said they turned to television or the radio. Others hurried home, presumably also to listen to the radio or watch TV; or phoned or visited friends and relatives to discuss the event; or explained that they just grieved, mourned, or "sat and thought about it." In reply to another question, 54 per cent of the public said they "felt like talking with other people about it," while 40 per cent "felt more like being by myself"; 6 per cent could not decide. It appears that the more people admired the late President, the more likely they were to want to be alone after they heard of his death. For example, 51 per cent of the Negroes, but only 28 per cent of Southern whites who were opposed to Kennedy in 1960, said they felt more like being by themselves. Thirty-seven per cent of the adults interviewed said they phoned or went to talk to somebody about the event; and, curiously, 38 per cent said that somebody phoned or came to talk to them about the assassination. These calls, in both directions, seem to be divided approximately equally between relatives and nonrelatives. Asked to compare their own reactions with those of other people, 30 per cent believed they were *more* upset than "most people," while only 8 per cent said they were less upset than others. Among Negroes, 49 per cent felt they were more upset, only 3 per cent felt less upset, whereas among Southern whites who did not prefer Kennedy in 1960, only 14 per cent felt more upset and 17 per cent felt less upset than most people.

The majority of all respondents could not recall any other time in their lives when they had the same sort of feelings as when they heard of President Kennedy's assassination. Of those who could think of such an occasion (47 per cent of the public), the majority referred to the death of a parent, close friend, or other relative. Only a third of the group mentioned the death of any other public figure; FDR was specifically named by about a fourth. And only 8 per cent of those who could recall a similar event referred to Pearl Harbor. Negroes and pro-Kennedy

Northerners were much more likely to compare Kennedy's death with that of a close friend or relative; fully 80 per cent of the Negro references were to such an occasion of personal grief. Southerners and non-Kennedy Northerners, when they thought of a similar event, referred more often than other groups to the death of Roosevelt or to Pearl Harbor.

In reply to the open-ended question, "When you first heard that the President had been shot, who did you think probably did it—that is, what sort of person?" only one out of five failed to name an immediate suspect. Almost half thought right away that it was the work of a crazed or fanatic individual. Twenty-nine per cent specifically mentioned mental illness (madman, crazy person, insane, mentally unbalanced, etc.), while an additional 17 per cent answered, "Some kind of crackpot," "nut," "fanatic," "extremist," and the like. In ideological terms, about a quarter of the population immediately suspected the work of a Communist, Castroite, or other leftist, while only half as many had the immediate reaction that the shot was probably fired by a segregationist or some other representative of the right wing. Negroes were the only exception to the latter case. Of the one-third of all Negroes who suspected an ideological motive for the assassination, two out of three blamed a segregationist; whites, whether North or South, pro-Kennedy or anti-, were much more likely to attribute the deed to a Communist or Castro supporter.

Interviewers next read a list of seventeen statements representing "the ways that some people felt when they first heard that the President was dead," and Table 1 shows the responses of the national sample. Perhaps the most striking finding, already foreshadowed by the comparison of Kennedy's death with that of a close friend or relative, and by the general failure to respond in ideological terms to the question of who killed him, is the immense tide of grief, loss, sorrow, shame, and anger that people felt when they first heard the news, and the relative infrequency with which political or personal concerns were mentioned.

The first reactions of nine out of ten Americans were sympathy for Mrs. Kennedy and the children, and deep feelings of sorrow that "a strong young man had been killed at the height of his powers." Furthermore, four out of five "felt deeply the loss of someone very close and dear," five out of six admitted to deep feelings of "shame that such a thing could happen in our country," and approximately three out of four

TABLE 1

Immediate Reactions to News of Assassination

Reaction[a]	Very Deepest Feeling	Felt Quite Deeply	Crossed My Mind	Never Occurred to Me
Felt so sorry for his wife and children	61%	31%	6%	2%
Felt sorry that a strong young man had been killed at the height of his powers	52	36	8	4
Felt ashamed that this could happen in our country .	50	33	10	7
Felt the loss of someone very close and dear	45	34	9	12
Felt angry that anyone should do such a terrible deed	44	29	14	13
Worried about how his death would affect the political situation in this country	19	28	32	21
Worried about how his death would affect our relations with other countries	16	28	33	23
Felt worried about how the United States would carry on without its leader	16	25	29	30
So confused and upset, didn't know what to feel . .	18	20	14	48
Thought it was done by some Communist or other radical to get rid of the President	13	15	40	32
Wondered if anybody could really be safe in this country these days when the President himself can get shot	10	11	29	50
Worried how this might affect own life, job, and future	9	11	17	63
Thought it was done by a segregationist or extreme right-winger	8	10	32	50
Hoped the man who killed him would be shot down or lynched	6	5	13	76
Worried whether person who did it would be a member of my race or religion and bring on persecution	3	3	12	82
Felt that in many ways the President had brought it on himself	2	2	11	85

[a] A seventeenth statement was, "Thought about the many tragic things that have happened to them and this was just another of them." It was intended to measure self-pity, a tendency to see the loss of the President only as another cross the respondent must bear. As seems obvious now, however, many or perhaps most respondents interpreted it as referring to the Kennedy family, and the meaning of the responses is obscure.

"felt angry that anyone should do such a terrible deed." These feelings were almost as characteristic of those who opposed the late President politically as of those who supported him.

These five immediate reactions, each one held by at least 73 per cent of the total public, were quite clearly dominant; in fact, none of the other twelve responses was characteristic of even half the people. In retrospect, it is unfortunate that we did not include some such item as, "I could hardly believe it; I thought there must be some mistake." Grief has been said to include "an initial phase of shock and disbelief, in which the sufferer attempts to deny the loss and to insulate himself against the shock of reality," and it is probable that the response of disbelief was as prevalent as those of loss, sorrow, pity, shame, and anger.[9] Almost half the *volunteered* comments to the question, "Were you more or less upset than most people?" included some reference to this reaction: "I couldn't believe that he was dead," "It seemed like a bad dream," "I just couldn't believe it," "It couldn't happen," "We thought it must be a joke," etc.[10]

The three next most frequent reactions were of worry and concern about the future of the nation. Forty-seven per cent immediately worried about the effect of the assassination on "the political situation in this country"; and the fact that this was mentioned by almost two-thirds of the Negroes and a solid majority of Southern white supporters of Kennedy suggests that they were thinking of the fate of the civil rights program rather than of presidential politics. Forty-four per cent worried about "our relations with other countries" and 41 per cent about "how the United States would carry on without its leader." The intensity of Negro reaction to the event is further underscored by the finding that two-thirds of this group, as compared with only 38 per cent of the general public, were "so confused and upset, [they] didn't know what to feel"; and that fully half of the Negro population, as compared with only 20 per cent of the general public, "worried how this might affect my own life, job, and future." One American in five "wondered if anybody could really be safe in this country these days, when the President himself can get shot"; this reaction was voiced by more than twice as many Negroes as whites. Only one person in nine said his first reaction was to "hope the man who killed him would be shot down or lynched."

The four days

The intensive coverage that radio and TV gave to the events following the assassination was unprecedented, and it is doubtful if the American public was ever before so saturated with details of a single event. The

[9] G. L. Engel, citing Freud and others, "Is Grief a Disease?" *Psychosomatic Medicine* (1961), *23*, 18–23.
[10] The Texas Poll of February 5, 1964, has reported answers to the open-ended question, "What was your first reaction to the news of the President's assassination?" "Disbelief" and "shock" were each mentioned by 42 per cent of the statewide sample. Sixteen per cent answered, "Sorrow, tears," and no other single emotion was given as first reaction by more than 10 per cent.

TABLE 2

Percentage Reporting Selected Symptoms Among the Adult Population

Symptom	A. During the four days						B. At time of interview					
	National sample (n=1,384)	Total Negro (n=165)	White pro-K north (n=568)	White pro-K south (n=184)	White non-K north (n=329)	White non-K south (n=138)	National sample (n=1,384)	Total Negro (n=165)	White pro-K north (n=568)	White pro-K south (n=184)	White non-K north (n=329)	White non-K south (n=138)
Didn't feel like eating	43	58	52	38	31	26	12	25	14	8	7	6
Smoked much more than usual	29	40	33	34	19	21	10	16	11	10	6	4
Had headaches	25	43	28	24	17	12	9	23	10	8	4	4
Had an upset stomach	22	26	28	17	14	14	5	6	7	6	2	4
Cried	53	62	61	53	42	34	20	31	26	16	12	6
Had trouble getting to sleep	48	68	50	53	36	39	18	32	20	17	10	9
Felt very nervous and tense	68	80	72	69	57	56	24	44	26	25	14	15
Felt like getting drunk	4	11	4	1	3	1	1	4	1	1	1	—
Felt more tired than usual	42	61	43	46	32	34	15	23	17	19	9	10
Felt dizzy at times	12	30	12	12	6	5	4	10	4	4	2	2
Lost temper more than usual	19	28	23	13	13	10	4	9	6	2	1	3
Hands sweated and felt damp and clammy	17	26	19	20	8	10	4	9	6	6	1	3
Had rapid heart beats	26	44	30	28	13	16	6	17	6	9	2	4
Felt sort of dazed and numb	57	57	65	64	46	47	20	29	25	18	13	10
Kept forgetting things	34	56	39	35	19	22	12	26	14	12	6	7
Felt none of these	11	4	8	11	18	18	50	29	43	56	63	66

fact that most places of employment closed early Friday afternoon, that a weekend intervened between the assassination and the funeral, and that Monday was proclaimed a day of national mourning permitted most people to devote full time for four days, if they chose, to the accounts broadcast by the media. And they did so choose. By his own estimate, the average adult spent 8 hours on Friday, 10 hours on Saturday, 8 hours on Sunday, and 8 hours on Monday watching television or listening to the radio. These are median times. We did not even attempt to measure the additional hours people must have spent reading the newspaper accounts and discussing the tragedy with family and friends. One would have perhaps expected attention to the media to flag somewhat as the days progressed, but this does not seem to have happened to any significant extent. On any one of the four days, a minimum of 95 per cent of the public spent some time listening to the radio or watching television, and on Saturday, Sunday, and Monday, approximately a quarter of the people devoted 13 or more hours to this activity.[11]

Political opponents of Kennedy spent less time with radio and TV than did his supporters, but even this group averaged 6 or 7 hours per day. Fourteen per cent of the public said they "had to turn off their sets at times because they couldn't stand hearing so much tragic news"; 34 per cent said they "wanted to stop hearing about the news but just couldn't get themselves to turn off the set"; 18 per cent said they found themselves watching or listening "more than they really wanted to"; and 15 per cent (28 per cent of the Negroes) said they were not able to watch or listen as much as they would have liked to.

Following the initial phase of shock and disbelief, and "a stage of developing awareness of the loss, marked by the painful effects of sadness, guilt, shame, helplessness, or hopelessness," the process of grief is characterized by crying, by a sense of loss and emptiness, by loss of appetite, sleep disturbance, and sometimes somatic symptoms of pain or other discomfort.[12] Table 2A indicates the prevalence of a variety of physical and emotional symptoms among the adult population during the period between the President's assassination and his funeral.[13] It will be

[11] In the telegraphic survey following the death of Roosevelt on a Thursday, only 88 per cent said they listened to the radio *at any time* on Friday, Saturday, or Sunday.

[12] Engel, p. 18.

[13] Many of these items were included in the present questionnaire because they had been asked earlier in the course of another study, and base lines were therefore available. The data from the two studies are not readily comparable, however, and further analysis is required.

noted that only one person out of nine reported none of the symptoms, that two out of three said they "felt very nervous and tense," that 57 per cent "felt sort of dazed and numb," and that a majority confessed there were times during the period when they cried. Almost half the public reported trouble getting to sleep, and over 40 per cent said they "felt more tired than usual" and "didn't feel like eating." Negroes and Kennedy supporters were more likely to experience such symptoms than persons politically opposed to the late President, though few even of the latter were entirely immune.

Of course, one cannot assume that all these symptoms stemmed directly from the assassination. At any given time, there are doubtless millions of Americans who feel nervous and tense, have trouble sleeping, or feel more tired than usual. But that a very large proportion of the ailments reported above were indeed a response to the unusual strains of the four days is indicated by Table 2B, which reports the proportions who still manifested the various conditions at the time of the interview, from two to five days after the funeral. A prompt and marked recovery had clearly occurred. Fully half of the population were by this time free of all the symptoms inquired about; no more than a quarter of the people reported any one of them; and half of the conditions were now characteristic of only one person in ten or less. Again, the symptoms were more long-lived among Negroes and Kennedy supporters than among his opponents. For example, only one in three anti-Kennedy Southern whites now reported any of the conditions, while more than two out of three Negroes were still suffering one or more of them.

Although hardly unaffected by the four days' events, the nation's children do seem to have been considerably less upset than their parents. It was presumed that teenagers would react in much the same manner as adults and that children under the age of four would not be directly affected. But we were curious about the emotions of the four-to-twelve age-group and the way in which parents of such children attempted to explain the assassination. A little over a third of the households (36 per cent) included one or more children of these ages, and, after ascertaining the sex and age of each such child, interviewers asked: "How upset was [each child]—very upset, somewhat upset, or not upset at all?" Adding together all children aged four to twelve, we find that 23 per cent were described as very upset, 45 per cent as somewhat upset, and 30 per cent as not upset at all. (The reactions of 2 per cent were not known to the respondent.) Although a total of 68 per cent were thus described as upset to some extent, it is perhaps more appropriate, in the light of adults' reports of their own reactions, to note that approximately a third of the children of this age-group were not upset at all and that only about one in four was "very upset" by the assassination.[14] And, like the adults, they seem to have recovered quickly. Asked whether, at the time of the interview, any of the children were still upset or whether they had all "gotten over it by now," only 15 per cent of the parents of such children said that any of them were still upset.

Two-thirds of respondents with children aged four to twelve in the household said they attempted to explain to the children what had happened, but the nature of the explanations seems to have varied widely. The most frequent response, offered by 39 per cent of those who said they tried to explain, was not really an explanation at all, but simply a recital of the facts: "A man shot the President," "President Kennedy is dead," etc. In another 16 per cent of the cases, the answer was either vague or irrelevant ("we tried to explain," "I showed him the newspaper"), or it developed that the child had actually received his explanation by means of radio or TV or at school. Thus, personal explanations of what had happened appear to have been attempted in fewer than one-third of the households with children in this age-group. Six per cent of those who said they tried to explain gave religious explanations ("President Kennedy is in heaven," "it was God's will"); 9 per cent explained that he had been killed by someone mentally ill ("he was shot by a crazy person"); 13 per cent explained that a "bad," "mean," "cruel," "wicked" man had done the deed. Five per cent explained to the children what a great man Kennedy was, and 6 per cent told them how terrible and tragic his death was ("we should all feel sad"). Four per cent stressed the historic nature of the event ("something always to remember," "something to tell your children about"), and the same proportion used the occasion to explain the American form of government and, in particular, the fact that the Vice-President would now assume the office.

Probably from the earliest times, a major function of religion has been

---

[14] "Upsetness" increased with the age of the child. Only 39 per cent of the preschoolers, but 72 per cent of the six-to-nine age-group and 85 per cent of the ten-to-twelve group, were described as very or somewhat upset. Girls were more inclined to be upset than boys up to age ten, but thereafter no sex difference was observed.

to provide solace to the bereaved; and the United States, at least as far as church attendance is concerned, is a more religious nation than most.[15] Even aside from the spontaneous prayers and meditation occasioned by the violent death of a beloved President, the frequent references to the Deity by national leaders and the ecclesiastical elements of the funeral would lead one to expect an upsurge of religious feelings and behavior among the general public. There seem to be no national data concerning the frequency, occasions, and content of people's prayers. But, in response to the question, "Did you yourself say any special prayers at any time during this period?" three-fourths of the national sample answered "Yes."[16] By far the most frequent objects of prayer (of 59 per cent of those who prayed) were the late President's wife, children, and immediate family. One-third of those who prayed said their prayers for the repose of the late President's soul. About a third of the group prayed for the welfare of the nation, and about a fourth for the new President, that he might have the strength and wisdom required to carry on. Many in the group, of course, prayed for more than one of these objects.

Yet, in contrast to the impression one may have received that the churches were flooded with people during this period and that there was a deepening of religious conviction among Americans as a result of the event, neither of these seems to have occurred. When asked, some days after the national day of mourning on Monday, "Have you attended any church or religious service since President Kennedy was assassinated?" half the sample answered "No." The 50 per cent affirmative is thus very little higher than the average church attendance (46 per cent) reported by Gallup in 1962 and 1963.[17] It is true that there was some increase in frequency of attendance during the period. Almost half of

[15] At a time when Gallup found 50 per cent of the American public attending religious services in a particular week, his British affiliate reported only 14 per cent in that country (American Institute of Public Opinion release, April 15, 1957).

[16] Though neither the samples nor the question wordings are identical, two other studies have produced very similar results. In reply to a questionnaire self-administered in late 1963 by a random sample of Christian church members in the California Bay Area, 75 per cent said they prayed "quite often" or "regularly once a week" or more (unpublished data from "A Study of Religion in American Life," University of California Survey Research Center). And in the 1958 Detroit Area Study, it was found that 71 per cent told interviewers they pray more often than once a week (personal communication from Gerhard Lenski, Study Director). A more recent Gallup report (Feb. 7, 1964) states that 63 per cent of a national sample pray "frequently."

[17] AIPO release, Dec. 29, 1963.

those who did attend said they went to more than one service, and a third of the attenders (one-sixth of the population) said their attendance was greater than usual. No significant change, however, was observed in response to the question, "How strongly do you feel about your religious beliefs—very strongly, strongly, moderately, not so strongly, or not strongly at all?" The proportion answering "very strongly" rose only 3 per cent, from 40 per cent on a June 1963 national survey to 43 per cent on the present study, and the proportion answering "strongly" stayed constant at 26 per cent.

Attitudes toward the assassination

While the major purpose of the NORC survey was to obtain a quick reading on the emotions and behavior of the American people in the days immediately following a sudden national crisis, a number of other questions probed the public's attitudes toward the assassin and the assassin's own killer, and toward the basic causes, if any, of the tragic events. Because of the speed with which the questionnaire was constructed and the lack of opportunity to pretest, these questions were often of the broad open-ended type and were not always well-pointed toward a specific issue. Certain of the findings are of some consequence, however, and we summarize them briefly here.

As was indicated by the earlier presentation of the immediate reactions of the public, there was no consensus about the ultimate responsibility for the assassination. When asked, "In your own opinion, who or what should really be blamed for the assassination of President Kennedy—aside from the man who actually fired the gun?" 41 per cent either had no opinion or blamed only the assassin. Only one person in five answered in ideological terms, 15 per cent blaming Communists or leftists, and 5 per cent right-wingers or segregationists. About one person in four placed the ultimate blame on the public generally or on the social environment. Thus, 10 per cent referred to a "climate of hatred" in the country, 8 per cent said "we're all to blame, we must all share the responsibility," and 6 per cent spoke of societal tensions, declining morality, social unrest, and other social factors.[18]

---

[18] This group of answers seems to provide the only possible evidence of guilt feelings on the part of the public in this survey. If guilt is indeed a typical grief reaction, either the public failed to experience it in the case of President Kennedy or it is too subtle an emotion to be revealed by normal survey research methods.

Fourteen per cent specifically blamed the assassination on poor security measures. The lack of consensus apparent in the spontaneous replies to the open question is evident also in the responses to direct questions that asked whether specific groups were in any way to blame. At the time they were interviewed, 37 per cent thought Castro or Cuba was in some way to blame, and 32 per cent believed Russia was in some way responsible. Twenty-six per cent attached some blame to "segregationists," 15 per cent to "the people of Dallas," and 15 per cent to "John Birchers or other right-wing extremists." Twenty-two per cent thought the Secret Service was to some extent at fault, and 6 per cent attached blame to "Negroes in this country."

Two other open-ended questions asked whether respondents thought the assassination had "taught the American people a lesson of any kind" and whether they could see "any good at all coming from the events of last week." Three-fourths of the public thought some kind of lesson had been learned, 25 per cent specifically stating that there must be less hate and intolerance, more love and understanding, among all Americans. Other answers were scattered. Sixteen per cent pragmatically said that the lesson was to adopt better security measures to protect our leaders. Nine per cent saw the lesson as a blow to American complacency and pride, and a spur to greater humility henceforth, but an equal number drew the opposite conclusion and stressed in their answers the need for more patriotism and harsher treatment of subversives. In response to the other question, half the public could see no good at all emerging from the events in Dallas. Eighteen per cent thought there would be less hate and greater unity among Americans, while 10 per cent expected that Kennedy's program would be carried on. No other "goods" were mentioned by more than 5 per cent of the people. On neither of the two questions were there any large intergroup differences, save that Negroes were more likely to say that the events taught people the consequences of hate and intolerance.

At the time of the interview, 72 per cent were "pretty much convinced" that Lee Harvey Oswald was the assassin; 28 per cent had some doubt that he fired the gun. There was no consensus on why the assassin, whoever he was, had done the deed. One-third attributed the action to mental illness, 16 per cent blamed Communism or left-wing sympathies, 3 per cent blamed right-wing sympathies. Twelve per cent thought the assassin had a grudge against the President or against the government, and another 12 per cent answered generally that he hated everybody, was disgruntled or unhappy, or was seeking an unspecified revenge. Interestingly, 12 per cent of the public volunteered the opinion that the assassin was paid to do the job, and another 11 per cent thought he had been ordered or persuaded to do it by some unspecified group. Somewhat surprisingly, only 24 per cent said, in reply to a direct question, that the assassination was the work of one man; 62 per cent of the public thought "other people were involved too"; and 14 per cent were uncertain. The overwhelming majority (81 per cent) were convinced that the assassin's target was really the President; 10 per cent thought "he might have been after somebody else"; and 9 per cent expressed no opinion.

Reactions to the shooting of Oswald himself provide reassuring evidence of the continued faith and belief of the great majority of Americans in the traditions of justice and fair play. We noted earlier that very few people indeed mentioned hatred of the assassin or a desire for revenge among their first reactions to the assassination of the President. Now, when asked to describe in their own words their feelings when they first saw or heard of the shooting of Oswald, less than 20 per cent gloated over his death or expressed regret that he did not suffer more. About a third specifically stated their sorrow that he had been deprived of due process and a fair trial, while another third regretted that his death now made it impossible ever to learn the truth.[19] With respect to his slayer, Jack Ruby, a majority (53 per cent) specifically stated in their own words that he should stand trial, receive due process, and let the court decide his fate; 15 per cent said he should be executed; and 20 per cent that he should be punished or treated just like anyone else. Only 4 per cent expressed the belief that he should be punished lightly or go free. Asked what they expected Ruby's fate would be, the majority felt he would be severely or appropriately punished, 13 per cent thought he would probably be punished lightly or go free, and 9 per cent expected a successful plea of insanity. A comparison of respondents' wishes with their expectations concerning Ruby reveals, among those for whom such comparison was possible, that 27 per cent expected him

[19] Many of the foregoing findings were also reported by Gallup and Harris in their December 1963 news releases. Thus, Gallup found only 29 per cent who believed the assassin "acted on his own." Harris found 26 per cent who had doubts that Oswald fired the gun, and only 5 per cent who were "glad Oswald got his due."

to get off more easily than they would like, and 9 per cent expected him to be punished more severely than they believed he should be. The majority (63 per cent) expected him to be treated appropriately.

Asked to rate Kennedy as President, fully half of the adult population, during the days after his funeral, called him "one of the two or three best Presidents the country ever had," and an additional 28 per cent described him as "better than average." Only 2 per cent termed him "somewhat below average" or "one of the worst Presidents the country ever had." Ninety-seven per cent of Negroes considered him above average, as did 90 per cent of his white Northern supporters and 78 per cent of his white Southern supporters. Among those whites who did not support him in 1960, 65 per cent of Northerners and 44 per cent of Southerners at the time of the interview called him better than average. This, of course, contrasts strongly with the last Gallup reading of his popularity while he was alive. In a release dated November 10, it was reported that a relatively modest 59 per cent approved of "the way Kennedy is handling his job as President," 28 per cent disapproved, and 13 per cent were undecided. When shown a card listing sixteen adjectives and asked which four best described the late President, he was seen by large majorities in the NORC survey as "intelligent" (80 per cent) and "courageous" (66 per cent).[20] About half the public chose the words "hard-working" (52 per cent), "sincere" (48 per cent) and "a good speaker" (47 per cent). Thirty per cent perceived him as "strong" and 22 per cent as "wise." Only about one person in five selected the adjective "young" to describe him, only 10 per cent, "liberal," and only 4 per cent, "conservative."

Finally, it may be stated that at this time the American public revealed a command of presidential history that is surprising in light of public opinion surveys that have long shown considerable ignorance of political facts. Eighty-eight per cent correctly named FDR as the last President to die in office, and, when asked to name other Presidents who had been assassinated, 91 per cent named Lincoln, 62 per cent named McKinley, and 47 per cent named Garfield. This high level of knowledge

[20] Courageousness was apparently also attributed to Roosevelt with considerable frequency upon his death. "Many commentators and newspapers remarked that the President was a 'fearless man' and Congressman Lyndon Johnson said, 'He was the one person I ever knew—anywhere—who was never afraid.'" Orlansky, p. 253.

undoubtedly reflects the educational effects of the mass media, to which the public was so heavily exposed during the four days.

Discussion

What can we conclude from these data? Further analysis is obviously required, but a number of important findings are already apparent. In no particular order of importance, the following conclusions seem warranted:

1. The increasing size and urbanization of the population, and the ubiquity of radio and television, now make it possible for virtually 100 per cent of the public to become aware of a crucial event within a very few hours. Hardly anyone is so isolated from his fellow citizens or so cut off from the mass media that he will not quickly receive the word. It is doubtful that this was the case even twenty years ago, at the time of Roosevelt's death.

2. The President's assassination seems clearly to have engaged the "gut feelings" of virtually every American. Events on this order are extremely rare. Survey after survey has consistently shown that most people are normally preoccupied with the health and problems of their own families, and those of their friends and neighbors. These are the things they talk about and worry about. A sizable proportion follow national and international events, many of them very closely, but their interest is largely that of a spectator watching a game. The election of an Eisenhower, the defeat of a Stevenson, a revolution in Cuba, the death of a Stalin, or the launching of a sputnik—such infrequent events, in contrast to the ordinary run-of-the-mill news, arouse the interest of almost everyone, but even they do not produce the cessation of ordinary activities, the almost total attention to the event, and the actual physical symptoms we have described here.

3. It is important that even political opponents of the late President shared the general grief. Despite stories of elementary school children being asked, like those in China, to applaud the assassination, it is clear that any such reactions were quite deviant. Sixty-two per cent of the Southern whites who opposed Kennedy in 1960 "felt the loss of someone very close and dear." At least two out of three of them felt sympathy, sorrow, anger, and shame for their country. Despite the acrimony of political debate, few Americans condone violence as a civic weapon;

indeed the great majority actually seem to come to the support of political opponents in times of national crisis. Gallup polls, for example, showed a sharp rise in Eisenhower's "approval rating" after the U-2 incident and the collapse of the Paris summit meeting in 1960, and a similar increase in Kennedy's rating immediately after the disastrous "Bay of Pigs" Cuban invasion in 1961.

4. We may note the tendency to personify the event. The assassination generally evoked feelings similar to those felt at the death of a close friend or relative; rarely was it compared to other times of national crisis. Immediate reactions were most often personal—sympathy for the President's wife and children, sorrow that "a strong young man had been killed," anger at the assassin, personal shame that such a thing should happen, and feelings of loss of a capable leader—rather than concern about the political consequences of the event. Perhaps great events can be meaningfully grasped only through personal symbols, such as Colin Kelly became in the days following Pearl Harbor, General MacArthur in the Philippines defeat, or Dwight D. Eisenhower on D day. The multitudinous political ramifications of such events cannot be easily comprehended; we seek instead a more familiar referent. At such times, too, our attitudes are strongly swayed by emotion, and our emotions tend to seek a human object rather than an abstraction.

5. Perhaps because people responded to the assassination in personal terms, their reactions appear to have followed a well-defined pattern of grief familiar to medical practice: an initial phase of shock and disbelief; a developing awareness of the loss coupled with feelings of sadness, sorrow, shame, and anger; the onset of physical symptoms such as tears, tenseness, sleeplessness, fatigue, and loss of appetite; and, finally, a gradual recovery in the course of which these symptoms disappear and a normal state of well-being is reestablished. Had the public *not* reacted to the assassination in some such terms as these—had substantial segments rejoiced over the event, had the people been obsessed by guilt, had they cynically brushed off the shocking news, or had their physical symptoms of grief unduly persisted—there would be some cause for alarm. But the immediate reactions seem normal, and the rapid recovery of both adults and children from the symptoms of grief that were so strikingly prevalent during the four days appears to be quite consistent with usual reactions to the death of a loved one.

6. The almost universal expressions of regret and grief, and the beatification of President Kennedy even by political opponents, are not at all unique under the circumstances. William McKinley, for example, is today generally regarded as a rather mediocre President, but the worldwide tributes to his administration and character that immediately followed his assassination are startlingly familiar. "A universal spasm of grief passed from end to end of the land. From far eastern Maine to the western land of gold, from the great lakes of the north to the great gulf of the south, the sentiment of deep regret, the feeling of intense sadness, filled every soul. Never was a man more deeply and widely mourned, not even the sainted Lincoln, nor the warmly esteemed Garfield. . . . The whole nation swung downward into the vale of grief, only slowly to rise again from under the force of that dread blow."[21] "The awful sound of the assassin's bullets seemed to reverberate throughout the world. To every American home the news brought a sense of personal bereavement. To the royal palaces of Europe it brought a shock of horror and amazement. . . . The State Department was flooded with cable messages of anxious inquiry and sincere sympathy from the King of England, the Emperor of Germany, and the governments of all parts of the world."[22]

Lest the reader conclude that such intense sorrow is reserved for assassinated presidents, it should be pointed out that the deaths from *natural causes* of presidents and other chiefs of state also have tended to set off waves of anguish in the populace. There is very little doubt that the death of President Roosevelt brought forth reactions of nearly the breadth and intensity of those brought forth by the Kennedy assassination.[23] This is hardly surprising because Roosevelt was indeed a heroic figure for much of the public. What really jolts the situation into perspective, though, is the evidence of rather extravagant displays of grief at the death of President Harding, a man of far less heroic stature. "Nothing could have been a more shocking surprise. At the big hotels

[21] Alexander K. McClure and Charles Morris, *The Authentic Life of William McKinley* (1901), p. vii.
[22] Charles S. Olcott, *The Life of William McKinley* (Boston, 1916), II, 321.
[23] See Orlansky for a vivid description of public reactions. (The degree of correspondence between the Orlansky account and the present report is remarkable.) See Filmore H. Sanford, "Public Orientation to Roosevelt," *Public Opinion Quarterly* (1951), *15*, 189–216, for an indication of the esteem in which Roosevelt was held.

dancing was immediately stopped and a hush and gloom settled over the crowds, who slowly began to leave. . . . Cabarets and hotel dining rooms were quickly deserted." "Meyer London, Socialist Congressman: 'Oh, what a calamity. This is a tremendous shock. . . . Politics are now forgotten in the love all factions had for him as a man.' " "Colonel Theodore Roosevelt, Acting Secretary of the Navy: 'He gave his life to the service of our country as truly as anyone in our history.' " "Jewish leaders compared Harding with Moses dying before he reached the Promised Land."[24]

Unfortunately, no surveys were conducted following the deaths of presidents like Harding and McKinley, and we do not know how much credence to place in the admittedly impressionistic contemporary accounts. We really cannot judge from such accounts how widespread intense emotional responses actually were; journalists and eulogists may well tend to exaggerate the extent of such phenomena for effect. In any case, the widely experienced sense of bereavement following Kennedy's death was not nearly as unusual a phenomenon as many of us believed at the time.

Of course, even if the general level of public grief were roughly the same regardless of the personal characteristics of the deceased chief of state, it does not necessarily follow that the same types of people would in each instance feel the loss most intensely. One might speculate that practically every President has tremendous appeal for certain segments of the population and is accepted with only a moderate degree of enthusiasm by the remainder. It would seem likely that the deaths of certain Presidents might bring forth the most intense emotional reactions from, for instance, older people residing in small towns, whereas the deaths of others would affect mainly younger groups residing in the metropolises. The fact that the Negro population seemingly reacted more intensely than the white population in the case of both Kennedy's and Roosevelt's deaths does not necessarily result from greater emotional lability on the part of Negroes. Both these Presidents happened to have an unusual appeal for members of minority groups.

There is not space here to examine and comment on all the various explanations for the intensity of emotion brought out by the death of a "ruler." We shall restrict ourselves to one of the more popular models.

[24] Orlansky, pp. 263–64.

This involves the displacement of childhood feelings of dependency from one or both the subject's parents onto the incumbent chief of state. Anxiety, the manifestations of which are difficult to distinguish from grief, is an almost inevitable consequence of the separation by death from the source of succor. It should be noted, though, that this explanation derives primarily from the observation of patients undergoing psychoanalysis. Such an interpretation is probably useful in accounting for the post-assassination behavior of such patients. It may also give us insight into the feelings of certain limited parts of the general population. Nevertheless, it seems to us that this view of the relationship between a citizen and the chief of state is far less appropriate in the case of President Kennedy than it was in the case of President Roosevelt.[25] It is more difficult to picture the youthful, fun-loving Kennedys as serving *in loco parentis* than it was the Roosevelts or the Eisenhowers. The apparent similarity of the reactions to the deaths of Roosevelt and Kennedy may mask appreciable dissimilarity in the feelings toward the two men. The following quotations point up facets of the leader's appeal that may be of particular relevance in understanding the appeal of Kennedy and the meaning of his loss.

Perhaps a more important source [than the parental surrogate function] of appeal made by the leader to his following lies in the vicarious gratification of their yearnings through his presumed traits and achievements. The splendor, the power, the flame of the leader are shared imaginatively. New elements of meaning enter the lives of those who are emotionally impoverished. The everyday disparities and injustices of social life, and sometimes the lacks and incapacities of personal life, fade out of the center of concern. ... The tendency to compensate for one's deficiencies by sinking them in the glorious achievements of more fortunate mortals may be an ever-present feature of social life.[26]

The President, in short, is the one-man distillation of the American people just as surely as the Queen is of the British people; he is, in President Taft's words, "The personal embodiment and representative of their dignity and majesty."[27]

---

[25] Democratic Representative Lyndon B. Johnson of Texas was quoted as having made the following statement upon receiving the news of President Roosevelt's death: "He was just like a daddy to me always; he always talked to me just that way." *Ibid.*, p. 243.
[26] Sidney Hook, *The Hero in History* (New York, 1943), p. 22.
[27] Clinton Rossiter, *The American Presidency*, rev. ed. (New York, 1960), p. 16.

Lincoln is the supreme myth, the richest symbol in the American experience. He is, as someone has remarked neither irreverently nor sacrilegiously, the martyred Christ of democracy's passion play. And who, then, can measure the strength that is given to the President because he holds Lincoln's office, lives in Lincoln's house, and walks in Lincoln's way? The final greatness of the presidency lies in the truth that it is not just an office of incredible power but a breeding ground of indestructible myth.[28]

7. It is good to document the relative infrequency of ideological fervor in the public's replies. One wonders what would have been the reaction in 1953 if an active leftist with a Russian wife had been charged with the assassination of the President of the United States. Perhaps one of the accomplishments of John F. Kennedy, in his few years as America's leader, was to dampen the fires of extremism rather than to feed them. It would seem that, even at the most generous estimate, only a minority of the public blamed the assassination even indirectly on Communists, and no more than a fourth, at the most, attributed it to the activities of right-wingers or segregationists. The "lesson" of the assassination was seen much more often as the evil harvest of hatred and intolerance than as a demonstration of a need for harsher security measures and stepped-up efforts to "catch the Communists."[29]

8. The attitudes toward Oswald and Ruby are heartening in their evidence of the public's sense of justice and fair play. At the time of the assassination, when it is evident that Americans were under great emotional strain, only 11 per cent "hoped the man who killed him would be shot down or lynched"; the thoughts of nine out of ten lay quite elsewhere. The great majority expressed an evidently sincere sorrow and regret over the murder of Oswald. And, far from there being any acclaim of the man who shot him, only 4 per cent held the view that Ruby

---

[28] *Ibid.*, pp. 102–3.

[29] Cf. McClure and Morris, p. 447: "Immediately upon the arrest of the assassin of President McKinley and the news that it was an attempt of anarchists, active and strenuous measures were taken to ferret out the conspiracy, if there were any, and to arrest the conspirators. Immediately, in Chicago, Ill., Paterson, N.J., and other large cities, the police located suspicious characters and those affiliated with anarchistic organizations. In Chicago nine men were arrested and lodged in jail upon very strong suspicion that they had criminal knowledge, at least, of the crime. Emma Goldman, whom the assassin had named as the author of writings and speeches by which he was inflamed, was also arrested and held to answer to the charge of inciting to murder, but was later discharged for lack of evidence."

should be punished only lightly or set free; most felt, not that he should be summarily executed, but that he was entitled to his day in court and should be treated just like anyone else charged with a similar crime. The public's expectations that justice would be done—in spite of the two shocking acts of violence—are also noteworthy. Relatively few believed that Ruby would be punished unduly severely or unduly lightly.

9. The consistency of our findings is marred by one anomaly—the fact that a majority of the public expressed the belief that the assassin did not act alone, that "other people were involved." A fact-finding committee of the Anti-Defamation League of B'nai B'rith has taken similar results from Gallup and other surveys to mean that most Americans believe the slayings of Kennedy and his alleged assassin "were the result of organized plotting." The committee attributes this situation to the activities of extremist groups, "which for years have been preaching the existence of plots and conspiracies in United States life."[30] A "conspiratorial" orientation toward public events was undoubtedly quite common during the McCarthy era and even now is readily employed by a substantial portion of the population. As one observer recently put it, "It takes a high degree of sophistication, Freud wrote, to believe in chance; primitive fears are allayed more easily by a devil theory of politics."[31] Resort to a conspiratorial diagnosis would seem to be particularly functional in the case of the Kennedy assassination because most people do not easily use the concept of mental illness to explain behavior—especially if the actor displays self-control and appears to be cognitively rational.

But aside from the lack of any other evidence in our survey to support a conspiratorial interpretation of the assassination, what makes the particular finding anomalous is that the majority who do say "other people were involved" do not seem to take their belief very seriously. Were people truly convinced that a ring of plotters and assassins had carried out the acts, one would expect a public outcry and official actions designed to bring the malefactors to justice. But even though the presumed accomplices of the assassin were still at large, few people seemed particularly concerned about discovering their identities and capturing

[30] *New York Times*, Feb. 1, 1964.
[31] Daniel Bell, *The End of Ideology* (New York, 1960), p. 193.

them. In another survey conducted by NORC one month later, hardly anyone mentioned the apprehension of the plotters as one of the "important problems facing the country."

Rather than indicating widespread paranoia and demonstrating the consequences of extremist propaganda, expression of the belief that others besides Oswald were involved would seem to us to have a more mundane foundation. People need to have explanations of important events and, in many cases, "cabalism" provides the most easily understandable and accepted one.[32] It is hard for most people to understand the psychic processes of a mentally ill person who seemingly acts at random; it is much easier to ascribe the event to an organized conspiracy with a conscious goal. Moreover, the conclusion that mentally ill people not responsible for their behavior are at large among us, and are capable of capriciously ending the life even of a President, is both bizarre and threatening. Presumption of some sort of conspiracy removes some of the caprice from the situation and thus provides a less threatening interpretation, especially if one does not really take it too seriously.[33] It is, of course, recognized that many extremists of both right and left normally interpret the course of events as a series of intrigues and have vigorously espoused such a view of the assassination. Our point, however, is that mere assent to such an interpretation in no way implies the effectiveness of extremist propaganda.

10. Finally, we introduce a table suggesting that the assassination of the President and the subsequent, televised shooting-down of his assassin in a police station had practically no effect at all, even in the short run, on certain basic beliefs and values of the American people that one might have thought would be profoundly upset by such startling and bizarre events. We have already noticed that people felt no more or less strongly involved in their religion after the assassination than they did before. Table 3 shows also the results of certain other questions that we included in our interview schedule because earlier national norms were

[32] Robert E. Lane, *Political Ideology: Why the American Common Man Believes What He Does* (New York, 1962), pp. 113–30.

[33] Almost every crime in the Chicago area that cannot be explained by some such obvious motive as sex or robbery is commonly ascribed to the conspiratorial activities of the "mob" or syndicate. Winick has reported that only 14 per cent of his sample failed to associate "the mad bomber" of New York City with some political group and that almost three-quarters pictured him as a Communist, Socialist, Anarchist, or Fascist (Charles Winick, "How People Perceived 'The Mad Bomber,'" *Public Opinion Quarterly*, 1961, 25, 33).

available and because we thought responses to them might be highly susceptible to influence by the assassination.

It may be seen that none of the beliefs show any marked change, and this is perhaps the most important finding of all. One might have expected an increase in anti-Communist feelings or a sharp decline in the belief that "most people can be trusted." But, in spite of their almost total preoccupation with the event and the strong emotions and even physical symptoms that it produced, Americans did not change their views of the world. The assassination of their President did not seem to make them more or less anti-Communist, it did not affect their attitudes toward civil rights, and it did not erode their basic optimism about other people's motives. These attitudes are not inflexible; three of them, at least, have shown substantial changes in the past. Willingness to allow Communist Party members to speak on the radio dropped from 45 per cent in 1946 to 36 per cent in 1948 and to 19 per cent in 1953. White support of public school integration increased from 30 per cent in 1942 to 48 per cent in 1956 and to 63 per cent before the assassination. Belief that most people can be trusted dropped from 68 to 57 per cent between the summer of 1952 and the fall of 1953, and then went back up to 75 per cent by 1957.

We can only speculate why the particular beliefs shown in Table 3 did not undergo any measurable change in response to the assassination. It should be noted, though, that each of the earlier changes referred to took place over an interval of at least two years. Since the questions were not administered either frequently or regularly, we cannot alto-

TABLE 3

Effect of Assassination on Selected Basic Beliefs

	Before Assassination		After
Belief	Date	Per cent agreeing	Per cent agreeing
Feel strongly or very strongly about religious beliefs . . .	6/63	66%	69%
Most people can be trusted	4/57	75	77
Communist Party members should be allowed to speak on the radio	4/57	17	18
Death is like a long sleep	1/63	55	59
Death is not tragic for the person who dies, only for the survivors	1/63	82	82
White students and Negro students should go to the same schools (whites only)	6/63	63	62

gether rule out the possibility that our smooth trend line may mask
some sharp fluctuations in the response. But from all we know about
the behavior of these belief patterns, it seems much more likely that
short-run changes in the past have been quite small, and that the larger
shifts we have cited represent the accumulation over time of many
smaller changes in the directions indicated.[34]

Our experience with sharp shifts of opinion in response to major
events is based almost entirely upon types of survey questions that are
rather different from those at issue here. Cantril's paper on opinion
trends in World War II offers some cases in point.[35] For instance, the
percentage expecting that Britain and France would win the war dropped
more than 15 per cent in about one week's time in May 1940, in response
to the German invasion of the Low Countries. A similar drop was
recorded over about a two-week period in April 1941, when Athens
fell to the Axis. Such questions have a large cognitive component and
it is probably not surprising that responses to them should have been
highly sensitive to the day-by-day news of the war. Had we asked in the
present study about the need for increased security of the Presidential
person or about reactions, favorable or unfavorable, to Lyndon B. Johnson, or about the prospects of Goldwater's being elected President in
1964, we, too, might have found a shift of 10, 15, or even more percentage points from earlier findings. We have already noted that approval
of Kennedy's performance as President showed a notable climb after
the assassination.

But we also note in Cantril that there was a sudden 10-point increase
in the proportion who thought it "more important to help England than
to keep out of war" during a brief period in July–August 1940, immediately following the initiation of mass air raids on Great Britain.
This question has far less cognitive component than "Who will win the
war?" and indeed seems somewhat comparable to our question on school

---

[34] We know so little about how such items behave normally because they are almost
never repeated over short intervals. Most investigators apparently assume that they are
too stable to warrant frequent inclusion in interview schedules. A clear lesson from the
present research endeavor is that such inquiries should be replicated frequently so as
to establish norms of change for a variety of survey items. Then, when we wish to assess
the impact of a particular event, we shall have available a better-understood instrument.
[35] Hadley Cantril, "Opinion Trends in World War II: Some Guides to Interpretation,"
Public Opinion Quarterly (1948), *12*, 30–44; Bernard Berelson, "Events as an Influence
Upon Public Opinion," *Journalism Quarterly* (1949), *26*, 145–48; Alfred M. Lee, "Public
Opinion in Relation to Culture," *Psychiatry* (1945), *8*, 49–61 (esp. p. 55).

segregation in the intensity with which opinions were held and in the deep-seated attitudes it engaged. A possible explanation of the disparate behavior of the two items lies in the fact that responsible leadership— notably Roosevelt—interpreted the events of the summer of 1940 to the public in a way that made wartime intervention seem more relevant and necessary. In contrast, no responsible leader interpreted the assassination to the public in a way that made changes in the items we are here considering seem relevant or necessary. Had a responsible Senator or FBI official urged the need of an anti-Communist crusade; had a charismatic evangelist used the occasion to call for a "return to religion"; had some leader on either side of the race issue managed to relate the assassination to civil rights in a way that the public could comprehend—then, some of these beliefs might have changed. But none of this happened.

Finally, though few Americans condone political violence, they are not unaware of its past occurrence or its future possibility. Assassination of a British King or Prime Minister would be unprecedented in modern times, and English reactions might well be different in several respects. But the United States has a rather recent history of lawlessness on the Western frontier; practically every American knows that Lincoln and other Presidents were shot; and there were probably few who would have denied the possibility of a Presidential assassination some time in the future. If so, it would follow that when the majority said, "Most people can be trusted," in 1957, they were allowing for the violence and disorder that from time to time are reflected in the society. The assassination, then, was such an incident, but it required no change in the basic belief that most people can be trusted.

Charles M. Bonjean, Richard J. Hill, and Harry W. Martin

Reactions to the Assassination in Dallas

Two days after the assassination of President Kennedy, a group of social scientists met in Washington.[1] Among the investigations suggested at this meeting was a survey of Dallas residents. This article reports the findings of that survey, which was conducted in Dallas November 28–30.[2]

Interviews were obtained from 212 Dallas residents. The multistage sampling procedure began with a random selection of census tracts, followed by a random selection of blocks within the chosen tracts. Quota controls for sex, age, and employment status were used within selected blocks to decide which persons to interview.

The interview schedule employed was a modification of the instrument developed by the National Opinion Research Center for its national study of reactions to the assassination. The interviews required from 15 to 99 minutes to complete, the median being 35 minutes.

This report on the Dallas data describes the diffusion of news of the assassination, immediate and prolonged reactions, and attitudes toward the assassination. Each topic is discussed first for the total Dallas sample and then for each of the following social categories:

1. *Socio-economic status.* The measure of social status employed was

---

[1] For a description of these discussions, see the article by Sheatsley and Feldman in this volume.

[2] This research was made possible by a grant from the Hogg Foundation for Mental Health, Austin, Texas. We wish to acknowledge the major role played by Alexander L. Clark in helping to direct the survey. Jack P. Gibbs and J. Gordon Shaw assisted with the sampling design and procedure, and Dr. Shaw provided much information about the social and political characteristics of Dallas. We are indebted to Robert L. Stubblefield, who facilitated this research in many ways and gave support to the field work in a tense community situation.

Hollingshead's Two-Factor Index of Social Position.[3] This index assigns an individual to one of five social classes on the basis of his occupation and education. The social-class distribution of the sample is as follows:

a. Class I. The 5 per cent of the Dallas sample assigned to this class by the index are the elite of the city. They are the business and professional leaders living in the "best" residential areas. Most are college graduates.[4]
b. Class II. The 16 per cent of the sample assigned to this class are primarily managers and lesser-ranking professionals. Most have had some formal education beyond high school.
c. Class III. This somewhat heterogeneous middle class includes 26 per cent of the Dallas sample. Most are salaried administrative or clerical employees or small business owners.
d. Class IV. This "working class" is the largest stratum in Dallas (and in most other communities where the index has been used)—32 per cent of the sample is found here.
e. Class V. The bottom stratum of the class structure in Dallas includes 21 per cent of the sample. These individuals are semi-skilled and unskilled workers with the least education.

Of the 212 Dallas respondents, 203 supplied information sufficient to place them into one of the above classes; the remaining nine respondents are excluded from this segment of the analysis.

2. *Race.* The responses of whites are compared with those of Negroes. In the Dallas sample there were 189 whites (89 per cent), 21 Negroes (10 per cent), and two "others" (1 per cent). In the analysis below the "others" are excluded.[5]

3. *Sex.* There were 104 males (49 per cent) and 108 females (51 per cent) in the sample.

4. *Political preference.* Respondents were asked, "In the 1960 election, did you prefer Nixon or Kennedy for President?" Kennedy was the

---

[3] August B. Hollingshead, *Two-Factor Index of Social Position*, privately mimeographed, 1957.

[4] The characteristics of these classes are described in detail in August B. Hollingshead and Fredrick C. Redlich, *Social Class and Mental Illness: A Community Study* (New York, 1958), pp. 69–135.

[5] Negroes apparently are underrepresented in the sample. According to the 1960 U.S. Census, Negroes constituted 14 per cent of the metropolitan-area population, 15 per cent of Dallas County, and 19 per cent of the City of Dallas.

TABLE 1

Class Differences in Communication Behavior and Reactions to the Assassination

Characteristics	Class I–II	III	IV	V
I. Heard the first news:[a]				
1. Within half an hour after the assassination . . .	81%	98%	74%	79%
2. From radio or television	30	49	43	48
3. When alone	19	26	20	21
4. When with relatives	36	53	46	47
5. At home	30	45	39	41
II. Reactions after hearing the news				
6. Unable to continue usual activities	33	34	52	48
7. Felt like being by themselves	26	32	35	55
8. Contacted by others	77	51	17	26
9. Contacted others	40	40	35	19
III. Responses to "What sort of person" question				
10. Gave any relevant response	86	64	39	22
11. Suggested a "right-winger"	28	11	5	0
12. Suggested a "left-winger"	2	8	15	0
IV. Religious responses				
13. Said special prayers	77	72	68	52
14. Prayed for Governor Connally	2	0	3	48
15. Attended religious services	65	45	38	21
16. Attended religious services more than usual	26	8	5	5
V. Responses to questions about blame				
17. "All of us"	35	15	8	5
18. "Climate of hatred"	33	11	8	0
19. "Russia"	23	38	26	29
20. "Segregationists"	16	9	18	29
21. "Birchers or other right-wingers"	26	28	14	12
VI. Responses to questions about consequences				
22. Suggested the assassination would bring us together, reduce hate and intolerance	26	21	18	5
23. Could see no good coming from it	30	30	61	69
24. Said we learned need for less hate and intolerance	28	38	18	17
25. Said we learned need for better security for leaders	0	9	9	17
VII. Opinions about the assassin				
26. Were "pretty much" convinced Oswald did it . . .	86	83	74	52
27. Thought motivation was mental illness	49	45	20	19
28. Thought motivation was Communism	5	19	12	5
29. Thought motivation was money	9	7	6	19
30. Thought others were in on a plot	51	74	71	62
31. Sure the assassin was aiming at Kennedy	95	92	82	64
VIII. Reactions to Oswald's death				
32. Thought Oswald was killed to suppress the truth .	9	4	15	12
33. Felt shocked or stunned	23	15	14	7
34. Thought Ruby should be executed	30	17	14	10
35. Thought Ruby should be imprisoned	7	13	2	10
IX. Evaluation of Kennedy				
36. Agreed Kennedy was one of our best Presidents . .	40	42	64	57

[a] $p < .001$ for all comparisons of Class III with other classes in the first five rows.

preference of 57 per cent, while 32 per cent indicated they preferred Nixon. Eight per cent did not remember, 2 per cent answered "other," and 1 per cent did not respond. Those preferring Kennedy will be compared with all the others in the discussions of reactions to the assassination and attitudes about it.[6]

Diffusion of the news in Dallas

The news of the assassination spread rapidly through the Dallas population.[7] Two-thirds of the sample heard the news within 15 minutes after the President was shot. By the time the President was pronounced dead, one half-hour after he was shot, 84 per cent had heard of the event. Within the following hour, another 11 per cent were informed; all respondents had learned of the event by 6 P.M.

Interpersonal communication was the most important source of the first news. Fifty-seven per cent of the sample received word of the assassination through personal messages or phone calls. Television and radio informed 26 and 17 per cent of the sample, respectively. No one first learned of the event through the press.

Not only was interpersonal communication the most important source of the first news, it was also almost as rapid as learning from the mass media. Eighty-nine per cent of those who heard from other persons had been informed within an hour of the first news release; 97 per cent of those learning from radio and 98 per cent of those learning from television heard the news during that time. These differences are not statistically significant at any commonly accepted level.

Most respondents were at home or at work when they first heard of the assassination (39 and 38 per cent, respectively). The remainder were in public places such as stores or restaurants (10 per cent), in someone else's home (4 per cent), or in a car (1 per cent). Less than a fourth (22 per cent) were alone when they first heard the news. The rest were with relatives, co-workers, friends or acquaintances, or strangers or neighbors, in that order.

[6] The two nonrespondents were excluded. This retrospective "preference for Kennedy in 1960" does not reflect accurately the voting behavior of Dallasites in 1960. The Nixon-Lodge ticket received 62 per cent of the Dallas County vote in 1960. A poll reported in the *Dallas Morning News* of July 24, 1960, showed Nixon-Lodge preferred by 35 per cent, and Kennedy-Johnson by 45 per cent; 19 per cent were undecided. The retrospective inflation of preference is also reported by Sheatsley and Feldman, p. 151, n. 4.
[7] For a report on the diffusion process in Dallas and comparison with diffusion characteristics for other news, see Richard J. Hill and Charles M. Bonjean, "News Diffusion: A Test of the Regularity Hypothesis," *Journalism Quarterly* (1964), *41*, 336–42.

Class differences. Consistent differences were found between the way that the news diffused to members of Class III and the way it diffused to members of other classes. Class III members were likely to have heard the news before members of the other classes (see Table 1, section I).[8] They relied more heavily on radio and television than members of the other classes, which perhaps explains in part why they heard the news first. They were more likely to have been alone, and also more likely to have been with relatives. They were least likely to have been with co-workers (29 per cent compared with 46 per cent of Class IV, $p < .001$). They were the most likely to have been at home. It is possible that these differences are as much a function of sex as of social class, since Class III had the most female respondents (68 per cent, compared with 51, 50, and 36 per cent of Classes I–II, IV, and V, respectively). However, the class that most resembles Class III in behavior is Class V, which had the most male respondents.

Racial differences. White persons were likely to have been informed of the assassination earlier than Negroes. Within one half-hour of the event, 85 per cent of the whites, compared with 67 per cent of the Negroes, knew about the event. This is particularly surprising given the fact that Negroes were more likely to have heard from radio or television (57 per cent of the Negroes compared with 41 per cent of the whites). Negroes were somewhat more likely to have been alone (33 per cent compared with 21 per cent) and, if with others, less likely to have been with relatives (27 per cent compared with 46 per cent).

Sex differences. Women were likely to have been informed of the assassination before men. Of the 108 women, 89 per cent heard the news within the first half-hour, while only 76 per cent of the men were informed during that time. Women were more likely to have heard the news on television (37 per cent compared with 15 per cent), while men were more likely to have heard it on the radio (23 per cent compared with 11 per cent). Men were more likely to have heard through interpersonal channels (62 per cent compared with 52 per cent). Women were more likely than men to have heard the news in a private home and less likely to have heard at a place of work. Although the sample is not sufficiently large to make the necessary multivariate analyses, we believe that the differences in media use between men and women and

[8] Unless otherwise noted, all differences that are discussed are statistically significant at the .05 level.

possibly between the social classes can be attributed to the fact that women were more likely to be at home and have access to television. We would hypothesize that there would have been no difference between men and women in learning from the media (and perhaps in time of learning) had the event not taken place during working hours. Indeed, those persons who were in private homes were more likely to have heard about the event from television. Fifty-six per cent of those in private homes heard in this manner, while 34 per cent were informed interpersonally. Persons who heard the news outside of private homes were more likely to have first heard of the event from other persons (72 and 86 per cent of those at work and in public places, respectively).

Reactions to the event in Dallas

The immediate reaction of most members (58 per cent) of the Dallas sample was to discontinue their usual activities. Most of those who were able to carry on their daily activities found it more difficult to do so. Only 6 per cent of the total Dallas sample were able to carry on "pretty much as usual." Most (73 per cent) of those who were not able to continue what they were doing turned to television and radio. Most (56 per cent) "felt like talking with other people about it," and 36 per cent felt "more like being by myself"; 8 per cent "could not decide." Forty-three per cent said they phoned or went to talk to somebody about the event— their spouses, friends or acquaintances, parents, and neighbors, in that order. Forty-five per cent were contacted by others.

When asked if they could think of any other time in their lives when they had the same sort of feelings as when they heard of the assassination, 62 per cent replied that they could not. Of those who could think of such an occasion, 50 per cent cited the death of a close relative, 19 per cent cited the death of President Roosevelt, and 13 per cent cited the attack on Pearl Harbor.

When the respondents were asked who they thought had probably shot the President, one person in four had no idea. Slightly more than a fourth of the sample thought the assassin was either "mentally ill" or "some kind of crackpot." Relatively few answered the question in ideological terms—7 per cent suspected the extreme left (Russia, Castro, a foreign agent, or a spy), and 9 per cent suspected the radical right.

Interviewers read a list of 17 statements representing "the ways that some people felt when they first heard the President was dead," and

TABLE 2

Immediate Reaction to News of the Assassination

Immediate Reaction	Felt very deeply or quite deeply	Crossed my mind	Never oc-curred to me
1. Felt so sorry for his wife and children	90%[a]	5%	5%
2. Felt ashamed that this could happen in our country . . .	86	5	7
3. Felt sorry that a strong young man had been killed at the height of his powers	83	9	8
4. Felt the loss of someone very close and dear	72	8	19
5. Felt angry that anyone should do such a terrible deed . .	68	11	20
6. Worried about how his death would affect our relations with other countries	42	29	29
7. Worried about how his death would affect the political situation in this country	41	25	34
8. Was so confused that I didn't know what to feel	40	9	49
9. Felt worried about how the United States would carry on without its leader	33	29	37
10. Thought about the many tragic things that have happened to them and this was just another of them	25	23	52
11. Was worried how this might affect my own life, job, and future	24	18	58
12. Thought it was done by some Communist or other leftist radical to get rid of the President	24	31	44
13. Wondered if anybody could really be safe in this country these days when the President himself can get shot . . .	20	30	50
14. Thought it was done by a member of an extreme right-wing or conservative group	15	27	56
15. Hoped the man who killed him would be shot down or lynched	9	10	81
16. Worried whether the man who did the killing would be a member of my race or religion, and let loose persecution of people like me	7	11	81
17. Felt that in many ways the President had brought it on himself	3	13	83

[a] Those who gave no response have not been included, and therefore some rows do not add up to 100 per cent.

asked which of these came closest to the respondents' feelings. As Table 2 indicates, the five most frequent immediate responses were sorrow for the President's wife and children, shame that it could happen in our country, sorrow that a strong young man had been killed at the height of his powers, feeling the loss of someone very close and dear, and feeling angry that anyone should do such a terrible deed. No other response was characteristic of a majority of the sample.

The next most frequent reactions were worry about the future of the nation. Forty-two per cent worried about how the President's death would affect our relations with other countries, and almost the same percentage worried about how it would affect the political situation in this country. One person in three worried about how the United States would carry on without its leader.

Almost everyone (99 per cent) spent some time watching television or listening to the radio on Friday. The mean time devoted to this activity on the day of the assassination was 8.7 hours. Media broadcasts occupied a great portion of the respondents' time for the following three days as well—an average of 9.9 hours on Saturday, 8.6 hours on Sunday, and 7.6 hours on Monday. Although almost everyone gave some time to the media on all four days, there was a slight increase in the percentage devoting no time to radio or television with each succeeding day—1.4 per cent on Friday, 2.8 per cent on Saturday, 3.3 per cent on Sunday, and 7.5 per cent on Monday. Almost one respondent in five (18 per cent) said they had to turn off their sets at times because they could not stand hearing so much tragic news; 40 per cent said they wanted to stop hearing about the news but just could not get themselves to turn off the radio or TV set; 23 per cent said they watched or listened more than they wanted to; and 11 per cent said they were not able to watch or listen as much as they would have liked.

Physical and emotional symptoms experienced by the Dallas sample during the period between the President's assassination and funeral are summarized in Table 3, column A. A majority of the Dallas sample recalled experiencing one or more of the following: "felt very nervous and tense," "felt sort of dazed and numb," "cried," "had trouble getting to sleep," and "didn't feel like eating." A near majority "felt more tired than usual." Only 4 per cent of the sample experienced no physical or emotional symptoms.

One week after the assassination, only one symptom was still being experienced by more than a third of the Dallas sample. As Table 3, column B, shows, 36 per cent of the sample still felt very nervous and tense. The second most common symptom one week later was crying, still characteristic of 20 per cent. A majority (58 per cent) experienced no symptoms at this time.

One-third of the Dallas respondents had children who were between the ages of 4 and 12. Although the data on the reactions of children were obtained from the parents and are less complete than the adult data, a

Table 3
Per Cent Reporting Physical or Emotional Symptoms

Symptom	All respondents		Whites	Negroes	Males	Females	Persons who preferred Kennedy in 1960	Persons who preferred Nixon or other in 1960
	During four days following assassination	One week after assassination						
	(A)	(B)	(C)	(D)	(E)	(F)	(G)	(H)
Felt very nervous and tense	82%	36%	78%	75%	75%	81%	80%	74%
Felt sort of dazed and numb	69	14	68	40	53	76	80	69
Cried	56	20	50	75	27	74	59	45
Had trouble getting to sleep	53	17	44	60	39	61	54	40
Didn't feel like eating	52	15	47	60	36	60	58	36
Felt more tired than usual	50	18	33	25	36	56	47	36
Kept forgetting things	35	8	33	40	24	41	37	47
Smoked much more than usual	34	8	32	25	38	27	36	27
Had rapid heartbeats	32	6	29	40	27	33	33	26
Had an upset stomach	26	6	25	25	14	35	31	26
Had headaches	26	7	22	40	13	35	30	18
Lost my temper more than usual	21	3	20	20	20	20	21	16
Hands sweated and felt damp and clammy	19	4	17	30	10	25	20	16
Felt dizzy at times	14	7	11	30	8	18	17	7
Felt like getting drunk	3	1	3	5	5	2	1	5

few tentative conclusions may be offered. Children appear to have been less emotionally upset than adults. Exactly one-third of the children were described as having been "not upset at all"; 21 per cent were described as being "very upset." One week after the assassination, 82 per cent of those children who were "upset" during the four days immediately following the event were described as "all over it."

Two-thirds of the respondents with children in the 4-to-12 age-group said they attempted to explain to the children what had happened. But many of them (30 per cent) simply relayed the facts to their children. Attempts to explain the facts varied from explaining that the assassin was mentally ill to discussing our form of government, including the nature of the presidency. None of the parents in the Dallas sample offered a religious explanation to their children; however, many in the sample turned to religion immediately after the assassination.

Special prayers were said by 68 per cent of the sample. When asked what they prayed for, the most common responses were: his family (54 per cent), our country (34 per cent), for the repose of the late President's soul (22 per cent), and for the strength and wisdom of the new President (19 per cent). Still, only 42 per cent of the sample attended religious services in the week following the President's assassination. Of those who did, 62 per cent said they went to more than one service, and 22 per cent said their attendance was greater than usual.

Class differences. Lower-class members tended to be more upset than members of the other classes (see Table 1, section II). About half of the former but only a third of the latter could not continue their usual activities. Not only were lower-class members more likely to feel like being by themselves, but the data indicate that they probably were alone immediately after the assassination. On the other hand, upper-class members were more likely both to contact and to be contacted by others about the news than were members of the other classes.

The higher the respondent's social class was, the more likely he was to offer some idea about the "sort of person" who assassinated the President, and to suggest the assassin was a "right-winger" or a "Bircher." (See Table 1, section III.) The lower his social class was, with the exception of Class V, the greater was his tendency to label the assassin a "left-winger" or "Communist." Class V members were less likely to answer in ideological terms than members of the other classes.

As Table 4 indicates, some class differences are found in the responses

TABLE 4

Per Cent Who Felt "Deeply" the Immediate Reactions to News of the Assassination

Immediate reaction	Class				Whites	Negroes	Males	Females	Persons who preferred Kennedy in 1960	Persons who preferred Nixon or other in 1960
	I–II	III	IV	V						
1. Felt the loss of someone very close and dear	77%	72%	65%	81%	69%	100%	69%	75%	83%	58%
2. Worried about how his death would affect the political situation in this country	35	36	44	52	39	57	49	33	45	40
3. Worried about how his death would affect our relations with other countries	32	38	58	52	40	57	48	36	45	41
4. Felt so sorry for his wife and children	95	87	89	88	89	95	87	94	91	89
5. Felt worried about how the United States would carry on without its leader	23	26	33	45	31	48	31	35	34	34
6. Felt sorrow that a strong young man had been killed at the height of his powers	79	81	88	81	84	76	81	85	89	73
7. Felt angry that anyone should do such a terrible deed	81	75	62	50	72	33	73	63	66	77
8. Hoped the man who killed him would be shot down or lynched	7	11	8	5	9	10	9	9	12	6
9. Thought about the many tragic things that have happened to them and this was just another of them	30	30	20	21	27	5	16	33	25	26
10. Felt that in many ways the President had brought it on himself	5	4	2	5	4	0	4	3	2	7
11. Thought it was done by a member of an extreme conservative or right-wing group	30	9	12	12	15	5	19	10	16	15
12. Thought it was done by some Communist or other leftist radical to get rid of the President	16	22	24	33	25	5	27	20	24	23
13. Felt ashamed that this could happen in our country	88	85	86	88	86	86	87	86	90	84
14. Was worried how this might affect my own life, job, and future	9	17	29	43	21	48	24	24	29	18
15. Worried whether the man who did the killing would be a member of my race or religion, and let loose persecution of people like me	5	7	8	9	6	14	8	7	9	3
16. Wondered if anybody could really be safe in this country these days when the President himself can get shot	9	17	29	19	19	29	14	25	24	14
17. Was so confused and upset that I didn't know what to feel	28	36	45	50	38	62	35	44	43	32

to the first hearing of the news. Members of the highest class grouping were more likely to have felt angry that anyone should do such a terrible deed and more likely to have thought it was done by a member of an extreme conservative or right-wing group. Members of the two lower classes were more likely to have worried about how the President's death would affect the political situation in this country, worried about how it would affect our relations with other countries ($p < .01$, Class I–II compared with IV and V), worried about how the United States would carry on without its leader ($p < .01$, Class I–II compared with V), worried about how it might affect their own lives, jobs, and futures ($p < .001$, Class I–II compared with V; $p < .01$, Class I–II compared with IV, and III with V), wondered if anybody could really be safe in this country these days when the President himself can get shot, and were more likely to be so confused and upset that they did not know what to feel ($p < .01$, Class I–II compared with V).

Class III members spent more time than members of the other classes watching television or listening to the radio on Friday and Saturday (9.0 hours on Friday compared with 8.2, 8.0, and 7.8 hours for members of Classes I–II, IV, and V, respectively, and 10.5 hours on Saturday compared with 10.3, 10.0, and 9.3 hours for members of Classes IV, V, and I–II, respectively; $p < .01$, Class III compared with V). On Sunday, Class III members continued to spend the most time watching television or listening to the radio, but the differences between classes were not significant. By Monday, Class IV members were spending more time with the electronic media than other class members, but Class III members were still spending more time than were Class V and Class I–II members ($p < .01$, Class IV compared with all others, and III compared with V). Although the differences were not significant, there was a greater tendency for respondents in the lower social classes to turn off their sets at times because they could not stand hearing so much tragic news (characteristic of 14, 17, 19, and 24 per cent of Classes I–II, III, IV, and V, respectively). Class I and II members were more likely than members of Classes V and III to feel they were watching or listening more than they really wanted to, and members of Class V were the most likely to feel they were not able to watch or listen as much as they would have liked.

The higher the social class was, the greater was the tendency to say special prayers during the four days immediately after the assassination. (See Table 1, section 4.) The most noticeable differences in prayer content by social class were the following: Class I–II members were more likely to have prayed for the repose of the President's soul than were members of the other classes, Class III members were more likely to have prayed for the nation, Class IV members for Kennedy's family, and, most strikingly, Class V members for Governor Connally. Also, the higher the social class was, the more likely the respondent was to have attended church or religious service during the week after the President's assassination ($p < .01$, Class IV compared with I–II; $p < .001$, Class V compared with I–II). Higher-class members indicated that this was more than they usually attended. No significant differences were found between classes in the physical and emotional symptoms experienced following the assassination, although there was a tendency for the symptoms to last longer among members of the lower classes.

Racial differences. Roughly the same proportion of whites and Negroes discontinued their usual activities after hearing of the assassination. A greater percentage of whites (83) than Negroes (63) watched television or listened to the radio. The average time spent watching television was greater for whites than for Negroes on all four days: 8.3 hours against 5.9 hours on Friday, 10.0 against 7.5 on Saturday, 8.8 against 7.5 on Sunday, and 7.8 against 6.5 on Monday. Whites were more likely to say that they watched more than they really wanted to, and Negroes were more likely to say they were not able to watch or listen as much as they would have liked.

As Table 4 shows, there were significant differences in the immediate responses of Negroes and whites to the assassination. Negroes were more likely to have "felt the loss of someone very close and dear," to have "worried how this might affect my own life, job and future," and to have been "so confused and upset that I didn't know what to feel." They were less likely to have "felt angry that anyone should do such a terrible deed," to have "thought about the many tragic things that have happened to them [the Kennedy family] and this was just another of them," and to have "thought it was done by a member of an extreme conservative or right-wing group."

Significant differences were also found in the physical and emotional responses (see Table 3, columns C and D). Symptoms more characteristic of Negroes were crying and feeling dizzy at times. Whites were more likely to have "felt sort of dazed and numb."

Sex differences. Women were more likely than men to discontinue their usual activities after hearing of the assassination (69 per cent compared with 46 per cent). Of those who did continue their usual activities, women were more likely to indicate that they found it difficult to do so (77 per cent compared with 47 per cent). The great majority of both sexes turned to radio and television, although women spent more time listening to the radio or watching television on each of the four days following the assassination. Women averaged 8.8, 10.9, 9.9, and 9.2 hours of viewing on Friday, Saturday, Sunday, and Monday, respectively; men averaged 7.5, 8.9, 7.4, and 6.1 hours on those days. Women were more likely to have been contacted by others and to have contacted others immediately after the assassination. Less than a third of the men (30 per cent), but 59 per cent of the women, were contacted by others. One-fourth of the men and 42 per cent of the women telephoned or talked to someone about the assassination on the day it took place.

Table 4 shows that the immediate-response patterns of men and women were fairly similar. Only two of the observed differences were significant. Men were more likely to worry about how the President's death would affect the political situation in this country, and women were more likely to have thought about the many tragic things that had happened to the Kennedy family and that this was just another of them.

Table 3, columns E and F, shows there were striking differences between men and women in their physical and emotional responses to the assassination. Of the 15 physical and emotional symptoms investigated, only three were more characteristic of men than of women (smoked much more than usual, felt like getting drunk, and lost my temper more than usual), but none were significantly so. By contrast, women were significantly more likely to indicate they didn't feel like eating, had headaches, had an upset stomach, cried, had trouble getting to sleep, felt more tired than usual, felt dizzy at times, had their hands sweat and feel damp and clammy, felt sort of dazed and numb, and kept forgetting things.

Women were more likely to have turned to religion after the assassination than men. Special prayers were said by 84 per cent of the women and 52 per cent of the men. Of this group, women were more likely to have prayed for Kennedy's family (47 per cent compared with 26 per cent of the men), whereas the men were more likely to have prayed for Oswald (52 per cent compared with 24 per cent of the women).

Political preference differences. Political preference in 1960 did not seem to differentiate between those who could and those who could not continue their usual activities. Still, the data lend some support to the generalization that the assassination had greater impact on those who said they preferred Kennedy. When asked, for example, if they could think of any other time when they had the same sort of feelings as when they heard this news, 64 per cent of them mentioned the death of a family member; the same response was given by only 29 per cent of those who had not voted for Kennedy.

Table 4 shows that those who preferred Kennedy were more likely to have "felt the loss of someone very close and dear," to have "felt sorrow that a strong young man had been killed at the height of his powers," and to have "worried about how this might affect my own life, job, and future."

Fourteen of the 15 physical and emotional symptoms investigated were more characteristic of those who preferred Kennedy in 1960 than they were of the others (see Table 3, columns G and H). The only symptom found with greater frequency among those who did not vote for Kennedy was to have "felt like getting drunk." Significantly more characteristic of the Kennedy supporters were "didn't feel like eating" and "had headaches."

Attitudes of the Dallas sample toward the assassination

Both poll-type and open-ended questions were used to determine if the respondents "blamed" anyone (other than the assassin) for the tragedy. When asked, "In your opinion, who or what should really be blamed for the assassination of President Kennedy—aside from the man who actually fired the gun?" the majority (54 per cent) either did not know or blamed only the assassin. The next most common response (29 per cent) placed the blame on the public generally or on the social environment; 15 per cent thought we were all to blame, 13 per cent suggested something like a "climate of hatred," and 1 per cent suggested "tensions." Seventeen per cent of the sample answered in ideological terms: 12 per cent blamed the extreme left and 5 per cent blamed the right. The only other view held by more than 3 per cent of the sample was that poor security measures were to blame, which 6 per cent suggested. When seven specific groups were suggested by the interviewer, a different response pattern was found. At the time of the interview, 30 per cent thought Castro or Cuba was in some way to blame, and 29 per cent thought Russia in some way responsible. One person in five blamed Birchers or other right-wing extremists, and 19 per cent thought segregationists were in some way responsible. The secret service was blamed by 17 per cent, Dallas residents by 12 per cent, and Negroes by 7 per cent.

Almost three-fourths of the sample thought that the assassination "taught the American people a lesson." About one respondent in four said the lesson learned was the need for less hate or intolerance. One in ten suggested the need for humility, less pride, less complacency, or something similar. On the other hand, only half the sample could see "any good at all coming from the events of the last week." Seventeen per cent thought the assassination would bring us closer together, reducing hate and intolerance.

One week after the assassination, 75 per cent were "pretty much convinced" that Lee Harvey Oswald was the assassin, 12 per cent "had some doubt," and 1 per cent were "pretty much convinced" he was not the assassin. When asked what they thought "led the killer to do it," 29 per cent cited mental illness or personality disorder, 24 per cent either did not know or responded in an irrelevant manner, 10 per cent mentioned Communism or Communist sympathies, 9 per cent thought he was paid to do it, 8 per cent indicated "hatred," and 6 per cent thought he was ordered or persuaded to do it by an unspecified source. Most respondents (66 per cent) thought the assassination was the work of more than just one man. Only 15 per cent thought it was the action of only the assassin himself, and another 19 per cent did not know. Seven respondents in ten were convinced that the assassin was really trying to hit the President rather than someone else, although 17 per cent thought he "might have been after" Governor Connally.

When asked, "What were your feelings when you first heard that Oswald himself had been killed?" the most frequent response was regret that his death made it impossible to learn the truth (26 per cent). Almost as many (25 per cent) said they were sorry he was denied a fair trial. Other frequent responses included mention of the Dallas police department (16 per cent), shock (15 per cent), feelings that Oswald got what he deserved, including sorrow that he did not suffer more (14 per cent), and feelings that he was killed to suppress the truth (10 per cent).

When asked about Jack Ruby, Oswald's slayer, 37 per cent said that he should stand trial, receive due process, and let the court decide his fate, but 42 per cent thought he should be executed, imprisoned, or, more generally, "punished." Only 1 per cent said he should be punished lightly or go free. When asked what they thought would actually happen to Ruby, they showed no consensus. The most frequent response (17 per cent) was that he would be executed. Following, in order, were light or no punishment (13 per cent), a successful plea of insanity (11 per cent), imprisonment (9 per cent), and conviction without specification of punishment (6 per cent). Over a third indicated they had no idea what would happen to him.

When asked, one week after the assassination, how they would rate Kennedy as a President, 52 per cent called him "one of the best." A fourth rated him as "better than average," 13 per cent as "about average," 3 per cent as "below average," and 1 per cent as "one of the worst." When they were handed a list of adjectives and asked to select the four that best described President Kennedy, "intelligent" was selected by 83 per cent of the respondents. Following, in order, were "courageous" (56 per cent), "sincere" (50 per cent), "good speaker" (49 per cent), and "hard working" (49 per cent).

Class differences. Members of the several social classes differed in their responses to the open-ended question, "In your own opinion, who or what should really be blamed for the assassination of President Kennedy?" (See Table 1, section V.) The higher the social class was, the greater the tendency for respondents to blame "all of us" ($p < .001$, Class I–II compared with IV and V) and to place the blame on a "climate of hatred" ($p < .01$, Class I–II compared with IV; $p < .001$, I–II compared with V). Significant differences also were found among the responses to the seven groups listed as being potentially responsible for the assassination. Class III members were the most likely to blame "Russia." Class V members were the most likely to blame "segregationists in this country." Class III members were the most likely to blame "Birchers or other extreme right-wingers."

The higher the social class was, the more likely respondents were to suggest the assassination would bring us together, reducing hate and intolerance ($p < .01$, Class I–II compared with IV and V; see Table 1, section VI). Conversely, the lower the social class, the greater the proportion indicating they could see no good coming from the assassination and subsequent events ($p < .001$, Classes I–II and III compared with V; $p < .01$, I–II and III compared with IV). There also were class differences concerning any "lessons" the American people may have learned from the assassination. Class III members were the most likely to suggest the need for less hate or intolerance. Class V members were the most likely to suggest the need for better security measures for our leaders ($p < .01$, Class I–II compared with V).

The higher the social class was, the more convinced the respondents were that Lee Harvey Oswald was the assassin ($p < .01$, Class V compared with I–II and III; see Table 1, section VII). When they were asked what they thought motivated the killer, differential responses were also noted. The higher the social class was, the more frequently mental illness was mentioned ($p < .01$, Class I–II compared with IV and V, III compared with IV). Class III members were the most likely to suggest "Communism." Class V members were the most likely to suggest that the assassin's motive was money—that he was paid. Class I–II members were the least likely to think others were involved in an assassination plot. The higher the social class was, the greater was the percentage convinced the assassin was really trying to hit the President ($p < .01$, Class III compared with IV; $p < .001$, I–II compared with V).

When asked "What were your feelings when you first heard that Oswald himself had been killed?" Class IV members were the most likely to respond that he was killed to suppress the "truth," and Class I–II members were the most likely to say that they felt shocked or stunned (see Table 1, section VIII). When asked what should be done with Ruby, Class I–II members were the most likely to indicate he should be executed, and Class III members were the most likely to suggest that he be imprisoned. Class IV members were the most likely to rate Kennedy as one of the best Presidents (see Table 1, section IX).

Racial differences. Whites were more likely to place the blame for the assassination on some group or person, and Negroes were more likely to give a "don't know" response to the question (76 per cent compared with 34 per cent of the whites). But when respondents were asked if specific groups were in any way to blame, no significant racial differences were observed.

Whites and Negroes gave similar responses about whether the assassination had taught the American people a lesson of any kind, but Negroes were more likely than whites to indicate they saw "no good" at all emerging from the events in Dallas (76 per cent compared with 46 per cent).

Whites were more likely to be "pretty convinced" that Oswald was the slayer (78 per cent compared with 38 per cent). Negroes more frequently thought the assassin was paid (24 per cent compared with 10 per cent of the whites). When asked what should be done with Ruby, responses were similar with one significant exception: 19 per cent of the whites suggested he should be executed, but no Negro did.

Negroes were more likely than whites to rate Kennedy as one of the best presidents (76 per cent compared with 46 per of the whites). They also were more likely than whites to describe President Kennedy as being "strong" (57 per cent compared with 29 per cent). Whites, on the other hand, were more likely to label him as "courageous" (58 per cent compared with 29 per cent).

Sex differences. In general, there was considerable similarity between men's and women's attitudes toward the assassination. Significant differences were found for only two items. Women were more likely to blame "the people of Dallas" (when it was suggested to them) than were males (17 per cent compared with 8 per cent), and were also more likely to select the term "courageous" (63 per cent compared with 48 per cent), whereas men were more likely to describe President Kennedy as "wise" (25 per cent compared with 13 per cent) and "liberal" (17 per cent compared with 7 per cent).

Political preference differences. Although there were no significant differences in the responses to the open-ended question about blame for the assassination, two differences were found between those who supported Kennedy in 1960 and those who did not in their responses to the groups suggested by the interviewer. Those who supported Kennedy were more likely to blame "the people of Dallas" (18 per cent compared with 4 per cent of the others). Those who did not support Kennedy were more likely to blame Castro or Cuba (38 per cent compared with 25 per cent).

Although both groups were about equally convinced that Oswald was the assassin, they had different opinions about why he committed the act. Those who did not support Kennedy in 1960 were more likely to suggest mental illness (44 per cent compared with 28 per cent) and Communism (18 per cent compared with 8 per cent). Kennedy supporters were more likely to give a "don't know" response (33 per cent compared with 16 per cent). Those who did not support Kennedy were more likely to think the man who shot the President was really trying to hit him rather than someone else (92 per cent compared with 81 per cent).

When asked about Ruby's fate, those who did not support Kennedy were more likely to believe Ruby would be executed (57 per cent compared with 30 per cent) or to believe that Ruby would successfully plead insanity (19 per cent compared with 8 per cent). Again, Kennedy supporters were more likely to say they did not know (40 per cent compared with 26 per cent).

As would be expected, those who supported Kennedy in 1960 were more likely to rate him as one of the best presidents (70 per cent compared with 26 per cent of those who did not support him). The groups also differed in the adjectives they selected to describe President Kennedy. Kennedy supporters were more likely to describe him as "strong" (35 per cent compared with 14 per cent) and "wise" (26 per cent compared with 8 per cent). Those who did not support Kennedy in 1960 were more likely to describe him as "liberal."

Summary

Our purpose has been to present a detailed description of the reactions of Dallas citizens to the tragic event that occurred in their city. We have used social class, sex, race and political preference as variables to indicate differences in the behavior of various social categories within the community. Many differences have been identified; certain general findings also emerge.

The great impact of the news is shown by a number of the findings. The normal activities of a majority of the respondents were interrupted. Most of those who tried to continue their normal routines found it hard to do so. Almost everyone wanted more information and turned to the mass-media sources to get it. How much the event preoccupied the respondents is shown by the amount of time they devoted to radio and television during that long weekend; 34.8 hours was the average reported by our respondents. Although we lack exact data, it seems reasonable to assume that many additional hours were spent on reading about the event or discussing it with others. The picture that emerges is that the event immediately captured the attention of the Dallas population and held it throughout the weekend.

Most of the Dallas sample could not compare the assassination to any previous experience. It gave rise to extensive and intensive emotional reactions. The respondents felt grief, shame, sorrow, and anger. Many physiological reactions were also common. All the data indicate the experience was traumatic.

There is also evidence that the public found it hard to comprehend the tragedy. Not only were the majority unable to relate the event to previous experience, but many could not give any explanation for the assassin's behavior; almost half said they were "so confused and upset that I didn't know what to feel," and most said they were "sort of dazed and numb." The typical experience seems to have been initial shock or confusion, followed by sorrow, grief, and shame, and accompanied by such physical symptoms as insomnia, fatigue, and tears.

The residents of Dallas used few ideological clichés to explain the event. Only after ideological causes were suggested by the interviewer did any significant number of respondents agree that such forces might have been behind the event. When respondents were asked to fix the "blame" for the tragedy, fewer than one person in five responded in ideological terms.

Similarly absent was any strong desire for vengeance. Few hoped the assassin would be "shot down or lynched." A quarter of the sample expressed sorrow that Oswald was denied a fair trial, and many in the sample said special prayers for him. The response to the murder of Oswald also reflects the sample's respect for orderly institutional process. Far from being acclaimed as a public hero, Jack Ruby was condemned by the vast majority. Only three respondents believed that he should be punished lightly or should be permitted to go free.

Much more analysis of the responses of the Dallas subgroups has to be done before a complete description can be offered. The evidence does indicate that differences in social class, race, and sex are related to differences in the way that the mass media and interpersonal channels are used to obtain information, and to the way in which the respondents reacted to the assassination and the events following it. However, until multivariate analysis of these data can be completed, only tentative conclusions can be offered.

Roberta S. Sigel

Television and the Reactions of Schoolchildren to the Assassination

Children as well as adults mourned, grieved, and participated in the general sense of bereavement after the death of President Kennedy. This was to be expected. It would be naïve to assume that children are totally isolated from the political environment, or that political attachments begin only with adolescence or adulthood. Long before the adult may assume political responsibilities, the child has begun to develop political values, preferences, and attachments.[1] Political behavior is learned just as all social behavior is, and much of it can be traced back to childhood socialization. To ignore children's reactions to political events, therefore, is to overlook an important source for the origins and understanding of adult political behavior.

The agents of childhood socialization are many. Prominent among them are adults (parents, teachers, etc.) and the mass media. Television especially has proved to be an important source of childhood learning as well as entertainment.[2] In this study we attempt to increase our knowledge of children's views of the assassination by comparing them with the views of adults and by observing the impact television had on children during those four days.

In undertaking such an investigation, one could only wish that the literature on children's political socialization were more plentiful. The

Support for this investigation came from grants from the National Institute of Health (MH10112-01) and from the Society for the Psychological Study of Social Issues. The comparison of children's and adults' reactions on pp. 205–10 of this article is expanded in Roberta S. Sigel, "An Exploration into Some Aspects of Political Socialization," in Gilbert Kliman and Martha Wolfenstein, eds., *Children's Reactions to the Death of a President* (Garden City, N.Y., 1965).

[1] Herbert H. Hyman, *Political Socialization* (Glencoe, Ill., 1958).
[2] Wilbur Schramm, Jack Lyle, and Edwin B. Parker, *Television in the Lives of our Children* (Stanford, 1961), pp. 24–117.

value of studies undertaken in times of crisis depends in no small measure on the base lines established in less stressful times. Few such base
lines exist. The literature on children's knowledge of politics, as well as
their interest and involvement in it, is not much better developed. Herbert Hyman reviewed the major pre-1959 findings in *Political Socialization*. Generally speaking, political socialization studies concern themselves with partisanship and are usually comparisons of the parents'
partisan preferences with their children's.[3] Some studies have concentrated on children's views of specific political issues, such as rights of
labor, civil rights, etc.[4] Recent studies have investigated children's views
of the President and other authority figures.[5]

There are two recent studies of great importance that deal with the
role of television in the lives of children.[6] But these studies do not tell us
much about children's reactions to national events, because as a rule
children tend to avoid news programs and documentaries.[7] True, children of superior intelligence and higher-class background tend to watch
more public affairs programs. But the average amount of time children
voluntarily spend watching programs on important questions of the day
is very small indeed.

No news avoidance was possible during the four days. Children
viewed either the assassination coverage or nothing. We are thus confronted here with a type of situation not previously researched.

Three factors stand out in all the above literature. 1. Politics has low
salience for children. 2. Children and adolescents tend to share their

[3] For example, Eleanor E. Maccoby, Richard E. Matthews, and Anton S. Morton, "Youth
and Political Change," *Public Opinion Quarterly* (1954), *18*, 23–39.

[4] For example, Richard Centers, "Children of the New Deal: Social Stratification and
Adolescent Attitudes," *International Journal of Opinion and Attitude Research* (1950),
4, 315–35.

[5] Robert D. Hess and David Easton, "The Child's Changing Image of the President,"
Public Opinion Quarterly (1960), *24*, 632–44; Robert D. Hess, "The Socialization of
Attitudes Toward Political Authority: Some Cross-national Comparisons," prepared for
the S.S.R.C. Inter-American Meeting of Sociologists, Princeton University, September
10–12, 1962; Judith V. Torney and Robert D. Hess, "The Child's Idealization of Authority," presented to the American Psychological Association, St. Louis, August 30, 1962;
Fred I. Greenstein, "Children's Political Perspectives: A Study of the Development of
Political Awareness and Preferences among Preadolescents," Yale U. Library, 1959, unpublished doctoral dissertation.

[6] Schramm *et al.*, *Television in the Lives of our Children* (Stanford, 1961), and Himmelweit *et al.*, *Television and The Child* (London, 1958). A similarly comprehensive study
was made in Japan, but since we know so little about Japanese culture and socialization,
we do not know if it is really comparable with the two other studies. The study was done
by T. Furu, *Television and Children's Life* [sic], Japan Broadcasting Company, 1962.

[7] Schramm *et al.*, p. 39, and Himmelweit *et al.*, p. 120.

parents' partisan and ideological preferences. 3. Children have very idealized and trusting views of political authority figures in particular and the government in general. Of course, adults also trust the essential reasonableness and justice of our political system.[8] But far from idealizing political officeholders, many adults tend to view them with suspicion, if not outright cynicism.[9] Except for this last, adults' and children's views of politics tend to be very similar.

Two of my goals were to see how the events of November 22 affected children and to see what role television performed in structuring children's reactions. We therefore developed ten hypotheses to be tested by questionnaires given to schoolchildren in grades 4 to 12 in metropolitan Detroit.

Hypotheses about assassination reactions

Little systematic data exist about how adults or children cope with death and bereavement in general. Even less is known of "the generalized massive bereavement which occurs at the death of certain public figures, such as kings, presidents, or entertainment idols like Valentino. One can perhaps assume that the bereavement in these situations is qualitatively different from that experienced by close relatives, yet it is nevertheless genuine."[10]

1. Since children learn not only the appropriate social reactions but also the appropriate political ones from adults, we would expect that children's reactions to the death of the President would show great similarity to adults' reactions. Children, in addition, have reasons of their own for grieving over the loss of a President. In their political world, he ranks extremely high and is seen as a benevolent leader who protects and cares for them.[11] His death might well be a traumatic experience partially threatening the child's sense of political security.

2. I also expected that children, especially younger children, would

[8] See, for example, Robert E. Lane, *Political Ideology: Why the American Common Man Believes What He Does* (New York, 1962).
[9] This point is made most emphatically by Murray B. Levin in *The Alienated Voter* (New York, 1960). A somewhat different position is taken by Paul F. Lazarsfeld, Bernard Berelson, and Hazel Gaudet in *The People's Choice* (New York, 1948), p. 38, and still another one is taken by William C. Mitchell in "The Ambivalent Social Status of the American Politician," *Western Political Quarterly* (1959), *12*, 683–98.
[10] Robert N. Wilson, in Alexander H. Leighton, John A. Clausen, and Robert N. Wilson, *Explorations in Social Psychiatry* (New York, 1957), p. 306. Edmund H. Volkart writes, on p. 285 of that volume, "No summary analysis of the social psychiatry of bereavement and separation can be made, since none as yet exists."
[11] See Greenstein, "Children's Political Perspectives."

show less concern over the murder of Oswald than adults. This assumption was based on the fact that notions such as due process of law, "every man is entitled to a fair trial," etc., are rather abstract and are acquired only with increasing maturity. Another reason would be that children recoil less from the use of violence and aggression than adults. Mastery of aggressive impulses is one of the things children have to learn.

3. Those children who grieved most over his death would probably be children whose identification with the late President was strongest. Thus we would expect Democrats and Negroes to express more grief than Republicans and whites. Children from working-class families would probably show more bereavement than those from managerial ones, since the President's policies may have seemed more beneficial to wage earners and to disadvantaged groups.

4. The amount and type of bereavement behavior shown would probably vary with age and sex. Older children and boys of all ages would be considerably more reluctant to demonstrate great emotional reaction over the death. Children presumably would express the above reactions by such behavior as:

a. Grief, shock, and disbelief that such a thing could happen to the President;
b. Fear for the security of themselves, their group, and/or the country;
c. Lessened faith in the omnipotence of the President and possibly in the stability of the government;
d. Psychosomatic complaints usually associated with stress, tension, and bereavement, such as loss of appetite and sleep, occasional headaches, etc.;
e. Anger, hostility, and aggressive feelings toward the person who caused the loss to the child.

These reactions would be mitigated or counterbalanced by three other factors:

a. Children's propensity for sustained grief is probably somewhat less well-developed than that of adults, since children tend to be more egocentric and more readily distracted by other events than adults;
b. Children generally are rather apolitical and not greatly preoccupied with happenings in the political world;
c. Children have a benign view of the political world and express great trust in the ability of our government to look after children.[12]

[12] Greenstein reports, for example, that children tend to see power figures, such as the mayor, as providers of children's needs (he puts swings in the park).

Hypotheses about the role of television

The NORC study and others have shown that people everywhere spent an extraordinarily large amount of time in front of their television sets. Television probably served a variety of purposes, such as: 1, confirming the news; 2, supplying information about the happenings; 3, providing catharsis, especially for those who watched it a great deal; 4, alleviating anxiety about the continuity of the government and the competence of the new President; and 5, crystallizing the appropriate cues and guides for correctly interpreting the meaning of the events and for portraying emotions and reactions appropriate for the situation.[13] Combining these observations with our knowledge of children's TV habits led to six hypotheses:

1. Since children's reactions to the assassination were expected to be very similar to those of adults, we expected that children too would have been drawn to television. We predicted that they watched more than usual and did not mind missing their favorite shows. Granted the coverage did not provide the entertainment and adventure of their customary favorites, it provided pomp and circumstances, release of emotion, relief for anxiety, and information that lent meaning to the extraordinary and unexpected.

2. The amount a child watches television depends on his age and social class. Younger children and children of lower-class parents watch more. Older children watch less because they have many other outside and outdoor activities, and have more homework.[14] Middle-class children read more books, participate in more organized activities, and in general watch less.[15] We expected that this pattern would hold for this sample during the weekend, except that higher-class children would increase their watching relatively more than lower-class children because of their greater concern for public affairs.

3. People whose feelings of loss were particularly intense (e.g., Democrats and Negroes) would probably increase their viewing more because they were in greater need of catharsis.

[13] Bradley S. Greenberg, "Diffusion of News About the Kennedy Assassination," pp. 89–98 in this volume.
[14] Both the American and the British studies confirmed that TV watching drops with adolescence, but the drop is less sharp in Britain. See Schramm *et al.*, p. 248, and Himmelweit *et al.*, p. 99.
[15] The British study (Himmelweit) did not find the pronounced class differences found in the American one (Schramm) except for the very young.

4. Children who worried most about the country's future or that of their family or group would watch television a great deal in order to get reassurance that all was well.

5. Different children would recall different parts of the coverage as having impressed them most. We can interpret this differential recall as a function of the meaning of the event for the children. Those most bereaved would remember the sadness of the funeral or possibly the Oswald murder. Emotional release in one case would come from sorrow and in the other from the expression of aggressive feelings.

6. Because of the type of coverage offered by all networks, television watching would influence the children's knowledge of the events; those who watched a great deal would be better informed than those who watched little.

Methodology

To test these hypotheses, a written questionnaire was administered to primary and secondary school children. The questionnaire consisted of 11 items from the Hess-Easton study on children's images of the presidency, 17 items from the NORC national survey that centered on adults' reactions, and an additional 45 items that I constructed, some of which inquired into children's television viewing.[16] In some instances the NORC language seemed quite adult, so I simplified it for children, but kept the meaning and intent unchanged.

The 45 new items were designed to gain insight into a great variety of questions related to political socialization.[17] Only those items that inquired into children's television watching during the weekend and those items that reflected children's reactions to the events are reported here. The children were asked what they remembered most about what they saw on TV and how they felt about the cancellation of their regular programs. They were also asked how much TV they usually watched and whether or not they increased their watching during those four days. Some questions were included to gain some indication of how television

[16] Hess and Easton, "The Child's Changing Image." The national sample used by NORC actually had a sizeable Detroit subsample (173) but we decided against using it for comparative purposes because it was an almost exclusively Negro sample drawn from the inner city.

[17] E.g., understanding of the presidency, of the relationship of the President to the general governmental structure, and of American concepts of justice. We also inquired into the degree of children's political knowledge of President Kennedy specifically.

affected knowledge. Two indices were constructed, one for assassination knowledge and one for general political knowledge.

To evaluate the relationship between personal upset and television viewing, two more indices were constructed, one for political anxiety and one for emotional intensity. The anxiety index was made up of all those questions that indicated a child's worry about the future of the country (e.g., "worried how the U.S. would get along without its leader"). The emotional intensity index combined all those that told about a child's personal affective reaction to the event (e.g., "I cried" or "I had a headache").[18]

The questionnaire was administered within 21 days after the assassination, to 1,349 school children in metropolitan Detroit, from 10 public and 3 private schools. (Extensive pretesting had to be forgone in the interest of rapid administration of the questionnaire.) Their teachers were not present during the administration. The children were told that the test was to explore their reactions to certain public events, that it was in no way related to their school standing, and that their answers were anonymous. Grades six and up completed the questionnaire in the customary manner, but each item was read aloud to the fourth-graders, who answered each item as it was read. Care was taken that each child answered each question. A cross section of the metropolitan Detroit school population is represented by the sample, including all social classes and ethnic groups.

Comparison of children's and adults' reactions

The most interesting phenomenon here is the similarity of adults' and children's responses. Table 1 clearly shows that grief, sympathy (for Mrs. Kennedy and the children), shame, and anger were voiced by more than two-thirds of both the adults and the children. Worry about the country, however, was also expressed by a majority. These figures are not exactly comparable to those of NORC because each child was given only two check-off choices, whereas NORC provided four. Children would seem to have worried more than adults about the future of the country and especially about how the country would get along without its leader (children 59 per cent, adults 41 per cent), but this may well be merely a reflection of the different construction of the question. In any case,

[18] On the political anxiety index the highest possible score was 5, and on the emotional intensity index it was 11.

TABLE 1

Comparison of Children's and Adults' Reactions

Reaction	Adults[a] (n = 1,384)			Children (n = 1,349)	
	Felt it deeply or very deeply	Crossed my mind	Never occurred to me	Felt that way	Did not feel that way
Felt the loss of someone very close . . .	79%	9%	12%	71%	25%[b]
Worried what would happen to our country	47	32	21	65	31
Worried what would happen to our relations with other countries	44	33	23	62	34
Felt so sorry for his wife and children . . .	92	6	2	93	4
Felt worried how the U.S. would carry on without its leader	41	29	30	59	37
Felt angry that anyone should do such a terrible thing	73	14	13	82	15
Hoped the man who killed him would be shot or beaten up	11	23	76	40	55
Felt ashamed that this could happen in our country	83	10	7	83	15
Was so confused and upset I didn't know what to feel	38	14	48	43	52
Felt in many ways it was the President's own fault	4	11	85	16	80
Hoped the next President would be better	—	—	—	36	59
I did not feel bad	—	—	—	13	81

[a] From NORC figures.
[b] Rows add to less than 100% because all children did not respond.

it is next to impossible to measure or compare intensity of emotions. It is doubly difficult when we deal with two groups as different as adults and children.[19]

Parents tended to underestimate the extent to which their children were upset. According to NORC, 32 per cent thought children were "not upset at all" and only 23 per cent thought they were "very upset." Table 2 shows that children were considerably more upset. Children's symptoms were strikingly similar to adults'. They reported about the same incidence of headaches, loss of appetite, trouble going to sleep, etc. Here we must, however, bear in mind that this is children's recall two weeks after the event and may well represent their perception of how

[19] The figures for adults are mostly from the paper by Sheatsley and Feldman in this volume. Some are from direct correspondence with Peter H. Rossi, Director, National Opinion Research Center.

TABLE 2

Symptoms of Adults and Children During the Weekend

Symptom	Adults (n = 1,384)	Children (n = 1,349)
Didn't feel like eating	43%	37%
Had headaches	25	22
Had an upset stomach	22	18
Cried	53	39
Had trouble getting to sleep	48	45

they think they should have felt rather than their real reactions. The younger children reported the most severe reactions; high-schoolers seemed to have suffered far less from headaches, loss of appetite, etc. Children of all ages professed to having cried less than adults (39 and 53 per cent, respectively). This is the only affective behavior on which the two groups vary so widely. Boys of all ages almost unanimously deny having cried. If we were to believe the children, 81 per cent of all the crying was done by girls.

The original items in this study, especially the open-ended ones, offer further insight into children's reactions. When asked to tell in their own words how they felt when they heard the news, 52 per cent said they could not believe it. Shock and disbelief are usually the first reactions of a grief-stricken person. Sheatsley and Feldman regret not having asked this question because they think "it is probable that the response of disbelief was as prevalent as those of loss, sorrow, pity, shame, and anger."[20] These data agree with them. Sadness was the other frequently reported sensation (30 per cent said they felt sad or bad), but anger, shame, and disgust were mentioned very infrequently. Obviously then, disbelief (shock) was the most salient emotion. Sixty per cent of the children and 53 per cent of the adults could not recall ever having felt that way before. Of those children who did, most had experienced the death of a relative or friend or possibly of an animal. Unlike adults, they never mentioned a public event or the death of a public figure. Death was thus very personal for them.

How did children interpret the events, compared to adults? Both children and adults were quite sure Oswald had killed the President (see Table 3), although 49 per cent of the children thought he might have

[20] Sheatsley and Feldman, p. 157.

TABLE 3

Comparison of Adults' and Children's Interpretation of the Events

Interpretation	Adults[a]	Children
Felt certain Oswald killed the President . . .	72%	75%
Undecided about it (have some doubts or don't know)	28	19
Why did Oswald do it?[b]		
Insanity	33	15
Paid to do so	12	5
Communists behind it	16	6
Dislike for Kennedy	12	14
Disliked government	—	4
Hatred	14	5
Don't know	15	38
Segregationist	3	c
Hated Connally	6	c
Ordered to do so	11	c
Miscellaneous	8	10
Who is to blame for the President's death?		
Oswald	d	73
Security measures	22	2
Russia or the Communists	15	.3
No one person	—	5
Hatred, bigotry, fanaticism	10	3
No answer	e	5
The public in general	25	c
We are all to blame	8	c
Tension and decline of morality	6	c
Castro or Cuba	37	c
People of Dallas	15	c
Birchers	15	c
Negroes in this country	6	c
Miscellaneous	—	4
Did the assassin plan it alone?		
Alone	24	35
With others	62	46
Don't know	14	18
Who do you think planned it with him?[f]		
Ruby		19
Russia		3
Communists		4
Miscellaneous		15
No answer or don't know		5
How did you feel when you first heard Oswald was killed?[b]		
Glad	12	19
Now we will never know	34	24
Should have had trial	30	16
Sorry for his family	5	1
Didn't care	g	6

TABLE 3—*Continued*

Interpretation	Adults[a]	Children
Thought it unfair	g	4
Killing always bad	g	1
Felt a bit bad	g	7
Felt bad or unhappy	g	13
Miscellaneous	37	4
No answer or don't know	4	5

[a] Data for adults obtained from Sheatsley and Feldman's paper.
[b] Answers are not quite comparable because children's question was open-ended.
[c] No child volunteered this response.
[d] Answers are not comparable because question wording was very different.
[e] NORC figures were not broken down this way.
[f] Percentages are less than 100 because only those are listed who said he planned with others.
[g] No adult volunteered this response.

been found innocent at a later trial. Adults and children alike were at a loss to explain why he had done so. More than twice as many adults (33 per cent) as children (15 per cent) attributed it to mental illness. Also, far more adults than children attributed it to Oswald's Communist leanings (16 and 6 per cent respectively). Several other items in the table also indicate that more adults than children took a conspirational view of the assassination. Thus, when asked who was to blame for the President's death, children (in an open-ended question) tended to think exclusively of Oswald. Russia and Communism were mentioned by only four children. Nor did they mention Castro, Cuba, or extremists of the right or left. Thus it would seem that children viewed the event with a refreshing absence of suspicion. Nor did children express much of the generalized guilt feelings to which some adults seem to have been prone. Not one child answered "we are all to blame," but 8 per cent of the adults did, and only 7 per cent of the children blamed the American public, compared with 25 per cent of the adults. Children seem to have seen the event in a simple and concrete way: blame must be put on the man who pulled the trigger. Many children in addition were at a total loss to explain why anyone would want to do such a thing (38 per cent as contrasted with 9 per cent of the adults).

Where children showed themselves most distinctly different from adults was in their reactions to the assassin and to the Oswald-Ruby aftermath. Oswald put attachment to American norms of justice and due process of law to a severe test—a test many children could not pass. For example, only 11 per cent of the adults hoped the man who shot the

President would be shot down, but 41 per cent of the children hoped so. It was the younger children especially who expressed this hope: 66 per cent of the fourth-graders did so. Only 17 per cent of the twelfth-graders felt this way, which is more comparable to the adults' feelings. Similarly, only 16 per cent of the children expressed regret that the murder of Oswald deprived him of due process of law (33 per cent of the adults did), which is, of course, in keeping with the previously cited aggressive feelings that children had toward the President's assassin. When asked by an open-ended question how they felt about Oswald's death, 19 per cent (the same as for adults) spontaneously said they were "glad" Oswald was shot, 6 per cent said they did not care, and 24 per cent expressed regret that "now we will never know" (compared with 33 per cent of the adults). And yet, 85 per cent knew Ruby was wrong to kill Oswald even if he was the assassin. Children's reactions thus showed a certain amount of ambivalence. They seem to have felt extreme hostility toward Oswald even while they were aware that what Ruby did to him was wrong.

The similarity between adults' and children's responses can be interpreted as a sign of a fairly complete socialization of children into the American political value system. The only difference is that children's regard for due process and human life is less well-developed. The aggressiveness children displayed toward Oswald indicates that socialization into such crucial parts of the American value system as the concept of justice takes place relatively late in a child's life, around adolescence. There is reason to believe that the child's first attachment to the political system is to its chief political personages, such as the President—that only later does the child acquire the system's political values and norms.

Differential involvement and reactions to the event

Even though all children love and admire the President, children who identify more with the President, be it for partisan or other reasons, might feel his loss most severely. Negro and white reactions were compared on the assumption that Negroes would have particularly strong reasons for mourning the President's death. Sheatsley and Feldman comment that adult Negroes seem to have shown more pronounced grief over the President's death than any other population group. This seems to hold even among school children. Almost without fail, the Negro children were considerably more upset and worried (see Table 4), and many a small child wrote in spontaneously that he or she worried "how my folks will get along now." One Negro girl attending a high school in the worst part of the city wrote: "It was as though my father had died all over again." Negro children showed much more hostility than white children toward the assassin and much more worry about how the United States would get along without its leader. They worried more about what would happen to our country domestically. These differences between Negroes and whites lead us to infer that in the minds of Negro children, Kennedy was intimately associated with the fate of the Negro, and hence their worry and concern were so much greater.

Similarly, we predicted that children who said they would vote Demo-

TABLE 4

Reactions of Children by Social Groups

When I heard the President was dead I:	This is how I felt			
	White (n = 1,006)	Negro (n = 342)	Democrats (n = 459)	Republicans (n = 231)
Felt the loss of someone very close and dear .	69%[a]	81%	79%	63%
Was so upset and mixed up, I did not know what to feel	44	40	38	47
Was mad that anyone should do such a terrible thing	81	84	86	81
Cried	40	40	44	34
Worried about what would happen to our country	63	74	67	69
Felt sorry for his wife and children	94	91	92	94
Hoped the man who killed him would be shot or beaten up	36	54	50	38
Did not feel bad	10	23	10	17
Did not feel like eating	27	39	41	32
Worried what would happen to our relations with other countries	64	64	64	61
Felt in some ways it was the President's own fault	15	18	14	18
Had trouble getting to sleep	42	52	48	40
Hoped the next President would be better . .	30	55	38	39
Felt ashamed that this could happen in our country	86	75	78	82
Had a headache	21	23	21	23
Worried how the U.S. would get along without its leader	55	70	66	58
Had an upset stomach	17	22	17	20

[a] The difference between these percentages and 100 per cent is accounted for largely by the other response, "I did not feel this way." Failure to check an item accounted for an average of four per cent of the children.

TABLE 5

Children's Estimates of Their Viewing Habits

Children	A lot every day	A little every day	Hardly at all
All children ($n = 1{,}349$)	38%[a]	39%	22%
Children of Blue-collar fathers ($n = 578$) . . .	49	39	11
Children of White-collar fathers ($n = 653$) . . .	26	40	33
4th-graders ($n = 264$)	68	25	5
6th-graders ($n = 281$)	51	41	7
8th-graders ($n = 339$)	39	44	16
10th-graders ($n = 249$)	12	46	41
12th-graders ($n = 216$)	10	38	50

[a] Rows add to slightly less than 100 per cent because a small number of children did not answer the question.

cratic if they were old enough to vote would show more signs of grief and fear over the future of the country than those who did not identify with the President's party. Table 4 indicates that this was indeed the case, although it showed up mostly in the area of emotional responses. Democratically inclined children reported more trouble sleeping, loss of appetite, crying, etc. More of them also "worried how the U.S. would get along without its leader" (Democrats 66 per cent, Republicans 58 per cent). More of them showed feelings of aggression toward Oswald (Democrats 50 per cent, Republicans 38 per cent). All children love all American Presidents, but Democratic children love Democratic Presidents more and Republicans, presumably, would love Republicans more. Thus, even in death and tragedy, children are partisan, though this is certainly not very marked.[21]

Television viewing

By their own estimates, most children are *not* heavy users of television. Whether their parents would agree with them is another question. As predicted, older children and those of the higher classes were among the lightest consumers. Only 38 per cent of all children called themselves heavy users (they said that they watch a lot every single day), but the rest (61 per cent) considered themselves occasional or infrequent users (see Table 5). However, on the fateful weekend, 98 per cent of the chil-

[21] Sheatsley and Feldman also noted that supporters of the late President seemed more upset than his former opponents.

TABLE 6

Change in Television Watching During the Four Days

Children	Watched more than usual	About the same as usual	Less than usual
All children ($n = 1,349$)	82%[a]	12%	5%
Children of Blue-collar fathers ($n = 580$)	78	15	6
Children of White-collar fathers ($n = 656$) . . .	86	8	5
4th-graders ($n = 264$)	81	13	6
6th-graders ($n = 281$)	74	18	8
8th-graders ($n = 339$)	79	14	5
10th-graders ($n = 249$)	90	5	3
12th-graders ($n = 216$)	90	6	4

[a] Rows add to slightly less than 100 per cent because a small number of children did not answer the question.

dren watched television, and 82 per cent of the children watched much more than usual. The older children increased their viewing considerably more than the younger; older children generally show more interest in public affairs (see Table 6). Adolescents have viewing tastes, political attentiveness patterns, and political preferences similar to those of the adult world in which they operate.[22] No wonder, then, that they are similar in their attention to the media as well.[23] More upper-class children, usually low in television watching, increased their viewing. Being low users to begin with, they quite naturally increased their viewing more, but the findings can also be interpreted as showing, once again, that for children as for adults, interest in public affairs is greater in the upper classes.[24] Interestingly enough, more girls increased their viewing than boys. Generally we have come to expect boys to show more interest than girls in public events and news.[25] It is quite possible, however, that the stark drama and tragedy of the event removed it from the realm of the political. Nor did children object to the cancellation of the regular programs. Only 11 per cent felt television should have continued with some children's or regular programs.

The third hypothesis about television was that those most aggrieved

[22] See, for example, Hyman, *Political Socialization.*
[23] Exact comparisons of adolescents and adults are unfortunately not possible, since we asked different questions. NORC asked respondents to estimate the number of hours spent daily in front of television. We asked for a comparison.
[24] See, for example, Schramm *et al.*
[25] Fred I. Greenstein, "Sex-Related Differences in Childhood," *Journal of Politics* (1961), *23*, 353–71.

would increase their watching the most. Apparently this is what took place among adults. NORC, for example, reported heavier use of television among supporters of President Kennedy than among his opponents.[26] Three groups were singled out as likely to be most aggrieved: Negroes, Democrats, and those scoring high on the emotional intensity index. It was difficult to test this hypothesis because few people in our sample did not increase their viewing. In addition, since most Negroes and Democrats were habitually heavy television users (no doubt because they were mostly members of the lower classes), it was even more difficult to find many really low users among them and see how their viewing patterns changed on November 22.[27] Another difficulty in interpreting these particular findings is with the specific question itself. Our question that asked children to estimate whether or not they watched "more TV" than usual failed to give us an absolute measure of how much more, either proportionally or in terms of hours, each child or group of children had watched.[28]

While these data are thus not exactly comparable to NORC's, a classification of children into seven groups, comprising two groups of heavy users, three groups of moderate viewers, and two groups of light viewers, nonetheless gives us a good relative measure of children's use of television during those four days. As predicted, more Negroes than whites were in the two heavy user groups (43 and 23 per cent, respectively). Few members of either race were found in the two light-user groups over the weekend. The same was true for partisanship: more Democrats (41 per cent) than Independents (26 per cent) or Republicans (22 per cent) were found among the two heavy-user groups.[29] It would follow, then, that people who had reason to mourn the President more watched television more.

We found a similar relationship between general emotional upset and increased viewing by dividing all the children into groups based on the

[26] Sheatsley and Feldman, p. 159.
[27] We did attempt such an analysis and found that the relationship remains the same even if we look only at those children who ordinarily are *low* television consumers. Low TV-viewing Negro children did *not* increase their watching noticeably more than low TV-viewing white children, who did increase their watching over the weekend. We observed the same unexpected similarity between Democratic and Republican children.
[28] Schramm comments on the difficulty encountered in asking children to estimate how much time they spend viewing and on their tendency to underestimate time actually spent. See Schramm *et al.*, p. 29 and Appendix III.
[29] Controlling for race and partisanship simultaneously did not alter the relationship.

degree of emotional upset they reported. The emotional intensity index yielded a maximum score of 11. We classified as most upset the group that scored 8 to 11 (13 per cent of the total population), as moderate the group that scored 4 to 7 (62 per cent), and as least upset the group that scored 1 to 3 (24 per cent). In the most upset group, the moderate group, and the least upset group, 44, 29, and 19 per cent, respectively, reported maximum viewing. This supports our hypothesis.

Our hypothesis that children who worried most about the future of the country would watch the most was not borne out. Increased television watching may, however, have contributed to faith in the competence of the new President. A majority (56 per cent) of generally low television consumers who increased their watching felt President Johnson would be just as good a President as Kennedy. Among low watchers who did not increase their watching, only 45 per cent thought so. By dividing the children into groups according to the amount of television watched, we can observe slight but regular increases in confidence in Johnson with each increase in viewing. Of course, there is no way of telling whether children who needed reassurance more watched more or whether those who felt reassured could more comfortably watch more. But it is conceivable that the frequent references to Johnson's past achievements and the many pictures showing him taking over the command of the government convinced children that the new President knew what he was doing and that the government would not founder.

Differential recall of television programs

The funeral was the best remembered event (36 per cent), followed by the death announcement itself (17 per cent), and news about Mrs. Kennedy and the children (15 per cent). These three items were followed by the Oswald shooting (7 per cent) and the commentators and the general coverage (6 per cent). Neither President Johnson's inauguration, the foreign dignitaries, nor the church services were mentioned by very many. Children of all ages and backgrounds mentioned the funeral more than any other presentation. There was much pomp and circumstance to the funeral ceremonies, and children are said to be fond of pomp and circumstance. Children are also said to be fond of excitement, shootings, and violence, yet it was not the violent aspects of the Dallas weekend (such as the episodes in the police station) that were remembered best, but the funeral.

We had thought that those who felt the most upset or bereaved would recall the funeral (or possibly the Oswald shooting) more than less upset people. We performed two analyses to test this hypothesis. The television offerings recalled by people high on the emotional intensity index were compared with those recalled by people low on the index, and Negroes' and Democrats' recall was compared to that of whites and Republicans. No pattern whatsoever relating emotional upset and recall was visible. The hypothesis was confirmed for Democrats and Negroes, who mentioned the funeral more often than Republicans and whites. This is some evidence that those who felt the most bereaved would recall the funeral more than those who felt less bereaved.

Younger children recalled the funeral and death announcement best, while older children mentioned Mrs. Kennedy, the sad look on people's faces, the television coverage, and Oswald's killing. For girls, Mrs. Kennedy and her family were the second most frequently recalled feature. Children of parents in managerial or professional occupations more frequently mentioned Mrs. Kennedy, the death announcement, and the commentators than those from blue-collar families.

Television watching and assassination knowledge

We had thought that children who watched the most would also be the most knowledgeable about the events of the weekend. But so many watched so much that this hypothesis was difficult to test. The assassination knowledge index, constructed to test accuracy of information, yielded a maximum score of eight, which 81 per cent of all children obtained. The people who habitually did not watch much and did not increase their watching did score lowest on assassination knowledge (only 42 per cent scored 8), but there were very few of them. Eighty-eight per cent of the habitually moderate watchers who continued to watch moderately got the maximum score, and 72 per cent of the habitually heavy watchers who increased their watching even more also got it. Although children who watched the least had less information, very heavy television watching did not increase knowledge any more than moderate watching. It seems that increased watching was only partially related to greater knowledge.

No relationship of any magnitude was found between general knowledge and television watching. Ten per cent of the children got the maximum score, 6, on the general knowledge index, but no great differences were found between light and heavy users of television. Thus, although television helped all children acquire knowledge about the assassination, it did not enhance their knowledge of political events that took place before the assassination, especially those during the late President's term in office.

The Oswald-Ruby episode and the world of the TV Western

We were struck by the similarity of the Oswald-Ruby episode to those a child watches day after day on television, especially the favored Western. In these Westerns, the bad guy comes to a bad end; he meets his fate. But only occasionally does he meet his fate in a courtroom at the hands of judge and jury. More frequently the avenger (usually the good guy) has no choice but to shoot the bad guy down or roll him over a cliff.

In the eyes of children, Oswald was clearly the bad guy of Dallas. Over and over they heard the Texas law enforcement officials (replete with the same ten-gallon hats and boots children know so well) declare that they had enough incriminating evidence against Oswald to ask for the death penalty and that they felt confident "we will get it." What, then, did Ruby do but gun down a man who by the standards of the Western deserved no better fate?

True, school and other institutions teach children the need for a fair trial, due process, etc. Nonetheless, there was the possibility that quite a few children would be so caught up by the Wild West atmosphere of the episode that they would forget book-learning and would not consider Ruby's deed criminal. Although this was found for some children, it was not for most. True, children were less upset than adults over Oswald's murder. Only 16 per cent volunteered that "we must not take the law in our own hands," and 3 per cent said that "two wrongs don't make a right." Quite a few, however, spontaneously told us that they were glad he died (19 per cent) or that it did not bother them one bit (6 per cent). Children who were glad to see Oswald shot were a minority. Most were convinced that Oswald was the President's assassin, but they also knew he was entitled to a trial, not to "mob justice." And they used the same impersonal standard of justice for Ruby. Eighty-three per cent said that even though "everyone saw Ruby shoot Oswald and . . . Ruby

TABLE 7

Television Watching and Aggressiveness

Social class and television usage	Hoped that Oswald would be shot or beaten up	
	Yes	No
Blue-collar children who are heavy users ($n = 276$) [a]	61%	39%
Blue-collar children who are light users ($n = 280$)	46	54
White-collar children who are heavy users ($n = 162$)	57	43
White-collar children who are light users ($n = 456$)	21	79

[a] Children who did not reply to all of these questions were excluded from this analysis.

confessed doing it," Ruby still had to be tried in court. There is no attempt here to make a hero out of Ruby (85 per cent said what Ruby did was wrong), but neither is there an attempt to deny him the safeguards of the American judicial system.

It is true that those children who prescribed otherwise, particularly those who were glad to see Oswald shot, were more frequently younger or from the lower classes. These are the very children who normally watch television the most. One might be tempted to attribute their greater aggressiveness to the highly aggressive content of television programs, but the research literature on this point is inconclusive.[30] It would seem equally plausible that more aggressive children will be more drawn to television simply because it provides such an abundant fare of aggression and violence. Since aggression in our society is somewhat more accepted among lower-class people, children of such families would be more drawn to television than those from middle-class families, where aggression is frowned upon or arouses feelings of guilt.[31]

Among those children who were happy to see Oswald killed (in both the check-off and the open-ended questions), high watchers predominate, even if one controls for social class (see Table 7). On the open-ended question ("How did you feel when Oswald was shot?"), in each social class heavy viewers consistently approved somewhat more of Oswald's murder and were consistently less concerned either over Oswald's being denied a trial or over the immorality of the killing.

[30] See, for example, the review of the literature by Eleanor E. Maccoby, "Effects of the Mass Media," in Martin L. Hoffman and Lois W. Hoffman, *Review of Child Development Research* (New York, 1964), pp. 323–48.
[31] See, for example, Allison Davis and Robert Havighurst, "Social Class and Color Differences in Child-Rearing," *American Sociological Review* (1946), *11*, 698–710.

Summary

Children's emotional and behavioral reactions to the events of November 22 were similar to those of adults. They too grieved and mourned and watched television for longer periods than usual. Many of their political reactions to the event were also similar to adults', although fewer children attributed conspirational overtones to the event. More of them, especially the younger ones, showed aggression toward Oswald and less concern over his murder. This aggressiveness was interpreted to mean that the internalization of such norms as due process, respect for individual life, etc., is acquired later in a child's socialization process than other political attitudes such as respect for authority.

Both those children who usually watch much television and those who usually watch little increased their viewing over the weekend and did not object to the cancellation of the regular programs. The heaviest watchers did not seem noticeably better informed than moderate viewers about the weekend. Impressively large numbers of children were accurately informed on almost everything that happened. Television also seems to have reassured children about the stability of the government and the competence of the new President.

One particular type of television fare, the Western, does not seem to have affected children's concepts of right and wrong, justice and injustice. Children did not condone Ruby's action. They saw that Ruby must be accorded the rights of due process of law just as they saw that those rights should have been accorded to Oswald.

We still know little about the role television might have in shaping the political imagery of our children.[32] Do the crime thrillers, Westerns, and other dramas that children prefer affect in any way their faith in authority? Do they shape children's understanding of the operations of justice, or alter their view of how a political society allocates power and prestige? If television is one of the socializers of children, then we must begin to know whether or not it is a political socializer as well. And if it is a political socializer, we must know for what type of political world it socializes children.

[32] Himmelweit *et al.*, pp. 221–62.

Fred I. Greenstein

College Students' Reactions to the Assassination

The striking response by Americans in all walks of life to the assassination provides a unique vantage point for gaining insight into the nature of citizens' attachments to their leaders. Psychoanalysts have argued that the emotional ties between citizens and their leaders are strong and deep-seated, that public responses to governmental authority are based on powerful orientations acquired early in childhood to family authority figures. This view has, however, not been widely accepted by social scientists who devote themselves to the study of mass political attitudes and behavior.

As a result of countless studies of citizens' reactions to day-to-day political happenings, social scientists have concluded that for the great bulk of the population, meaningful life experiences occur mainly in the face-to-face environment. The wider environment, including the political system, is only dimly perceived and does not elicit strong feelings and attachments. It would be possible to document this point at length, but a few illustrations should suffice. As election day approached in October 1952, only 37 per cent of a national sample acknowledged being "very interested" in the presidential campaign, and at all times many citizens readily report that they are not interested in politics. In September 1963, when the question of President Kennedy's Republican opponent had become a topic of extensive press speculation, a Gallup poll determined that 42 per cent of their national sample had not heard of Goldwater, 67 per cent of Romney, 72 per cent of Scranton, and 93 per cent of Hatfield. Nixon and Rockefeller were unknown to 16 per cent of the sample.[1] Confronted with much data showing the lack of citizen involvement in politics, social scientists find it difficult to accept theories that suggest that objects in the political environment play an important role in individual psychic functioning.

Yet the massive public response to the assassination makes it clear that public attachments to at least some political figures are deeper and more complex than the public opinion polls would indicate. The President's assassination unloosed powerful and widespread feelings of shock, grief, and anxiety. Earlier deaths in office of Presidents seem to have evoked similarly strong feelings.[2]

INTERVIEWS WITH COLLEGE STUDENTS

This paper attempts to unravel the nature of male college students' reactions to President Kennedy's assassination. It touches only briefly on the more fundamental question: what *prior* psychological attachments existed toward the chief executive? An understanding of these continuing but not readily visible attachments may well provide insight into certain fundamental sources of political cohesion.

The main source of data for this report is four group interviews, each lasting somewhat more than two hours, and held between November 23 and 26, 1963, with groups of about a dozen undergraduates at Wesleyan University.[3] The first three interviews were with volunteers from three fraternity houses, the fourth with a seminar group. These "natural groups" had had prior associations with each other; in the case of many members of the fraternity groups, the actual events of the assassination period had been experienced in common. No claim can be made that these groups are statistically representative. Rather, excerpts from the interviews will be used to illustrate what is essentially a typological discussion.

We encouraged the students to reconstruct both the situations in

[1] For a brief summary of the literature on public involvement in politics see Fred I. Greenstein, *The American Party System and the American People* (Englewood Cliffs, N.J., 1963), chap. 2.

[2] For references to the research on earlier deaths, see the article by Sheatsley and Feldman in this volume.

[3] Interviews were conducted by Nelson W. Polsby and myself. For another report on these interviews, which expands on certain of the observations discussed here, see Fred I. Greenstein, "Young Men and the Death of a Young President," in Gilbert Kliman and Martha Wolfenstein, eds., *Children's Reactions to the Death of a President* (Garden City, N.Y., 1965).

which they had learned of the assassination and their immediate behavior, thoughts, and feelings. We gradually broadened the discussion
to accommodate any statements the students were willing to proffer,
taking account each day of such unfolding events as Oswald's murder
and Kennedy's funeral. The interviewing was informal. It was our clear
impression that the students felt strongly impelled to discuss their
thoughts and feelings, and that the group setting was not inhibiting but
allowed expression of responses that at least some of the students would
have found difficult to express individually to the interviewers.

THE PHENOMENOLOGY OF RESPONSE

The statements that follow describe aspects of the phenomenology of
response to the assassination. While the form of presentation stresses
stages of response to the assassination, it should not be assumed that
all respondents experienced all of the "stages," or that actual responses
were neatly sequential.

Speed of communication

The speed with which news of the assassination spread and the great
prevalence of face-to-face news transmission provide one indication of
the intensity of the response to this event. The first reports of the event
over the mass media were received by only a small proportion of the
students, but interpersonal relaying of the news was extraordinarily
rapid. The few physically isolated students who were not a part of this
immediate communications network were aware that their experience
had not been typical.

I think it was about 1:30, or it must have been shortly after, it came out on
television. I heard of it by way of a person who had heard of it from our
[fraternity house] cook, who was listening to the radio.

I was ... with about seven other fellows. [A student] came into the lounge
and ... said, "The President's been shot and so has the Vice-President." And
immediately you had to believe this because no one would just come into the
lounge and make this announcement in front of seven or eight people.

After receiving the first report, especially if it came by word of mouth,
one immediate impulse was to seek confirmation from television or radio. Another impulse, discussed below, was to establish contact with

others, especially by talking about the assassination. These contacts contributed to the rapid relaying of the news.[4]

Disbelief and credulity

By far the most commonly reported initial comments were expressions of disbelief: "It can't be true!" This response was so stereotyped that one might suspect that it reflected undergraduate skepticism. But as the studies of responses to Roosevelt's death show, expressions of disbelief on such occasions are quite general.[5] On closer examination, these assertions of disbelief do not even seem to express skepticism: they have none of the quality of reservation of judgment. Rather, they have the quality of denial, of inability and unwillingness to assimilate the communication.

When I first heard of it ... it was just total disbelief. I said this was all right for 1905, this is all right for 1914, but this just doesn't happen in 1963, not to the President of the United States. Even last night [November 22] I could see a dignitary riding along in a car and getting shot and then I could see John Kennedy. I had these two little spheres, but I could never make them coincide.

[The first report] was just the fact that he had been shot and I initially thought, well, he might have just been wounded. It's nothing really serious. They'll patch him up and he'll be all right. But then it came across that he was dead. I still, of course, didn't believe it; it just wouldn't sink in.

A variation on the pattern of initial disbelief was the interpretation of the first word-of-mouth report as a joke. "When X came in ... I just thought he was kidding. ... Even when I *did* believe he was shot, for some reason or other, I seemed just to have a mental block against the fact that he would ever die."

At another level, or at a slightly later stage, the response is often one of credulity. One might assume that college students would tend to sus-

---

[4] This rapid pattern of face-to-face communication is also described in Delbert C. Miller's report of college student communication about Franklin Roosevelt's death, "A Research Note on Mass Communication," *American Sociological Review* (1945), *10*, 691–94. Only about 15 per cent of Miller's respondents learned of Roosevelt's death directly from the mass media. The lower frequency of word-of-mouth communication in the general population is doubtless due to less population density than on the college campus.
[5] Harold Orlansky, "Reactions to the Death of President Roosevelt," *The Journal of Social Psychology* (1947), *26*, 239–40.

pend judgment in the face of imperfect information. Yet commonly the first additional communication, whatever its source, was accepted as confirmation of the report.

S: I'd just taken a nap and had woke up and went to . . . call up a friend of mine to find out what he was doing that night. He [asked] did I hear the President was shot? And I said, "You're kidding!" He said, "No, I'm not . . . it's on television, go put it on." There was Walter Cronkite starting to talk and I said, "Jesus, it's true!" and I hung up the phone and went in and started listening to the report.

I: You mean even before you heard him you felt it was true?

S: Yeah. Once I saw the special news apparatus, and . . . I knew it should be a regular program and here's a special show. Obviously now, he's not kidding. It must be true.

Occasionally students deny having felt disbelief, suggesting that the disbelievers were in some way shunning reality.

I had no disbelief at all. This [disbelief] seemed to be apparent with most people you talked with later on: they just couldn't believe it. But being confronted with the news so dramatically, my heart sank. For some reason, as soon as you knew he was shot in the head, you just knew that he was dead.

Rumors

Rapid face-to-face transmission of the news combined with credulity (after initial disbelief) would seem an almost certain prescription for rumors. Most of the students did report hearing rumors. Usually these were not of local origin, however. With a few exceptions, they were the same rumors that appeared in the first radio and television reports.

I: Did any of you pick up any rumors about Johnson?

S_1: He had a heart attack, and McCormack had a heart attack too.

S_2: There was a rumor for a while, it was over the television, that Johnson had been shot; he'd been seen going into the hospital clutching his arm or his side or something like that.

The media themselves dispelled these rumors almost immediately. A much more sustained and highly developed flow of rumors followed Roosevelt's death in office.[6] It may be that the difference can be accounted for by the time of President Kennedy's assassination, at the

---

[6] *Ibid.*, pp. 258–59.

end of the work week, and the magnitude of the television coverage. After the first rapid interpersonal dissemination of the news, attention became focused on the authoritative information sources.

Self-consciousness

Students' descriptions of their first feelings and thoughts after accepting the report of the assassination have a common undertone: the event seems to have engendered a substantially increased sense of one's own subjectivity. Students were able to describe in quite vivid detail their immediate state of mind. What follows are some of the specific kinds of feelings and thoughts referred to.

"*Shock*." The word "shock" is perhaps the single most-used term in the press reports of public responses to both Kennedy's and Roosevelt's death. They have some of the same stereotyped quality that we find in the assertions of disbelief. One senses that for many individuals the surge of feeling set off by learning of the President's death is not easily verbalized; hence the retreat to a simple formula. Students, like others in the population, speak of having been "shocked," but they seem more able to present relatively differentiated descriptions of the sensations summed up by the term, including various physical concomitants of their emotional responses.

I heard a radio going . . . I heard something about three shots, the president, etc., and this didn't affect me too strongly because . . . we are kind of used to news bulletins. . . . It struck home when . . . one of the commentators mentioned that he had asked . . . O'Donnell, the President's aide, "Is he alive or dead?" and O'Donnell had said, "No comment." And the stomach just dropped right out.

S: I didn't believe at first . . . then I thought, well, my God, it can't happen here and it can't happen now. This sort of thing just isn't done in these United States. And I immediately thought, you know, a civil war or something. Then I got very angry, physically and emotionally sick, you know.
I: Sick how?
S: Well, my legs were shaking. First I smacked the wall and then I just kind of shook and then I sat down . . . I just kind of shook all over and then I was just emotionally blah, just exhausted.

No immediate response; numbness. Some students report, often with a sense of surprise, that they had no immediate feelings. Their statements suggest initial numbness, possibly out of an incapacity to absorb the implications of the information and to deal with the emotions which were aroused. Usually students went on to describe a "slow burn" effect, and a later—sometimes considerably later—surge of feelings.

Actually I don't think it really hit me until the next day when I read it in the New York Times and somehow, when you read it, it comes out to you so much more plain.

I turned on the radio, the words came in . . . that President Kennedy is dead and I . . . sort of sat there gazing into space. I don't think I realized that it really happened. I don't think it hit me emotionally hard until that night when we started discussing it and everything.

Unreality. The increased consciousness of one's inner subjectivity often seemed to be accompanied by a sense of the unreality or strangeness of the external environment, both the events being reported from Dallas and the student's immediate surroundings.

[It was] like watching a movie in a way. In the sense that there wasn't any connection with you and I felt really no participation in the events . . . like recalling a dream.

I was looking at it almost from a distance . . . My first reaction, actually, didn't concern the assassination at all . . . I looked at all the people around and my first reaction was just the complete somberness of the whole situation there.

Comments on the strangeness of the immediate environment stressed the silence and solemnity of other people. A few students said with surprise (and possibly irritation) that people *did* seem to be acting normally, implying that manifestly different behavior should have been expected. The preception of the strangeness of the face-to-face environment was presumably based on realistic observation of the actions of others. But it also seemed to be a function of, among other things, the dazed feeling stimulated by the first news report and a greatly heightened sensitivity to details of other people's behavior, which resulted from a need to confirm one's own responses by observing and discussing the responses of others.

It can't happen here. The news media carried many reports of statements like "This sort of thing just isn't done in these United States."

This probably is the most clear-cut instance of a response explicitly connected with the fact of assassination rather than with the simple death of the chief executive in office. Among our respondents, two rather different motivations seemed to be behind the response: feelings of insecurity generated by a major breach in the public order and a sense of national embarrassment in the international arena.

We're always pushing how civilized we are . . . then here in the United States a President gets assassinated. And then what really almost infuriated me and really worried me was when Oswald was shot yesterday . . . It can't help but hurt us . . . in the eyes of the world.

In the last two interviews, the students increased their attempts to interpret the weekend. At this point, several of them took issue with the "how-could-it-happen here?" response.

There is murder going on all along. I couldn't see this thing, people not realizing that it could happen.

A regime was toppled in South Vietnam a month ago and both leaders were shot . . . The premier in Japan [was] knifed to death by a fanatic. [I wonder] if . . . a non-American would feel that this was as much of a shock. I mean, it shouldn't happen here, but that it can happen here should seem a possibility.

Who was guilty? Much attention was devoted to the problem of who the President's assassin had been: the students followed the intricacies of Oswald's activities and career in considerable detail. The most common initial interpretation of the murder, especially before information about Oswald was available, was that it had been politically motivated and that "rightists" or segregationists were responsible. Some conservatives reported their relief in learning Oswald's identity, and some liberals their regret.

It eventually produced for me a little bit of relief when he was shown to have tied in a little bit with the Fair Play for Cuba thing. It was a lot easier for the country as a whole to take it that way than if it had been the extremism that was causing so much trouble in the country already.

As soon as he was dead, my immediate hope was that it was done by a rightist and it could be shown to be so, so that then we would find some good in his death, at any rate, by being able to discredit the radical right.

Two students from conservative backgrounds, one a southerner and another a westerner who comments "everybody... I know at home, they're all John Birchers," reported calling home and feeling relieved to learn that their parents and friends had been disturbed and upset by the assassination.

Anger, hostility, and aggressiveness. Some students reported that anger was part of their first reaction to the assassination; for others, anger appeared relatively late, as part of an increasing realization that the President was dead and that nothing could be done about it. The unfocused nature of the anger was striking. It took the form of a diffuse flailing out, a sense of frustration at one's inability to control events.

I became ... immediately angry. It was a very deep and physical anger.... I slammed the wall and broke blood vessels in my hand when I found out that he had actually died.... An action like [assassination] is so final and so noncontrovertible that I felt that my own political rights had been violated.

S: It was sort of rage and impotent anger that I couldn't do anything and yet it was really absurd.
I: Were you angry at someone?
S: No, not really anyone in particular, just at the very act....

Often the anger was directed toward more or less irrelevant objects. One student said, "I was really angry, very angry. It was irrational, but I was really mad at Texas." Another said, "Immediately I seemed to get mad at people around [in the fraternity house]. I don't know why—probably because, you know, at various times you [got] into arguments with them about [Kennedy], or something like that." A student who had heard the news while shopping at a Middletown store began looking for a friend who had gone downtown with him so that they might return to the campus; he said, "I went back on the street looking for X ... I was really mad ... I kept walking back and forth and I said to myself if X doesn't come along, I'm going to bust somebody. Really." His friend added, "I wanted to tell Y. I think we had a very interesting parallel. We were separated from each other. I think we both wanted to find each other, but we were so confused that we couldn't. Y mentioned that he was angry at me, and I think that's true. I hadn't thought about it before, but I think I was very angry at him, too." As we shall see, a certain amount of diffuse anger was also felt toward Johnson, who at first seemed to some almost to be usurping the President's role.

Instrumental calculations. After the first emotional response and the first wave of recognition that the President had died, there was a great deal of practical speculation about what the consequences of his death would be for domestic and foreign politics. What kind of man was Johnson? Would Kennedy's legislative program be enacted? Who would be the nominees of the two parties for the 1964 elections? Occasionally students reported that their immediate thoughts after learning of the assassination were about its political ramifications, sometimes with surprise that they could entertain instrumental considerations under such circumstances: "About the first thing that hit me when we had just heard that he'd been shot . . . I was thinking if he lives through this, nobody will ever be able to beat him now."

Associations with other deaths. By the college years not everyone has had experience with the death of family members or friends. The students who had, regularly reported that the feelings evoked by the presidential death were as great as *or greater than* those evoked by deaths of personal acquaintances. This is perhaps the most telling evidence that citizens *do* develop exceptionally deep attachments to leaders.

Well, a friend of mine [died in an accident] several years ago. We had a room near each other in the [dormitory] that year and we were real good buddies, and when he died I found out about it sort of matter-of-factly—somebody assumed that I already knew—and I felt sort of guilty that one of my reactions was that, well, X's gone, you know. And, in a way it was, how could he do that to me? How could he leave me? In the loss you felt that there was a personal anger . . . and this is very similar to what I felt about Kennedy, and yet with Kennedy it was not only me, but the whole country. It was not so much that Kennedy was dead, but that I was without a friend and a leader, and so was the whole country. It had become sort of queer. Well, my mother's been in the hospital recently, you know, and kind of ill. In a kind of a way I felt that it would be better if she had died rather than Kennedy.

The only experience I've had with death is that my grandfather died after two years of the state that Joseph Kennedy is in now and it wasn't pleasant. And at the time I vividly recall that I was sorry, but not upset like this, like I was Friday. . . . Somehow I felt when I heard this news like . . . someone real close to me had died. It's something . . . I've tried to explain to myself and I can't.

Actions

From the very first reports through the funeral of President Kennedy on Monday, the assassination produced marked changes in behavior.

Many students described the immediate consensus that led to the cancellation of Friday afternoon classes. A few attempted to continue studying, but had difficulty doing so. "I tried to do work. I tried to tell myself, if it's true, there's nothing you can do but just go on and try to keep on doing work, but I felt pretty sick about it." For at least one student, the change in routine resulting from the assassination was itself emotionally disturbing.

I was on my way to go to class. I remember . . . thinking, what should I do? Where should I go, what should I do? And then almost immediately thinking this is ridiculous. Obviously there's nothing left for me to do but go to [class], because there's nothing I can do about it anyway. And we got to the room and there was a feeling among four or five people in the class that the class should be called off. And I remember reacting to that suggestion with something awful close to . . . anger. The idea that we can't let this thing upset us that much. You know, we've got to have our class. There's no point in letting this destroy the social order.

Communications behavior

By far the major type of action stimulated by the assassination was communication, both at a personal level and by means of the mass media. Much behavior that at first glance would seem to have as its goal acquiring and exchanging information actually was affectively motivated. Especially at the face-to-face level, transmission of information was secondary to the need to establish contact with others.

Whom a person wanted to be in contact with at the time is doubtless an illuminating indication of his interpersonal relationships. Students referred to the desire to telephone a fiancee or to be with a friend with whom they customarily talk politics.

I wanted to call my fiancee something terrible . . . I mean here's someone I'm very close to mentally and emotionally and so forth. I just had to . . . echo around some more.

S_1: I wanted to talk to somebody, to try and verify this . . . Well, my first reaction was to go up and ask [S_2]. To be consoled.

S_2: Yeah, even after it happened [S_1] wasn't there [at the dormitory television set] for a while. You know, we talk about politics a lot together and I had this feeling that I wanted to talk to him about it.

When Roosevelt died, Johannsen found that numerous coeds at Skidmore College felt the need to call their parents. One of the girls commented "I just had to talk to my father; I felt as though I had just lost him."[7] Our respondents generally were quite explicit in *denying* the desire to call their parents. Many acknowledged that they had had telephone conversations with their parents over the weekend, but maintained that the call was not spurred by the President's death. Some students who denied that *they* wanted to call home attributed this desire to other students.

S₁: I tried to call home [Friday night], but I tried to call the night before too.

S_1: I tried to call home [Friday night], but I tried to call the night before too.

S_2: Same here. I tried to call my girl because I hadn't written her in a while. I tried to call her the night before too.

I: So you had no impulse to call your girl, or to call home?

S_2: Because of this? No. Especially not. Other people talked about calling home and I said, "What in the world do you want to call home for?"

S_3: I did call, but I was planning to anyway. I'd been planning to, but I always put things off.[8]

Face-to-face communication shades off into mass communication behavior, since most of the television viewing took place in group contexts and was accompanied by extensive discussion.

The really grotesque thing was, I guess, Friday night sitting listening to the radio—the same stuff over and over again and I have the feeling that somehow—well, it was the obvious thing that if we listened to it long enough we'd believe it. And the other feeling was that we were sort of sounding each other out on how to respond to the whole thing. How do you act about it, you know?

Television viewing and radio listening were a constant backdrop to the weekend's experience. Irving Janis has pointed out the similarities between the intense media attention during the assassination weekend and the compulsive staring that has been observed at disaster sites; in both cases the behavior seems to be a working-through process, an attempt to come to grips with emotions stirred by a gross disturbance in the environment.[9] That the television viewing had compulsive aspects

[7] Dorothea E. Johannsen, "Reactions to the Death of President Roosevelt," *The Journal of Abnormal and Social Psychology* (1946), *41*, 221.

[8] From the remarks of S_2 and from the examples quoted above of students from anti-Kennedy backgrounds who were reassured by calling home, it is clear that *some* students consciously sought to establish contact with their parents. One also feels that students like S_3, in spite of their denials, were at least prompted by the assassination not to put off calling.

[9] Irving Janis, personal communication.

was clear from students' descriptions of their inability to cease viewing in spite of tedium and distaste at the nature of the news coverage.

S_1: The whole coverage is really bad. I don't know why we sit there and watch it.

S_2: I stayed right up until the network went off.

S_3: I don't know. It's just something like this creates . . . kind of like a vacuum in your head of all the things you're used to and you just have to fill it up.

S_4: I kept waiting for something that would make me more hopeful or feel better about it. It never came, of course, but you're tied to the TV set in hopes that it would.

S_5: After the TV went off last night, I thought about . . . why I had spent the whole day and it struck me that I was waiting for somebody to explain why this happened.

Developing feelings and afterthoughts

Most of the responses described so far occurred immediately after the respondents learned of the assassination, or only shortly later. In some cases these responses continued, perhaps in attenuated form, throughout the weekend. And throughout the weekend there were responses to specific events as they unfolded—the shooting of Oswald and President Kennedy's funeral, for example. In addition, there is an interesting class of responses that can be considered afterthoughts.

Recurrent disbelief. Throughout the weekend students frequently said "I still can't believe that it happened," adding that "of course" they realized that the President *was* dead. "One thing I'd like to know, everytime someone here [in the Saturday interview] says 'Kennedy's dead,' I get a little of the same initial shock and I have to say to myself, Yeah, that's right, Kennedy's dead. I just wonder if this occurs to other people [general nods of assent]." Even more than the initial responses of disbelief, these statements seemed to reflect a stereotyped way of gradually accommodating the emotions stirred up by the assassination and of beginning to reconstruct one's loyalties and one's cognitions about the central authority of the political system.

Undoing fantasies. Statements of disbelief may also contain an element of undoing the event: "If I don't accept it, perhaps it will prove not to have happened." Direct undoing fantasies were reported.

S_1: Didn't anybody think of being there and seeing a gun pointing out of a window, or throwing himself over Kennedy's body, or something? Or maybe sacrificing yourself?

S_2: I saw Kennedy bending over to tie his shoe just as the guy was pulling the trigger, you know, therefore the bullet missing, hitting the side of the door or something.

S_3: Yeah. In my own mind I tried dozens of different ways to recreate the moments just before the assassination so somehow it could have been avoided.

Humor. Occasionally, somewhat hesitantly, humor broke the generally tense tone of the weekend's preoccupation with the assassination. For example, a student reported a fraternity brother's comment that the Kennedy impersonator, Vaughn Meader, now was "out of a job. . . . It took two and a half hours after [the assassination] was announced [for there to be a joke]. I looked at my watch."

Life is continuing. A later counterpart of the perception of unreality and strangeness immediately after the assassination was the reflection that nothing *has* changed, that life and the political system will continue. A student reported the following thoughts at a swimming practice Friday afternoon.

S: You kind of wondered [that] the usual routine of swimming practice seemed to go on even though the President had been killed and yet this went on.

I: Does this seem strange?

S: It didn't seem strange. I remember noticing over the . . . weekend that no matter who died the sun came out and the stars were there and everything material sort of went right on being and this sort of thing kept right on happening. . . .

The notion that life *should* change in some gross fashion was present in the occasional superstitious observations connecting Kennedy's death to other events: a fire that took many lives in Ohio, the rainy weather of November 23, Aldous Huxley's death, etc. Students invarably were at pains to stress their disbelief in such superstitious connections. In this, judging from the literature on Roosevelt's death, they probably differ from other population groups in which magical thinking can more readily be accepted.[10] However, the conspiracy theories discussed below may be equivalent to superstitious explanations. In both cases the fortuitousness of the event is denied and there is a primitive attempt to restore orderliness and predictability to the world.

10 Orlansky, pp. 259–60.

Responses to the key protagonists

John F. Kennedy. It was in their descriptions of President Kennedy and of the depth of their feelings about his death that students were most likely to portray their own responses as those of male college students.

I was at a White House meeting for a bunch of guys who'd been working in Washington during the summer . . . before last. . . . We were all invited to the White House [on] a beautiful spring kind of day at the end of summer, and Kennedy came out and stood up on a platform—there must have been thousands of us there—and you know, it's just so amazing, he had this tan —he'd been in Washington quite a while as I understand—but he had this beautiful tan on and he started there speaking in the clipped way he has . . . about the need for people to go into government service, and then right out of the blue he says, quoting a historian out of something or other . . . he just quoted a paragraph, you know, just click, click. . . . You got this idea of somebody who's completely dedicated himself to the service of his country, who feels very emotionally about service, and yet who controls it and guides it through intellect. . . . This is the kind of guy whom we could identify with, who was as we hoped we might be some day.

Other aspects of "the Kennedy image" and the context of the assassination also contributed to the response. Some of the students had heard Kennedy speak at an Amherst-Wesleyan football game earlier in the year.

When I saw him—it just sort of excites you and I know that this happened to people all around me even if they were against him. . . . Just seeing the President excited them. . . .

The thing that really hit me was watching a tape of the morning before it happened. He had a speech in Fort Worth, he was there talking to these people . . . he came outside and cracked a joke about Jackie as he does a lot of times, or as he did a lot of times, and then he went out and shook hands with the people. Then you see him walking back in the way he walks with that sort of jaunty look back over his shoulder, smiling and waving to everyone, just obviously loving the public, obviously loving being out in it. . . . You see the Kennedy that's become a fixture in this country. . . . Then, all of a sudden, boom, he's gone.

Although Kennedy's personality and the suddenness of his death were important components of the response, it also was clear (sometimes only after a good bit of probing) that his status as incumbent President was necessary if not sufficient to evoke the intense feelings.

I: Ask yourselves, what if this had been Johnson, or Warren, or Stevenson? Would ... classes have stopped? ... What would your reaction be?

S₁: I don't think it would have been the same.

S₂: No, because the *President* has been assassinated. The President of the United States has just been murdered. That's something in itself.

S₃: I think it's because the act of shooting the President is not only an act against the person, it's sort of an act against the office of the Presidency, or you react that way.

I: Were you conscious two or three days ago of being that powerfully attached to the President?

S₄: Not at all. It brings a reassessment of your opinions. ... I don't think many people had any ... serious, final image of Mr. Kennedy. This brought as a sudden shock that you have to make a final image, because it *is* final, absolute. It's very hard to describe. But it couldn't have been the same with anyone else.

Mrs. John F. Kennedy. Responses to Mrs. Kennedy also were much colored by the respondents' status as young men and college students.

S₁: Very quickly after I accepted the death I also felt the loss of Jacqueline Kennedy, who I think has [played] an important part.

I: In what way?

S₁: In American society—very gracious, intelligent, speaks three languages ... an ideal hostess ... and attractive.

S₂: This is what the college guy would like to marry.

Throughout the weekend attention to Mrs. Kennedy's actions and deportment bordered on the obsessive. The students clearly were drawn to observe her in detail, although some recoiled from their own attention.

S: There was a report on the radio giving the facts surrounding the actual incident—talking about the blood on her dress and her reaching down and kissing the lifeless lips of her husband. This just revolted me.

I: What revolted you exactly?

S: I think the fact of intruding into her personal affairs. This is something while it has to do with the whole nation, this is perhaps a greater personal loss to her than any of us can imagine. The whole idea of it just simply revolted me.

Lyndon B. Johnson. The Kennedy family occupied the foreground of attention during the assassination weekend, but it seemed possible for people fully to indulge their grief only because of the smooth, automatic succession of the Vice-President. Although the effect of the automatic succession was to reassure people, a number of students report an immediate reaction of resentment toward Johnson, partly because of his Texas background, partly because he seemed ("irrationally," the students acknowledged) to be somehow usurping the presidential role.

S_1: I didn't think anything much about him when he was Vice-President.... I first realized that I really had a sort of a resentment towards him as soon as he was inaugurated and they started calling him President Johnson. I don't know. I can't really explain this at all, because I don't resent the man ... But I somehow still [Monday] can't help but feel a little bit of resentment when they talk about President Johnson instead of President Kennedy.

S_2: I felt this resentment, too, a little bit.... It wasn't that I didn't feel he was a capable person, either.

The resentment and doubts about Johnson, when they existed at all, were quickly eliminated by most of the students. It was common for students to acknowledge that merely by assuming the mantle of office Johnson had improved himself in their eyes. In public opinion research, the term "*fait accompli* effect" is used to refer to the tendency of people to improve their opinion of a candidate once he has been elected to office.[11] One rarely sees the *fait accompli* effect operating as rapidly and visibly as it did after the Kennedy assassination.

I thought, "Oh my God, what are we going to do with Johnson in there!" And then I thought and thought. Well, gee, I was kind of impressed a little earlier with him, you know, before he was Vice-President I didn't think he was such a bad guy. Maybe things aren't going to be so bad after all.

You found yourself clinging to him all of a sudden.

Getting to Johnson, this strikes me again, the fact that we immediately began to think of Johnson in slightly better terms than we have before ... I at least began to think things like, well, he was the man who put the two civil rights bills through the Senate, the first time this had been done since the Civil War, he was a Roosevelt New Dealer, and so forth.

Just the fact that he was in the presidency gave him a sort of deification.

[11] Hadley Cantril, *Gauging Public Opinion* (Princeton, N.J., 1944), pp. 37–38; I. H. Paul, "Impressions of Personality, Authoritarianism, and the *Fait Accompli* Effect," *Journal of Abnormal and Social Psychology* (1956), 53, 338–44.

Oswald-Ruby. The students expressed little hostility toward Lee Oswald, either before or after his murder. The general consensus was that a quite convincing circumstantial case had been made for Oswald's guilt, although many students maintained lingering doubts and suspicions that there was more here than met the eye.

I can't feel a real visceral anger toward the assassin for some reason ... [The] suddenness of it all keeps out the other idea.

I don't think people are really attributing political motives to the Oswald killing of Kennedy. I think people are really just impressed and floored and it's knocked [them] out flat. I ... think that people aren't really feeling anger towards Marxists or far rightists or anybody like that.

The most strongly expressed feelings, which of course were exacerbated by the shooting of Oswald, were that redress had to be by legal process. Ruby was uniformly described with contempt by the students, and none of them expressed sympathy with his murder of Oswald. Yet it should be noted that here, as in a number of other instances, an unacceptable motive (wanting to see Oswald killed) *was* attributed to others.

Post mortem

The funeral. The telecast of President Kennedy's funeral had been seen by most of the respondents in our Monday and Tuesday interviews. This ceremony seemed to reduce tension and concern markedly and to turn people toward the new state of affairs, in which John F. Kennedy no longer was an actor.

It's funny that the funeral function ... really had its effect on me. ... I was so affected by this thing, watching the television day in and day out, hour after hour. I began to realize, okay, Kennedy is dead and on we go.

Everything else had been so senseless, so lacking in form or anything. At least here were people bearing up under something and carrying this thing to a conclusion; there was a little bit of nobility to this whole thing.

Tuesday-morning conspiracy theories. National surveys indicate that a majority of the public expressed the belief that the assassin did not act alone, that other people were involved. In our interviews, although some skepticism about Oswald's guilt was expressed throughout the weekend, it was not until Tuesday morning, the day after the funeral, that full-blown conspiracy theories were presented. Two students voiced their belief that a conspiracy had taken place and elaborated on their views at some length, although neither had an explicit theory of the nature of the putative conspiracy. Many other students seemed willing to entertain the conspiracy hypothesis. One student commented, "I'm convinced that there's some kind of a conspiracy somewhere. The events seem to fit in so nicely, and in the frame of European assassinations in the past. This is the kind of thing that happens—you hire an assassin and somebody assassinates the assassin. This is what has happened in the past, at least this is what I've heard." Another had become reasonably convinced on the basis of a casual conversation with a man who

was sure that if there were not underworld ties, there were international ties to this sequence of events. . . . It struck me at first as awfully fictitious and then I thought about it a minute and I think I was reacting under the impression of what had happened this weekend and was a little disillusioned about our civilization at this stage. . . . All of a sudden it seemed to me very real and very possible and something like this could actually be underlying . . . especially the rumors about how Oswald was in Mexico visiting the Cuban and Russian embassies. I immediately wanted to think, well it's a plot of some sort. . . .

Sheatsley and Feldman argue that such interpretations, "rather than indicating widespread paranoia," represent a primitive attempt to arrive at an emotionally unthreatening explanation. My impression is that this fits the conspiracy explanations offered by the students. The explanations were presented with an air of detachment quite unlike the emotional descriptions of responses earlier in the weekend. When pressed to suggest what might be done to uncover the conspirators, the students had little to offer and did not seem to feel that an exhaustive investigation of their hypotheses was imperative.

CONCLUDING REMARKS

The main purpose of this paper has been to characterize various aspects of the response by our college student interviewees to President Kennedy's death. The quotations from the interview transcripts provide some immediate sense of the quality of the responses.

We have noted several points at which the collegiate status of the students seems to have colored the way they experienced the assassination and its aftermath. For many of them, Kennedy evidently was (whether or not they had consciously acknowledged it before his death) a reasonably heroic figure and an exemplar. His youth, energy, and the intellectuality associated with him led many students to identify themselves with his activities and aspirations. His attractive wife also clearly had engaged their attention. In most respects, however, our college students seem to have experienced the assassination as adults generally did.

Perhaps the most interesting question is one that can only be answered inferentially from data on responses to the assassination: what prior (i.e., "normal") orientations toward the President were tripped off by his sudden death? The reactions of this college group suggest at least two dimensions of ongoing orientation toward President Kennedy.

1. It became clear from the interviews that part of the attachment to Kennedy was *personal*, comparable in many respects to personal attachments to friends and relatives. There is no evidence that Kennedy was viewed in parent-like terms. Indeed, as Sheatsley and Feldman comment, it is "difficult to picture the youthful, fun-loving Kennedys as serving *in loco parentis*."[12] Nevertheless, the magnitude of grief was as great, if not as enduring, as would be expected for the death of a family member or a very close friend. Clearly something about the President's symbolic position and the public's repeated exposure to him leads people to incorporate him into their private worlds, into their selves.

2. It also was evident that for most people something more than private loss was felt. The death of the President was profoundly disturbing because it was a major fissure in the social order. Without this familiar figure in his regular position at the head of state, the security of the nation, both domestically and internationally, seemed problematic. Evidently, then, at least in our political system, the incumbent chief executive is a reassuring symbol of social stability. *He* is empowered to watch over the nation. *Our* day-to-day lack of interest in the minutiae of national and international politics is tolerable partly because we know that someone—a symbol of the entire machinery of government—*is* in charge. Personification of the President as the nation's guardian is a simplification of reality comparable to the conspiracy theories that sprang up after the assassination, and, doubtless, it also functions to lend order to an otherwise threatening disorder.

---

[12] Sheatsley and Feldman, p 171. Cf. David Kirschner, "Some Reactions of Patients in Psychotherapy to the Death of the President," *Psychoanalytic Review* (1964–65), *51*, 125–29.

S. Thomas Friedman and John Pierce-Jones

Attitudinal Strategies in American Undergraduates' Interpretations of the Assassination

There can be little doubt that the assassination of President Kennedy and the events of that weekend shocked the people of the United States and the world. Extremely complicated feelings of instability and uncer-tainty, fear and melancholy, hostility and guilt, seized many people, even as such feelings seized those people in India whose responses to other catastrophes have been described by Prasad and by Sinha.[1]

If it is true that most Americans did not expect the President to be shot in Dallas, the very occurrence of that tragedy and the people's almost immediate knowledge of it should, theoretically, have caused some psychological discordance in them. In other words, the event on November 22 probably produced a state of "cognitive dissonance," Fes-tinger's construct describing the condition in which one experiences two discordant cognitions: perceptions, items of information, beliefs, and the like.[2] According to Festinger, cognitive dissonance evokes ac-tivities that tend to reduce the experienced dissonance.

Attitudinal strategies

If the foregoing analysis of the American psychological condition at the time of President Kennedy's assassination is correct, then many per-sons must have engaged in much dissonance-reducing activity after the murder. When perceived events run counter to expectations (whether

[1] J. Prasad, "A Comparative Study of Rumors and Reports in Earthquakes," *British Journal of Psychology* (1950), *41*, 129–44; D. Sinha, "Behavior in a Catastrophic Situa-tion: A Psychological Study of Reports and Rumors," *British Journal of Psychology* (1952), *43*, 200–209.
[2] L. Festinger, *A Theory of Cognitive Dissonance* (Stanford, Calif., 1957).

these are explicitly formulated or merely implicitly held), one seeks to comprehend that experience. Moreover, it appears likely that the essential process is one in which people actively invoke various more or less pertinent concepts from their available repertoires to use as attitudes and beliefs about the experienced events. This means, in effect, that human beings tend to use certain attitudes in varying degrees, as "strategies" by which they close the gap between the dissonant cognitions. To such attitudes we have assigned the term "attitudinal strategies."

Many social scientists raised the following two general questions, among others, shortly after the assassination of the President. What attitudinal strategies were invoked by Americans to interpret the assassination? In view of various groups' widely different prior evaluations of President Kennedy, to what degree were each of the various attitudinal strategies employed by persons of different ages, religious groups, income levels, political preferences, and the like?

These questions presuppose that Americans had available to them, at the time of the President's murder, certain common attitudinal strategies that could be invoked to interpret the event. Various theoretical analyses of the several processes involved in dissonance reduction and experience construction, as well as considerations of the functions of attitudes, point to certain general strategies that should be identifiable in people's attitudes and beliefs about calamitous events.[3] For example, a strategy that ranges from some degree of denial, such as skepticism, at one extreme to acceptance of the occurrence of an event at the other should occur nearly universally. So, too, should variable dispositions to blame an apparent calamity on specific agents (e.g., Lee Oswald), on broader groups (e.g., Southerners), or on a more or less amorphous and anonymous collectivity (e.g., "all of us").

If such placing of responsibility and blame is likely to have been among the general strategies invoked by Americans to interpret the assassination, we should also expect countertendencies to have occurred —tendencies to absolve various agents and groups (e.g., Texans) from guilt and to defend them against accusations of it. Another obvious and general strategy should have been to interpret the crime as an idiosyn-

[3] Festinger, *Cognitive Dissonance*; G. A. Kelly, *The Psychology of Personal Constructs* (New York, 1955); D. Katz, "The Functional Approach to the Study of Attitudes," *Public Opinion Quarterly* (1960), *24*, 163–204; I. Sarnoff, "Psychoanalytic Theory and Social Attitudes," *Public Opinion Quarterly* (1960), *24*, 251–79.

cratic and unrepresentative act, one quite out of keeping with the "true national character." Such a strategy could, in theory, be used to protect beliefs that presidential assassinations are improbable and that the citizenry can be trusted not to eliminate duly constituted leaders by violence. On the other hand, the society in which the assassination occurred could have been to some extent viewed as a "lawless" one in which the preconditions of violence might occur more or less readily. Finally, it does not seem improbable that there might have been widespread, if variable, tendencies to construe any unforeseen catastrophe as somehow "fated," as predetermined and beyond prediction and social control.

Research purposes and hypotheses

For this research we assumed that the measurable variance in attitudes and beliefs about the assassination and the associated events would fairly well represent the strategies people used to comprehend those events.[4] We thought the several strategies described above would probably have been among the principal ones invoked. More specifically, we anticipated that these strategies would be revealed as statistically independent (orthogonal) dimensions by factor analyses of American university students' attitudes. We predicted that undergraduates of universities located in widely separated regions of the nation would use certain common strategies (e.g., ascription of responsibility to Americans collectively), though they would differ in the degree to which they used each strategy.

The first purpose of this study was, then, to find out if such strategies as we had anticipated could indeed be identified and measured. A second purpose was to test the hypothesis that similar sets of strategy factors, frames of reference used to comprehend the assassination, were invoked by people in widely separated parts of the country. A third purpose was to find out if various subgroups of university undergraduates differed in the degree to which they used each of the several strategies.

Method

An attitude questionnaire (AQ) was constructed using items that three judges considered relevant to the attitudinal dimensions we want-

[4] This study was supported in part by a grant from the Hogg Foundation for Mental Health at The University of Texas. We are grateful to the Foundation, its director, Dr. Robert Sutherland, and its associate director, Dr. Wayne H. Holtzman, for their interest in this investigation.

ed to measure. The *AQ* consisted of 23 statements, each of which required a response on a 7-point bipolar scale (neutral point omitted) ranging from "strongly agree" to "strongly disagree." Two additional items required an estimate of the number of people in the United States who might plan and carry out a presidential assassination, and an estimate of the number of Americans who might have approved of the murder of Lee Harvey Oswald. We also used a biographical data sheet for information about personal and social background factors (e.g., sex, age, parental income, home city), and 20 rating scales of the semantic differential type to be filled in for four persons central to the assassination and for four other figures then prominent on the American political scene. The instrument was administered during early December 1963 (at the University of Texas and Pennsylvania State University) and in early January 1964 (at the University of Illinois, Chicago, and the University of Oregon).[5] Students answered anonymously; their interest and cooperation appear to have been almost uniformly strong.

Subjects. Data were gathered from undergraduate students in four state universities. At the University of Texas 557 students from different departments and colleges were examined, and from this pool a stratified random sample of 358 students was selected as representative of the university's total undergraduate population in terms of sex, year in school, and the college in which the student was enrolled. Regrettably, the representativeness of the samples from Illinois ($n = 196$), Oregon ($n = 148$), and Pennsylvania State ($n = 107$) could not be assessed. The total sample numbered 809. For certain analyses, the entire pool of subjects was employed; for others, these 809 subjects were differentiated into smaller groups by university, age, sex, and other factors.

Procedures. All correlation coefficients between all pairs of the 25 *AQ* items were computed, both for the four university samples separately and for the total sample. The correlation matrices thus obtained were subjected to factor extraction by the principal axis method, and those factors having eigenvalues of 1.00 or higher were rotated by Kaiser's varimax method.[6] The final rotated factor matrices were then examined in order to identify and describe the individual attitudinal strat-

---

[5] We are profoundly grateful for the ready cooperation of Drs. Dale B. Harris, Pennsylvania State University, Eli Lippman, University of Illinois, Chicago, and Richard A. Littman, University of Oregon, who accepted the task of gathering data from appropriate samples at their respective universities.
[6] H. F. Kaiser, "The Varimax Criterion for Analytic Rotation in Factor Analysis," *Psychometrika* (1958), *23*, 187–200.

TABLE 1

Final Varimax Rotated Matrices of Orthogonal Factors in Attitude Questionnaire Items

AQ Item	I. Collective responsibility				II. Regional responsibility				III. Sympathy for Jack Ruby				IV. Fatalism			
	UT[a]	UI	PS	UO	UT	UI	PS	UO	UT	UI	PS	UO	UT	UI	PS	UO
1	—	—	—	—	—	—	—	—	−73	—	—	−81	—	—	71	—
2	—	—	—	—	—	—	—	—	−76	—	—	−70	—	—	79	—
3	—	—	67[b]	—	—	—	—	—	—	—	—	—	—	54	—	—
4	—	—	—	—	—	—	—	—	—	—	43	—	67	—	—	—
5	—	—	—	—	—	—	—	—	—	—	—	—	36	—	—	—
6	—	—	—	—	—	—	—	—	—	71	—	—	—	—	—	88
7	—	—	—	—	62	—	−74	—	—	—	—	—	—	—	—	—
8	—	—	—	—	—	—	—	—	—	—	—	—	—	—	—	88
9	—	—	—	—	−34	84	−73	—	—	—	75	—	−52	—	—	—
10	79	85	76	80	—	—	—	78	—	—	—	—	—	—	—	—
11	54	52	47	47	—	—	—	—	—	—	—	—	—	—	—	—
12	47	—	—	—	—	—	—	34	—	—	—	—	—	—	—	—
13	−36	—	—	—	—	—	—	—	—	—	−51	—	—	−45	−34	—
14	—	—	—	—	—	—	—	—	—	—	—	—	—	—	—	—
15	—	—	—	—	72	84	−83	—	—	71	—	—	—	—	—	—
16	—	—	—	—	42	—	—	62	—	—	—	—	—	—	—	37
17	—	—	—	—	—	—	—	—	—	—	—	—	—	—	47	—
18	77	84	87	88	—	—	—	81	—	—	—	—	—	—	—	—
19	—	—	—	—	—	64	−36	—	—	—	—	—	—	—	—	—
20	84	87	80	89	−69	—	—	—	—	—	—	—	—	—	—	—
21	—	—	—	—	—	—	—	—	—	−68	—	—	—	—	—	—
22	—	—	—	—	—	—	—	37	—	—	−72	—	—	—	—	—
23	—	—	—	—	—	—	—	—	—	—	—	—	−71	—	—	—
24	—	—	—	—	—	—	—	—	—	—	—	—	—	52	—	—
25	—	—	—	—	—	—	—	—	—	—	—	—	—	70	—	−35
Variance[c]	11%	11%	12%	11%	7%	9%	10%	9%	6%	7%	7%	7%	6%	6%	7%	8%

TABLE 1—Continued

AQ Item	V. Police efficiency				VI. Veridical cognition				VII. Texas responsibility				VIII. Lawlessness in society			
	UT	UI	PS	UO	UT	UI	PS	UO	UT	UI	PS	UO	UT	UI	PS	UO
1	—	—	—	—	—	—	—	—	—	—	—	—	—	—	—	—
2	—	—	—	—	—	—	—	—	—	−73	—	—	—	—	—	—
3	—	—	—	—	−50	—	—	—	—	−71	—	—	—	—	—	—
4	—	—	—	—	—	—	—	—	—	—	—	—	—	—	—	−81
5	—	—	—	−76	62	—	—	—	—	—	−37	—	—	−71	—	—
6	−89	−88	—	—	—	—	—	—	—	—	—	—	—	—	—	—
7	—	—	—	—	—	—	—	—	—	—	—	—	—	—	−79	—
8	−89	−92	—	—	—	—	—	84	—	—	—	—	—	—	—	—
9	—	—	—	—	—	—	—	—	—	—	—	—	—	—	−80	—
10	—	—	—	—	—	60	—	—	—	—	—	47	−71	—	—	—
11	—	—	—	—	—	—	—	—	—	—	—	—	—	—	—	—
12	—	—	—	—	—	—	—	—	—	—	—	—	—	−42	—	—
13	—	—	—	—	—	—	—	—	—	—	−50	—	—	—	—	—
14	—	—	−45	—	—	—	—	—	—	—	—	75	—	—	—	—
15	—	—	—	—	—	—	—	84	—	—	—	—	34	—	—	—
16	—	—	—	—	—	—	87	—	—	—	—	−53	—	—	—	−36
17	—	—	—	—	—	41	—	—	—	—	—	—	—	—	—	—
18	—	—	—	—	58	—	—	—	—	−44	—	—	−42	—	—	—
19	—	—	—	—	—	—	—	—	—	—	−83	48	—	—	—	−36
20	—	—	—	—	—	—	72	—	—	—	—	—	—	—	—	—
21	—	—	−59	75	—	—	—	—	—	—	—	—	—	−41	—	—
22	—	—	—	—	—	—	—	—	—	—	—	—	−62	—	—	—
23	—	—	—	—	—	68	—	—	—	—	—	—	—	—	—	—
24	—	—	—	—	—	—	—	—	−70	—	—	—	—	—	—	—
25	—	—	66	—	−38	—	—	—	−58	—	—	—	—	—	—	—
Variance[c]	8%	8%	6%	6%	6%	6%	7%	7%	5%	6%	5%	6%	6%	5%	7%	6%

[a] UT, University of Texas; UI, University of Illinois; PS, Pennsylvania State University; UO, University of Oregon.
[b] Decimals have been omitted before all factor loadings. Only loadings numerically greater than ±.34 have been included.
[c] Percentages of total AQ variance are expressed to the nearest whole per cent.

TABLE 2

Items in Eight Common Factors in Attitude Questionnaire
Responses of the Total Sample

Loadings	Item no.	Item	Per cent of total variance
Factor I		Collective responsibility	11%
.86	22.	Each and every one of us is partially responsible for the assassination of President Kennedy.	
.82	19.	The idea of collective responsibility for the killing of President Kennedy must be applied to all the citizens of the United States.	
.82	11.	There is a lot of truth in the assertion of certain columnists that we are all responsible for the behavior of Lee Oswald.	
.50	12.	The climate of lawlessness in the country, as demonstrated by the flouting of the law by the Governors of certain southern states, contributed to the assassination of the President.	
Factor II		Regional responsibility	8
.74	20.	The assassination of President Kennedy could have taken place only in the South.	
.74	10.	The assassination of President Kennedy could have taken place only in Dallas.	
.71	16.	The assassination of President Kennedy could have taken place only in Texas.	
.37	15.	Jack Ruby should be given a medal for saving the State of Texas a lot of trouble and expense.	
Factor III		Sympathy for Jack Ruby	6
.73	7.	When you strip away the verbiage and sob-sister stuff, what Jack Ruby did was a fitting and proper end for Lee Oswald.	
.63	15.	Jack Ruby should be given a medal for saving the State of Texas a lot of trouble and expense.	
.62	24.	About what proportion of the total U.S. population, in your opinion, approve Jack Ruby's slaying of Lee Oswald?	
−.36	21.	Jack Ruby's shooting of Lee Oswald is just as serious a crime as Oswald's shooting of President Kennedy.	
Factor IV		Fatalism	6
.78	1.	In a basic way, all events happen for the best.	
.72	2.	There is a course in human events that made President Kennedy's assassination inevitable.	
−.43	18.	If President Kennedy had not gone to Dallas, he undoubtedly would be alive today.	
Factor V		Police efficiency (Criticism of police)	5
.70	9.	The Dallas police were negligent in making it possible for Jack Ruby to kill Lee Harvey Oswald.	
.69	23.	The Secret Service was negligent in not taking greater precautions in Dallas.	
−.49	4.	The police of Dallas, Texas, did an excellent job in apprehending Lee Harvey Oswald.	

TABLE 2—*Continued*

Loadings	Item no.	Item	Per cent of total variance
Factor VI		Veridical cognition	6%
.70		5. There is no doubt in my mind but that Lee Harvey Oswald was guilty of assassinating President Kennedy.	
.55		13. He who strikes at our President strikes at all of us.	
−.45		21. Jack Ruby's shooting of Lee Oswald is just as serious a crime as Oswald's shooting of President Kennedy.	
.36		4. The police of Dallas, Texas, did an excellent job in apprehending Lee Harvey Oswald.	
Factor VII		Texas responsibility	7
.90		8. The idea of collective responsibility for the killing of President Kennedy must be applied to all the citizens of Texas.	
.89		6. The idea of collective responsibility for the killing of President Kennedy must be applied to all the citizens of Dallas.	
Factor VIII		Lawlessness in society	5
−.74		17. Certain columnists are right when they suggest that tragedies of this sort are to be expected from time to time and that we just have to take them in stride.	
−.58		14. There is no relationship between the treatment given Adlai Stevenson in Dallas about a month ago and the assassination of President Kennedy in the same city.	
.35		21. Jack Ruby's shooting of Lee Oswald is just as serious a crime as Oswald's shooting of President Kennedy.	
.34		12. The climate of lawlessness in the country, as demonstrated by the flouting of the law by the governors of certain southern states, contributed to the assassination of the President.	

egy factors obtained. Next, the five separate factor matrices were compared empirically by the factor-matching method of Ahmavaara.[7] This method yields "invariance coefficients," based on the cosines of the angles of vectors, such that values numerically greater than ±.90 imply similarity that approaches identity between two factors, one each from the matrices being compared, while values numerically smaller than ±.70 indicate a lack of similarity between the two factors. All possible pairs of factor matrices among the five basic matrices were compared by this method. For our purposes only those factors that yielded an

[7] Y. Ahmavaara, *Transformational Analysis of Factorial Data* (Helsinki, Finland, 1954), and *On the Unified Factor Theory of Mind* (Helsinki, Finland, 1957). This method has been described by J. Pierce-Jones, J. V. Mitchell, and F. J. King in "Configurational Invariance in the California Psychological Inventory," *Journal of Experimental Education* (1962), *31*, 65–71.

invariance coefficient numerically greater than $\pm.75$ were considered matching factors. These procedures were used to test the propositions that certain attitudinal strategies could be identified and measured as statistical factors, and that similar sets of strategies (factors) were employed by different groups of students drawn from different regions of the nation.

Attitudinal strategy factors employed

The rotated matrices of factor loadings obtained by analyzing all correlations among the 25 AQ items for each sample are shown in Table 1. In addition, Table 2 shows the percentage of the total AQ variance accounted for by each factor in the combined sample of 809 students. The names we have assigned to each rotated factor for the total sample, based on a careful consideration of the content of AQ items that loaded numerically greater than $\pm.34$, are provided in Table 2, together with the specific items contained in each factor.

There were eight common factors in the entire student sample.[8] Our reasons for naming factors I, II, IV, and VIII as we did should be clear from the content of the items in Table 2. Since agreement with any one of the items in factor II implied a tendency to agree with the others, they probably measured a strategy that placed blame on the region in general, rather than specifically on Texas or Dallas. In factor III, the negative response to item 21, that is, denial that the two shootings were equally serious crimes, apparently implied approval of Ruby's act and a concomitant tendency to estimate that many other Americans also approved of it. Factor V might perhaps have been called "Criticism of police." Factor VI was difficult to interpret because of the complexity of the items that defined it. The name we have chosen is not very satisfactory, since some of the items seem to involve ethical judgments as much as veridical cognition, but it does take care of item 5, which had the highest factor loading. It is very interesting that factor VII separated from factors I and II to define a strategy that blamed the assassination specifically on Texas and on Dallas; it is even more interesting that this strategy seemed to be used by Texans as well as non-Texans (see Table 3).

---

[8] The only AQ item that is not in the tables or text of this article is item no. 3, which read, "The assassination of President Kennedy is a good indicator of our real national character." There was a ninth factor, but since it was defined by only one item, the question on the number who might attempt an assassination, it has been left out of this analysis.

TABLE 3

Factor Similarities Between the Total Sample and Each of the
Four State University Samples

Factors in total sample	Matching factors found in analysis for			
	Texas	Penn State	Oregon	Illinois
I. Collective responsibility	×	×	×	×
II. Regional responsibility	×	×	×	×
III. Sympathy for Jack Ruby	×	×[a]	×[a]	×
IV. Fatalism	×	×	×	×
V. Police efficiency	×			×
VI. Veridical cognition	×[a]			
VII. Texas responsibility	×[a]	×	×	×
VIII. Lawlessness in society	×	×[a]	×[a]	

[a] Invariance coefficient between .70 and .75, denoting a low but not zero similarity of factors by Ahmavaara's method.

Ahmavaara's factor-matching method was applied to all possible pairs of factor matrices from the four samples and the total sample to test the prediction that similar attitudinal strategies would occur as factors in samples from all over the nation. Table 3 indicates the number of *common* factors found for the total sample of students, which were matched by factors found for each of the university samples. Six Texas factors, six Illinois factors, four Oregon factors, and four Pennsylvania State factors were virtually identical (i.e., the invariance coefficients were numerically greater than ±.75) with factors for the total group. These factors would be increased by two for Texas, Penn State, and Oregon if invariance coefficients of .70–.75 were accepted as indicative of some factor correspondence.[9] The results from the factor-analytic and factor-matching studies appear to support the conclusion that Americans (at least, university students) from different regions of the United States tended to comprehend the assassination by invoking several measurably similar attitudes and beliefs.

Variables influencing the use of eight common factors

Although our respondents generally appear to have come to grips with the assassination of President Kennedy along similar lines, it does *not*

[9] Interested readers may obtain complete sets of the tables of factor loadings and invariance coefficients for this study by addressing their requests to John Pierce-Jones, Director, Personnel Services Research Center, The University of Texas, Austin, Texas.

TABLE 4
Mean Standard Factor Scores for Subsample Groups

Groups compared	Mean standard scores of groups on factor							
	I	II	III	IV	V	VI	VII	VIII
A. Regional groups								
Universities								
Texas $(n = 358)$ . . .	.04	−.17	−.14	.19	−.08	.20	−.03	−.24
Penn $(n = 107)$	−.05	.26	.11	−.16	−.13	−.03	.15	.08
Ill. $(n = 196)$	−.05	.14	.13	−.05	.17	−.16	.07	.26
Ore. $(n = 148)$	.02	.03	.09	−.28	.07	−.25	−.13	.17
F-ratios	.45	7.49[c]	4.45[b]	9.54[c]	3.54[a]	9.82[c]	2.08	13.70[c]
Home City								
East $(n = 97)$	−.06	.14	.03	−.19	−.08	.04	.12	.02
M'west $(n = 194)$ . . .	−.03	.12	.12	−.02	.17	−.17	.07	.29
West $(n = 144)$	.04	.04	.07	−.28	.04	−.26	−.13	.19
Tex., rural $(n = 67)$ . .	.23	−.24	−.17	.21	.02	.33	−.06	−.11
Tex., urban $(n = 246)$.	−.02	−.14	−.11	.16	−.10	.14	−.02	−.24
Dallas $(n = 35)$	−.01	−.28	−.19	.24	−.10	.44	−.25	−.50
F-ratios	.87	3.76[b]	1.97	5.42[c]	1.91	7.07[c]	1.43	9.44[c]
B. Personal-social background groups								
Sex								
Male $(n = 514)$	−.09	−.03	.04	−.08	−.10	.06	.00	−.05
Female $(n = 278)$ . . .	.18	.00	−.09	.15	.19	−.11	−.03	.12
F-ratios	13.30[c]	.19	2.73	10.01[c]	15.67[c]	5.24[a]	.20	5.53[a]
Religious Affiliation								
Jewish $(n = 79)$	−.01	−.12	.35	.00	.33	.05	−.10	.45
Catholic $(n = 146)$ . .	.01	.03	.00	.01	.12	.03	−.08	.14
Ecclesiastical								
Protestant $(n = 237)$	.05	.00	−.11	−.01	−.03	.01	−.03	−.03
Denominational								
Protestant $(n = 222)$	−.01	−.08	−.11	.18	−.15	.17	.06	−.24
F-ratios	.13	.72	5.24[b]	1.57	5.45[b]	1.09	.81	11.03[c]
Political Preference								
Republican $(n = 181)$.	−.21	−.08	.01	.07	−.07	.00	−.07	−.22
Independent $(n = 294)$	−.04	.00	−.11	.03	−.01	−.16	−.04	.06
Democrat $(n = 297)$ . .	.20	−.03	.08	−.09	.09	.16	.08	.06
F-ratios	10.57[c]	.47	2.73	1.69	1.71	7.49[c]	1.55	5.73[b]
C. Liberal-conservative groups								
Politics								
Conservative $(n = 205)$	−.21	−.11	−.01	.11	.02	.04	−.10	−.25
Moderate $(n = 269)$ . .	−.03	−.06	.07	.08	−.04	.08	.00	.00
Liberal $(n = 314)$ . . .	.17	.08	−.07	−.13	.04	−.08	.04	.18
F-ratios	9.42[b]	2.94	1.49	5.04[a]	.48	2.04	1.26	11.41[c]
Economics								
Conservative $(n = 286)$	−.08	−.15	.03	.13	.00	−.03	−.08	−.19
Moderate $(n = 226)$ . .	−.06	.01	.07	.02	−.05	.09	.00	.13
Liberal $(n = 276)$ . . .	.14	.10	−.11	−.14	.05	−.02	.05	.10
F-ratios	4.17[a]	4.95[b]	2.35	5.00[b]	.62	1.08	1.19	8.92[c]
Race Relations								
Conservative $(n = 174)$	−.30	−.16	.10	.02	.09	.16	−.12	−.25
Moderate $(n = 143)$ . .	−.03	.10	.04	.24	−.08	.06	−.07	−.10
Liberal $(n = 472)$ . . .	.13	.00	−.06	−.08	.00	−.07	.05	.13
F-ratios	12.39[c]	3.04[a]	1.66	5.80[b]	1.05	3.44[a]	2.20	10.43[c]

[a] $p < .05$. [b] $p < .01$. [c] $p < .001$.

follow that students from different regions, with different politics, and so on, employed each of the strategy factors to the same extent.

Eight standard factor scores, each having a mean of zero and a standard deviation of 1.0, were computed for each of the 809 students in the total sample. These factor scores were based upon the items, and their factor loadings from the analysis of the combined samples, that defined each of the eight common factors. The factor scores for each person were then analyzed by single classification analyses of variance to test the third general proposition, namely, that various distinguishable subgroups of undergraduate students differed in the degree to which they used each attitudinal strategy to comprehend the assassination of President Kennedy.

Regional differences. Table 4, section A, shows the mean standard factor scores and F-ratios obtained by comparing the subgroups determined by, first, the four state universities and, second, six different regions that the home cities of the students are located in, on each of the eight factors. Statistically significant differences ($p < .05$) occurred between the four universities and between home regions on several attitudinal factors.

It is especially noteworthy that significant regional differences were *not* found for factor I (collective responsibility) or factor VII (Texas responsibility), a fact that points to regional similarities in the degree to which "all of us" were deemed responsible for the assassination, and to an apparent absence of tendencies in the regions sampled to blame Texas. Nonetheless, significant regional differences did occur on factor II (regional responsibility). The pattern of mean scores indicated that Easterners and Midwesterners tended to hold the South guilty, but Texans tended to deny that idea. Texans did, however, show a significantly stronger preference than non-Texans for a fatalistic (factor IV) interpretation of the assassination, and invoked social lawlessness (factor VIII) as an interpretive strategy significantly less.

It is, perhaps, not surprising that Texans tended to obtain higher scores than other groups on factor VI (veridical cognition), since the murder of the President did take place in Texas. Finally, although interuniversity comparisons suggested that Texans were significantly less sympathetic toward Jack Ruby (factor III) and more critical of the efficiency of the police (factor V), the results from the more detailed comparisons of the home city regions showed no statistically reliable differences for these strategies between Texans and others. Hence, these findings are inconclusive as evidence about whether or not Jack Ruby's case might have been given a less sympathetic hearing in Texas than elsewhere.

Personal-social background differences. We analyzed the variance in the eight common factors between the subgroups determined by sex, religious affiliation, and political preference. The results obtained are summarized in Table 4, section B. Men and women differed significantly on five of the eight factors, and the other two subgroups on three each.

The pattern of statistically significant differences supported the generalization that the women had a stronger sense of collective responsibility for the assassination (factor I), used more fatalistic interpretations (factor IV), were less skeptical about the events (factor VI), seemed more likely to blame the assassination on social lawlessness (factor VIII), and seemed to be less critical of the police (factor V). Religious groups were found to differ significantly on factors III, V, and VIII. For factor V (police efficiency) and factor VIII (social lawlessness), the sharpest cleavages occurred between the Jews and the Denominational Protestants (i.e., Baptists, Methodists, and Disciples of Christ). These differences, as well as that observed for factor III (sympathy for Jack Ruby), appear to mean that Jewish students, more than other undergraduate religious groups (especially the Protestants), interpreted lawlessness as a cause of the assassination and showed sympathy for Jack Ruby, and that Jewish and Catholic students were more critical of police action than Protestants. The political preference subgroups showed significant differences on factors I, VI, and VIII. Democrats apparently used the collective responsibility construction and accepted the events as veridical more than Republicans. The Republicans were less likely than others to see social lawlessness (factor VIII) as a cause of the assassination. We also took each respondent's report of his family's income for the preceding year as an imperfect criterion that might allow comparisons across economic levels. These comparisons indicate that, by and large, students from varying economic circumstances differed little if at all in their use of most of the strategy factors.

Liberalism vs. Conservatism. Self-rating scales were used to elicit the relative liberalism-conservatism of each respondent. One such rating was obtained for each of three domains of human affairs—politics, economics, and race relations. Although these three self-descriptions were highly intercorrelated, we decided to maintain the tripartite distinction for further analysis. We used these self-ratings to establish three groups of subjects—conservatives, moderates, and liberals—in each of the three domains, and analyzed the variance between the resulting nine subgroups for each of the eight common factors. The results are summarized in Table 4, section C.

Liberals used the strategy of collective responsibility for the assassination (factor I) significantly more than the other two subgroups in all three domains. Those who rated themselves as conservatives in all three domains tended to reject blaming the South (factor II) for the assassination significantly more strongly than liberals. The most valid general interpretation of our results for factor IV appears to be that liberals in all three domains invoked a fatalistic interpretation of the murder of John Kennedy significantly less than conservatives. Finally, liberals were significantly more likely to believe that lawlessness in society (factor VIII) was a part of the cause of the assassination.

Summary and Conclusions

The three general hypotheses this research was designed to test were substantially supported by the results. A complex set of identifiable, measurable, independent attitudinal strategies was employed by our respondents to comprehend the assassination of President Kennedy. Except for the interpretation that the assassination was an "idiosyncratic act," the strategy factors that we initially anticipated were, indeed, among the common ones identified by factor-analytic studies. Factor-matching investigations showed that these factors were ubiquitously employed. The particular strategies called into play by individuals' experiences of the assassination were highly general, but the evidence from many analyses of variance in these strategies (measured by standard factor scores) indicated that patterned differences in the *degree* to which these strategies were used was a function of such factors as the person's university, area of residence, sex, religious affiliation, political preference, and self-rating on liberalism-conservatism. The chief patterns seemed to be as follows:

1. Collective responsibility for the assassination was assumed by people from all the regions studied. This strategy was used significantly more by women, Democrats, and liberals than by their opposite numbers.

2. There was less assumption of regional responsibility, or guilt, by Texans and conservatives than by Easterners, Midwesterners, and liberals.

3. There was more sympathy for Jack Ruby among non-Texans and Jews than among Texans and Protestants.

4. Women and Texans accepted the idea of the fatalistic determination of events significantly more than men and non-Texans.

5. There was less criticism of the police agencies by non-Texans, liberals, and women than by Texans, conservatives, and men.

6. There was more acceptance of the events as veridical among men, Texans, Jews, and Democrats than among women, non-Texans, Protestants, and Republicans.

7. There were no significant differences whatsoever among any of the groups compared in the degree to which they ascribed responsibility for the assassination to Texas. In other words, the Texans in our sample asserted or denied such responsibility just as much as non-Texans.

8. There were pervasive differences in the degree to which the concept of lawlessness in society was invoked as a strategy to account for the assassination. This strategy emerged as the only one that significantly discriminated between all personal-social background groups. Lawlessness in society was invoked more often by non-Texans, by Jews and Catholics, by Democrats and Independents, and by liberals.

Finally, we think that, apart from whatever light this study may have shed on American reactions to the assassination of the President, it may also have outlined a rationale and a general method for systematic investigations of the ways in which individuals attempt to come to grips with sudden disasters and social changes.

James S. Coleman and Sidney Hollander, Jr.

Changes in Belief in the Weeks Following the Assassination

An event becomes a public event when it focuses the attention of a body of persons, who thereby constitute a public. Such events, by their very focusing power, are the principal agents in creating a public from a heterogeneous assortment of persons. In this sense, President Kennedy's assassination was one of the first events to have a world public, one of the first to create such a public.

When such an event focuses attention, a powerful potential is created. Before the event, men's thoughts, emotions, and actions move in diverse directions, and largely counterbalance one another. After the event, they come to be aligned along one dimension, either in two opposing directions, thus producing a potential for conflict, or in a single direction, producing a potential for unitary action. The assassination, had it provided some object for the emotions it aroused, might have produced either of these responses. As it was, the event provided no object, other than the temporary one of Lee Oswald and the subsequent tragicomic one of Jack Ruby. Yet even without an object, the emotions of many people centered on this event. We investigated these emotions and their course during the weeks following the event. The investigation was an attempt not to recreate their substance, but rather to examine their structure in the public. This paper will thus be less a contribution to history than to the general analysis of responses to public events.

Unified and diversified reactions

Whenever the attention of a large public is focused on a single event or set of events, some reactions are alike among the various members of the public, and some are different. Nearly all persons, when they learned of the assassination, experienced similar feelings of shock and horror. Yet from that point on, reactions differed. Some immediately saw it as a bitter action by the radical right; others saw a Communist plot to overthrow the government. As events progressed, some turned their anger on Oswald, some on the Dallas police, some on Ruby. In some emotions and attitudes people were united; in others they were divided.

A sample of 345 persons from the standard metropolitan area of Baltimore were interviewed by telephone at three different times.[1] The first interview was one week after the assassination (Friday to Monday of Thanksgiving weekend), the second was three weeks after, and the third was seven weeks after. The questions were fourteen agree-disagree statements, identical in form, which were asked during all three interviews. Since the pressure of events did not permit the usual exploration and hypothesis formation, the questions were developed from the personal observations of about half a dozen researchers collaborating on this study. Several items were suggested in a memorandum issued by a group of social scientists who met in Washington on Sunday, November 24.[2] The questionnaire was briefly pretested. The statements represented states of feeling, possible explanations of the assassination, and possible consequences. A few were extraneous to the immediate situation but were included to measure changes anticipated over the study period.

The statements were:

C. Guns and violence are too much a part of American life.[3]
D. The assassination is a disgrace to our country in the eyes of the world.
E. I suspect the Communist countries had something to do with it.
G. What has happened shows the power of the country to pull together.
H. Too much has been made over the assassination.

---

[1] The sample began as 600, but was reduced sharply by attrition, since only 4 days were allowed at each interviewing period for the interviews. The sample was drawn randomly from the telephone book, and rough quotas were assigned to obtain, within the household, appropriate distributions of age and sex. The final sample cannot be called representative, even of the telephone households in Baltimore, because of the high attrition. But since the intent was not to describe quantitatively population characteristics, but rather to examine trends and qualitative variations among different portions of a public, a random sample of a well-defined population was less important.

[2] For an account of this group, see the paper by Paul B. Sheatsley and Jacob J. Feldman in this volume.

[3] The letters identifying the statements are those used in the questionnaire. Missing letters were for statements that were not repeated during all three interviews.

I. It leaves the country without a leader.
J. It shows how much prejudice and hatred there is.
K. It's useless to look for meaning in a thing like this.
N. The tragedy to the families means more to me than the effect on the country.
O. It shows there's a lot of political unrest in this country.
P. It's too shocking to know what to think.
Q. It shows we have too much freedom in this country.
R. Of course it's a terrible thing, but it doesn't affect me personally.
S. I don't feel as safe personally as I did before.

The possible responses to each of these questions were "agree strongly," "agree somewhat," (don't know, if volunteered), "disagree somewhat," and "disagree strongly," scored 4, 3, 2, 1, and 0, respectively. The scores were averaged over the sample or subsample.

A unified response by a public is by definition one in which all respond alike. Obviously, no statement of the type listed above will receive a perfect consensus. The amount of consensus on any statement can be measured by the variance of the responses. Thus for two statements, the variance was about 1.0, but for others it was greater than 2.0. The two statements about which there was most unanimity were "What has happened shows the power of this country to pull together," with which most people strongly agreed, and "It leaves the country without a leader," with which most people strongly disagreed. The distribution of the responses to these two statements in Table 1 indicates this unanimity. Table 1 also shows the three items that had the least consensus (variance of 2.2 or greater).

The high-consensus sentiments were also extreme.[4] In the two above, there was not only high consensus, but consensus on *strong* agreement and *strong* disagreement. While it is certainly possible to produce a high consensus with everyone in the middle, this event did not. In fact, a listing of all the responses with a variance of 1.8 or less includes all the responses whose mean score was outside the range between "somewhat agree" and "somewhat disagree," and only one response inside that

[4] Such a phenomenon can result from truncating the range of response at one end. But clearly in this case the response categories were identical for all statements, and their content was derived from the ambient preoccupation with the events. To be sure, both the consensus and the extremity of response could have been reduced by artificially extending the range for the answers to include "violently agree" and "violently disagree," or something of the sort. But this extension would then destroy comparison with the other statements.

TABLE 1

High and Low Variance in Responses

Statement	Agree strongly	Agree somewhat	Don't know	Disagree somewhat	Disagree strongly
G. Pull together 237	70	18	5	15
I. No leader 11	21	10	48	255
P. Too shocking 126	77	21	58	63
O. Political unrest 101	77	39	59	69
J. Prejudice 153	76	22	48	46

range. (All the responses are shown in Table 2 according to the sizes of their variances.) This one response was to the statement that Communist countries were involved, about which many people were undecided. As we shall see shortly, this indecision resolved itself. Responses to this statement shifted more (away from suspicion) than those to any other in the whole list. Undoubtedly, there were many more such shifts in the few hours immediately following the event, but by the end of a week, the sentiments on which there was high consensus were, in general, strongly decided: the country *can* pull together; we are *not* without a leader. These attitudes had already gone through the process that was yet to come for the fears about any involvement by Communist countries.

What were the responses that showed high variance? Most people thought the assassination was a disgrace to the country in the eyes of the world, but a sizeable minority disagreed strongly. Most people thought it showed how much prejudice and hate there is, but others refused to define it that way. Most thought it showed political unrest, but others disagreed. These are the kinds of definitions of an event that create diversity of response, even for an event that produced emotions as uniform as this one.

Shifts in consensus and diversity

Yet not all the processes that stabilized these attitudes had occurred by the end of the first week. There were shifts of some sort in most of the attitudes. It will give some insight into the dynamics of public opinion to find out what these were.

Two kinds of shifts must be studied. The first kind, shifts in the mean score, are of most interest for study of the content of the reaction itself;

the second kind, shifts in the consensus or diversity of response, are of most interest for study of the structure of public opinion and of how that structure develops. It is the latter that interests us here. Table 2 summarizes the changes in mean scores and variances during the six weeks between the first and third interviews.

In examining these shifts in consensus, a curious fact emerges. The variance increased on all but three attitudes; and those three were among the four with the *lowest* initial variance. Thus we find just the opposite of a statistical regression effect: the variances that were initially lowest became lower still, the highest ones higher still.

These three attitudes, that the country *does* pull together, that we are *not* without a leader, and that there is *not* too much freedom, all indicate a kind of closing of ranks in the face of danger. They continued to develop consensus throughout the seven weeks covered by these interviews. Most of the other attitudes shifted toward less consensus. As people came, in their own minds and their own social groups, to reexamine the event, it took on ever more diverse meanings for them. This is evident from several attitudes for which the mean score changed less than the variance: that the event showed prejudice and hate, that it

TABLE 2

Means and Variances for the Fourteen Statements

Statement	First interview		Second interview		Third interview		Change between first and third interviews	
	Mean	Variance	Mean	Variance	Mean	Variance	In Mean	In Variance
Variance 1.8 or below[a]								
G. Pull together . . .	3.5	1.0	3.6	0.7	3.7	0.6	+0.2	−0.4
I. No leader	0.5	1.1	0.5	1.1	0.4	0.9	−0.1	−0.2
H. Too much made of it	0.6	1.3	1.1	2.2	1.1	2.1	+0.5	+0.8
Q. Too much freedom	0.7	1.5	0.6	1.4	0.6	1.4	−0.1	−0.1
R. Doesn't affect me .	0.9	1.7	1.1	1.9	1.2	2.1	+0.3	+0.4
S. Don't feel safe . .	0.9	1.8	0.8	1.7	0.8	1.9	−0.1	+0.1
E. Communist	2.0	1.8	1.4	1.8	1.3	2.2	−0.7	+0.4
Variance 1.9 or above								
N. Family tragedy . .	1.6	1.9	1.5	2.0	1.3	2.2	−0.3	+0.3
C. Guns and violence .	3.0	1.9	2.7	2.3	2.7	2.5	−0.3	+0.6
K. No meaning . . .	1.3	2.1	1.5	2.3	1.5	2.5	+0.2	+0.4
J. Prejudice	2.7	2.2	2.6	2.4	2.4	2.6	−0.3	+0.4
D. Disgrace	2.9	2.2	2.7	2.5	2.7	2.5	−0.2	+0.3
O. Unrest	2.2	2.3	2.1	2.6	2.1	2.8	−0.1	+0.5
P. Too shocking . . .	2.4	2.4	2.4	2.3	2.1	2.5	−0.3	+0.1

[a] At time of first interview.

showed political unrest, that it indicated that guns and violence are too much a part of American life, and that it was a disgrace to our country. Initially, some persons reacted one way to each of these statements, and others reacted the opposite way. As they continued to redefine the event in the context of their own personalities and experiences, this diversity increased. For example, the statement, "It shows how much prejudice and hatred there is," is one that different persons would naturally be predisposed to respond to differently, depending on whether they wanted to see it as an act of prejudice or not. But initially the shock of the act was so strong that it inhibited persons from disagreeing strongly with that statement—to disagree was to view the event dispassionately. Seven weeks after the event, dispassion was more acceptable. Thus initially only 46 disagreed strongly and 153 agreed strongly, but on the third interview 82 disagreed strongly, an increase of 36, and 126 agreed strongly, a decrease of only 27. For some statements, such as the one about political unrest, both extreme categories increased.

Of special interest is the shift shown by the suspicion that Communist countries were involved. This suspicion, which was already held by only a minority a week after the event, further declined sharply over the next weeks. But in this decline there was a countermovement, shown by the increase in the variance. In the first interview, 45 per cent of those who agreed with this suspicion agreed strongly; by the third interview, a smaller proportion held this suspicion (25 per cent compared with 38 per cent earlier), but of these, 53 per cent held the suspicion strongly. Although there was a general movement away from suspicion of Communist countries, the minority that held this suspicion held it even more strongly.

Two of the attitudes that initially showed a high consensus (that *not* too much has been made of the assassination, and that it *does* affect me personally) greatly increased their diversity, unlike the others that initially showed a high consensus. These attitudes reflect intensity of involvement, and exhibit the effects of both the passion of the event and the ensuing dispassion. In time, the possibility of dispassion emerged, freeing those whose principal concerns were elsewhere to say too much *has* been made of it, and it does *not* affect me personally. Thus these attitudes show the different rates at which people recovered from the intense involvement that all experienced in the beginning.

The differences shown by these various responses suggest a differential in the dynamics of opinion shift among the attitudes or categories of attitudes. It is as if they required varying periods of incubation. For example, responses to the statements, "too much has been made of it," and "it doesn't affect me personally," indicate (negatively) how much attention was concentrated on the event. The mean scores for both of these increased, showing a drop in attention, and they sharply increased their variance. The statements on guns, Communism, prejudice, and unrest elicited beliefs about possible causes of the event, and consequent negative attitudes toward those causes. Each of these beliefs was already held by a minority, which continued to shrink, though the variance of the responses increased. "Too much freedom" is similarly a possible cause; and not only the belief in it declined, but also the variance of the responses. The statements about "pull together," "no leader," and "don't feel safe" all concerned consequences of the event for society. On these the variance decreased or increased only slightly, showing greater consensus, and the mean scores became even more extreme than at first. Indeed, there is reason to believe that these items had passed their peak by the time they were formulated into the research design.[5] These similarities and differences point strongly to the need for a theory of public opinion that includes such components and that does not lump all psychological variables into the general category of "opinion."

Differential reactions by subgroups

The results suggest not only that attitudes shift toward stability, as indicated in the previous section, but also that they shift at different rates among different population subgroups. Various demographic characteristics of this population were examined for their relation to the responses to this event. These included sex, race, age, education, religion, and political preference (voted for Kennedy or Nixon in the last election). Several of these characteristics did not seem to be related to differences in the responses, but one that did, for nearly every attitude, was education.

Three educational groups were separated: those with less than high school education, high school graduates, and those with some college. The mean scores for each of these educational groups at each interview

[5] Sheatsley and Feldman think that one probably common immediate reaction, disbelief, was so fleeting that it escaped inclusion in their study despite their focus on immediate reactions.

TABLE 3

Mean Scores for Persons With High, Medium, and Low Amounts of Education

	Education								
	High			Medium			Low		
	Interview:			Interview:			Interview:		
Statement	1st	2nd	3rd	1st	2nd	3rd	1st	2nd	3rd
G. Pull together	3.5	3.6	3.7	3.4	3.6	3.8	3.5	3.6	3.7
I. No leader	0.3	0.2	0.2	0.4	0.4	0.3	0.7	0.7	0.5
H. Too much made of it .	0.7	1.3	1.1	0.7	1.0	1.0	0.6	0.9	1.3
G. Too much freedom . .	0.4	0.3	0.3	0.7	0.5	0.6	1.0	0.9	0.8
R. Doesn't affect me . .	0.7	0.9	0.9	0.8	1.1	1.0	0.9	1.3	1.5
S. Don't feel safe . . .	0.5	0.6	0.5	0.7	0.5	0.5	1.2	1.2	1.1
E. Communist	1.5	0.9	0.8	1.9	1.3	1.1	2.4	1.7	1.6
N. Family tragedy . . .	1.4	1.3	1.2	1.4	1.4	1.3	1.9	1.6	1.4
C. Guns and violence . .	2.7	2.3	2.1	2.9	2.6	2.7	3.2	3.1	3.2
K. No meaning	1.2	1.7	1.5	1.2	1.3	1.4	1.5	1.6	1.6
J. Prejudice	2.2	2.0	2.0	2.7	2.5	2.4	3.1	3.0	2.7
D. Disgrace	2.7	2.4	2.4	3.0	2.7	2.7	3.0	3.0	3.0
O. Unrest	1.8	1.6	1.5	2.1	2.1	2.1	2.6	2.4	2.5
P. Too shocking	1.6	1.8	1.6	2.3	2.3	1.9	3.0	2.8	2.5

are given in Table 3. The college group was less suspicious of Communism, but also less likely to define the event as showing prejudice and hate; it was less likely to say there was political unrest, and less likely to say there was too much of guns and violence. In short, the college-educated were less likely to see *any* object as the cause of the event. They were also less likely to say that we were without a leader or that the event was a disgrace in the eyes of the world.

One consistent element does appear in these responses: the more educated persons' responses are less extreme. Another way of seeing this is to examine the direction of shifts in the responses. In general, we can say that with time passions and emotions subsided toward their pre-assassination levels. Thus in every case we can think of the earlier response as being the more passionate, and the direction of the shift as being away from passion, toward calmness.

When the responses are viewed this way, we see that in every case but two ("doesn't affect me" and "no meaning"), the more educated groups gave the least passionate response. For those attitudes in which the subsequent movement was down, they were initially the lowest; for those items in which the subsequent movement was up, they were initially the highest. Why should those with the most education show the least intensity in their responses to this event? Much research has shown that these are precisely the persons most aware of events, most responsive to their environment.

One of the fundamental differences between peoples at different levels of civilization is the intensity of their emotions. Travelers visiting less civilized parts of the world are constantly confronted with a welter of violent sounds and actions that reflect violent emotions. In the summer of 1964, one read in the newspapers of a riot in Peru over a soccer match in which more than 100 persons were killed, and of riots in New York in which one or two persons were killed. One early report in Europe of the New York riots rumored "hundreds killed"; this was inconceivable, despite the seriousness of the disorders, but the report about Peru was entirely conceivable.

The historian Huizinga, writing about the Middle Ages, titles his first chapter, "The Violent Tenor of Life," which he sees as a fundamental contrast to the present.[6] He describes this violent tenor of life as expressed in every way: in the intensity of sound, smell, and color; in the frequency of violent action and of bloody consequences; in the absence of quiet even at night.

Such violent emotion can express itself also in the response to a public event. It was widely remarked after the assassination how calmly the American people had taken this event. Indeed, this calm had been characteristic of the three preceding presidential assassinations, including Lincoln's, which by its context might have been expected to be otherwise. It may be that under similar circumstances any people would react in so orderly a fashion. Yet this is the kind of event that can—and in many cases of history does—provoke the most kinds of disorder.

The suggestion, then, is that the intensity of the responses of those at different educational levels differed because of the civilizing effect of education. Formal education is perhaps the principal civilizing device society possesses, and it appears in this case that it tempered the extremity of the response.

Either of two things could be meant by this phrase, "tempered response." It could mean that the average position of the more educated group is not as extreme as that of the less educated group. But it could also mean that the response has shifted less, and that it will subsequently

[6] J. Huizinga, *The Waning of the Middle Ages* (New York, 1954).

TABLE 4

Demographic Analysis of Responses

Statement	Women Interview: 1st	2nd	3rd	Men Interview: 1st	2nd	3rd	Persons who voted for Kennedy Interview: 1st	2nd	3rd	Persons who voted for Nixon Interview: 1st	2nd	3rd	Negroes Interview: 1st	2nd	3rd	Whites Interview: 1st	2nd	3rd
E. Communism	2.2	1.6	1.5	1.8	1.2	1.0	2.7	2.6	2.4	2.1	2.1	1.8						
P. Too shocking	2.7	2.8	2.3	2.2	2.6	2.0	1.1	1.0	0.9	0.6	0.5	0.6						
S. Don't feel safe	1.1	1.1	0.9	0.6	0.5	0.6							1.4	1.6	1.7	0.8	0.7	0.6
O. Unrest	2.6	2.5	2.4	2.0	1.7	1.8							2.9	3.2	3.0	2.2	2.0	2.0
R. Doesn't affect me	0.7	1.0	1.1	1.1	1.2	1.4												
J. Prejudice	3.1	2.9	2.7	2.3	2.5	2.3	2.9	2.8	2.6	2.5	2.4	2.2	3.5	3.5	3.5	2.6	2.5	2.2
H. Too much made of it							0.4	0.8	1.0	1.2	1.8	1.6						
I. No leader							0.7	0.6	0.4	0.3	0.3	0.3	0.9	1.3	1.0	0.5	0.4	0.3

shift less. We do not know what the response to these statements would have been before the event; we cannot know how far the response has shifted. But we can ask how much the response subsides in the time covered by the interviews and for which group it subsides most.

The evidence is less clear here. For seven of thirteen statements, the response of the less educated group shifts more over time than that of the college group; for four of them, the college group shows more shift; and for two, the shift is equal. Thus, although the evidence is less clear, it suggests "tempered" response not only in the sense of a less extreme position, but also in the sense of a less extreme shift away from an existing position.

Sex shows the same kind of tempering effect as education. Men show a more tempered response than women. On six of the fourteen statements, men and women initially differed more than 0.3. Their responses to these six are shown in Table 4. These figures show that in every case, the direction of the shift in the women's responses in the second and third interviews is in the direction of the men's initial response. The women's responses were more extreme for all six statements. They suspected Communism more, they felt more that it showed prejudice, they felt less safe, they saw more unrest, they more often saw it as too shocking to know what to think, and they less often felt that it didn't affect them personally. This is somewhat surprising, for although women are sometimes characterized as more emotional than men, they are less involved in politics and public affairs. In political disorders, it is men who act violently, not because they are more emotional than women, but because they are more involved in public life. The stronger responses of women to these statements indicate that the assassination was as much a private and personal event as a political one. The greater impact of the assassination upon women shows how much it was defined as a personal tragedy rather than merely as an event in public life. For although the woman is more embedded in the family than is the man, this event reached all the way in and touched her even more intensely.

Another indication of the personal, pervasive, and nonpolitical nature of this event is the absence of large differences between persons who voted for Kennedy and persons who voted for Nixon. For only five of the fourteen statements were there initial differences greater than 0.3 between Kennedy and Nixon voters, and for only one of these ("too much has been made of it") was there a large difference. As Table 4 shows, on each of these five statements the Nixon voters showed both a less extreme reaction and less subsequent shift, like the college educated and like men.

Thus in all three of these cases, the principal difference in the responses of the different groups is in their intensity. Even for statements that should have revealed ideological differences, such differences were blanked out, and only differences in intensity remained. (For example, Nixon voters were very slightly *less* likely to suspect that Communist countries were behind the event.)

Differential shifts

For all the demographic characteristics studied above, although initial reactions differed somewhat among the subgroups, the subsequent shifts in attitudes and their general direction were similar. Yet in an earlier section, it was evident that as time passed, the diversity or variance in the responses of different persons increased for most of the statements. This means that for some attitudes there were merely shifts away from the extremes, which spread people out along the continuum. But for others there was simultaneous movement in *both* directions. For example, statements I, N, O, and S got more responses in both extreme categories at the third interview than at the first. The question thus arises: which groups showed differential directions or rates of change in their responses to the statements? The general answer to this question lies beyond the scope of this paper, but one important illustration can be given, that of race.

The initial reactions of Negroes to several of the statements differed from those of whites. Negroes were even less likely than whites to say that too much had been made of the event, were even more likely to see it as a disgrace to the nation, were more likely to see it as too shocking to know what to think, and were more likely to suspect Communist involvement. Their more intense or extreme reactions to these statements were like those of women, the less educated, and the Kennedy voters, and their subsequent shifts parallelled those of the whites: they subsided toward less intensity.

On another set of statements, however, Negroes not only differed initially from whites, but also changed their reactions differently. These are shown in Table 4. The initial reactions of Negroes to these statements show considerably more intensity and anxiety than those of whites. But the reactions of the whites shifted toward a *less* anxious position, whereas the reactions of the Negroes shifted toward more anxiety, or did not shift at all. Thus Negroes not only were initially more likely to see prejudice and hate in the assassination, but they also saw just as much prejudice and hatred seven weeks after it as one week after, whereas the whites perception subsided. They initially felt less safe than the whites; their fears increased over the next six weeks, but the whites' fears decreased. They were more likely to feel the country had no leader and more likely to see political unrest; although the whites' emotions on these matters subsided slightly, the Negroes' were slightly *higher* at the third interview than at the first. For all these statements, the data point to an initial fear and anxiety that existed for both whites and Negroes, that subsided for whites, but did not subside for Negroes.

This increase in fear and anxiety reminds us of what might have been. The reactions to this event subsided and we are led to think of this subsiding as the natural change. Yet it is no more natural than the opposite. If there had been some object for reaction, or if the subsequent weeks had brought internal or international disturbances (of whatever origin), then the fears and emotions could have continued to build. For every event, there is a period during which the intensity of involvement and the focusing of attention increase, and what we know of this process suggests that the rate of incubation increases as the rate of information diffusion and social interaction increases. Furthermore, incubation was completed at different times for different types of response and for different subgroups. In this case, Friday and Saturday were the period of increase for most persons. But the increase can continue for a long time and can lead to violence and disorder. It is often not recognized that such a period of increase always occurs, even after an event such as this one, which was so quickly disseminated. Thus, the "natural" course of public opinion after an event includes both an increase of attention-focusing and a decrease.[7] The crucial question is how long the increase continues, and how high it rises. In this case, it rose very high, but it did not last very long, possibly because there was so much social interaction

[7] A good illustration of the period of increase occurred for one of the authors on Friday afternoon, two hours after the event. He was scheduled to give a visiting lecture at another university. Despite the event, the schedule was maintained, he gave the lecture, and there was full attendance. Yet a day later, it would have been inconceivable to carry out the lecture as scheduled. Similar instances occurred in many places, where an activity was continued Friday that could not have been on Saturday.

and such intense exposure. One might even speculate that the intense exposure provided by television reduced the danger of expanding violence and disorder by compressing the period of increasing involvement into a very short time.

Even for this event, in which the course of public opinion had this rising and falling structure, there are some curious variations that are little understood. Certainly the most important and puzzling of these is the difference between public opinion in the United States and in Europe. Outside the United States, there was not the same intense involvement throughout the four days that was experienced by nearly all Americans. There has also been a slower decline in publications about Kennedy, in rumors, in suspicions that the facts are not known, and in a belief that Oswald either was not the killer or was the tool of a larger plot. A traveler outside the United States is quickly aware of a continued attention to Kennedy that is far greater than in the United States, of an unwillingness to close a book that Americans have firmly closed. It is unclear even which of the two phenomena requires explanation: the rapid decline in the attention paid by Americans, or the continued attention in other countries. Even without explanation, the difference reminds us of the different courses public opinion can take and of our meager knowledge of its dynamics.

Monroe J. Miller and Roger S. Zimmerman

Immediate and Subsequent Reactions in Manhattan

We did this study to try to answer some questions about people's reactions to the assassination of President Kennedy. We wanted to know, what were some of the factors that made for differences between the reactions of different groups? What fears and emotions did people express in a national crisis? To tap these reactions, we began interviewing within one hour after the assassination. Forty-six interviews were conducted on the day and evening of the assassination in lower midtown Manhattan. Fifty more were conducted three-and-one-half weeks later at the same time of the day and in the same area of the city. We used the same questions for both sets of interviews, except that those persons in the second sample were first asked to recall their opinions at the time of the assassination and then to give their current opinions.

The questionaire asked whether the assassination would or would not have any effect on the international situation, on the civil rights movement, and on United States prestige. The fourth question asked whether the assassin belonged to a group or acted on his own. The final question asked what punishment Oswald deserved. Those who recommended death, torture, or non-legal punishment were put into one category, and those who were willing to accept whatever verdict was arrived at by due process of law were put into another.

The results of the interviews are presented in Table 1. In the total sample, nearly as many people felt there would be little or no effect on the various issues as felt there would be some effect. It is necessary to examine both the recollected and the current opinions of those inter-

TABLE 1

Immediate and Subsequent Reactions to the Assassination

Respondents thought the assassination:	White sample			Negro sample			Total sample		
	Early ($n=29$)	Retrospective ($n=32$)	Late ($n=32$)	Early ($n=17$)	Retrospective ($n=18$)	Late ($n=18$)	Early ($n=46$)	Retrospective ($n=50$)	Late ($n=50$)[a]
1. Would affect international situation	41%	50%	34%	82%	67%	56%	57%	56%	42%
2. Would affect civil rights	48	72	41	65	89	67	54[b]	79[b]	50
3. Would affect U.S. prestige	33[b]	66[b]	53	93	67	61	55	66	56
4. Was the work of a group	45	56	31	56	67	22	49	60	28
5. Merited severe punishment	44[c]	—	3[c]	82[c]	—	11[c]	59[c]	—	6[c]

[a] There are some minor reductions in n's for specific questions.
[b] $p < .05$ by χ^2 test.
[c] $p < .001$ by χ^2 test.

viewed. The recollected opinions of the total sample about the first, third, and fourth questions show some similarity to the opinions about those questions that were stated on the day of the assassination. A sharp difference is noted on the civil rights issue, however. During the weeks between the two interviews, the mass media stressed that there would be no change in the administration's civil rights policy, so there would seem to be little reason for opinions to have become retrospectively more extreme. On the other hand, President Johnson was considered a Southerner by many, which may have somewhat influenced opinions, and some of the mass media played up the post-mortem identification of President Kennedy with the civil rights movement.

The percentage of those who thought the various issues would be affected declined between the two sets of interviews. This is true both for the first and second interview samples (Early and Late columns), and for the two measures of the second sample (Retrospective and Late columns). There was, however, no difference between the two samples in the effect on United States prestige that was expected. That percentage does decrease from the recollected to the current opinions in the second sample.

For some reason, more people remembered thinking that a group was involved than had actually thought so in our first sample. The specific

groups that the second sample held responsible were considerably different from those named by the first sample, who mainly suspected extreme right-wing or segregationist groups. The people in the second
sample said they had been equally suspicious of right-wing and Communist groups. It seems unlikely that the second sample had had suspicions that were so different from those of the first sample; intervening
information probably influenced their recollections. The major current
suspicion of the second sample was of a Communist or Cuban group;
very few believed a segregationist or extreme right-wing group was involved. Fully 28 per cent of these respondents still believed some group
was involved, even though the mass media consistently played down the
idea.

One of our hypotheses was that more Negroes than whites would
think the assassination would affect the civil rights movement. Another
was that Negroes would give more extreme replies to the question about
Oswald's punishment. More Negroes than whites in both samples did
expect the assassination to affect the civil rights movement. Second,
nearly twice as many Negroes as whites in both samples recommended a
punishment more severe than would be obtained from due process of law.
In fact, Negroes generally expected greater effects on all the issues,
sometimes by as much as 60 per cent more than the whites (on U.S.
prestige). The percentage who expected effects consistently decreased
from the retrospective opinions to the current ones, and it decreased
more for whites than for Negroes on all but the fourth question, where
the exact opposite was found. We interpret this response as meaning
that Negroes were more emotionally involved by the assassination and
also felt more threatened by it.

We paid attention not only to the content of the respondents' replies,
but also to their emotional tone. All respondents were classified for each
question by whether they had answered "yes," "no," or "don't know."[1]
Then the tone of their response was examined. On the day of the assassination, those who replied "No, no effect expected" to the various questions seemed to demonstrate the least emotion. They appeared to be
uninvolved or else convinced that few or no lasting effects would result
from the assassination. "No, I don't think that there will be any effect"
and "I think that Johnson will carry out his program" demonstrate this

---

[1]There seemed to be a reasonable amount of consistency in the responses to the various
questions. The majority of those who replied "yes" to one question replied "yes" to all
the others.

attitude. These people were a minority. Those who replied with "don't know" answers showed two emotional patterns. Some were like those who replied "no" in that they showed relatively little emotion, but they had not yet decided what they thought and seemed to be weighing the alternatives. They had not yet gathered enough information to come to a "rational" conclusion, or at least were not about to commit themselves. Then there were those who seemed too upset to give any answer; e.g., "I don't know, I just don't know what to think," and "Who can say? It's impossible to believe this has happened."

Those who thought there would be effects showed a great deal of emotion. Many seemed so upset that they spoke without any attempt to mask or rationalize their feelings. They exhibited the greatest need to share their thoughts with others. Here we heard, "It will definitely affect the international situation. It has to. He was fighting for humanity, for a fair deal for the people. This must make such a bad impression," and "This will hurt the international situation. This affects everybody. He was a great man with a great future." Many in this group also expressed anger, usually not directly, but in the general tone of their responses. The anger was most obvious in their responses to the question, "What should be done to the assassin when he is captured?" Typical responses were "String him up," or "Kill 'im," or "Take him out and shoot him."

Another factor was the atmosphere during the afternoon and evening when we did the first interviews. It was difficult to characterize, but it might be called one of "frantic quiet." In a city like New York, the every-day noise in the street can be overwhelming; on this day, there was no tumult, no noise. Not everybody seemed to be busy going somewhere. People were completely willing to stop and talk, perhaps to seek additional information. People gathered around news stands or radios to hear what little more they could. People with portable radios were surrounded by listening crowds. Few people hesitated to talk about their personal feelings. When approached, the respondents immediately began to tell us how impossible it was that such a thing had happened. Their confusion and bewilderment may perhaps be seen best in their responses to the question, "When did you first hear about the assassination of the President?" Very few people gave a direct answer. Most began to talk about their disbelief or shock or other feelings. Many seemed to become more concerned as the interview progressed, as if the enormity of the event were just then beginning to seep through their initial shock.

Norman M. Bradburn and Jacob J. Feldman

Public Apathy and Public Grief

One of the problems that has persistently intrigued commentators on the American political scene is the apparent apathy of the average citizen about political events.[1] The large proportion of eligible citizens who do not vote in most elections, the vast numbers of people who are unaware of even the most hotly debated issues, the difficulties faced by citizen groups in trying to rally popular support for a particular piece of legislation—these phenomena are too well known to the student of American politics to need documentation. As Morris Rosenberg has pointed out:

> In terms of amount of time spent in political discussion or activity, amount of money spent for political causes, amount of thought devoted to political affairs, and degree of wholehearted emotional involvement, politics is probably far less important than the family, job and career, friendship relationships, and entertainment. . . . This apathy is truly monumental.[2]

And yet, there are events that cut through the apathy and chronic "know-nothingness" as if the public were hard of hearing and had suddenly turned on its collective hearing aid. The assassination of President Kennedy was such an event.

The traumatic nature of the assassination, the extent and depth of the public response, and the rarity of comparable public reactions to phenomena remote from personal lives suggested that an inquiry into reactions

[1] This investigation was supported by Public Health Service Grant MH09183 from the National Institute of Mental Health.
[2] Morris Rosenberg, "The Meaning of Politics in Mass Society," *Public Opinion Quarterly* (1951), *15*, 5–15.

TABLE 1

Selected Items Indicating Reactions to Assassination

Reactions on first hearing President was dead	Per cent reporting "Very deepest feeling"		
	National sample (n = 1,384)	Washington (n = 194)	Detroit (n = 172)
Personal grief			
Felt so sorry for his wife and children	61%	54%	57%
Felt sorrow that a strong young man had been killed at the height of his powers	52	53	72
Felt the loss of someone very close and dear	45	40	73
Personal indignation			
Felt ashamed that this could happen in our country	50	44	51
Felt angry that anyone should do such a terrible deed	44	49	55
Political consequences			
Worried about how his death would affect the political situation in this country	19	19	40
Worried about how his death would affect our relations with other countries	16	14	32
Felt worried about how the U.S. would carry on without its leader	16	9	45
Other reactions			
Worried how this might affect their own life, job, and future	9	4	27
Thought it was done by some Communist or other radical to get rid of the President	13	6	14
Thought it was done by a segregationist or extreme right-winger	8	9	19
Hoped assassin would be shot down or lynched	6	4	13
Symptoms during four-day period	Per cent answering "Yes"		
Felt very nervous and tense	68%	64%	82%
Felt sort of dazed and numb	57	53	54
Cried	53	62	65
Had trouble getting to sleep	48	34	65
Didn't feel like eating	43	40	66
Felt more tired than usual	42	42	58
Smoked much more than usual	29	28	37
Had rapid heart beats	26	13	32
Had headaches	25	21	41
Had an upset stomach	22	18	21
Hands sweated and felt damp and clammy	17	9	17
Felt dizzy at times	12	5	22

to the assassination might cast some light on the problem of public apathy. In this paper we attempt to do two things. First, we try to specify the exact nature of the response to the assassination—what it was and, more particularly, what it was not. Second, we examine differences in the reactions of several groups in order to find out which parts of the population reacted the most intensely. In examining these differential reactions, we are most concerned with comparisons between groups that have in the past generally appeared to be politically apathetic and groups that have shown more political involvement.

This paper is based on two subsamples of respondents from a larger panel study of behavior related to mental health that the National Opinion Research Center has been conducting during the past year. One of the principal goals of that research has been to study the effects of significant events in the larger environment on individual psychological well-being. In particular, it has been concerned with the effects of political and social crises on the individual's mood and anxiety level. At the time of the assassination, we had nearly completed a second wave of interviewing in four different communities in metropolitan areas of the United States. Immediately after the assassination, NORC began making plans for a nationwide study of reactions to the assassination. In constructing the interview schedule, questions that had been used in the panel study were added to the assassination questionnaire in order to generate data for comparison. In addition to the nationwide sample, a subsample of respondents in two of the communities who had been interviewed during October was reinterviewed with the same questionnaire that had been used in the national study. Thus, for each of the respondents, we have data from the post-assassination interview, from a wave of interviews conducted in October 1963, and from a wave conducted in February and March of 1963. For comparative purposes, we have norms based on a national sample interviewed during the week following the assassination. The samples consisted of 194 people living in a suburban county of the Washington, D.C., metropolitan area, and 172 people living in the inner city of Detroit. All of the respondents in Detroit were Negroes and almost all of those in the Washington area were white.

Sheatsley and Feldman have reported the extremely deep and intense reactions of the national sample in an article in this volume. In this paper we wish to specify in more detail the nature of the responses and to gauge more precisely their depth. Table 1 gives the distributions of

TABLE 2

Distribution of Responses to Interviews in March, October, and November 1963
(Per cent "Yes")

Symptoms	Washington (n = 194)					(Detroit (n = 172)				
	I Mar.	II Oct.	Diff. II−I	III Nov.	Diff. III−II	I Mar.	II Oct.	Diff. II−I	III Nov.	Diff. III−II
Nervous and tense .	57%	50%	−7%	64%	+14%	45%	42%	−3%	82%	+40%
Trouble sleeping . .	21	20	−1	34	+14	30	20	−10	65	+45
More tired than usual	24	21	−3	42	+21	30	25	−5	58	+33
Smoked more than usual	11	8	−3	28	+20	8	8	0	37	+29
Mean score on grief index . .	1.12	.98	−.14	1.67	+.69a	1.13	.93	−.20	2.42	+1.49a
Rapid heart beat . .	13	12	−1	13	+1	15	14	−1	32	+18
Upset stomach . . .	23	23	0	18	−5	18	23	+5	21	−2
Felt dizzy	16	10	−6	5	−5	30	23	−7	22	−1
Headaches	44	46	+2	21	−25	50	46	−4	40	−6
Hands sweated and felt damp and clammy .	15	11	−4	9	−2	13	15	+2	17	+2
Mean score on anxiety index .	1.11	1.03	−.08	.65	−.38a	1.25	1.22	−.03	1.33	+.11

a $p < .001$.

the responses to questionnaire items for the national sample and for the two samples with which we will be concerned in this paper. Part 1 of the table presents responses to a list of various ways people may have felt when they first heard that the President was dead. Responses were given on a four-point scale ranging from "very deepest feeling" to "never occured to me." It can be seen here that the modal response was one of personal grief over the event and of sympathy for the President's family. Reactions to the event are almost entirely in terms of the personal tragedy involved and are almost devoid of any concern about the political implications of the act. However, the Negro sample in Detroit showed both the most grief and the most concern over possible political consequences. The depth of the reaction, both personal and political, shown by the Negroes appears to be in large part a function of Kennedy's identification with the civil rights movement and of fear that his death might have negative consequences for it.

The second part of Table 1 presents data about certain emotional or psychological reactions during the four days. Many of these items are derived from traditional scales of anxiety symptoms, such as the Neuropsychiatric Screening Adjunct developed by Shirley Star in *The Ameri-*

can Soldier.[3] Again, the most frequent responses are those that psychiatrists describe as being typical of grief: nervousness, feelings of numbness, crying, trouble getting to sleep, and loss of energy and appetite. Here we might also note the relative infrequency of such symptoms as dizziness, sweating hands, upset stomach, and headaches, which are traditional somatic indicators of anxiety.

The distinction between grief and anxiety reactions is not clearly made in psychiatric literature. Indeed, it perhaps cannot be precisely made because of a frequent anxiety component in grief reactions. In this particular study, however, we can clearly delineate the type of reactions experienced by our respondents. In general, they are similar to those described by Engel as being characteristic of normal grief.[4] Table 2 presents the distribution of responses to the symptom items during the three different interviews, I (March 1963), II (October 1963), and III (post-assassination).[5] Between March and October there were small changes, some negative, others positive, in the per cent reporting various symptoms. Between the interviews conducted just before the assassination and those conducted immediately afterward, there were, however, very marked increases in nervousness, trouble sleeping, tiredness, and smoking, and, for Negroes, also in rapid heart beats. On the other hand, there were small changes in upset stomachs, dizziness, sweating hands, and, for whites, in rapid heart beats. There was also a considerable percentage decrease in headaches reported by those living in the Washington area, but not by the Negroes in Detroit. The decrease in headaches may be further indication of the external focusing of emotion that is characteristic of grief at the loss of a loved one, as contrasted with the turning inward of emotion in anxiety reactions.[6]

Although most symptoms of normal grief may also, under certain circumstances, be symptoms of anxiety, the converse is not true; i.e., few of the symptoms of anxiety are also symptoms of grief. Thus, in order to be better able to investigate differential reactions, it was convenient to construct two indices that summarized the responses. The first index,

[3] S. A. Stouffer, A. A. Lumsdaine, M. H. Lumsdaine, R. M. Williams, M. B. Smith, I. L. Janis, S. A. Star, L. S. Cottrell, *Studies in Social Psychology in World War II, Vol. IV: Measurement and Prediction* (Princeton, N.J., 1949).

[4] George L. Engel, "Is Grief a Disease?" *Psychosomatic Medicine* (1961), *23*, 18–23.

[5] Three items, "felt sort of dazed and numb," "cried," and "didn't feel like eating" are omitted from the following tables because they were not asked in the pre-assassination interviews.

[6] See Otto Fenichel, *Psychoanalytic Theory of Neuroses* (New York, 1945), p. 253.

which might be called a grief index, consists of four of the items, for which panel data were available, that are similar to those described by Engel as being characteristic of grief: nervousness, trouble in sleeping, loss of energy, and increased smoking. The index score was obtained by giving a person 1 point for each of the symptoms he reported and then adding up the number of points. Thus, each person could obtain a score between 0 and 4 on the index. The second index, which similarly might be called an anxiety index, was scored similarly for each of the remaining five symptoms, which are generally considered indicative of anxiety. Scores on this index thus ranged from 0 to 5. By using the two indices, we can compare changes that occurred within different subgroups of our samples.

As can be seen from Table 2, the mean score on the grief index changed very slightly between March and October, but increased quite significantly between the October and November interviews. The second order differences, i.e., between III–II and II–I, are also significant ($p < .05$) for both samples.

The mean score for the anxiety index remained about the same between March and October for both samples. Between the October and November interviews, the mean for the index declined significantly for the Washington suburban sample, and increased slightly, but not significantly, for the Detroit sample. One must be cautious in interpreting the changes in this index because it is heavily influenced by the decline in the report of one item, headaches, and does not change consistently for both samples. The stability of both indices between March and October and the sharp rise in the grief index, compared with the inconsistent changes in the anxiety index, however, indicate that the reactions were specifically those of grief, and that we can at least say there was not a widespread increase in anxiety in the population.

How might the course of events after the assassination have differed had anxiety been more prevalent? It has been suggested that scapegoating is a common mechanism to release anxiety. Under such conditions, certain segments of the population are widely blamed for all social evils, the belief being that the removal of these agents of the devil from society will bring back the idyllic conditions of an earlier era. Such a belief, which Neumann calls the conspiracy theory of history, has been the basis of various movements in American history such as the Know-Nothing Party of the 1850's, the Ku Klux Klan, and more recently, the John Birch Society.[7] Parsons has ascribed the witch-hunts of the McCarthy period to the strains of rapid social change in the post-war period.[8] The assassination of the President by an admitted Communist sympathizer would seem likely to set the stage for a resurgence of fears about Communist infiltration and of the interpretation of all contemporary problems as being due to the Communist conspiracy. But such a reaction did not come.

The lack of a generalized anxiety reaction, which lack is indicated by our data, would be consistent with the absence of a witch-hunt reaction toward Communists or Communist sympathizers, and with the absence of any noticeable public reaction against those groups or individuals who were most likely to have been in a plot with Oswald. Sheatsley and Feldman have pointed out that, at the time of the interviews, the majority of the people in the country believed that Oswald had been part of a larger plot. At the same time, however, there was a noticeable lack of concern with ferreting out the plotters or taking action against those groups with which Oswald had been associated. The fact that the popular reaction appears to have been almost totally one of grief suggests an explanation, at the psychological level, of the fact that there was little anti-Communist sentiment. If one function of such witch-hunts is to allay widespread anxiety, the absence of anxiety reactions to this event meant that one of the essential motivations for such a mass movement was lacking. One suspects that attempts to start such a movement would have gotten little response from the population.

Turning now from the question of the nature of the reaction to that of differential reactions among subgroups in the population, we should note first that Negroes appeared to show greater grief than whites. The change in the grief index for the Negro respondents in the Detroit sample is significantly greater ($p < .001$) than the change for the respondents living in the Washington area, almost all of whom are white. Since Negroes have traditionally been considered to be politically apathetic, one might cite this difference as evidence that those who are normally apathetic were responding deeply to this event. On the other hand, in view of the recent agitation in the civil rights movement, one

---

[7] Franz Neumann, "Anxiety and Politics," in M. R. Stein, A. J. Vidich, and D. M. White, eds., *Identity and Anxiety* (Glencoe, Illinois, 1960).

[8] Talcott Parsons, "Social Strains in America," in D. Bell, ed., *The New American Right* (New York, 1955).

TABLE 3

Reactions Upon First Hearing of the President's Death, by Sex, Education, and Sensitivity to News

	Washington						Detroit					
	Sex		Education		Anything in news upset you?		Sex		Education		Anything in news upset you?	
Reactions	Male (n=82)	Female (n=112)	H.S. grad. or less (n=132)	Some College (n=62)	Yes (n=78)	No (n=116)	Male (n=63)	Female (n=109)	8th grade or less (n=79)	Some H. S. (n=93)	Yes (n=101)	No (n=71)
Personal grief												
Felt loss of someone close and dear	36%[a]	42%	43%	37%	45%	36%	64%	79%	76%	71%	78%	67%
Felt so sorry for his wife and children	38	65	58	44	57	52	65	81	77	73	75	74
Felt sorry that a strong young man had been killed at the height of his powers	44	58	55	45	59	47	69	73	73	71	72	71
Political consequences												
Worried about how his death would affect the political situation in this country	15	22	20	18	26	15	40	40	44	37	41	40
Worried about how his death would affect our relations with other countries	10	18	15	15	20	11	33	32	32	33	34	31
Worried about how the U.S. would carry on without its leader	4	13	9	8	8	10	43	47	44	46	45	47

[a] Per cent who reported the reaction was their "very deepest feeling."

could argue that the Negroes are emerging from their political apathy and that their greater reaction to the assassination is an indication of their awakening involvement in the political process. One indicator, the proportion voting in 1960, rates the Negroes in Detroit as highly active, with 85 per cent reporting that they voted in the 1960 Presidential election. Whatever their degree of political involvement, however, it is likely that the depth of the reaction shown by Negroes to the President's assassination was in large part a function of his identification with the civil rights movement.

To investigate further the possible effects of political apathy, we will consider three types of differences that have been suggested as related to political involvement: sex differences, differences in educational level, and differences in emotional reactions to events in the news. Before proceeding with the analysis, a word about this last distinction is in order. In the interview conducted in October, respondents were asked if there had been anything in the recent national or international news that had upset them or made them tense. Respondents who answered "yes" to this item gave as examples civil rights incidents in the South, the March on Washington, the Supreme Court decision on prayers in schools, and the then recent overthrow of the Diem regime in Viet Nam. We have used responses to this item as a measure of general sensitivity to political events. We would expect that those who reported having become upset or tense over events of somewhat less dramatic import than the assassination would more likely be emotionally involved in political events.

There is no consistent relationship among the three variables. In the Washington suburb, men were a little more likely than women to be upset about things in the news, but in Detroit, men were somewhat less likely to be upset. In Detroit, those who were upset by something in the news were somewhat more likely to be more educated, but this is not true in the Washington suburb. In each of the communities, the average education of men and women is about the same.

On the whole, we would expect that people who are less emotionally involved in the world about them, particularly in the political world, would show less reaction to the assassination than those who are more involved. We might note here that, at least for sex differences, there is another hypothesis that is equally credible. Since women are reputed to be more emotional than men, women would react more to the assassination, even though by most criteria they are less politically involved than men. Or one could hypothesize that the two tendencies would cancel each other out, thus producing no differences between men and women. Such is the sophistication of our theories that we have a plausible explanation for any possible outcome, or, to put it more crudely, we don't have any idea which way the differences will go.

Table 3 presents the data for the three statements about personal grief and the three about political consequences separately for sex, education, and sensitivity to events in the news.[9] Table 3 shows that, on the whole, women in both Washington and Detroit were more likely than men to feel sorrow and personal loss. In Washington, women were somewhat more likely than men to express worry over the effects of the assassination on the political situation, but the differences were small, and were nonexistent in the Detroit sample. In Washington, those with less education were consistently more likely than those with more education to feel sorrow and personal loss, but the education groups did not differ significantly in worrying about political consequences of the assassination. In Detroit there was little difference between the education groups in either type of response to the assassination. This lack of difference may be in part due to the fact that the respondents in Detroit were on the average so much less educated that the distinction between more and less educated had to be made in terms of whether they had been to high school, rather than in terms of college.

Turning now to those who had reported being upset by something in the news, we see that in Washington these people on the whole were more likely to report feeling sorrow and personal loss, and on two of the three political items were more likely to have worried about the political consequences of the assassination. In Detroit, however, those who had reported being upset by something in the news showed no significant difference from those who did not so report.

Considering the effects of these three variables, then, we would say there is little evidence that those who might be less concerned with events beyond their personal worlds responded less to the assassination than those who presumably were more involved in the world around them.

Let us look, now, at the specific emotional and physiological responses

[9] Only the results for the personal grief and political consequences items are reported. The differences for the personal indignation and other reactions show a similar pattern.

that on the basis of the panel data we have shown to be the character-istic reactions. If one were to look only at the post-assassination means reported in Table 4, one would conclude that women showed consider-ably more grief than men. When one controls for the previous levels of the symptoms, however, one finds that men also displayed much grief, and that there was very little difference between men and women in the amount of change exhibited. Thus, for example, if one looked only at the per cent who reported feeling nervous and tense in a post-assassina-tion interview, one would find 70 per cent of the women, but only 55 per cent of the men. Such a difference, however, masks the fact that in an interview a month before, 68 per cent of these women reported being nervous and tense, but only 26 per cent of these men did. Thus, the men increased 29 percentage points in reported nervousness, while the wom-en increased only two percentage points. When we look at the mean values for the grief index, we see that both men and women showed significant increases in grief symptoms, and that women showed a slightly greater increase than men. The difference between the increases shown by men and women, however, is not statistically significant. The total picture is one of considerable grief felt by both men and women, with very little evidence that women felt it more than men.

Table 4 also shows that in the Washington suburb there was a greater

TABLE 4

Mean Grief Index Scores Before and After the Assassination

Sample	Subsample	Oct. 1963	Nov. 1963	Diff. Nov. — Oct.
Washington	Men $(n = 82)$	.77	1.37	+.60[a]
	Women $(n = 112)$	1.14	1.90	+.76[a]
Detroit	Men $(n = 63)$	.71	2.09	+1.38[a]
	Women $(n = 109)$	1.05	2.60	+1.55[a]
Washington	High school graduate or less $(n = 132)$	.97	1.74	+.77[a]
	Some college $(n = 62)$	1.02	1.53	+.51[a]
Detroit	8th grade or less $(n = 79)$	1.00	2.33	+1.33[a]
	Some high school $(n = 93)$	.87	2.49	+1.62[a]
Washington	Upset by any news in Oct. $(n = 78)$ . .	.96	1.76	+.80[a]
	Not upset $(n = 116)$	1.00	1.62	+.62[a]
Detroit	Upset by any news in Oct. $(n = 101)$.	.95	2.44	+1.49[a]
	Not upset $(n = 71)$	.91	2.41	+1.50[a]

[a] $p < .001.$

change in the grief index for those of less education than for those of more, although again the shift is significant for both groups. Although the difference between the increases for these two groups is greater than for men and women, it is still not statistically significant. In Detroit, however, the tendency was in the opposite direction, those with more education showing more emotional reaction. As we pointed out earlier, this difference between the two samples may be only apparent, because of the different dividing lines used. Since the respondents in Detroit are, on the average, considerably less educated than those in Washington and, in general, show a greater reaction on almost all the indicators of grief, their greater reactions may be in part due to their lower education. There is evidence from the national study, however, that even controlling for educational level, Negroes showed more grief than whites.

Finally, Table 4 shows that those who had reported being upset over something in the news were no more likely to show grief than those who had not been upset. Both groups showed a significant increase in grief responses to the assassination.

Changes in the mean of the anxiety index do not show any significant subgroup differences. Within each of the three control variables, the mean declines significantly for the Washington sample, but irregularly for the Detroit sample.

Discussion

What, then, can we conclude from our data? A conservative interpretation would suggest that there was no appreciable difference in the degree and depth of reaction to the assassination between those who are more and those who are less engaged in their environment. A somewhat more liberal interpretation of the data might suggest that those who traditionally have been thought of as more apathetic—Negroes, the less educated whites, and women—displayed deeper, more emotional reactions than those who have traditionally been thought of as politically involved. No matter which interpretation of the data one accepts, however, the question remains: why did this event provoke such deep reactions among those who are so often untouched by the events of the political world?

In trying to explain the differences between the usually observed reactions to major political events and the widespread emotional response to the assassination, we would like to make two points. The first is that a concept like apathy really involves several dimensions. As Riesman and Glazer have pointed out, a lack of political activity is not the only, or even the best, indicator of apathy.[10] Emotional involvement must also be considered in judging whether a person is apathetic or not. The fact that affect is a psychological variable and is therefore difficult to measure makes it almost impossible for the observer to tell confidence in the efficacy of the governmental process from indifference to political events. We live, after all, in a representative democracy, and delegate the responsibility for political decisions and administration to elected representatives. As long as the system works reasonably well, the bulk of the citizenry is content to leave the governmental officials alone to cope with the problems of running the government as best they can. The fact that many people do not manifest great interest in or knowledge about political matters does not necessarily mean that they do not care about what happens. It may mean only that they are not terribly interested in the details of what their elected representatives, whom they believe to be doing a relatively good job, are doing on their behalf.

The situation is somewhat analogous to a person's view of his health. As long as one is healthy, one is not overly concerned with bodily functioning. General confidence that the body will continue to do its work properly without outside tinkering has given rise to a view that the public is, in fact, indifferent to its health. Indeed, from the point of view of many public health officials, the public is extremely apathetic about health matters. When things begin to go wrong, however, either with the body or the body politic, people are quite capable of taking steps to see that things are put right. As Davies points out:

[People] may be expected to get aroused when state action threatens ... their particular individual or group values. To expect more is to assume a measure of involvement, perspicacity, farsightedness, and perhaps meddlesomeness that is not the endowment of ordinary mortals.[11]

That it may sometimes be too late by the time one realizes something is wrong is not to say that one is indifferent about one's health or about politics, but merely that one has been too confident about the adequacy of the body's functioning.

[10] D. Riesman and N. Glazer, "Political Apathy: Its Social Sources and Subjective Meaning," in B. Rosenberg, I. Gerver, and F. W. Howton, eds., *Mass Society in Crisis* (New York, 1964).
[11] James C. Davies, *Human Nature in Politics* (New York, 1963), p. 55.

Our knowledge about people's emotional reactions to major political events is very slight when contrasted with our knowledge about people's understanding of these events. Although the distinction between emotional concern about an issue and public interest in it has been made by many writers, as Lane indicates, the two dimensions are usually combined into one concept. The justification for such a procedure is the pragmatic one that "questions on 'interest' and 'concern' tend to select out the same populations and to be related to behavior in roughly the same way."[12] But the public's lack of declared interest in political events or information about them may be a very imperfect indicator of their concern about such events, particularly since the use of such an indicator almost always leads to such truisms as that the better educated are more knowledgeable, as indeed they are about almost everything (at least everything that social scientists seem to consider worth studying). As an example of a situation in which the distinction between knowledge and concern can lead to different conclusions, we can cite a study of the Cuban crisis of October 1962.[13] In this study those with more education were more likely to have correct information about the Cuban situation, but those with less education were just as likely to be worried about the consequences of the crisis. Knowledge about events may not be very highly correlated with emotional concern about them.

The second point we wish to make is that the death of a President is a special kind of political event. The death of someone we know and love produces intense feelings of loss, feelings that even the strongest of us do not like to face very often. In these days of the nation-state, the death of the head of state is particularly disturbing because, as the personalized symbol of the nation, he is the object of much of the emotional component of love of country. As far as we can tell from historical records, the death of the President, whether from natural causes or murder, has always provoked large-scale emotional responses in the population. We suspect that the large extent of the grief is caused by the simultaneous loss of a loved person by all the citizens. This collective confrontation of the death of the national leader is as rare as it is disturbing, and appears to trigger off very profound emotional reactions in almost all men, no matter what their status in society.

[12] Robert E. Lane, *Political Life* (Glencoe, Illinois, 1959), p. 134.
[13] David Caplovitz, "Worry over the Cuban Crisis," in N. Bradburn and D. Caplovitz, *Reports on Happiness* (Chicago, 1965).

Part IV

---

*The Impact of the Assassination on
Political Cognitions*

Norma Feshbach and Seymour Feshbach

Personality and Political Values: A Study of Reactions to Two Accused Assassins

This study is concerned with the relationship between personality predispositions, social attitudes, and the reactions to the assassination of President Kennedy and to the central figures of the ensuing events.[1] Although grief over President Kennedy's death was often compounded by horror at the shooting of Oswald, the latter response was by no means as common as the former. During the first hours after the murder of Oswald, we became aware that there were not only some adults and adolescents who were indifferent to this additional tragedy, but also some who were actually pleased by it. With the help of the Dallas authorities, they had judged him guilty and were now gratified that he had received his just deserts, sparing the public the great expense of a trial.

Our first problem, then, was to identify those people who were unmoved or even pleased by this second lawless killing. This inquiry led to additional questions, about variations in the motivations attributed to Oswald and Ruby, in perception and judgment of Ruby, and in responses to the President's death. Sources of these variations were sought in personality characteristics, political affiliation, sex, punitive attitudes toward delinquents and toward members of radical political groups, and, finally, child-rearing values. Our key assumption was that preference for aggressive alternatives in one's personal life—that is, aggressive personality attributes—is associated with preference for aggressive alternatives in one's social life and value system. Although this proposition is clearly

[1] This study was carried out as part of a research project supported by research grant MH08317-01 from the National Institute of Mental Health, United States Public Health Service.

related to the theorizing that has been done about the authoritarian personality, it is much simpler and more modest in its implications.[2]

METHOD

Two days after the funeral of President Kennedy, a questionnaire that included a personality inventory was administered to 315 undergraduates at the University of Colorado and to 64 residents of the town of Boulder, Colorado.[3] The 179 male and 136 female students, who were enrolled in introductory psychology classes, completed the questionnaire during a regular classroom session. One month later, several items from the questionnaire were readministered to the college sample. Because the relative marginal frequencies for the town and college samples were quite similar, because the town sample was more homogeneous in its responses, and because there were so few in the town sample, the analyses reported in this paper are mostly based on the college sample.

The items included in the questionnaire were designed to yield data on the following:

1. Sex, age, place of birth, grade-point average, and religious and political affiliations.

2. Child-rearing experiences and attitudes, including the respondent's punishment history as a child, attitudes toward various disciplinary techniques, and closeness to his father.

3. Political attitudes toward Communists, Cuba, and Castro.

4. Attitudes toward delinquents, assessed by a short, fictitious case history of a juvenile delinquent, about which the respondent answered a series of questions tapping punitive-rehabilitative attitudes toward the delinquent. This measure was included not only because it measures attitudes toward criminal behavior, but also because it is a sensitive index of displaced aggression.[4]

5. Reactions to Kennedy, Oswald, and Ruby, various aspects of which were assessed by about half the items, excluding the personality inventory.

[2] T. W. Adorno, et al., The Authoritarian Personality (New York, 1950).
[3] The authors wish to thank John Gillis, Tish Greiner, Bette Lang, Gilda Kauvar, and Marshall Rosenshine, who freely donated their time as interviewers.
[4] H. Kaufman and S. Feshbach, "Displaced Aggression and its Modification Through Exposure to Antiaggressive Communications," Journal of Abnormal and Social Psychology (1963), 67, 79–82, and "The Influence of Antiaggressive Communications Upon the Response to Provocation," Journal of Personality (1963), 31, 428–44.

6. The following four personality scales, consisting of MMPI-type items, were included at the end of the questionnaire. Satisfactory reliabilities have been established for each of these scales.

a. Neurotic undercontrol was measured by a 22-item scale based upon a preliminary instrument developed by Block at the University of California, Berkeley. It was designed to assess impulsiveness and inability to delay gratification.

b. Aggression anxiety was measured by a 21-item scale constructed by the authors and designed to assess the degree to which aggressiveness is inhibited.

c. Covert aggression was measured by a 15-item scale based upon Bendig's revision of the Buss-Durkee aggression questionnaire.[5] The items are concerned, for the most part, with hostile affect.

d. Overt aggression was measured by an 11-item scale, derived from the revised Buss-Durkee inventory and primarily concerned with overt aggressive behavior.

In order to facilitate the analysis of the personality data, the distribution for each instrument was split approximately into quartiles. Because of the differences between males and females on the various scales, the quartile division was done separately for the male and female distributions. The lowest and highest quartiles were then compared.

RESULTS

Town sample marginals will be presented with those of the college group. However, unless otherwise noted, the analyses are based on the college sample. Reactions to Kennedy, to Oswald, and to Ruby will be reviewed in sequence, each of these being considered in turn as a dependent variable.

Reactions to Kennedy's death

Reports of strong emotional disturbance over the death of President Kennedy were almost universal. In response to one question, 91 per cent of the sample said they were extremely shocked. In response to a second, 62 per cent said they were extremely upset and 31 per cent fairly upset by

---

[5] A. W. Bendig, "Factor-analytic Scales of Covert and Overt Hostility," *Journal of Consulting Psychology* (1962), *26*, 200; A. H. Buss and Ann Durkee, "An Inventory for Assessing Different Kinds of Hostility," *Journal of Consulting Psychology* (1957), *21*, 343–49.

TABLE 1

Analysis of Immediate Reactions to President Kennedy's Death

Group	Extremely upset	Fairly upset
Townspeople $(n = 64)$	75%	22%
All college students $(n = 315)$	62	31
Male Democratic students $(n = 66)$	59^b	38
Male Republican students $(n = 76)$	52^a	38
Female Democratic students $(n = 42)$	90^{ab}	7
Female Republican students $(n = 61)$	72^a	25
Strongly favored Kennedy's policies $(n = 122)$ . . .	75^b	25
Moderately favored them $(n = 114)$	57^b	39
Moderately opposed them $(n = 45)$	60	36
Strongly opposed them $(n = 20)$	45^b	10

^{a} $p < .05$, comparing figures in the same section of the same column.
^{b} $p < .01$, similarly.

the President's death. The degree of unanimity on the first question does not provide much variance for further analysis. Nevertheless, there was a significant, although not surprising, sex difference on this item: 97 per cent of the females and 87 per cent of the males said they were extremely shocked.

In addition to genuine distress, the forces of propriety and social conformity undoubtedly contributed to the 93 per cent of the students who said they were extremely or fairly upset; only 7 per cent of the responses were distributed among the remaining five answers. However, despite the massing of responses, even the choice between extremely and fairly upset proved to be linked to a number of variables. Here again there was a sex difference: 80 per cent of the females, but only 56 per cent of the males, said they were extremely upset by President Kennedy's death. Both Republicans and Democrats were very upset by the assassination.

However, there were other differences between the two groups, particularly among the female students, where significantly more Democrats (90 per cent) than Republicans (72 per cent) reported being extremely upset (see Table 1). A question about Kennedy's policies turned out to be a better indicator than political affiliation. Of those who strongly supported the late President's policies, 75 per cent were extremely upset and 25 per cent fairly upset by his death. They contrasted sharply with the small group of respondents who were strongly opposed to his policies, of whom only 45 per cent were extremely and 10 per cent fairly upset. Of the various personality measures, only the aggression anxiety index yielded consistent and statistically significant differences on this question for both males and females. About 25 per cent more high anxiety than low anxiety students stated that they were extremely upset by the assassination.

Reactions to Oswald's death

Table 2 shows that, as might be anticipated, both the town and college samples were far more upset by Kennedy's death than by Oswald's. The

TABLE 2

Analysis of Immediate Reactions to Oswald's Death

Group	Extremely or fairly upset	Little upset	No feeling or pleased
Townspeople $(n = 64)$	48%	26%	26%
Students:			
Male $(n = 179)$	38[b]	31	30[b]
Female $(n = 136)$	61[b]	20	16[b]
Neurotic undercontrol			
Low-scoring males $(n = 37)$	57[b]	32	11[b]
High-scoring males $(n = 44)$	20[b]	27	52[b]
Low-scoring females $(n = 39)$	66[b]	27	7[b]
High-scoring females $(n = 39)$	43[b]	31	26[b]
Covert aggression			
Low-scoring males $(n = 38)$	63[b]	24	14[b]
High-scoring males $(n = 34)$	27[b]	29	45[b]
Low-scoring females $(n = 31)$	67	13	20
High-scoring females $(n = 31)$	48	19	32
Overt aggression			
Low-scoring males $(n = 39)$	46	36[a]	19[b]
High-scoring males $(n = 29)$	38	14[a]	48[b]
Low-scoring females $(n = 33)$	60	30	6
High-scoring females $(n = 23)$	47	22	22
Degree upset by Kennedy's death			
Extremely upset males $(n = 95)$	52[b]	32	15[b]
Fairly upset males $(n = 69)$	23[b]	33	44[b]
Extremely upset females $(n = 102)$	60	20	17
Fairly upset females $(n = 30)$	50	27	23
Attitude toward children's fistfighting			
Would encourage it $(n = 106)$	44	22	32[a]
Would discourage it $(n = 199)$	50	29	20[a]

[a] $p < .05$, comparing adjacent, paired numbers in the same column.
[b] $p < .01$, similarly.

townspeople were significantly more disturbed by both deaths than the college men. Although Democrats and Republicans responded similarly, 61 per cent of the women, compared with 38 per cent of the men, said they were extremely or fairly upset by Oswald's death. Whether this sex difference merely reflects the social norm that permits women in our culture to acknowledge emotions more freely than men or whether it points to a genuine difference in affective involvement and responsiveness cannot be ascertained from these data alone.

An examination of the personality correlates yielded several predicted differences in the responses to the killing of Oswald. Both male and female subjects who scored high on neurotic undercontrol were substantially less upset by Oswald's death than those who scored low. In fact, fully half the males who scored high indicated that they were indifferent to or pleased by the murder of Oswald. This kind of person is typically explosive and impulsive, with limited ego control. Psychoanalytic theory suggests that the affective relationships of such a person are likely to be shallow and his empathic responsiveness minimal. It is consistent with this interpretation that significantly more of those who scored high on neurotic undercontrol (24 per cent) than of those who scored low (11 per cent) reported that their father did not spend enough time with them when they were children.

The findings for the aggression anxiety variable were similar for both deaths, but the differences only attained the $p < .10$ level of significance. The measures of aggression proved to be more discriminating, especially for the males. Many more of the males who scored high on covert and overt aggression than who scored low reported feelings of indifference or pleasure at Oswald's death. Those respondents who had a minimum of bitterness and aggression were the most upset by the shooting of Oswald. Hostility much more than aggression anxiety determined the reaction to Oswald's murder, but not to Kennedy's.

The males showed a strong, positive relationship between the degrees of disturbance at Oswald's death and at President Kennedy's death. Although this association seems quite reasonable, we shall report additional evidence that different factors influenced the responses to the two deaths. Thus, significantly more respondents who encouraged fistfighting in youngsters for self-defense were pleased by Oswald's death than respondents who were less sanguine about fighting. No such relationship was found for the reactions to President Kennedy's death. We also examined the reasons given for Oswald's shooting of Kennedy, the reasons given for Ruby's shooting of Oswald, opinions about whether Oswald had accomplices, and the amount of time the father had spent with the respondent, but these were not significantly related to the reactions to Oswald's death.

Exposure to television and radio

We digress from our central theme to consider how much the respondents watched television or listened to the radio. The amount of voluntary exposure to the mass media during this period may reasonably be taken as an index of emotional involvement, although, to be sure, there were other factors. Table 3 shows that the town sample watched more television than the college sample on each of the three days following the President's assassination, although both groups reported equal access to television. This finding is consistent with the greater degree of emotional disturbance over both deaths reported by the town sample. Simi-

TABLE 3

Analysis of Time Spent on the Mass Media

	Nov. 23		Nov. 24		Nov. 25	
Group	More than two hours	Two hours or less	More than two hours	Two hours or less	More than two hours	Two hours or less
Townspeople ($n = 64$)	87%[b]	11%	75%[b]	24%	80%[b]	18%
Students ($n = 315$)	64[b]	35	53[b]	47	60[b]	39
Male Democrats ($n = 66$)	72[a]	26	68[b]	30	56	42
Male Republicans ($n = 76$)	56[a]	43	46[b]	55	52	48[a]
Female Democrats ($n = 42$)	74	24	57	40	71	26
Female Republicans ($n = 61$) . . .	59	41	51	49	69	31[a]
Neurotic undercontrol						
Low-scoring males ($n = 37$) . . .	75[a]	25	—	—	—	—
High-scoring males ($n = 44$) . . .	48[a]	52	—	—	—	—
Low-scoring females ($n = 77$) . .	77	23	—	—	—	—
High-scoring females ($n = 39$) . .	67	33	—	—	—	—
Aggression anxiety						
Low-scoring males ($n = 37$) . . .	—	—	—	—	30[b]	70
High-scoring males ($n = 40$) . . .	—	—	—	—	63[b]	38
Low-scoring females ($n = 30$) . .	—	—	—	—	63	37
High-scoring females ($n = 39$) . .	—	—	—	—	79	18

[a] $p < .05$, comparing adjacent, paired numbers in the same section of the same column.
[b] $p < .01$, similarly.

TABLE 4

Analysis of Suggestions About Oswald's Motives

Group	Suggested personal reasons	Suggested political reasons
Townspeople ($n = 64$)	43%	20%
Students ($n = 315$)	46	29
Male Democrats ($n = 66$)	48	24[a]
Male Republicans ($n = 76$)	41	44[a]
Female Democrats ($n = 42$)	58	17
Female Republicans ($n = 61$)	48	34
Covert aggression		
Low-scoring males ($n = 38$)	37	22[a]
High-scoring males ($n = 34$)	45	45[a]
Low-scoring females ($n = 31$)	48	29
High-scoring females ($n = 31$)	54	35
Overt aggression		
Low-scoring males ($n = 39$)	56	17[a]
High-scoring males ($n = 29$)	38	45[a]
Low-scoring females ($n = 33$)	54	30
High-scoring females ($n = 23$)	48	34

[a] $p < .05$, comparing adjacent figures in the same column.

larly consistent is the finding that significantly more Democrats than Republicans watched television or listened to the radio for more than two hours on the first two days after the assassination. A sex difference did not appear until the day of the President's funeral.

The analysis of the personality variables also yielded a fairly regular pattern over the three days. The significance levels vary, depending upon the particular day and the sex of the respondents, but we found that greater exposure to television or radio is associated with all four variables. The respondents with deeper empathic feelings and with the least hostility and aggression appear to have been more emotionally involved in the events.

Beliefs about Oswald's motives

An analysis of the reasons given for Oswald's shooting of President Kennedy is presented in Table 4. These data are derived from responses to an open-ended question. The first three reasons given (which comprised 99 per cent of all the reasons given) were coded and grouped into two broad categories: personal assertions, that Oswald did it because he was insane, fanatic, wanted to avenge a personal grievance, etc., and political assertions, that Oswald did it because he was a Communist, a conspirator, differed with the President over Cuba, etc.

The rationale behind this categorization was the assumption that aggressive and suspicious persons were more likely to attribute conspiratorial and political motives to Oswald than to think of him primarily as a warped personality. The analyses are based on the first reason offered by the respondent. Preliminary analyses that took the other reasons offered by the respondent into account yielded results similar to those yielded by the simpler analysis we finally used.

Table 4 shows that about twice as many Republicans as Democrats believed that Oswald shot Kennedy for political reasons, and that there was a weaker but statistically significant tendency for Democrats to think more in terms of personal factors. We found that the measures of neurotic undercontrol and aggression anxiety were unrelated to inferences about Oswald's motives. However, as with the degree of disturbance over the shooting of Oswald, differences in covert and overt aggression were significantly associated for males with the reasons offered for Oswald's action. Males high in aggression were much more likely than those low in aggression to attribute Oswald's attack on the President to political motives.

Beliefs about accomplices

A structured question that asked whether Oswald was part of a conspiracy was included in the questionnaire. Beliefs about whether Oswald had accomplices and about his motives should be closely related. Table 5 shows that 60 per cent of those who offered political motives believed that Oswald had accomplices, but only 35 per cent of those who offered personal reasons thought so. Even after eliminating from the political reason group those who explicitly asserted that Oswald shot Kennedy because he was part of a conspiracy, there were still 57 per cent of this group who felt that Oswald had accomplices.

Although the correlations for the reasons offered for Oswald's action are similar to those for the opinions about accomplices, they are not as strong for the latter. Only the differences between those high and low in overt aggression are statistically significant. Those high in overt aggressive tendencies were more likely to believe that Oswald had accomplices; those low in overt aggressive tendencies were more likely to believe that Oswald carried out the assassination by himself.

TABLE 5

Analysis of Beliefs About Accomplices

Group	Believed Oswald had accomplices	Had no idea about it	Believed Oswald acted alone
Townspeople ($n = 64$)	39%	22%	39%
Students ($n = 315$)	43	29	27
Male Democrats ($n = 66$)	35	35	27
Male Republicans ($n = 76$)	47	26	25
Female Democrats ($n = 42$)	45	29	26
Female Republicans ($n = 61$)	51	23	26
Overt aggression			
Low-scoring males ($n = 39$)	36	20	44[a]
High-scoring males ($n = 29$)	48	28	17[a]
Low-scoring females ($n = 33$)	27	36	36
High-scoring females ($n = 23$)	52	30	17
Reasons suggested for Oswald's act			
Personal ($n = 145$)	35[b]	31[a]	32
Political ($n = 92$)	60[b]	18[a]	21
Recommended action against Cuba			
Bomb, invade ($n = 45$)	64[b]	20	16[a]
Help, ignore, stop trade ($n = 249$) . .	40[b]	30	30[a]
Recommended action against Castro			
Execute ($n = 50$)	56[a]	28	16[a]
Ignore, remove, jail ($n = 245$)	40[a]	29	31[a]

[a] $p < .05$, comparing adjacent figures in the same column.
[b] $p < .01$, similarly.

Consistent political orientation is shown by the relationship between attitudes toward Cuba and opinions about Oswald's accomplices. The students who would like to invade Cuba and to execute Castro were much less likely to believe that Oswald acted by himself than those who favored less aggressive actions.

Perceptions of Ruby

Oswald was uniformly disliked. He had committed a grievous, reprehensible act, and the respondents undoubtedly reflected national sentiment in their intensely negative perceptions of him. But how did they perceive Jack Ruby, who also was an assassin? We gave the respondents adjective checklists and asked them to circle those adjectives they felt described Ruby's personality. It was evident from the frequencies with which the various adjectives were checked that Ruby's image was far from heroic. Considering those adjectives checked by at least 30 per cent of the sample, Ruby was perceived as irrational, emotional, irresponsible, bitter, stupid, childish, hostile, and radical. Only 22 per cent of the sample saw him as patriotic, and even fewer saw him as loyal. Not one respondent described him as noble, and very few felt that he was warm, dashing, brave, or even sociable. The respondents made an interesting and perhaps appropriate discrimination in that 38 per cent described him as hostile, but only 10 per cent described him as cruel.

A total score was derived for each respondent by subtracting the number of negative from the number of positive adjectives. The distribution of these scores and of the individual adjectives did not show any significant variation as a function of sex, political party, or personality traits. As might be expected, those who were most upset by Oswald's death entertained the most negative image of Ruby, but even here the difference between the most upset and the least upset attained only the $p < .10$ significance level. Regardless of the attitude expressed toward Oswald's death or toward Kennedy's, Ruby was predominantly perceived as immature, impulsive, and inadequate.

Beliefs about Ruby's motives

Beliefs about Ruby's motives were elicited by an open-ended question. As for the same question about Oswald, the first three reasons offered were coded. The figures in Table 6 are based upon the first reason given.

The most common explanation was that Ruby was angered and upset,

TABLE 6

Analysis of Beliefs About Ruby's Motives

Group	Reason suggested			
	Emotional	Revengeful	Patriotic	Conspiratorial
Townspeople ($n = 64$)	42%	19%	8%	9%
Students ($n = 315$)	39	23	13	13
Neurotic undercontrol				
Low-scoring males ($n = 37$)	46	14[a]	11	22
High-scoring males ($n = 44$)	31	34[a]	11	9
Low-scoring females ($n = 39$)	40	26	10	12
High-scoring females ($n = 39$)	41	20	15	8
Reasons suggested for Oswald's act				
Personal ($n = 141$)	41	18	11	9[a]
Political ($n = 92$)	31	27	16	18[a]

[a] $p < .05$, comparing adjacent figures in the same column.

and acted impulsively. A perhaps related reason, coded separately because of its frequency, was the suggestion (no doubt based on Ruby's
public statement) that he killed Oswald to avenge Mrs. Kennedy. Only
13 per cent of the college students suggested that Ruby's motive was
patriotism. The same percentage suggested that he and Oswald might
both have been members of a conspiracy.

The motives suggested for Ruby are more complex and varied than
those suggested for Oswald. Although respondents who gave political
motives for Oswald's action were significantly more likely to think that
Ruby was a member of a conspiracy, they also more frequently suggested
revenge and patriotism as motives. Attribution of patriotic motives to
Ruby would seem to be, at least on the surface, directly opposed to perception of him as a conspirator. Yet there might well be a functional
similarity between these two interpretations of his behavior, which is
more evident in the breakdown of the aggression variables. A greater
percentage of the high aggressive groups than of the low aggressive
groups, whether covert or overt, male or female, offered patriotic or conspiratorial motives. It is as if the initial response of the very hostile individual were to enhance Ruby by attributing patriotic motives to him or
to condemn him by perceiving him as a conspirator.

Opinions about treatment of Ruby

In addition to their opinion of Ruby, the respondents were asked what
they thought should be done with him. Although 15 per cent of both the
town and college samples felt they could not make any recommendation
until after the trial, the rest were willing to choose among the alternatives
provided. We were particularly interested in the factors associated with
the recommendation that Ruby be shot, and, secondarily, in those associated with the recommendation of a suspended or light sentence. Table 7
shows that about half the respondents felt that Ruby should be given a
long prison term. The college students again revealed a more aggressive
orientation than the townspeople in that 16 per cent of the former, but
only 6 per cent of the latter, were in favor of shooting Ruby. Republicans
and Democrats felt similarly about this, but significantly more males
than females thought Ruby should be shot. It is noteworthy that more
of the males also selected the most lenient option, the difference between
the sexes achieving the $p < .05$ level when the frequencies for suspended
sentence and short prison term are combined.

The personality variables, with minor exceptions, failed to discriminate on this question, perhaps because of the complicating effects of one's feelings about Oswald's death. While there was no relationship between recommendations for Ruby's punishment and feelings about President Kennedy's death, feelings about Oswald's death correlated predictably with recommendations about Ruby. Significantly fewer of those respondents who were not upset by the killing of Oswald favored shooting Ruby, and significantly more favored a short or suspended sentence.

Attitudes toward Castro and Cuba are more revealing. Thirty-four per cent of the respondents who would like Castro executed, but only 14 per cent of those who want him removed or left alone, thought Ruby should be shot. At the same time, the group that had the highest proportion of respondents who recommended a suspended sentence is this very group that favored Castro's execution. Similarly, the respondents who advocated the bombing or invasion of Cuba were also the ones who were likely to advocate either execution or a short prison term for Ruby. Those who favored strong aggressive action against Cuba took the most

TABLE 7

Analysis of Recommendations About Ruby

| | Ruby should: | | | | |
Group	be shot.	get a long sentence.	be put in a mental hospital.	get a short sentence.	get a suspended sentence.
Townspeople ($n = 64$)	6%[a]	53%	17%	6%	3%
Students ($n = 315$)	16[a]	50	10	6	3
Males ($n = 179$)	21[a]	44[a]	10	8	4
Females ($n = 136$)	11[a]	57[a]	10	4	1
Degree upset by Oswald's death					
Extremely or fairly upset ($n = 145$)	21[b]	55	6	2[a]	7[a]
Little upset ($n = 71$)	21[a]	53	17	1[b]	0[a]
Not much feeling ($n = 69$) . . .	7[ab]	54	14	16[ab]	7[a]
Recommended action toward Cuba					
Bomb, invade ($n = 45$)	31[a]	31[b]	11	13	4
Help, ignore, stop trade ($n = 249$)	16[a]	54[b]	10	6	2
Recommended action toward Castro					
Execute ($n = 50$)	34[b]	28[b]	12	10	8[a]
Ignore, remove, jail ($n = 245$) .	14[b]	54[b]	10	6	2[a]

[a] $p < .05$, comparing figures in the same section of the same column.
[b] $p < .01$, similarly.

extreme positions toward Ruby. They were either the most accepting of his aggressive act or the most ready to advocate extreme punishment.

Changes in attitudes

The results up to this point have been based upon the data gathered two days after the President's funeral. A number of items were readministered to 224 students from the initial college sample, and the new scores were subjected to detailed analysis. On the whole, stability of response rather than change was the rule. In addition, the changes in the scores were, with minor exceptions, not correlated with personality variables, sex, or political affiliation. Although these exceptions were significant, statistical regression effects could not be ruled out. Consequently, in Table 8 we shall simply summarize the changes that took place and not attempt to present breakdowns for particular subgroups.

On the first question, which dealt with attitudes toward President Kennedy's policies, there were significantly more negative than positive changes. It is possible that these shifts reflected genuine changes in attitudes toward the Kennedy program, perhaps resulting from an attempt to reduce the dissonance created by his loss. However, it seems more reasonable to assume that, given the social constraints and emotional upheaval produced by the President's death, respondents were motivated to feel that they were in greater agreement with the President's policies than they actually were. One month later they could feel freer to express their real opinions. The situation is reversed for feelings about Oswald's death. Immediate expressions of indifference and pleasure gave way with time to the respondent's belief that he was more upset than he really was. Here the assumption is that social norms operated to lower the accuracy of the second report.

TABLE 8
Changes in Beliefs One Month Afterward Among Students

Belief	No change	More	Less
Favored Kennedy's policies $(n = 223)$	70%	10%[b]	20%[b]
Upset about Oswald's death $(n = 222)$	47	35[b]	18[b]
Oswald had accomplices $(n = 222)$	54	12[b]	34[b]
Described Ruby favorably $(n = 224)$	25	51[b]	24[b]
Recommended severe punishment for Ruby $(n = 222)$	62	16	22

[b] $p < .01$, comparing figures in same row.

Whereas for the first two questions the respondent essentially had to recall his feelings, the remaining questions dealt with continuing situations that had immediate stimulus value. Changes on these questions were less subject to the distortions that may have influenced reports of feelings about the President's policies and about Oswald's death. One notes, for example, a substantial shift toward believing that Oswald carried out the assassination without accomplices. The shift probably reflects the reports carried by the mass media during this period. It is likely that the increased feeling that Oswald was not part of a conspiracy (thus eliminating Ruby as a conspirator) contributed to the positive shift in the impression of Ruby. At the same time, greater familiarity with Ruby may have also contributed to a more positive image of him. Recommendations about the treatment of Ruby remained relatively stable. The few shifts that did occur tended to be in the less punitive direction. Both at the time of the shooting of Oswald and one month later, the great majority of the respondents did not favor execution for Ruby.

DISCUSSION

In reviewing the data as a whole, one is impressed with the uniformity of the responses to the assassinations of President Kennedy and Oswald. Whether Republican or Democrat, male or female, college student or local resident, the respondent was likely to have been very upset by the sudden loss of the President, disturbed by the lawless killing of Oswald, and neither vindictive nor forgiving toward Ruby. The event produced massive effects, whose power was such that they dominated the responses and dwarfed the influence of preexisting personal factors. At the same time, there was some variability in reactions, which was not random but systematically related to demographic, attitudinal, and personality factors. Knowledge of a respondent's political attitudes, sex, degree of impulse control, and hostile tendencies enables one to predict idiosyncratic responses to this specific, concrete situation. Moreover, the data tie together the diverse feelings and opinions about the different aspects of the events into a consistent and meaningful pattern.

The particular independent variables that were selected for this study were aggressive impulses and attitudes in both interpersonal relations and the political realm. These variables proved to be systematically related to feelings about Oswald's death, to the amount of voluntary exposure to television and radio, to the motives imputed to Oswald and Ruby, and to the treatment recommended for Ruby.

The respondent who is ready to attack when frustrated is the one who was likely to be pleased by Oswald's death, to feel that Oswald's act was politically inspired, and to believe that Ruby was a patriot who should be let free with a suspended sentence or, contrastingly, a conspirator who ought to be shot. When one examines the personality characteristics of those respondents who wanted to execute Castro or invade Cuba, who believed that the assassination of the President was carried out by a Communist conspiracy, and who were extremely lenient or punitive toward Ruby, one finds the same hostile person.

Personality factors were nevertheless not the most important determinants of responses to the President's assassination or of positions on Castro and Cuba. We have already commented on the overriding significance of the situation presented by the two assassinations. The variations in response that did occur were influenced not only by hostility, impulsiveness, and aggression anxiety, but also by specific attitudes toward the principal figures involved. Respondents who were strongly opposed to President Kennedy's policies were less upset by his death than those who had supported him. Respondents who were very upset by the killing of Oswald perceived Ruby more negatively and were more disposed to recommend severe punishment than those who were indifferent to or pleased by Oswald's death.

Whether the variance in response was due to specific attitudes or to more general personality traits, the fact that the situation was not completely overwhelming, and that most respondents appeared to maintain their own typical attitudes and opinions, made it possible to discern systematic correlations between the reactions to President Kennedy, to Oswald, and to Ruby. Although the correlations observed were far from one-to-one relationships, it is encouraging that some part of the responses to a unique, socially significant event could be predicted from knowledge of more general predispositional variables. This study thus may have served three purposes: acquiring data on the validity of specific personality and attitudinal inventories, field testing a general hypothesis that links aspects of political behavior to personality variables, and enhancing our understanding of the meaning and impact of an important, historic event.

David O. Sears

Effects of the Assassination of President Kennedy on Political Partisanship

Political commentators have long been fascinated by the relative harmony prevailing in the American democratic system. Explanations have often focused upon the American two-party system, particularly on the role of the opposition party and its leaders. In the United States a defeated opposition usually accepts the will of the majority with relative calm, if not complete equanimity.[1] In general, differences of opinion appear not to be imbued with the irreconcilable, battle-to-the-death quality often present in partisan debate elsewhere.

To some the pacific quality of American politics indicates apathy or an absence of genuine and important differences of opinion between victor and vanquished. Available comparative data indicate, however, that Americans are among the most partisan of democratically governed citizens.[2] A perhaps more plausible explanation concerns leadership.

I wish to thank Mr. David Hoffman for conducting the experimental sessions, Miss Sura Boxerman for helping with the data analysis and Dr. Kent M. Dallett for arranging distribution of the premeasure. The research was supported by a grant from the National Science Foundation.

[1] See V. O. Key, Jr., *Public Opinion and American Democracy* (New York, 1961), p. 468. Several other studies have reported that partisans of a losing candidate upgrade their evaluation of the victor after an election. See I. H. Paul, "Impressions of Personality, Authoritarianism, and the *Fait Accompli* Effect," *Journal of Abnormal and Social Psychology* [*JASP*] (1956), *53*, 338–44; D. O. Sears and J. L. Freedman, "Organizational and Judgmental Modes of Cognitive Conflict Resolution," *American Psychologist* (1961), *16*, 409; B. H. Raven and P. S. Gallo, "The Effects of Nominating Conventions, Elections, and Reference-Group Identification upon the Perception of Political Figures," *Human Relations* (in press).

[2] G. A. Almond and S. Verba, *The Civic Culture: Political Attitudes and Democracy in Five Nations* (Princeton, N.J., 1963), p. 155.

A broad spectrum of possible leaders exists, from which almost any may be selected without spurring dissident elements of the population to revolt. Most important, opposition leaders are usually considered to be competent and acceptable rulers.

The pattern of acceptable opposition leadership is an important one. Potential deviations from it are met with alarm by partisans of the majority. Their concern is usually directed rather specifically toward two possibilities. One is that the opposition might lose its role as an acceptable alternative to the party in power if it should become dominated by leaders with extreme ideological positions. Liberals frequently expressed such a concern about the 1964 Republican presidential nomination. Each American political party is generally thought respectable by its opponents, a pattern that does not hold in many nations. Almond and Verba found that Democrats make many more favorable than unfavorable statements about Republicans, and vice versa, whereas in such countries as Italy and Mexico partisans are much more likely to make negative statements about their opponents.[3]

The other possibility is that opposition factions, if dominated by leaders with extreme ideological positions, might affect the locus of the "middle of the road." For example, Richard Rovere, in a despairing moment early in the 1960s, lamented that the "middle of the road" appeared to be about halfway between the relatively centrist John F. Kennedy and the indisputably rightist Robert Welch. Similarly, liberals feared that the nomination of Senator Goldwater in 1964 might broaden the spectrum of respectable political positions to include those previously almost unique to the extreme right wing.

To worry in this way about the "middle of the road" is to assume that the influence of a political opposition extends far beyond its own strong partisans, extends indeed to its opponents, or else it could not affect the "middle of the road." Of course, the substantial influence of preferred (and presumably positive) reference groups is well documented, and generally obeys a simple consistency principle.[4] The more a person is

[3] *Ibid.*, p. 131.

[4] See T. M. Newcomb, *Personality and Social Change* (New York, 1943) ; P. F. Lazarsfeld, B. Berelson, and H. Gaudet, *The People's Choice* (New York, 1948), chap. 4; A. Campbell, P. Converse, W. Miller, and D. Stokes, *The American Voter* (New York, 1960), chap. 12.

attracted to or identifies with a group, the more it can influence his opinions. The same holds for individual sources of information.[5]

Much less is known about the influence of nonpreferred (and presumably negative) reference groups. The consistency principle would seem to provide little reason to worry about their seductive powers, however. A negative reference group should positively influence the opinions of its followers, to be sure, but it should negatively influence the opinions of its opponents. Thus when an opposition party disagrees with the majority position, the disagreement should merely strengthen the resolve of the latter's proponents (i.e., have a boomerang effect).

This reasoning about the power of a political opposition has two important shortcomings, however. The first is that there is little empirical evidence about the influence of presumably negative reference groups or communicators, and what little evidence there is is somewhat contradictory.[6] The second is that the consistency principle offers no guidelines for the joint influence of preferred and nonpreferred groups when both take positions (whether they agree or disagree). And for a political opposition, this is the decisive situation.

A heuristic analogy might be made, however, with research on opinion discrepancy. Substantial evidence indicates that the more strongly a person disagrees with a propagandist, the more the person will change his opinions, but only up to a point. Given extreme disagreement, there is little influence on the person's opinions.[7] These findings are most easily explained by the notion that ideological positions are divided, in a given person's mind, into a "latitude of acceptance" and a "latitude of rejection." Positions acceptable to him may be defined as constituting a "latitude of acceptance," and the advocacy of one of these positions (usually little different from his most favored position) is likely to in-

[5] See C. E. Osgood and P. H. Tannenbaum, "The Principle of Congruity and the Prediction of Attitude Change," *Psychological Review* (1955), *62*, 42–55; L. Festinger, *A Theory of Cognitive Dissonance* (Stanford, Calif., 1957).
[6] See A. R. Cohen, "A Dissonance Analysis of the Boomerang Effect," *Journal of Personality* (1962), *30*, 75–88.
[7] C. I. Hovland, O. J. Harvey, and M. Sherif, "Assimilation and Contrast Effects in Reactions to Communication and Attitude Change," *JASP* (1957), *55*, 244–52; S. Fisher and A. Lubin, "Distance as a Determinant of Influence in a Two-Person Serial Interaction Situation," *JASP* (1958), *56*, 230–38; E. Aronson, J. A. Turner, and J. M. Carlsmith, "Communicator Credibility and Communication Discrepancy as Determinants of Opinion Change," *JASP* (1963), *67*, 31–36; J. L. Freedman, "Involvement, Discrepancy, and Change," *JASP* (1964), *69*, 290–95.

fluence his opinion positively. Positions he finds objectionable, on the other hand, may be defined as constituting a "latitude of rejection," and the advocacy of one of *these* positions (usually very different from his most favored position) is likely to have little success—if it does not actually have a boomerang effect.[8]

Political parties and leaders may be arrayed in people's minds in a similar fashion. If so, acceptable parties and leaders would presumably be able to influence their opinions positively, but objectionable parties and leaders would not. This reasoning yields two concrete hypotheses. First, the success of a political party's attempt to influence a person's opinions should depend upon whether it falls in his latitude of acceptance or his latitude of rejection. Therefore, if Almond and Verba's data are accepted, the nonpreferred major party in the United States should be able to influence the opinions of its opponents positively when no other information about the issue is available, whereas the analogous effort in Italy or Mexico should have no influence or a negative influence. Second, disagreement between two political parties on a given issue should produce some kind of a compromise response in a person if both parties fall within his latitude of acceptance, but should merely increase his adherence to the preferred party's position if the nonpreferred party falls in his latitude of rejection. The same principles should hold, of course, for arrays of political leaders.

Pilot research has supported these two hypotheses for American political parties. The research setting was designed to maximize the effect of the *source* of information on the respondent's opinions by minimizing the effect of his existing opinions on the issue and by making the source's position as clear as possible.[9] The present research, originally designed to replicate these findings and to extend them to political leaders, was suspended when the President was assassinated. Testing was resumed two weeks later because the procedure being used appeared to be relevant to two dimensions of public opinion presumably affected by the assassination.

First, many leaders declared a moratorium on political partisanship for the month of mourning. This situation offered an opportunity to

[8] M. Sherif and C. I. Hovland, *Social Judgment* (New Haven, Conn., 1962).
[9] The pilot research was conducted in the spring of 1963 with the help of Mr. Bruce Rubenstein, and will be reported in detail elsewhere. For the argument on which this approach is based, see R. E. Lane and D. O. Sears, *Public Opinion* (Englewood Cliffs, N.J., 1964), chap. 5.

assess the effects of the assassination and the mourning period on party-linked partisanship. For example, it might be thought that the assassination would decrease the influence of the preferred party on its supporters, and increase the influence of the nonpreferred party. Or it might have increased the influence of the Democratic party alone for a variety of reasons.

Second, the assassination was thought to affect popular feeling about moderation and extremism in American politics. Many expressed intense revulsion for political extremists. Others began to think that differences of opinion between men of goodwill were in fact trivial, and should be debated in more prudent terms. The assassination may thus have decreased opposition leaders' influence by rendering unacceptable those of more extreme persuasion. Or it may have increased opposition leaders' influence by focusing attention on a national consensus and by minimizing narrowly based factional partisanship.

Method

On October 1, 1963, we gave 244 students in an introductory psychology section during the regular class hour a premeasure questionnaire to determine their party preference and whether they thought certain prominent American politicians acceptable or objectionable. Seventy-six of these students were further tested in experimental sessions before the President's assassination, during November, and afterwards, during December. Two experiments were conducted. In the "party experiment" the subjects were presented with a series of positions allegedly taken by the Democratic party and/or the Republican party on hypothetical bills before Congress, and were asked to express their own opinion; they were given no other information about the bills. In the "political leader experiment," subjects made similar judgments based only on positions allegedly taken by political leaders whom they had previously rated as acceptable or objectionable.

Subjects. Almost all the subjects were freshmen or sophomores, and under 21 years of age. In the party experiment 24 Republicans were tested, 16 before and 8 after the assassination, and 24 Democrats were tested, 15 before and 9 after the assassination. In the political leader experiment all subjects were Democrats, 16 tested in November and 12 in December. The subjects volunteered for the experimental session as part of a course requirement of six hours' participation as experimental subjects.[10] The premeasure questionnaire and the experimental sessions were handled by different persons, and fairly intensive questioning revealed no subject who thought the two sessions were part of the same study.

Premeasure. The premeasure questionnaire consisted of three parts, two of which dealt with the students' feelings about sixteen American political leaders. These leaders had been selected, on the basis of extensive pretesting with another undergraduate class, as being relatively well known and as being approximately equally spaced on a liberal-conservative continuum. They were presented to the students roughly in order of decreasing liberalism and increasing conservatism, as shown in Table 1 (p. 313).

The students first rated these sixteen men on a five-point scale of "familiarity with [their] activities and beliefs." Next, they rated the men's political beliefs as "acceptable" or "objectionable," and indicated which man's beliefs were "most acceptable" and which "most objectionable." Each leader's name was followed by a short biographical sketch (about 75 words), which gave a brief personal history and was intended to support the rank order on the liberal-conservative scale. Finally, the student supplied his own name, sex, birthdate, college class, general interest in politics, and party preference. The strength of party preferences was determined by two items, each with a seven-point scale: the standard item used by the Survey Research Center[11] and the question "Which do you think is closer to your own point of view, the Republicans generally or the Kennedy Administration?" Responses to these two items were highly correlated in the class as a whole ($r = +.83$, $n = 244$). Those

---

[10] The use of undergraduates in social psychological research traditionally stimulates a standard set of claims and denunciations. These hardly seem directly relevant here. First, UCLA undergraduates may be rather similar to that segment of the American public that regularly is aware of and reacts to the positions taken by political leaders. That is, UCLA students may be fairly representative of the so-called "attentive public." In contrast, a random sample of the American public would not be representative at all of this more specialized "public." And second, the sample is small enough in any case that one would want to treat the findings as suggestive rather than as definitive. There is much speculation about public reactions to leadership in times of crisis, and, necessarily, rather little evidence. The resiliency and longevity of our system of government may someday depend upon such reactions, and it is useful, hopefully, to assemble whatever bits and pieces of evidence we can.

[11] A. Campbell, G. Gurin, and W. Miller, *The Voter Decides* (Evanston, Ill., 1954), pp. 217–18.

with scores of 4 or less, and 12 or more, were classified as strong partisans.

Procedure for the party experiment. Each subject was tested individually. The experiment was described as a "test of opinion formation based upon the receipt of an extremely limited amount of information." The subject was then shown a 13-point scale of support for or opposition to a hypothetical bill. The seven odd-numbered points were labeled.[12] The subject was then told that he would be presented with a series of trials, on each of which he would be given the Democratic party and/or the Republican party position on a hypothetical bill in terms of this scale. The subject was then to "indicate [his] reactions or feelings by calling out a number on this chart." Any one of the 13 points of the scale could be used to indicate his own position on the bill. Pointers were used to represent the parties' positions to the subject on each trial. Each trial represented a different hypothetical bill.

Forty-six trials were then given. On each trial, the positions taken by one or both parties were indicated by placing the party pointers on one or two of the labeled points on the scale. The subject then indicated his own position on the bill. He was given no other information about it.

The main body of the trials consisted of six blocks, with seven trials in each block. In one block the subject's party took each odd-numbered position from 1 to 13 and the other party's position was not given (notated for Democrats as $D_v R_0$).[13] In the second block the pattern was

[12] The two extreme points read as follows. 1: "I strongly support this bill, and expect to use all my influence to try to see that it is passed by Congress. It will meet an urgent need and cannot be postponed." 13: "I am strongly opposed to this measure, and expect to use all my influence to see that it is defeated. If the bill were passed, it would have very damaging consequences that we might not be able to repair." The sense of the intermediate points may be conveyed by the following excerpts. 3: "I support this bill . . . it could be postponed . . . highly desirable." 5: "I am mildly in favor of this bill . . . does not seem urgent . . . desirable measure . . . I will vote for it." 7: "I am undecided on this bill . . . good points and . . . bad points . . . quite equally balanced." 9: "I am mildly opposed to this bill . . . would do little harm . . . unnecessary . . . I will vote against it." 11: "I am opposed to this bill . . . no need for the measure, and it could do harm . . . highly undesirable."

[13] The notation system used for these trials is as follows. The party preferred by the subject is always given first, the nonpreferred party second; "D" and "R" stand, of course, for Democratic and Republican. The four subscripts used are "v," "0," "+," and "−." The subscript "v" means, "This party was varied, taking each of the odd-numbered positions from 1 to 13." The subscript "0" means, "This party's position was not given to the subject." The subscript "+" means, "This party was anchored throughout the block at strong support (position 1)." The subscript "−" means, "This party was anchored

reversed: the other party varied from 1 to 13 and the subject's party's position was not given (D_0R_v). In a third the subject's party was always at 1 (strong support) and the other party varied from 1 to 13 (D_+R_v). This pattern was reversed in a fourth block (D_vR_+). Finally, in the last two blocks, one party was anchored at 13 (strong opposition) and the other party was varied $(D_-R_v$ and $D_vR_-)$. In addition to these 42 trials, four were repeated in which only one party's position was given at position 1 or 13.

Two orders for the trials were constructed from a table of random numbers. The only restrictions upon the randomization were that no party should take the same position on two successive trials and that the two parties' positions should not be simply reversed on two successive trials. Each of these orders was used both forward and backward, yielding four orders for the trials. When the subject had completed all 46 trials, he was given a set of evaluative semantic differential scales for each party.[14]

Procedure for the political leader experiment. Substantially the same procedure was used for the political leader experiment, except that the leaders' positions were used instead of party positions. Also, because of a dearth of Republicans among UCLA undergraduates, only Democrats were used in this second experiment.

On the basis of the "acceptable" and "objectionable" ratings in the premeasure, seven political leaders were selected for each subject. These were picked to correspond to various points in the hypothetical latitudes of acceptance and rejection. The latitudes themselves were presumed to be zones of an underlying ideological dimension. Four "acceptable" politicians were selected for each subject. One was the "most acceptable" as indicated by the subject in his premeasure. A second was "highly acceptable," the next to "most acceptable" in the direction of greater liberalism (as defined *a priori* by the rank order used in the premeasure). A third was the "least acceptable," the most conservative man rated by the subject as acceptable. The fourth was "average acceptable,"

---

throughout the block at strong opposition (position 13)." For the "political leader" experiment, the same subscripts, with the same meanings, are used; the only change in the notation is the use of MA and O, meaning "most acceptable leader" and "other leader," respectively, as the main symbols.

[14] The exact items are given in P. H. Tannenbaum, "Initial Attitude Toward Source and Concept as Factors in Attitude Change Through Communication," *Public Opinion Quarterly* (1956), *20*, 413–25.

TABLE 1

Democratic Subjects' Response to Political Leaders on Premeasure

Leader's name	Per cent rating leader as:			Modal subject	
	Accept-able	Unfa-miliar[a]	Objec-tionable	Hypothetical latitudes	Special classification
Norman Thomas . .	1%	94%	5%	—	
Walter Reuther . . .	46	46	8		—
Hubert Humphrey .	69	24	7		—
Adlai Stevenson . .	93	0	7		Highly acceptable
John Kennedy . . .	100	0	0	Latitude	Most acceptable
Mike Mansfield . . .	69	31	0	of	—
Stuart Symington . .	38	50	12	acceptance	—
Lyndon Johnson . .	90	0	10		Average acceptable
Thomas Kuchel . . .	62	28	10		—
Nelson Rockefeller .	80	0	20		—
Henry Cabot Lodge .	62	10	28		Least acceptable
Richard Nixon . . .	20	0	80		Least objectionable
Robert Taft, Jr. . . .	12	72	16	Latitude	—
Barry Goldwater . .	10	2	88	of	Average objectionable
John Rousselot . . .	1	69	30	rejection	—
Robert Welch . . .	1	38	61		Most objectionable

[a] Given one of the two lowest familiarity ratings, whether also rated as acceptable or as objectionable.

the one in the middle of the range of those rated as acceptable. The remaining three were drawn from those rated as objectionable in the premeasure. The "most objectionable" had been indicated on the premeasure. A second was the "least objectionable," the most liberal of those whom the subject rated as objectionable. The last was the "average objectionable," the one in the middle of the range of those the subject had rated as objectionable. The political leaders used, and the selections for the modal subject, are shown in Table 1. No politician was selected for a subject who had given him the lowest or next-to-lowest rating on the premeasure familiarity scale.[15]

Four political leaders were used during each subject's experimental session. The "most acceptable" was used for each subject, and six combinations of the remaining six, taken three at a time, were used. The combination used for a given subject was determined arbitrarily by the

[15] That is, those excluded had been rated as follows: "I have heard his name, but I don't know anything about him," or "I have never heard of him before." The minimum familiarity included was "I have heard about him and am familiar with some things he has done, but I don't know much about him."

experimenter before the experimental session, without knowledge of which leaders were involved.

The experimental procedure was almost identical to that described above for the party experiment, except that the four political leaders replaced the two parties. Each subject received six blocks of seven trials each, in three of which his "most acceptable" man was anchored at 1 (strong support) and each of the other three leaders was varied from 1 to 13 (MA_+O_v). In the other three blocks, the "most acceptable" man's position was not given and each of the other three leaders was varied from 1 to 13 (MA_0O_v). In addition, each subject received three additional trials with the "most acceptable" man alone, at position 1 (MA_+O_0). As in the party experiment, the trials were presented in four different orders, and afterwards the subjects filled out evaluative semantic differential scales for each of the four politicians.

Dependent measures. There are several ways of describing subjects' responses during the experimental trials. Two main indices are used in the present analysis.

1. *Influence index.* The amount of influence a given party or leader has on a subject's judgments may be described by the slope of his responses as that party or leader moves from 1 (strong support) to 13 (strong opposition) within a given block of trials. If the subject also increasingly opposes the bill, the varying source has positive influence, and the slope of the subject's responses will be positive. If the subject increasingly supports the bill, however, the party or leader has negative influence, and the slope of the subject's responses will be negative. The influence index used here was computed for any given block of seven trials by subtracting the subject's responses when the party or leader was at 1, 3, and 5 from his responses when the party or leader was at 9, 11, and 13, and dividing by two. (This index is equivalent to an average slope over the block of trials, multiplied by a constant of 12.) Hence if the subject followed the varying party or leader perfectly, the index would be +12; if his responses were completely unrelated to the party's or leader's position, the index would be 0; and if the subject took positions exactly opposite to those of the varying party or leader, the index would be −12.

2. *Deviations from neutral.* Another important dimension of opinion formation under these conditions is the extent to which the subject regards the party's or leader's position as adequate information on which

to base his own opinion. If the source's position gave the subject no information, he would presumably respond "seven" (neutral); if it were completely adequate information, he would adopt either the source's position or its opposite. The amount of information yielded by the source's position has therefore been taken to equal the absolute distance between the subject's response and the neutral point, summed over the six trials of a given block on which the varying source took a nonneutral position.

A note on the assassination. As might be guessed from the relatively small proportion of the subject population actually tested, these particular tests were originally part of a larger experimental design, in which such factors as trial order, strength of party affiliation, and combinations of leaders were to be statistically controlled. This design was truncated by the President's assassination. The subjects scheduled for the afternoon of November 22 were not tested, nor were any others tested until December 6.

Every effort was made to repeat, after the assassination, exactly the same procedure used earlier. Therefore, the same experimenter used the same room, the same materials, the same experimental procedure, and so forth. Only two changes had to be made in the post-assassination session. In the premeasure John F. Kennedy had been selected most often as "most acceptable" (41 per cent of the students, followed by Stevenson, 23 per cent; Rockefeller, 13 per cent; and Goldwater, 8 per cent). In the post-assassination sessions, he was replaced arbitrarily either by Lyndon Johnson or by "the Kennedy Administration" whenever necessary. In addition, the "average acceptable" leader was no longer used, partly because Lyndon Johnson had been that leader for many subjects and partly because our main interest was in opposition leaders.

Results

Comparability of samples. It is possible that any differences between the November and December samples might be explained most simply by volunteer bias. However, the three post-assassination groups were almost identical to their respective pre-assassination groups on the background variables available: age, sex, college class, interest in politics, familiarity with political leaders, and strength of party preference. Only one difference even approaches significance: Democrats tested in the party experiment in December had stronger initial party preferences

TABLE 2

Mean Influence Index for the One-Party Trials

| | Party varied | | |
| | Democratic | Republican | |
Subjects	party	party	Partisanship
Democratic			
November $(n = 15)$	+7.88	+1.70	+6.18
December $(n = 9)$	+7.78	+0.11	+7.67
Change	−0.10	−1.59	+1.49
Republican			
November $(n = 16)$	+0.16	+7.25[a]	+7.09[b]
December $(n = 8)$	+2.31	+4.31[a]	+2.00[b]
Change	+2.15	−2.94	−5.09

[a] $F = 5.68, p < .05$. All p-values in this chapter are based on two-tailed tests.
[b] $F = 6.15, p < .05$.

than those tested in November $(p < .05)$. The dependent measures are therefore adjusted by covariance for this difference when appropriate in the analyses described below. Aside from this, there was no evidence of any volunteer bias, and the samples may be considered thoroughly comparable.

The influence of a single party's positions. As expected, the positions of either party, when presented separately, had positive influence before the assassination (using the binomial test, $p < .001$ for the preferred party and $p < .05$ for the nonpreferred party). Table 2 gives the mean influence index for the single-party trials, and illustrates the positive influence that even the nonpreferred party had under normal political conditions.[16] Strong partisanship was also present, of course. The preferred party was more influential than the nonpreferred party for 90 per cent of the subjects $(p < .001)$.

The clearest effect of the assassination was a weakening of Republicans' partisanship. Among Republicans, the difference between the two parties' influences declined $(p < .05)$, mainly because of a decline in Republican party influence. In contrast, Democrats' partisanship remained about the same. When Democrats' influence scores are adjusted by covariance, the slight increase in partisanship shown in Table 2 vanishes.

[16] The finding that the nonpreferred party had positive influence when considered alone repeats a finding from the spring 1963 pilot data. Tests of 24 subjects yielded $p < .01$ at that time.

Semantic differential ratings of the two parties yield the same conclusion: Republicans' partisanship became weaker, but the Democrats remained about as partisan as ever. The mean difference in ratings of the two parties declined from 9.51 to 2.77 among Republicans ($p < .025$) and from 7.20 to 5.87 among Democrats (not significant).[17]

These conclusions are not affected if differences in initial strength of party preference are considered. Strong and weak Republicans alike became less partisan, although the difference was significant only for the latter. Neither strong nor weak Democrats changed noticeably.

Compromise responses to both parties' positions. The nonpreferred party also appears to have positive influence, under normal circumstances, when both parties' positions are given. When the preferred party was anchored at strong support ($D_+ R_v$ and $R_+ D_v$), the varying positions of the nonpreferred party positively influenced 90 per cent of the pre-assassination subjects ($p < .001$ by binomial test). In the $D_- R_v$ and $R_- D_v$ trials the nonpreferred party influenced 97 per cent of the subjects positively ($p < .001$). Of course, the preferred party had an even stronger record of positive influence: *all* pre-assassination subjects were positively influenced in the $D_v R_+$, $R_v D_+$, $D_v R_-$, and $R_v D_-$ trials. Thus it seems that almost all subjects normally make a compromise response when confronted with the conflicting positions of the two major parties.[18] That is, the disagreement of the nonpreferred party does *not* normally produce a boomerang effect.

The assassination had no significant general effect upon the partisanship of these compromise responses, either among Republicans or among Democrats. However, it did interact with strength of initial party preference among Republicans. Strong Republicans became somewhat more partisan ($p < .10$) and weak Republicans became considerably less partisan ($p < .01$). As Table 3 shows, this difference between strong and weak Republicans was statistically significant ($p < .01$), but the number of cases involved was very small.

---

[17] This change reflects reduced evaluation of the Republican party and increased evaluation of the Democratic party, but only the former was significant ($p < .05$) because of the greater variability in the ratings of the Democratic party. Differences between the November and December samples are loosely described as "changes," although change was not measured directly, of course.

[18] Heavier weight is usually given to the preferred party's position in forming this compromise response, of course; witness the fact that about 90 per cent of the preassassination subjects were more influenced when their preferred party varied and the opposition party was anchored than when the roles of the parties were reversed.

TABLE 3

Mean Influence Index for Republicans in the Two-Party Trials

Block of trials	November	December	Change
Strong Republicans			
Republican party varies $(R_vD_+$ and $R_vD_-)$	+7.75	+9.08	+1.33
Democratic party varies $(R_+D_v$ and $R_-D_v)$	+2.54	+0.83	−1.71
Partisanship	+5.21	+8.25	+3.04[a]
Weak Republicans			
Republican party varies $(R_vD_+$ and $R_vD_-)$	+7.54	+4.05	−3.49
Democratic party varies $(R_+D_v$ and $R_-D_v)$ . . .	+3.54	+5.40	+1.86
Partisanship	+4.00	−1.35	−5.35[a]

[a] $F = 13.17, p < .01$.

Although the main changes were therefore among Republicans, Democrats were affected in one interesting way. They became more responsive to any opposition expressed by *either* party. Both parties became more influential when opposing the other's positive stand $(D_+R_v$ and $D_vR_+)$ and less influential when disagreeing with the other's negative position $(D_-R_v$ and $D_vR_-)$. This difference, presented in Table 4, is significant beyond the .05 level. Thus the main effect of the assassination on Democrats' responses to the two parties was to increase their uneasiness about a measure whenever either party expressed some opposition to it. This effect parallels a change in the response to certain opposition leaders, as will be seen below.

The assassination seems, in general, to have hurt the Republican party more than it hurt the Democratic party, since Republicans became less partisan and Democrats did not change. This was partly due to Repub-

TABLE 4

Mean Influence Index for Democrats in the Two-Party Trials

Block of trials	November	December	Change
Anchored party opposes bill			
Republican party varies (D_-R_v)	+ 3.90	+ 3.11	−0.79
Democratic party varies (D_vR_-)	+ 8.37	+ 8.22	−0.15
Total	+12.27	+11.33	−0.94[a]
Anchored party supports bill			
Republican party varies (D_+R_v)	+ 2.87	+ 3.89	+1.02
Democratic party varies (D_vR_+)	+ 7.27	+ 7.61	+0.34
Total	+10.14	+11.50	+1.36[a]

[a] $F = 5.79, p < .05$.

TABLE 5

Mean Absolute Deviation From Neutral in the Single-Party Trials

Block of trials	November	December	Change
Only Republican position given (R_vD_0)			
Response of Republicans	15.19	11.88	−3.31
Response of Democrats	9.93	5.00	−4.93
All subjects	12.65	8.23	−4.42[a]
Only Democratic position given (D_vR_0)			
Response of Republicans	8.75	10.25	+1.50
Response of Democrats	16.60	16.00	−0.60
All subjects	12.55	13.29	+0.74[a]

[a] $F = 5.98$, $p < .05$.

licans' lowered evaluation of the GOP. More importantly, the positions taken by the Republican party simply conveyed less information in the aftermath—Democrats and Republicans alike seemed to find them less meaningful. Table 5 shows the rather substantial decline in deviations from the neutral point during the trials in which only the Republican position was given. Evidently the subjects became considerably more reluctant to express an opinion based only on the Republican position. In contrast, there was a slight increase in willingness to take a stand based only on the Democratic party position. The difference between the two parties in this respect is significant ($p < .05$).

A possible clue as to why the assassination had greater impact on Republicans and on Republican party influence is provided by some incidental data. Each post-assassination subject was asked, "Do you think it is proper to criticize President Johnson and his administration?" If the subject said, "No," he was asked when he thought it would be proper. Sixty-three per cent of the Democrats felt criticism was quite proper "right now" (i.e., sometime during the last two weeks of the mourning period). In contrast, *no* Republican thought it proper until the end of the mourning period at the earliest ($p < .05$ by the chi-square test), and most thought it inappropriate before sometime the following year. Clearly, the Republican partisan was placed in a more difficult political position than the Democratic partisan.

In summary, then, the principal effects of the assassination upon the two political parties' effectiveness as reference groups seem to have been:

1. Republicans became less partisan, particularly those who were

weak Republicans to begin with. Democrats did not change in partisanship.

2. The Republican party became less attractive to Republicans.

3. Republican party positions became less useful to Republicans and Democrats alike as bases for forming opinions. They were no longer very helpful in distinguishing between good and bad programs.

4. Republicans believed in strict observation of the so-called moratorium on partisanship more than did Democrats; specifically, they felt obliged not to criticize the new administration.

5. Democrats became more sensitive to the expression of any opposition. That is, Democrats became more reluctant to support a program that either party opposed. They did not, however, become less willing to support unopposed measures.

The influence of a single leader. Positions taken by "acceptable" leaders were expected to have positive influence, and those by "objectionable" leaders to have negative influence, in the absence of any other information and under normal political circumstances. Pre-assassination responses to the single-leader trials were appropriate for testing this expectation. They provided general support for it, as Table 6 shows. Every subject presented with "acceptable" leaders' positions was positively influenced by them ($p < .001$ by binomial test). In contrast, 77 per cent of the subjects presented with "objectionable" leaders' positions were negatively influenced by them ($p < .07$). Thus the distinction between latitudes of acceptance and latitudes of rejection appears to have been a meaningful one for categorizing political leaders.

It might also be noted in passing that these data demonstrate the usually elusive "boomerang effect." The *range* of influences commanded by the "most objectionable" leader was from -5 to -15.5. Clearly, the

TABLE 6

Mean Influence Index for Single-Leader Trials (MA_0O_v)

Leader varied	November	December	Change
Highly acceptable	+ 7.83	+6.29	−1.54
Average acceptable	+ 5.29	—	—
Least acceptable	+ 1.72	+3.12	+1.40
Least objectionable	− 3.42	+0.58	+4.00
Average objectionable	− 4.65	−2.25	+2.40
Most objectionable	−10.64	−4.42	+6.22

pre-assassination subjects felt that distinguishing right from wrong, and good from bad, was a relatively easy matter. Anything the "most objectionable" leader supported was, ipso facto, wrong and bad; anything he opposed was, equally obviously, right and good.

The assassination increased the influence of "objectionable" leaders in these single-leader trials. These data are presented in Table 6. The most interesting effect, from a theoretical point of view, is the change of the "least objectionable" leader from negative to positive influence.[19] This suggests a broadening of the latitude of acceptance to include previously rejected leaders. Or, to put it another way, more opposition leaders seem to have been thought reasonable and trustworthy after the assassination than had been before it.

The "loyal opposition." The same general pattern of increased influence for "objectionable" leaders held in the two-leader trials, but none of the changes approached significance. The unique place of an opposition leader suggests, however, that we should pay attention to somewhat more specific kinds of influence. Two cases are of particular interest; both concern policy that has been strongly endorsed by majority leaders. One is a supportive or "consensus" stance. That is, a prestigeful opposition leader may be able to attract crucial support for a measure proposed by majority leaders, and thus be decisive in producing a general "consensus." The second (possibly more natural) is an opposition or "veto" stance. An opposition leader may be able to wield a decisive veto, and thus kill (or badly maim) a majority leader's program.[20]

[19] This change does not approach statistical significance on the influence index. However, it is more reliable for trials in which the "least objectionable" leader took the more extreme positions. Deleting the middle two trials (on which this leader took positions 5 and 9) from the influence index yields a marginally significant increment in influence after the assassination ($F = 4.94$, $p < .06$), as does consideration of only the two most extreme trials ($F = 4.34$, $p < .07$). Similarly, the increased influence of the "most objectionable" leader is not highly reliable on the influence index ($F = 2.98$, $p < .12$), but deleting the two middle trials again increases the significance level somewhat ($F = 3.65$, $p < .09$).

In general, the differences in the political leader experiment were not as significant as those in the party experiment. The magnitude of the differences, and the variability of the scores, were extremely similar in the two experiments. However, the number of subjects compared was smaller in the former, which apparently accounts for the difference in p-values. The differences should thus be interpreted more cautiously, although the pattern seems rather consistent, as will be seen below.

[20] See Austin Ranney and Willmoore Kendall, *Democracy and the American Party System* (New York, 1956), pp. 482–83, for a discussion of this feature of American politics as it applies to legislative action. The Kennedy Administration, whose legislative proposals were innovative (at least relative to prior legislation), could not count on a firm

The influence that these two kinds of stances have may be described by a question: Once we know that our most favored leader strongly supports something, what difference does it make to us if a given opposition leader voices his support or opposition? It can be characterized more precisely by the specific conditions of the experimental sessions. A leader has "consensus power" if his support for a given bill, when added to the support of the "most acceptable" leader, increases support for it (specifically when the difference, MA_+O_0 less MA_+O_+, is positive). Similarly, he has "veto power" if his opposition to a given bill, in the context of the "most acceptable" leader's support of it, increases opposition to it (specifically when the difference, MA_+O_- less MA_+O_0, is positive).

For both consensus power and veto power, the crucial factor before the assassination was the distinction between "acceptable" and "objectionable" leaders. The sharpest difference occurred for veto power. Each "acceptable" leader (highly acceptable, average acceptable, and least acceptable) was significantly able to weaken support for a measure backed by the "most acceptable" leader ($p < .001$, $p < .001$, and $p < .01$, respectively). None of the "objectionable" leaders (least objectionable, average objectionable, and most objectionable) had discernible veto power, however ($p > .60$, $p > .30$, and $p > .30$, respectively). The same pattern held for consensus power, although less dramatically. Each "acceptable" leader had significant or nearly significant consensus power ($p < .05$, $p < .02$, and $p < .07$, respectively). The "least objectionable" leader also had significant consensus power ($p < .05$), but neither of the other "objectionable" leaders did ($p > .15$ and $p > .70$, respectively). In general, the power to add support to, or weaken support for, programs advanced by a "most acceptable" leader seems therefore to be possessed almost exclusively by other "acceptable" leaders.[21]

The changes in this pattern after the assassination were similar to those outlined above for the single-leader trials. The main change was increased veto power for the "least objectionable" and "average objec-

---

majority in Congress. This put certain leaders and groups quite visibly in a "swing" position, and may have provided an almost ideal opportunity for the opposition minority to exercise the two powers in question. These experiments are not concerned with negotiations between legislators, of course, but with the consequences for popular thinking of the positions taken publicly by parties and leaders.

21 All "objectionable" leaders, and all but one "least acceptable" leader, were Republicans. Thus they were not only members of the nonpreferred party for these Democrats, but members of the party cast nationally in an opposition role.

TABLE 7

Increases in Veto and Consensus Power After the Assassination

Leader	Veto power[a]	Consensus power[b]
Highly acceptable	−0.52	−0.06
Least acceptable	+0.56	−0.19
Least objectionable	+1.78	−0.27
Average objectionable	+1.13	−0.58
Most objectionable	−0.21	−0.14

[a] Difference between November and December means of MA_+O_- less MA_+O_0. A positive number indicates increased veto power in December.
[b] Difference between November and December means of MA_+O_0 less MA_+O_+. A positive number indicates increased consensus power in December.

tionable" leaders (although only the change in the former approached statistical significance, at $p < .07$). The data are presented in Table 7. After the assassination these leaders began to approximate the veto power of "acceptable" leaders, attaining significance levels of $p < .15$ and $p < .01$, respectively.[22] The "most objectionable" leader enjoyed no such exaltation, however; his absence of veto power was as marked as ever ($p > .40$). Hence these changes are consistent with those discussed earlier. They give us additional reason to suppose that the assassination broadened Democrats' latitudes of acceptance to include the less "objectionable" opposition leaders.

However, opposition leaders' influence did not increase in all respects. There were no changes in consensus power for any leader. Hence mildly "objectionable" leaders were given blackballs, but evidently gained no importance as supporters of the "most acceptable" leader. This neatly parallels the change in Democrats' responsiveness to positions taken by the opposition party: as indicated above, the Republican party became more effective among Democrats only when it opposed programs supported by the Democratic party (see Table 4). Putting these findings together, Democrats after the assassination seem to have become more concerned with being sure that there was little *active* opposition to a program they supported. At least their opinions were more tentative and moderate if there was active opposition by mildly "objectionable" leaders or by either major party.

[22] These changes were not caused by any lessening of the "most acceptable" leader's influence because of post-assassination substitutions. Effects of the assassination on the MA_+O_0 trials were trivial ($p > .40$), as they were on semantic differential ratings of the "most acceptable" leader ($p > .50$).

"Extremist" leaders. Much was said after the assassination to condemn "extremist" leaders. Some blamed political extremism for the assassination; e.g., Chief Justice Warren said it was "a result of the hatred and bitterness that has been injected into the life of our nation by bigots." Many expressed the hope that the President's murder would diminish the power and respectability of extremist groups, whether through sorrow and guilt (e.g., Governor Edmund G. Brown of California: "[His] sacrifice may bring about a lessening of some of the hatreds in our country") or more vengeful rejection (e.g., Mayor Samuel Yorty of Los Angeles: "Maybe the American people will stop and think about the hate groups who encourage this type of thing, such as those who call Eisenhower a Communist and call Kennedy dirty names"). One might therefore expect extremist leaders to have less influence on the opinions of their opponents in the aftermath.

The "extremist" leaders denounced after the assassination were well represented by the "most objectionable" leader. For every post-assassination subject he was Robert Welch, founder and leader of the John Birch Society. The effects of the assassination upon his influence seem confusing. On the one hand, all "objectionable" leaders gained influence in the single-leader trials, and the "most objectionable" leader showed the largest gain of all (see Table 6). On the other hand, the "most objectionable" leader did not share in the increase in veto power, unlike the other "objectionable" leaders (see Table 7).

This paradox is easily enough resolved. The gain in influence in the single-leader trials is spurious. It merely reflects the change of a negative source into a meaningless one. The pre-assassination subjects took a neutral position on only 12 per cent of the trials in which the "most objectionable" leader took a nonneutral position. The post-assassination subjects, in contrast, took a neutral position on 42 per cent of such trials ($p < .08$ for the difference). Before the assassination Welch was an almost perfectly negative source. Afterwards, his positions communicated less definitive information—they were essentially irrelevant to the task of forming an opinion. That this difference was due to the assassination is suggested by the fact that the mean ratings of familiarity with the "most objectionable" leader could not have been more similar—2.7 on a five-point scale for pre- and post-assassination subjects alike.

The effects of the assassination on opposition leaders' influence upon Democrats seem, in summary, to be these:

1. The influence of all previously "objectionable" leaders was increased when their positions were the only available information.

2. This increase concealed two quite different effects: less "objectionable" leaders (mainly moderate Republicans) tended to change from negative to positive sources, but highly "objectionable" sources (mainly conservative Republicans) changed from negative to irrelevant and meaningless sources.

3. The veto power of previously mildly "objectionable" leaders increased, whereas that of highly "objectionable" leaders did not. The power to enhance support for policies backed by the "most acceptable" leader remained at pre-assassination levels.

Concluding remarks

An asymmetric reaction to the post-assassination political moratorium was suggested by the party experiment data. Republicans became considerably less partisan, but Democrats were just as partisan as they had been before the assassination. Weak Republicans in particular became less partisan. A combination of circumstances undoubtedly was responsible for this asymmetry. Perhaps most important was the fact that the new President quite explicitly assumed leadership of the country on a nonpartisan basis ("all the people"). Soon, however, he began a zealous drive for the enactment of the late President's highly controversial legislative program. Congressional opposition necessarily was unusually restrained. Hence pressures were placed on all, but most heavily on Republicans, to inhibit partisanship. The bind in which Republicans were placed was illustrated by their unanimous support of the moratorium— in contrast to the relatively meager support of it by Democrats.

Perhaps the credentials of Democrats were less subject to challenge; their grief for the murdered President, and loyalty to his successor, would not be questioned should they criticize administration policy. Possibly the same holds in many cases of mourning: the more indisputable one's esteem for the deceased, the more one may recall his vices as well as his virtues. Whatever the psychological dynamics in this case, the effect seems clear. The assassination left the partisan arena, at least temporarily, to the Democratic party.

The Democrats' responses to the assassination were, not surprisingly, rather different. Before the assassination a fairly clear distinction existed between "acceptable" and "objectionable" sources of information. "Acceptable" sources included the Democratic party, all Democratic leaders, and the Republican party along with some moderate Republican leaders (in the role of "least acceptable" leader).[23] "Objectionable" sources included the remainder of the Republican leaders used. The "acceptable" sources had positive influence, and the "objectionable" sources had negative influence: their positions were meaningful in either case.

This distinction was less clear following the assassination, and seems to have been replaced with something rather different. The Democrats became more reluctant to support a measure if either party opposed it. They were more influenced by moderately "objectionable" leaders' positions in the absence of any other information. And the moderately "objectionable" leaders had increased veto power over policies strongly supported by the "most acceptable" leader. In these respects the influence of opposition leaders was enhanced by the assassination. The value of their contributions to agreements across party lines was certainly heightened. On the other hand, it seems, if anything, to have decreased the importance of extreme conservatives. Democrats seemed to consider extremely "objectionable" leaders' positions as largely meaningless and irrelevant after the assassination.

One might speculate that the pre-assassination partisan dichotomy had been replaced by another. No longer was the important distinction that between the "good guys" and the "bad guys." Rather, there appeared to be a broad category of responsible men whose consent (whether by active agreement or passive acquiescence) was prerequisite to a Democrat's support of a program strongly endorsed by the President or his administration. The other category included only rather extreme Republican conservatives, whose positions seemed uninteresting and irrelevant, beyond the pale. By including previously "objectionable" Republican leaders in the broad category of responsible men, Democrats also might be said to have become less partisan after the President's murder. Furthermore, one would not envy the persuasion job facing any presidential candidate cast into this second category.

---

[23] This is not surprising, since, for almost three-fourths of the subjects, the "least acceptable" leader was Rockefeller, Lodge, or Nixon. At the time these men seemed to represent the dominant faction of the Republican party, especially in California. Senator Thomas Kuchel had recently won a stunning victory in the face of a general Democratic off-year sweep.

Lewis Lipsitz and J. David Colfax

The Fate of Due Process in a Time of Crisis

A common interpretation of the November events was that the United States, with a tradition of violence derived in part from frontier justice and in part from what has been called the "moralizing style of American Protestantism," had again experienced the by-products of that tradition.[1] The cults of violence and vigilantism—the seeking of a justice unencumbered by law—have often been manifested in events ranging from lynchings to fluoridation controversies. This led some observers to conclude that the assassination and the events that immediately followed it were in many respects archetypes of American experience.[2]

We decided to find out if the public reaction to the assassination actually was characterized by low-scale hysteria and vigilantism. To what extent did persons suspend whatever notions of justice and due process they might have held under less threatening circumstances, and what were the psychological and sociological characteristics of such persons? What are the implications of such reactions for the antagonistic traditions that are represented by the Fifth and Fourteenth Amendments on the one hand, and by vigilantism on the other? This paper is intended to shed some light on the public capacities for reason and unreason in a time of national crisis.

Between November 24 and 30, we interviewed 115 residents of Thread

[1] Daniel Bell, "The Dispossessed," in Daniel Bell, ed., *The Radical Right* (Garden City, N.Y., 1964), p. 18.
[2] Everett C. Hughes, for example, has pointed out that "the shooting of Oswald was done in almost the classic style of a lynching." That one could speak of a "classic style" in this genre supports the notion that a "routinization of violence" does in fact form a distinct tradition. *The Correspondent* (January–February, 1964), p. 5.

TABLE 1

Beliefs About Oswald's Guilt on Friday Night[a]

Certainty and reasons	Per cent of respondents ($n = 110$)[b]
Certain of Oswald's guilt	52%
Cite "evidence"	35
Mass media	11
Background and associations	4
Certain, no other information	2
Ambivalent: question of accomplices	6
Uncertain	42
Cite conflicting or insufficient evidence	24
People can't say	7
Didn't follow news	4
Uncertain, no other information	7

[a] The question was: By Friday night, right after the assassination, how certain were you that Oswald was the assassin? Why?
[b] In this and following tables, n's less than 115 are the result of noncodable responses, including "don't know."

City, a predominantly Catholic, New England manufacturing town of 15,000.[3] An analysis of this stratified sample of household heads provided the data for this paper.[4]

The dimensions of guilt

"In all likelihood there does not exist a single American community where reside 12 men or women . . . who presume that Lee Harvey Oswald did not assassinate President Kennedy."[5] For the student of opinion formation and for those concerned with the maintenance of civil liberties, the charge that Oswald could not have received a fair trial is an important one. In the hours following the assassination, the American people were exposed to the mass media in unprecedented numbers, and the media were initially monolithic in tone and content.[6] Conflicting evidence, editorial antagonisms, and countervailing arguments were largely

[3] The authors would like to acknowledge the assistance of Mrs. Anita Frankel and Mrs. Lewis Lipsitz in coding the interviews.
[4] Twenty-five of those included in the Thread City sample were actually residents of a nearby metropolitan area. They were included because, when examined in terms of authoritarianism, occupation, and education, they were not distinguishable from the Thread City sample.
[5] Mark Lane, "A Defense Brief for Oswald," *National Guardian* (December 19, 1963), pp. 5–9.
[6] The NORC study by Paul B. Sheatsley and Jacob J. Feldman in this volume reports that at least 95 per cent of the populace were exposed to radio or television in the four days following the assassination.

absent. It was unlikely that the media would generate opposing opinions in their audience. Rather, they were likely to channel opinions of different people in one direction (e.g., toward belief in Oswald's guilt) at different rates. Nevertheless, commentators were careful not to make unqualified statements that Oswald was guilty. Thus if Oswald were perceived as guilty at the close of that first day, the mass media were not the sole cause of this perception, but were a contributing factor along with the various personalities and social dispositions of the audience.[7]

A majority of the Thread City respondents reported that they were convinced of Oswald's guilt at the close of the first day. Table 1 shows that 52 per cent were certain, and another 6 per cent were uncertain only because they thought that Oswald had accomplices and might not be the only guilty party. Of the 42 per cent who were unconvinced of Oswald's guilt, 18 per cent said it was because they felt incompetent to judge or had failed to follow the news closely. The remaining 24 per cent who were doubtful cited the inconsistency of the evidence. For this period, in which radio and television were virtually the only sources of information, 11 per cent cited the media—and not any specific content —as a reason for believing that Oswald was guilty.

How much consensus of opinion about Oswald's guilt developed? The proportion of persons who reserved judgment dropped sharply in the next few days. By the time of the interview (approximately one week after the assassination, on the average), better than four out of five persons in Thread City were certain Oswald had been the assassin.

The increase in the total number of persons who were certain of Oswald's guilt was 24 per cent, as Table 2 shows. White-collar and blue-collar workers, authoritarians and nonauthoritarians alike, showed increases of over 20 per cent. Everyone tended to become more certain of Oswald's guilt. After one week, only the college-educated were less than 75 per cent convinced that Oswald was the assassin. Yet even in this group, which was likely to be more aware of the norms of due process, only one person out of three remained uncertain.

These data may bear out to some extent those who have feared the opinion-shaping effects of the mass media. In the days following the assassination, the pressures applied by the media substantially increased the certainty of Oswald's guilt in all sectors of the population. Of course, it is not clear what role informal-group pressures played in creating that

[7] The opinions expressed were retrospective, since the interviews were conducted from two to nine days after the assassination.

TABLE 2

Certainty of Guilt by Social Class and Personality

Sample	Certain on Nov. 22			Certain one week later[b]		
	Per cent	No.	Q[a]	Per cent	No.	Q
Total	58%	110		82%	108	
Occupation						
White-collar	53	51	.10	77	48	.16
Blue-collar	58	52		82	51	
Education in years						
13+	46	35	.36[c]	66	35	.64[d]
9–12	63	49		94	47	
0–8	67	21		81	21	
Authoritarianism[e]						
Authoritarians	62	47	.19	84	45	.15
Nonauthoritarians	53	59		80	60	

[a] Kendall's Q measures the "strength" of a relationship. See H. M. Blalock, *Social Statistics* (New York, 1960), pp. 231–32.
[b] The question one week later was: How do you feel about this now? Why?
[c] Q-score is based on a comparison between 13+ and 0–12.
[d] $p < .05$ by χ^2 test, comparing 13+ and 0–12.
[e] A five-question scale was employed to tap this psychological syndrome. All five questions were adaptations of standard questions from the original F-scale described in T. W. Adorno, *et al.*, *The Authoritarian Personality* (New York, 1950), pp. 224–62 (e.g., "Most people who don't get ahead just don't have enough willpower.") Those who agreed with 0–2 questions were classified as "Nonauthoritarians." Those who agreed with 3–5 questions were classified as "Authoritarians."

certainty. It is possible that those who still doubted were under more pressure to conform than those who were certain from the outset, especially because the mass media reinforced the convictions of the latter.

Vengeance and understanding

Part of the idea of justice is the idea of equal treatment. On November 22, Oswald was arrested for the assassination of the President; on November 24, Jack Ruby was arrested for the murder of Oswald. Yet a majority of people in Thread City felt that the crimes did not merit equal treatment. One comparison in Table 3 reveals this most readily: nearly 60 per cent of the sample wanted the death penalty or worse for Oswald, whereas only 20 per cent thought that Ruby should be executed. A particularly intense response to the President's death is revealed in the overly punitive, vengeful reactions of a significant portion of the respondents: 19 per cent felt that Oswald should have suffered or been tortured.

Even those who did not favor execution or suffering judged Oswald more harshly than Ruby. Only 17 per cent felt that Oswald should be tried by a jury, whereas nearly one-third believed Ruby should be. Clearly Ruby was not identified as an honorable or a heroic figure, but his crime was perceived as being within the traditional legal framework, whereas Oswald's was not. And although, as Daniel Bell has asserted, the "historic contribution of liberalism was to separate law from morality," it is nevertheless clear that in this instance most persons could not or would not make such a distinction, in spite of the legal similarity of the two crimes.[8]

TABLE 3

Prescriptions of Punishment for Oswald and Ruby[a]

Prescribed Punishments	Oswald (n = 106)	Ruby (n = 106)
Death	38%	20%
Torture, Suffering	19	0
	57[b]	20[b]
Life Imprisonment	18	16
Death, If Not Insane	3	4
Mental Institution	3	0
Short Prison Term	2	27
Released, Rewarded	0	2
As Determined By Jury	17	31

[a] The questions were: If Oswald (Ruby) were found guilty, what do you think should be done with him?
[b] $p < .001$.

Despite an apparent ambivalence about the killing of Oswald, all but 3 per cent of the respondents said they thought his murder was wrong. But when the reasons people offered for condemning the slaying are examined, the relationship between authoritarianism and punitiveness becomes evident. Among the nonauthoritarians, 69 per cent condemned the slaying of Oswald on legal-ethical grounds—e.g., everyone has a right to a trial, persons must be protected by the law, and no one has a right to kill. Among the authoritarians, 49 per cent condemned the murder on other than legal or ethical grounds—e.g., American prestige would be hurt, or with Oswald dead the truth might never be known. As Table 4 indicates, authoritarians who thought that Oswald should receive the death penalty were even less likely to condemn his murder on legal-ethical grounds.

[8] Daniel Bell, "Interpretations of American Politics," *Radical Right*, p. 71.

TABLE 4

Basis for Condemning Oswald's Death, Authoritarianism, and
Recommended Punishment[a]

	Authoritarians		Nonauthoritarians	
Basis of condemnation	Death, suffering ($n = 24$)	Other ($n = 17$)	Death, suffering ($n = 29$)	Other ($n = 33$)
Ethical-legal	38%[b]	71%[b]	76%	66%
Other grounds	62	29	24	34

[a] The question was: Do you feel what Ruby did was right or wrong? Why?
[b] $p < .05$ by χ^2 test.

As for Ruby's punishment, blue-collar workers (33 per cent) and those with less than college education (28 per cent) were more likely to recommend capital punishment than white-collar workers (13 per cent) and the college-educated (6 per cent).

The most striking point is that the different opinions *within* each of the demographic groupings showed great consistency. Among both white-collar and blue-collar workers, for example, the difference between those favoring the death penalty for Oswald and those favoring it for Ruby was 36 per cent. Similar differences were found within authoritarianism, education, religion, and age classifications.

Perceived conspiracy and punitiveness

As Robert Heilbroner has observed, the assassination confirmed one of the "wildest phantasms of the ignorant": an American President was reported killed by a Marxist Castro sympathizer.[9] What kind of an impact did this interpretation of the event have upon a public unaccustomed to dealing with the abstract principles of due process and civil liberties? How widespread was the idea that the events were conspiratorial? Who were the persons most likely to favor repression of certain groups, who were the ones concerned with the problems of civil liberty implied by these events?

Of the Thread City respondents, 40 per cent believed that the assassination was part of a conspiracy.[10] This proportion is particularly note-

[9] Robert Heilbroner, *The Correspondent* (January–February, 1964), p. 5.
[10] Since all interviews took place after Oswald had been shot by Ruby, the tendency to perceive a conspiracy may have increased.

worthy because the conspiracy notion was played down by the media in the days between the assassination and the interviewing. Twelve per cent believed that indigenous subversive groups—American Communists, pro-Cubans—were involved, while 8 per cent saw international Communism as responsible. The sense of conspiracy was generally diffuse, however, with 20 per cent of the responses referring to a miscellany of gangsters, segregationists, and anarchists.

When explicitly asked if they thought that a Communist conspiracy might have been behind the assassination, 40 per cent said it was a distinct possibility; only about half of these were unequivocally convinced, however. And slightly more than half the sample believed that restrictive measures should have been imposed on various groups.

The expectation that authoritarians and lower-class persons would be more likely to interpret these events in terms of a conspiracy was generally confirmed.[11] Table 5 indicates that authoritarians, blue-collar workers, and those with no college education supported the notion of a conspiracy and favored repressive action more than nonauthoritarians, white-collar workers, and better-educated respondents.

Clearly the opinions about conspiracy, investigations, and repression did not converge as much as those about Oswald's guilt. Within the various subgroups a wide range of opinion was found. Nevertheless, conspiratorial and repressive thoughts at this time of crisis were revealed by 54 per cent of the Thread City residents. The presence of such attitudes in so many people suggests that, given a slightly different configuration of events, the crisis might have resulted in popular hysteria and widespread witch-hunting.

Conclusions

The findings in Thread City show that questions about guilt and responsibility were quickly resolved in the week following the assassination. Oswald was judged guilty, his killer condemned. The belief that others, particularly Communists, might have been involved was held by many people, but there was little doubt that Oswald was the assassin.

Half the Thread City sample favored investigating and clamping down on particular groups. This represents a marked lack of consensus, for

---

[11] On the relationship of conspiracy thinking to social and psychological factors, see Seymour M. Lipset, *Political Man* (Garden City, N.Y., 1963), chap. 4; and Robert E. Lane, *Political Ideology* (New York, 1963).

TABLE 5

Conspiracy Beliefs by Occupation, Education, and Authoritarianism[a]

Sample	Held certain groups responsible			Advocated investigation of certain groups			Advocated control of certain groups			Believed Communists were involved		
	Per cent	No.	Q	Per cent	No.	Q	Per cent	No.	Q	Per cent	No.	Q
Total	39%	91		54%	72		54%	63		38%	89	
Occupation												
White-collar	23	40	.63[b]	40	35	.52[b]	41	32	.55[b]	20	41	.68[b]
Blue-collar	56	43		68	31		70	27		56	41	
Education in years												
13+	31	29	.27[b]	48	25	.24	38	24	.52	17	29	.62[b]
9–12	31	42		62	29		60	25		33	40	
0–8	77	17		56	16		77	13		82	17	
Authoritarianism												
Authoritarians	51	37	.43[b]	63	30	.31	74	27	.64[b]	54	39	.58[b]
Nonauthoritarians	29	51		48	40		38	34		23	47	

[a] The questions were: a. Do you feel that certain groups are responsible for the assassination? Which ones?
b. Do you feel that investigations should be made of any groups?
c. Do you favor a clamp-down on the activities of any groups?
d. Some people have suggested that the Communists were directly involved in the assassination. Others have said this isn't so. How do you feel about it?
[b] $p < .05$ by χ^2 test.

approximately half of the sample did not think such steps were necessary. It is perhaps not surprising to find that so many favored investigation and restriction. Herbert McClosky has reported, for example, that over a third of the population believe people should be forced to testify against themselves if there is great danger to the country, and that one-quarter believe that "in dealing with dangerous enemies like the Communists we can't afford to depend on the courts, the laws, and their slow and unreliable methods."[12] McClosky's surveys, of course, were not conducted in the tense and unusual atmosphere created by an assassination. It is worth noting McClosky's argument that if many people do not genuinely understand basic libertarian principles, they may end up undermining the very institutions they seek to defend. He points out that many of McCarthy's supporters did not reject democratic notions, but thought they were defending them by supporting the Senator.

In Thread City, at any rate, there seem to have been public capacities for both reason and unreason in the time of crisis. Vindictive and distrustful sentiments existed. That such attitudes were not activated was partly the result of attempts by political leaders to discourage them. It also seems probable that Oswald's death made less likely any popular persecution of the leftist groups with which he had been identified.

[12] Herbert McClosky, "Consensus and Ideology in American Politics," *American Political Science Review* (1964), *58*, 365.

Christopher J. Hurn and Mark Messer

Grief and Rededication

It may be precisely in its lack of readily observable long-term consequences that the assassination of President Kennedy is most significant for the student of society. The assassination has not become a political issue, nor have doubts about the identity or associations of the assassin crystallized into hardened and opposing interpretations. But if the assassination has been assimilated into the mainstream of American history, we should not assume that it was not a crisis for the society, or a threat to it. We suggest, rather, that it was assimilated because of the efficacy of the processes of reintegration that followed it.

The concepts of a "threat to society" and "reintegration" are both vague. Our argument is that both are fruitful starting points for a sociological analysis of the assassination. The death of President Kennedy presented a potential threat in at least two respects. First, different interpretations of the responsibility for the crime might have led to bitter recriminations between North and South or to persecution of various groups. Second, the violence of Kennedy's death led many people to question one aspect of their faith in their society and of their commitment to it. Thus, in answer to the question, "What was the first thing that came to your mind?" almost twenty per cent of our sample replied, "How could such a thing happen in this country?" or "What a terrible thing in this day and age!" A belief basic to law and order—

We are grateful to Scott Greer, Director of the Center for Metropolitan Studies, Northwestern University, for advice and encouragement without which this study would not have been undertaken, and to Dorothy L. Meier, Washington University, for her helpful criticism of an earlier draft of this paper.

that violence is something that happens elsewhere—was called into question.

If this interpretation is sound, we not only might expect general reintegrative processes to cope with the threat, but also should be able to specify in some detail the character of these processes. If people wondered whether the principles of nonviolence, respect for law and order, etc., were still valid, we would expect individual reaffirmation of these principles. We argue, therefore, that one of the main mechanisms of social reintegration after the assassination was individual rededication to social values.

The major independent variable in this analysis of rededicatory processes is the experience of grief. Our hypothesis is that persons who overtly exhibited grief were more likely to rededicate themselves to social values than those who did not. We do not refer to a difference between affected and unaffected respondents, but to the means by which our respondents handled the emotions universally aroused. Approximately half the respondents reported that their overt behavior after the assassination was almost entirely affective: they cried, prayed, expressed sorrow and shock, etc. The other half engaged in cognitive or evaluative behavior: they sought or gave information, discussed the consequences of the event, etc. Respondents classified as grief-stricken, then, were those who did *not* report cognitive or evaluative behavior.

Persons who simply broke down on hearing the news might not seem likely to be useful in the process of social reintegration. This is certainly true in cases of physical disaster.[1] After the assassination, however, grief responses seem to have been positively functional. Our hypothesis is that grief did not lead to anomie, but to a reaffirmation of fundamental values, and that this reaffirmation was part of the reintegration of American society.[2]

Methodology

Our data comes from self-administered questionnaires completed by a cross-section of two generations—mostly college students and their

---

[1] There is an extensive literature about the social reintegration that follows physical disaster. See, for example, Allen H. Barton *et al.*, *Social Organization Under Stress* (Washington, D.C.: National Academy of Sciences—National Research Council, 1963).

[2] The notion that grief at the death of a ruler might be functional is clearly contrary to the position put forward by Sebastian De Grazia in *The Political Community: A Study of Anomie* (Chicago, 1948). He cites "the death of the ruler" as an example of "acute anomie" (pp. 112–15).

parents—in the Chicago metropolitan area.[3] A response rate of about 85 per cent resulted in 1,728 usable questionnaires. The questionnaire was pretested four days after the assassination, and after revision, was administered to the student sample the following day. Parents completed the questionnaire during the Thanksgiving holiday. All the schedules were returned by Monday, December 2.

In spite of our efforts to get broad representativeness, the sample clearly cannot be generalized to the whole population, but perhaps it can be generalized to students and their parents in large metropolitan areas.

Results

Answers to two open-ended questions were used to classify the respondents into the grief and cognitive categories. The questions were, "What was the first thing you did after the assassination?" and (after asking the respondent whom he contacted immediately after hearing the news) "What did you do with this person?" Almost all the grief responses fell into one of three categories: "cried," "prayed," and (in answer to the second question) "expressed sorrow and shock together." The other major categories, "watched TV or listened to the radio," "asked for news," "gave news," and "discussed consequences," similarly accounted for over 80 per cent of the cognitive responses. Other, more ambiguous responses ("sought company," "talked about the event," etc.) were assigned to the grief or cognitive categories on the basis of other criteria. For example, because persons who answered "sought company" to the first question tended disproportionately to answer "expressed sorrow and shock" to the second, they were classified as grief-stricken. This procedure resulted in 905 (52 per cent) grief responses and 823 (48 per cent) cognitive responses.

The most serious criticism of this classification scheme is that it is based upon *overt* grief responses. For example, we found that 46 per cent of the 506 male students, 45 per cent of the 411 male adults, 67 per cent of the 397 female students, and 53 per cent of the 414 female adults, or 52 per cent of the total sample of 1,728, fell into the grief-

[3] The data presented in this paper were obtained from a survey conducted by the Center for Metropolitan Studies, Northwestern University, and supported by a grant from the National Institute of Mental Health. Only a small part of the data gathered in that study is considered here, and other members of the research group are not responsible for any errors we might perpetrate.

TABLE 1

Grief Responses by Location When News Was Heard

Sample	Alone		With friends		With family		With co-workers or fellow students		Other	
	No.	Pct.	No.	Pct.	No.	Pct.	No.	Pct.	No.	Pct.
Male students	83[a]	37%	60	38%	25	60%	220	48%	118	51%
Male adults	54	33	21	38	48	48	210	49	68	44
Female students . . .	43	58	43	70	24	63	182	65	105	73
Female adults	121	57	31	39	82	54	107	51	73	56
Total[b]	301	47%	155	47%	179	54%	719	53%	364	57%

[a] Read "Of the 83 male students who were alone when they heard the news, 37 per cent gave grief responses."
[b] Some of the items on the questionnaires were not always answered. Therefore, the total n for the tables is not always 1,728.

stricken category.[4] These figures do nothing to allay the suspicion that our classification yields differences that arise not from genuine differences in reactions to the event, but from differing *norms* about the acceptability of overt grief responses.

Fortunately, this conjecture may be tested. If most of the variation in grief responses between the age and sex categories is an artifact of the varying acceptability of overt grieving among these different groups, and if such grief responses are more acceptable among females than males, then males who were in a situation where these norms are most powerful—with co-workers, for example—should display less grief than males who were either alone or with their families. For females, on the other hand, little situational variation would be expected. Table 1 provides a test of this hypothesis. Persons of both sexes were more likely to grieve if they were with their families, and all but the adult females were *less* likely to grieve if they were alone. Further, males of both generations were *more* likely to display grief if they were with co-workers or fellow students. Differences between the percentages of males' grief responses in the various locations are no greater than the differences between the females' percentages.

Grief and rededication

Since our hypothesis is that there is a positive relationship between grief and individual rededication to social values, we must try to rule

[4] Comparing all males with all females, $\chi^2 = 49.1$, df $= 2$, and $p < .001$. Comparing all students with all adults, $\chi^2 = 15.8$, df $= 2$, and $p < .001$.

out the alternative hypothesis that the predicted relationship is an artifact of characteristics of persons who both exhibit grief and rededicate themselves. By introducing variables related to both grief and rededication, we hope to show that the alternative is less plausible than the principal hypothesis.

The measure of rededication was constructed as follows. Respondents were asked, "In the light of the President's assassination, do you think there is anything you *personally* should do?" and, if yes, "What is it?" Responses to the second question that were specifically partisan, that suggested increased security measures, or that suggested a campaign against extremists were considered nonrededicatory. There were two classes of responses that were considered rededicatory. The largest consisted of responses such as "improve my own life," "promote brotherhood," "be more tolerant," etc. The other consisted of responses such as "become a better citizen," "take a more active interest in the affairs of government," etc.

A second, less conservative measure of rededication was also examined. The respondents were asked whether they thought there was anything *people like them* should do. More of the sample responded affirmatively to this weaker measure of rededication (40 per cent, compared with 30 per cent).[5]

We found that 34 per cent of the 905 respondents who were classified as grief-stricken, but only 25 per cent of the 823 who reported cognitive behavior, gave rededicatory responses.[6] This confirmation of the research hypothesis becomes more convincing when other variables are controlled to rule out other explanations of the relationship. The following variables were examined: age, sex, social status, personal identification with Kennedy, and degree of political involvement.

Since grief responses were more frequent among females than males, we had to find out whether rededicatory responses were also. Table 2 examines the relationship between grief and rededication for each age and sex category. Males who gave grief responses gave a higher percentage of rededicatory responses. However, there was no such relationship for females.

---

[5] We computed both measures of rededication for all the tables shown below, but since our second, less strict measure had the same relationship to all of our independent variables, it is not reported here.

[6] $\chi^2 = 16.1$, df $= 1$, and $p < .001$.

We also tried to find out whether social status affected the relationship between grief and rededication. Because of missing data we had to use different measures of social status for students and parents. For parents, all those with high-school education or less were classified as "low status." For students our cutting point was those whose father's occupation was "small business owner" or "nonexecutive office worker"; these and all manual occupations were classified as "low status." Only about 10 per cent of our sample would be classified as "low status" by the more usual blue-collar, white-collar distinction, which would have made the subgroup comparisons in this paper impossible. Since we had found in a preliminary analysis that high social status was positively associated with rededicatory responses and negatively with grief responses (except for female students), we anticipated that the introduction of this variable would clarify the relationship between grief and rededication for both females and males.

Table 2 shows the results of this procedure. For persons with high social status, all the percentage differences in rededicatory responses for both the grief and the cognitive responses are in the predicted direction. For persons with low social status, on the other hand, not only are there two reversals of the relationship among females, but there are only slight percentage differences between the grief and cognitive categories for both male students and male parents. For both males and females with high status, therefore, grief is positively associated with rededica-

TABLE 2

Grief and Rededicatory Responses by Age, Sex, and Social Status

| | Rededicatory responses | | | | | | | | |
| | Male students | | Male adults | | Female students | | Female adults | | Total | |
Social status and response	No.	Pct.	No.	Pct.	No.	Pct.	No.	Pct.	No.	Pct.
High status										
Grief	91[a]	43%	97	24%	136	46%	95	32%	419	37%
Cognitive	121	28	131	15	57	46	90	26	399	26
Low status										
Grief	130	41	78	13	110	38	119	15	437	28
Cognitive	148	37	82	10	69	41	98	20	397	24

NOTE: Comparing both high- with low-status groups, $\chi^2 = 14.6$, df $= 8$, and $p < .01$. Comparing all grief with all cognitive responses, $\chi^2 = 13.8$, df $= 4$, and $p < .01$.
[a] Read "Of the 91 male students with high status who gave grief responses, 43 per cent gave rededicatory responses."

TABLE 3

Grief Responses by Identification, Involvement, and Status

	Grief responses			
	High political involvement		Low political involvement	
Social status and identification with JFK	No.	Pct.	No.	Pct.
High status, high identification	156[a]	60%	280	58%
High status, low identification	182	48	210	41
Low status, high identification	127	58	418	59
Low status, low identification	108	37	191	45

NOTE: Comparing all high- with all low-status respondents, $\chi^2 = 3.7$, df = 4, and $p < .5$. Comparing all high- with all low-involvement respondents, $\chi^2 = 4.0$, df = 4, and $p < .5$. Comparing all high- with all low-identification respondents, $\chi^2 = 38.9$, df = 4, and $p < .001$.
[a] Read "Of the 156 persons with high status and high identification who were high in political involvement, 60 per cent gave grief responses."

tion, for males with low status the relationship is less clear, and for females with low status the association is negative.

We next had to find out whether either grief or rededication is related to the respondent's identification with Kennedy or to his degree of political involvement. Respondents were asked, "When President Kennedy was killed, how well was he doing his job?" Those who answered, "As well as any of the outstanding Presidents," or "Very well," were classified as high identifiers. Those who reported that they were involved in arguments about the administration "once a month or more" were classified as high identifiers. Those who reported that they were "rarely" or "not at all" were classified as low in political involvement. Insofar as one element of grief is an experience of *personal loss*, we would expect that persons who identified with the President would give a high percentage of grief responses. On the other hand, we hypothesized that political involvement would be negatively related to the frequency of grief responses. Persons who were highly involved politically we would expect to handle the situation cognitively. Table 3, which shows the percentage of grief responses for three variables, identification, involvement, and social status, confirms the hypothesis about identification for both values of the other two variables and supports the hypothesis about involvement for low-status respondents, but not for high-status respondents. Among low-status respondents, high political involvement is negatively related to grief; among high-status respondents, the slight relationship is reversed.

We next had to examine the relationship of these same variables to rededication. Here we hypothesized that both identification with Kennedy and high political involvement would be positively related to rededication. If rededication is a response to a challenge of one's faith in the principles upon which one's society rests, then we might expect that politically involved persons, whose awareness of these principles is high, would rededicate themselves more frequently than persons who were not as politically involved. For somewhat different reasons, we would expect persons who identified with the President to rededicate themselves more frequently than those who did not identify. Identifiers, we suggest, were more likely not only to express grief (see Table 3), but also to grieve more intensely and, if the major hypothesis is correct, to rededicate themselves. Table 4 shows that political involvement is positively related to rededication for both high and low status, and high and low identification with the President. Likewise, identification with Ken-

TABLE 4

Grief and Rededicatory Responses by Status, Identification, and Involvement

| | Rededicatory responses | | | |
| | High political involvement | | Low political involvement | |
Responses, social status, and identification with JFK	No.	Pct.	No.	Pct.
Grief responses				
High status, high identification	94[a]	44%	161	38%
High status, low identification	87	36	87	37
Low status, high identification	74	42	247	30
Low status, low identification	40	28	86	20
Cognitive responses				
High status, high identification	62	36	119	24
High status, low identification	95	23	123	24
Low status, high identification	53	40	171	19
Low status, low identification	68	28	105	23

NOTE: Comparing all grief with all cognitive responses, $x^2 = 21.8$, df = 8, and $p < .01$. Comparing all high- with all low-status respondents, $x^2 = 7.2$, df = 4, and $p < .2$. Comparing all high- with all low-involvement respondents, $x^2 = 15.6$, df = 4, and $p < .01$. Comparing all high- with all low-identification respondents, $x^2 = 14.8$, df = 4, and $p < .01$.

[a] Read "Of the 94 persons with high status and high identification who were high in political involvement and who gave grief responses, 44 per cent gave rededicatory responses."

nedy is consistently positively related to rededication. Although we made no predictions about the relationship between social status and rededication, Table 4 shows that rededicatory responses are somewhat more likely to occur among persons with high status.

Comparing Tables 3 and 4, we see that only high identification with Kennedy is positively related to *both* grief and rededication. However, identification may not be the *only* variable that could show the association between grief and rededication to be spurious. For a full test of the hypothesis, we must see what happens when we control simultaneously for all three of our independent variables. The results of this analysis are also shown in Table 4.

Reading the table from top to bottom, we see that in six of the eight comparisons in each half of the table our general hypothesis is supported. The two exceptions, moreover, are not serious reversals of the relationships. None of our independent variables, either separately or in combination, appear to explain the relationship between grief and rededication. Thus, altogether for both high and low status and for both the grief and the cognitive category, the highest percentage of rededicatory responses occurs for persons of high political involvement and high identification with Kennedy, this percentage is higher in both cases for respondents classified as grief-stricken than for the others. Further, it may be noted that for the persons with high status, *all* the percentages for grief-stricken respondents are higher than any of the percentages for the other respondents.

The two final tests of our central hypothesis are cast in somewhat different form. Ideally, to verify the relationship between grief and rededication we should find out whether extreme grief is more closely associated with rededication than moderate grief. Although we lack a quantitative measure of grief, we can distinguish between grief-stricken respondents who wished to be alone when they heard the news and respondents who wished to be with others. Whether a desire to eschew social interaction represents more extreme grief is a moot point. However, this distinction between asocial and social grief responses is of some sociological importance. With Durkheim in mind, we might expect persons who preferred to express their grief with others to give a higher percentage of rededicatory responses. As Shils and Young argued, "this moral remaking cannot be achieved except by the means of reunions, assemblies, and meetings where the individuals, being closely united to

TABLE 5

Grief and Rededicatory Responses by Sociability

| | Rededicatory responses by | | | | | |
| | Those who wanted to be alone | | Those who wanted to be with their family | | Those who wanted to be with others | |
Response	No.	Pct.	No.	Pct.	No.	Pct.
Grief	266[a]	40%	347	30%	286	31%
Cognitive	209	32	256	24	356	20
Total	475	37%	603	28%	642	25%

N O T E : Comparing those who wanted to be alone with those who wanted to be with their family or others, $x^2 = 15.2$, df = 2, and $p < .001$. Comparing those who gave grief responses with those who gave cognitive responses, $x^2 = 14.4$, df = 3, and $p < .01$.
[a] Read "Of the 266 persons who wanted to be alone when they heard the news and who gave grief responses, 40 per cent gave rededicatory responses."

one another, reaffirm in common their common sentiments."[7] Table 5 indicates, however, that persons who wanted to be alone gave a higher percentage of rededicatory responses than persons who wanted to be with others. Again, in each situation persons classified as grief-stricken gave a higher percentage of rededicatory responses. These relationships proved consistent when controlled for age and sex and for the three independent variables, identification, involvement, and status.

These results force us back to the question, "Why?" We are led to search for a variable that mediates between grief and rededication and that renders the relationship somewhat more meaningful. One such variable, we hypothesized, was the degree to which the respondent felt personally involved in the responsibility for the assassination. Specifically, persons who regarded the assassination as the isolated action of a crackpot were less likely to feel personally involved in responsibility for the crime than persons who attributed the assassination to "the climate of hatred and violence in America." The latter, we predicted, would be both more likely to grieve and more likely to rededicate themselves. Table 6 suggests that this variable may indeed mediate between grief and rededication and that a sense of responsibility for the assassination may be one element in the linkage between grief and rededication.

[7] Emile Durkheim, *Elementary Forms of Religious Life* (London, 1915), p. 427; quoted by Edward Shils and Michael Young in "The Meaning of the Coronation," *Sociological Review* (1953), *1*, 67. See also A. R. Radcliffe-Brown, *The Andaman Islanders* (Cambridge, England, 1922), chap. 5.

TABLE 6

Grief and Rededicatory Responses by Social Responsibility

| | Rededicatory responses by | | | |
| | Those who blamed a crackpot | | Those who blamed a climate of violence and hatred | |
Response	No.	Pct.	No.	Pct.
Grief	328[a]	26%	143	45%
Cognitive	365	19	103	36
Total	693	22%	246	41%

NOTE: Comparing those who blamed a crackpot with those who blamed a climate of violence, $x^2 = 29.0$, df $= 2$, and $p < .001$. Comparing those who gave grief responses with those who gave cognitive responses, $x^2 = 6.5$, df $= 2$, and $p < .05$.

[a] Read "Of the 328 persons who blamed the assassination on a crackpot and who gave grief responses, 26 per cent gave rededicatory responses."

Conclusions

The assassination of President Kennedy brought the respondents, some of them for the first time perhaps, into an intense involvement with a public event. If the amount of involvement is not in question, both its character and its consequences are. Was this involvement with a public event essentially vicarious or did the respondents perceive a *connection* between public events and individual lives? The data suggest that between one-fourth and one-third of our respondents made this connection. For them the assassination was a true merging of social and individual concerns. Those who volunteered rededicatory responses perceived a relationship between a public event and the manner in which they and others had hitherto conducted their lives. They did not feel merely that "something should be done" or that people like themselves should rededicate their lives, but that they themselves should attempt to be more tolerant, promote brotherhood, and become better citizens.

There was a relationship also between the kind of involvement and rededicatory responses. Those whose reaction to the event was to seek or give information or to discuss the consequences of the assassination were less likely to rededicate themselves than those who reported that grief dominated their behavior immediately after the assassination. One of the consequences of grief, therefore, may have been to narrow the gap between personal and public concerns, to translate a social event into terms directly relevant to the individual.

Two explanations are suggested. Grief, by personalizing public events, by rendering them more immediate, facilitates articulation of personal and public concern. Second, the experience of grief after the assassination led to a heightened sense of responsibility for the crime, to an awareness that the respondent was personally involved in and even culpable for the assassination of the President.

We have only touched the surface of the question of why our presumed relationship between grief and rededication should exist. If grief articulates public events and personal concerns, we have suggested no general explanation of *how* it does. Here lie obvious opportunities for further research. We need to know more about the kind of grief experienced. Was it, as the NORC report suggests, a personal grief at the loss of "someone close and dear," or were the respondents experiencing grief, not so much as a personal loss, but rather on behalf of their society? Did persons grieve because the collectivity had lost its leader or because they had lost a man with whom they personally identified? These are important questions for future analyses.

Sidney Verba

The Kennedy Assassination and the Nature of Political Commitment

For God's sake, let us sit upon the ground
And tell sad stories of the death of kings.

Classic political history is the history of the life and death of kings. It is the intensely human drama of great men, for the king is a fallible mortal whom we can see and understand. But it is more than a human drama, for the king is also the symbol of society and nation, and is endowed with the highest religious significance.[1] And the king is the government as well; how he performs in peace and war determines how his nation and subjects live. Thus the life and death of kings merges the history of great institutions with the story of individual men, the secular ruler with the sacred symbol. Political life is endowed with religious significance. It engages us intellectually and emotionally. It is the fit subject for the Shakespearean tragedies.

Political science today studies the complex interaction of many highly differentiated individuals, groups, and governmental institutions; it differentiates between the individual personality and the social role. And the sacred and the secular are no longer linked; politics is viewed as a secular enterprise, at least in the developed nations of the West.[2] The unity of politics embodied in the person of the king is lost.

The events surrounding the Kennedy assassination may offer a unique

---

[1] On the dual significance of the king, see Ernst H. Kantorowicz, *The King's Two Bodies: A Study in Medieval Theology* (Princeton, 1957).

[2] Edward Shils and Michael Young argue that this is why social scientists have not paid sufficient attention to rituals like the British coronation. See "The Meaning of the Coronation," *Sociological Review* (1953), *1*, 63–81.

opportunity for the reintegration of our somewhat fragmented picture of the political system. This paper will attempt to link the more precise behavioral studies of the assassination to the functioning of the larger political system. Such a task is elusive; this essay can only touch some aspects of the problem and must remain more speculative than the studies of the reactions of individuals. But it is a worthwhile enterprise. The way the many aspects of politics were connected in the study of the lives of kings may have been too easy, but some such connection is needed.

The assassination crisis. Political crises are decisive moments in societies. They are moments when political institutions are called upon to function at new levels, when political activities take on a new intensity, and when the salience of political matters rises suddenly and substantially. Crises are often, but not always, generated outside of the political system—by economic collapse, by foreign attack, or in this case, by the violent act of a lone individual. They are important because they place in relief the institutions of the political system and the beliefs of its members; they bring to the fore what may have been implicit and unobserved in a society. Crises are often the major constitutive events of a political system. It is often at times of crisis that new institutions are formed and existing political institutions are tested to the full. It is only at such times of crisis and strain that one can observe the capacity of such institutions, and how they operate under such tests may determine their fate. Furthermore, it is during crises that most people learn about the nature of their political system. People not ordinarily involved in politics are suddenly deeply involved. They see the operation of the system in an intense light, and what they learn at the moment of crisis will determine what they believe about politics after the crisis.[3]

The particular nature of the Kennedy assassination crisis makes it possible to observe the total American political system in operation—insofar as it is meaningful to talk of observing an abstraction like a political system. This is because the crisis affected so many levels of American politics and society. It involved the top and central institutions of the American government—those having to do with the transfer of

[3] For a general discussion of the role of salient political crises in the development of political beliefs, see Sidney Verba, "Comparative Political Culture," in Lucian Pye and Sidney Verba, eds., *Political Culture and Political Development* (Princeton, 1965). See also Robert E. Ward and Dankwart A. Rustow, "Conclusion," in Ward and Rustow, eds., *Political Modernization in Turkey and Japan* (Princeton, 1964), pp. 65–68.

power, the succession to high office, and the most crucial decisions of policy that affect our nation. At the same time it involved all the intermediary institutions of the American political process: all levels of government, national, state, and local; various branches of government, military and civilian; and many nongovernmental institutions, notably the American political parties. Furthermore, the great role of the communication media in a modern political system was made explicit in the crisis. And lastly, it involved the micro-units of society—the families and groups of friends that clustered around television sets and reacted as groups to this event—as well as the members of the American society as individuals. Above all, the activities of individuals, of primary groups, of intermediary groups, of the mass media, and of the highest governmental institutions were all focused on the same event. And these various levels were constantly interacting with each other.

Despite all our information about how the members of the political system were affected by the crisis, we know very little about the impact of the crisis on the system itself. The difficulty here is the difficulty of generalizing from a single case. A crisis is a particular event in a particular social setting. Its impact depends in part on the nature of that setting. But using such a crisis as a basis for understanding its setting—in this case, understanding something about the nature of the American political community—involves knowing, ideally, what the impact of such a crisis might be in some other setting. One would want to know—and the question is intriguing—what the reaction to this crisis might have been in an America of 1953, during the height of the McCarthy era, or what the reaction might have been in some other country. We do not, of course, have such clearly comparable situations. But knowledge of succession crises in other societies can help to highlight the important characteristics of this particular succession crisis.

The crisis and institutional performance. Since we wish to examine the meaning for the American political system of the reactions to the assassination, we should mention one of the most obvious (and because obvious perhaps not sufficiently stressed) aspects of the crisis: the rapid and efficient formal transfer of presidential power. The chaos in the Dallas Police Department has tended to obscure the fact that the formal procedures for transferring power went so smoothly. There was almost no time during which the locus of executive power was uncertain, no major period of jockeying for power, and, indeed, little change in personnel or policy direction.

What may be more important is the extent to which the specific mode of institutional transfer was congruent with the basic values and expectations of the American people. We have detailed knowledge of what the American people thought about during the crisis and what inferences they drew from the crisis. At no time does it appear that anyone at any level of the society asked whether the institutions specified in the Constitution should or would operate. Criticism and doubt existed about the general tone of American political life or the activities of particular agencies, but the validity of the central institutional structure seems to have been taken for granted. Indeed, the questions that were not raised during the crisis illustrate how fundamental and implicit is the commitment to these political institutions. Compare succession crises elsewhere. It is not so much that the American military did not attempt to take control of the government; it is that no one even thought to ask where the military's support lay. And though there were many who suspected that a conspiracy lay behind the assassination, it was thought of as a low-level or external conspiracy—that is, few considered it a conspiracy generated within the American government in an attempt to change leadership or the direction of policy.

The reaction to the assassination and political commitment. The assassination crisis increases our understanding of various institutions of American politics because it allows us to see them operating in a time of strain. It increases our understanding of the American political process also, because it makes apparent certain patterns of political belief and commitment that in ordinary times remain latent and unobservable. The parallel drawn between the assassination crisis and Shakespearean tragedy is, I believe, more than a passing analogy. In Shakespearean tragedy, personal emotion and public performance, the fate of individual men and the fate of nations, the sacred and the secular, are linked. On the weekend of the crisis, these things were also linked in the minds of those observing—in some real sense, participating in—the events of the assassination.

Since *The Lonely Crowd* we have been wont to think of the emotional relationship of most Americans to the political life of their country as essentially "cool" and detached. Detached amusement or perhaps indignation is the appropriate posture. The assassination and the reaction to it reveal a level of emotional commitment that lay unnoticed beneath the surface. That there was an intense and almost universal emotional reaction to the assassination is amply revealed in the studies in this volume. And though the assassination was extremely important politically, as most observers seem to have been aware, the reactions were highly personal. Family imagery recurs in reactions to the event: people spoke with pain of the shattering of the Kennedy family, or felt as if they had lost a member of their own family. Ideological interpretations of the event and concern with the impact of the event on the American political process were much rarer.

The Kennedy assassination also illustrates the close meshing of the sacred and the secular in the top institutions of a political system. In a society in which the formal ideology is officially secular, in which ceremony is relatively underplayed (compared with societies having monarchic or aristocratic traditions), and in which the assassinated leader was of a minority and controversial religion, the close linkage of religious institutions to the events of the crisis weekend is particularly striking. As illustrated by the data in this volume, a large proportion of the American population responded to the assassination with prayer or attendance at special church services, and religious ceremony and imagery abounded in the events of the weekend.

What this suggests is that complete separation of church and state may be possible in only a formal sense. In a secular society where formal religious commitment is weak, the activities of the state may be the nearest one comes to activities of ultimate importance, activities that fundamentally determine matters of death and life and the quality of life. In short, governmental institutions may have significance of a religious kind. The awe inspired by the ultimate power of the church in more pious times may be akin to the awe inspired in modern secular societies by the ultimate power of the state.

Of even greater importance may be the particular role of the presidency in symbolizing the ultimate nature of state power. Recent studies have shown that the President plays a variety of roles not visualized in the Constitution. He is the symbolic referent for the learning of political commitment; children first become aware of political matters through an awareness of and diffuse attachment to the President.[4] As Durkheim pointed out, complex social collectivities, of which nation-states are the biggest and most complex, are not easily the direct objects of emotional

[4] Robert D. Hess and David Easton, "The Child's Image of the Presidency," *Public Opinion Quarterly* (1960), *24*, 632–44; and Fred I. Greenstein, "The Benevolent Leader: Children's Images of Political Authority," *American Political Science Review* (1960), *54*, 934–43.

attachment or commitment. Rather some common symbol that stands for the unit and with which people can identify is required. And such attachment is possible to the greatest degree "when the symbol is something simple, definite, and easily representable, while the thing itself [i.e., the social collectivity], owing to its dimensions, the number of its parts, and the complexity of its arrangements, is difficult to hold in the mind."[5] Durkheim was dealing for the most part with relatively simple societies and with the religious symbols that held them together. But what may be most interesting is the way this central symbolic role in a modern secular society is preempted by the political symbols that stand on the highest level for the society—in the American case by the presidency above all.

The presidential role is thus endowed with a religious quality. In many of the new nations of the world, where social change is more rapid and revolutionary than it has usually been in recent western history, scholars have noted the replacement of traditional religious beliefs by belief in a political religion.[6] Commitment to the political, because it replaces the total commitment to traditional religious patterns and arises as part of a general rejection of the traditional patterns, tends to take an all-or-nothing form. Politics demands complete dedication; political deviation is heresy. American society operates on a lower level of intensity. There is little intense commitment in either the religious or the political sphere; there is instead a pluralism of commitments and certainly less expression of political or religious emotion. (Interestingly enough, when there is intense religious commitment, as in some fundamentalist religions, it is often associated with extreme political views). But the relationship between religion and politics in the United States may be analogous to what it is in the new nations. Religion and politics in the United States are closely related to each other, and many of the functions that religion and religious symbolism perform elsewhere in holding society together are performed in the United States by the central political symbols. If in the new states a passionate political religion replaces an intense traditional religious commitment, in a modern society such as the United States a somewhat less intense political religion assumes some of the functions of a less intense religious system.

[5] Emile Durkheim, *The Elementary Forms of Religious Life* (London, n.d.), p. 211.
[6] David E. Apter, "Political Religion in the New States," in Clifford Geertz, ed., *Old Societies and New States* (New York, 1963).

What I am suggesting is that the absence of ritual in American politics, the absence of an aristocratic or monarchic tradition, and the
self-conscious secularization of political life may obscure the extent to
which political commitment in the United States contains a prime component of primordial religious commitment. The reactions to the assassination—the intense emotion, the religious observances, and the po-
litico-religious symbolism—are evidence (though hardly proof) that
such commitment exists. And the President is the appropriate focus of
this commitment, for like the medieval king he is the concrete human
individual whom one can see, on whom one can focus attention, and
with whom one can share common human emotions, and yet he is something transcending his concrete human aspects, for he is also the symbol
of the nation.[7] And as Durkheim stressed, the symbols of nationhood
are more than particular objects that are made to stand for something
larger; they are major constitutive elements of polities and societies.
Relatively simple social units whose functions are not very significant
for the participants and that can be easily visualized might survive
without some collective representation. But, as the frantic search for
symbols by leaders of the new nations indicates, nations are unlikely to
survive long without some such central symbols.[8]

But where does this central commitment to the symbols of nationhood
—in this case the presidency—and to the nation thus symbolized origi-
nate? Early socialization of children is one source, but periodic ceremonies and collective events that allow the members of the society
mutually to reinforce each other's commitment by collective activities
are another way. In the relatively simple societies of which Durkheim
wrote, this was accomplished by periodic reunions and ceremonials. In
a complex and widely extended society like the United States, a society
without the ceremonies of royalty, such reunions and common observances are somewhat rarer, though national elections and some national
holidays may be examples of such events. The assassination crisis is important here because it is probably the nearest equivalent in a large
modern nation-state to the kind of intense mutual rededication ceremony
that is possible in a smaller and simpler society. There are several fea-

[7] Kantorowicz stresses the important parallel between the dual human-transcendent nature of the King and the man-God nature of Christ. It is the dual nature that makes the
King such a dominant symbol.
[8] See, for instance, McKim Marriott, "Cultural Policy in the New States," in Geertz, ed.,
Old Societies.

tures that make it such a ceremony. The fact that it involved almost total participation is important. The figures on the universality of information and involvement are overwhelming as evidence of the ability of the mass media—television in particular—to link a large nation together. Furthermore, the media communicated not only information but shared emotion. It may not be the event itself that is most significant for this ceremonial aspect (though it took a special kind of event to focus so much attention and emotion); the fact that the reaction to the event was shared seems more important. It was in many cases shared by families gathered around television sets, it was shared in church services and other community ceremonials, but it was intensely and widely shared through the media themselves. Not only were the emotions of individual Americans involved, but they were made clearly aware of the emotions of their fellow Americans.

Kennedy the man and Kennedy the symbol. But can one really talk of the assassination crisis in terms of these vast national symbols? Certainly one aspect of the crisis was its immediate human quality. A particularly young and attractive President, the President's family—these are essential features of the event and the reaction to it. Does the intense emotional involvement reported in this volume indicate the importance of national symbolism and a deep emotional commitment to politics? Or does it simply suggest how people might react to the violent death of any personality as well known as President Kennedy?

The question is crucial but unanswerable. The assassination is not one of a recurring set of phenomena; hence one cannot ask whether the same reactions might emerge when the particular setting and participants differ. Indeed, the assassination (when thought of in relation to the overall American political system and not to the millions of individuals who reacted to it) is a prime example of that bane of the student of politics, the nonrecurring single case from which one can learn nothing but that is of such crucial political significance that one must try, nevertheless, to learn from it. One could try to answer the question in two ways. In the first place one could ask if such reactions would have arisen if the President had been a different person. One does not know, but there is evidence that the reaction to the death in office of previous Presidents was intense and by no means commensurate with what one would have expected on the basis of their personal characteristics.[9] Con-

[9] See the references to the reactions to the assassination of President McKinley and the death of Franklin D. Roosevelt in the essay by Sheatsley and Feldman in this volume.

versely, one could ask if such an intense reaction as followed the Kennedy assassination would have followed the violent death of some equally well-known personage who did not occupy the highest political office. Again one cannot answer definitely, but one suspects not. To some extent the question answers itself, for it is the very fact that Kennedy was the President that made his personal as well as public life so well known. The exposure of nonpolitical figures (say, from the entertainment world) may be great, but it tends to be more heavily stratified and limited to particular groups.

To determine the uniqueness of the event, one would have to partial out the various aspects of the impact of President Kennedy—his personal characteristics, his symbolic and semireligious position, his vast instrumental powers as President. But it is just because these three are in fact so inextricably linked that the assassination of a President is an intense event and the presidency itself such an important unifying institution.

I have focused thus far largely on the linkage between the individual man and the symbolic role of the presidency. Unlike, say, the British Monarch the American President has also a powerful instrumental political role. As Bagehot pointed out, the position of the monarchy above partisan politics enhances its symbolic potential by protecting it from the heat of political controversy. Not so the presidency. Yet there are, I believe, several reasons why the American President can perform a symbolic function despite his actual power position. For one thing, of course, the power itself is a source of the awe that the presidential role inspires. If the actual political power of the President makes the incumbent vulnerable to the sort of criticism that the British Queen's nonpolitical position protects her from, the political power also makes it unlikely that the American presidency would be subjected to many of the criticisms leveled at the royal family for its triviality and lack of function. Bagehot's separation of the instrumental and symbolic parts of the British government may cut both ways. Furthermore, the presidency may be viewed as essentially a nonpartisan office from whose incumbent one may expect at least a reasonably responsible performance. For one thing, the studies of early images of the President among children suggest that one first views him as a benign and diffuse authority figure, not as a figure of partisan controversy. And the reactions to the crisis itself show that there are few sharp differences between the adherents of the two major parties in their reactions to the assassination. It would be hard to find evidence that the crisis was in any important sense a partisan matter.

The effects of the crisis. Crises bring into relief certain aspects of political systems that might otherwise remain implicit and unnoticed. But such events not only make the characteristics of a political system clear, but also have a major effect on the system itself. A crisis, such as the assassination of the President, involves a sudden rise in the salience of politics among the public. Many people who were essentially apolitical or parochial suddenly become deeply concerned with and aroused by political matters. This sudden involvement of all the segments of society, including many whose involvement in politics is rare or intermittent, may involve some danger for the political system. As has been frequently pointed out, the last group mobilized—the group that is immune from all influence and political communication save the most intense—is a group of great volatility. Being somewhat unused to politics and being involved in politics only in the extreme, they are likely to react more emotionally than people with more experience. It is thus during crises that people learn the major lessons of politics, in the sense of forming basic impressions of their political system and of the other groups that make up the system.

Crises may, therefore, have major integrative effects on society or major disintegrative effects. They are likely to reinforce whichever of the two tendencies is stronger in the society. It has been pointed out, for instance, that the major crises in Italian history have been disintegrative ones—that is, each major crisis from the Risorgimento through the Resistance to the founding of the current Republic has had the effect of alienating one social group from others and from the political elite.[10] Evidence suggests that in American politics great crises tend to have integrative effects—at least in foreign affairs. Anything that increases the salience of the presidency, even such a blunder as the U-2 incident or the Bay of Pigs invasion, seems to lead to a more favorable evaluation of the presidency. This would seem to bear out the basic symbolic importance of the presidency: if events cause one to think about the presidency, the result is increased commitment.

There is little doubt of the integrative effect of the assassination. Par-

---

[10] See Joseph LaPalombara, "Italy: Fragmentation, Isolation, Alienation," in Pye and Verba, eds., *Political Culture.*

tisanship declined in intensity, as the study by Sears shows. The opinions of the American people about Kennedy's presidency soared after the assassination. The crisis had an integrative effect on the American political system in several ways. In the first place, the fundamental institutions of the American political process were put to a test before the entire public. If it is true that such institutions work at least in part because people believe they will work, then the fact that so many people saw them work in this particular case probably increases their future effectiveness. Second, the crisis demonstrated the reliability of a variety of intermediary institutions in our society. In particular, I believe it demonstrated the reliability of the mass media. That a crisis of this sort did not create greater anxiety about the stability of the American government probably depends largely on the fact that channels of mass communication were available that were objective and, what may be more important, were *believed* to be objective by the American public. To see the importance of such rapid and reliable communication facilities, one has only to imagine what the crisis would have been like without them. Furthermore, the other intermediary institutions that were involved in the crisis—such institutions as the American military and the two opposing political parties—all demonstrated their basic commitment to the norms of the democratic system. Lastly, the crisis was integrative in that it involved the collective and largely self-conscious sharing of a significant emotional experience by a national population. Not only did the individual American mourn, but the mourning went on in groups, and in a communication context that made it apparent to all that they were sharing this experience with most others around the country. In a sense the crisis was the occasion for an unexpected rededication ceremony.

The emotion triggered by the Kennedy assassination was an intensely private emotion, akin to the emotion at the death of a close relative. But it had an important public dimension. It was directed at a public object, it was shared, it was overtly expressed in a society in which such overt expression is rare. That the emotion was so intense and took such a public form was, I believe, due to the particular political nature of the event. It is unlikely that the assassination created emotional commitment on the spot. Rather it brought to the fore a preexisting commitment—a commitment fundamental to the political community in the United States.

There has been a tendency to assume that politics is linked to deep emotional and religious commitments only in traditional societies, in which the sacred and the secular are intertwined, or in societies dedicated to mass mobilization in which commitment to the central institutions of the state becomes dominant and replaces any other. But such deep commitment may also be important, though less apparent and overt, in modern pluralistic societies. The emotional context of the assassination partakes somewhat of the commitment found in smaller traditional societies. It was shared within the primary units of society; it was a primordial and implicit commitment shared by most members of the society and probably acquired during early socialization. Though it was greater in extent—it covered a vast nation and was communicated largely through the "impersonal" mass media—yet one could not describe the reaction as a "mass" response. It was an emotional experience mediated by many nongovernmental institutions, in particular the religious institutions and the family, and above all it was not an emotional commitment that implied a rejection of other commitments.

Perhaps the most important aspect of the reaction to the assassination is the way it illustrates the complex admixture of the rational institutions of politics with the more traditional, religious, and indeed somewhat magical aspects of political commitment. The transfer of power to the new President is a rational-legal procedure in which the limits to individual initiative and on the individual personality are great. Yet it is through this procedure that the symbolic and charismatic aspects of office are also transmitted.

What holds a complicated and pluralistic political society like the United States together? We used to think it was a common democratic ideology, but lately we are not so sure. Americans apparently do not think of politics in any but the vaguest terms; the commitment to democratic values in any overt sense does not appear to extend much below the level of slogans.[11] The reactions to the assassination support this view—there is little overt ideological content to the reactions.

But this may not mean that common beliefs are irrelevant to the political system. What the Kennedy assassination may show is that the

[11] See James W. Prothro and C. W. Grigg, "Fundamental Principles of Democracy: Bases of Agreement and Disagreement," *Journal of Politics* (1960), 22, 276–94; Angus Campbell *et al., The American Voter* (New York, 1960), chap. 10; and Herbert McCloskey, "Consensus and Ideology in American Politics," *American Political Science Review* (1964), 57, 361–82.

level of commitment to politics is both more intense than that revealed by the usual public-opinion-surveying techniques, and of a somewhat different order. For one thing, it is a diffuse emotional commitment not closely related to any particular political ideology, issue, or controversy, which may be why it is so inadequately tapped by the usual issue- or election-oriented public opinion studies; and it is a commitment that lies beneath the surface of ordinary day-to-day politics. As such, it may be the kind of primordial emotional attachment that is necessary for the long-term maintenance of a political system. It is not the rather fragile support that is based solely on a calculation of interests; it is support based on a longer-run, less rational sort of attachment.

And the fact that it is latent and unrecognized under ordinary circumstances is also important. The ordinary operation of politics in a pluralistic country like the United States involves many compromises, much juggling and reconciliation of values, and many activities in which the finer points of principle are ignored. Such may be the price of pluralism. But the man who approached such a political system with his deepest moral commitments close to the surface could only retreat in disgust or remain cynically fascinated with the process he observed. Thus a deep emotional commitment to politics may be unstabilizing if it is constantly in the foreground, but it may also be unstabilizing if it is not somewhere in the background.[12] What the assassination indicated is that such a commitment exists and can be brought to the fore. But a comparison of the emotional tone of political discussion before the crisis and during it—a comparison clearly reflected by the data in this volume—shows that the emotional commitment is not a part of the ordinary day-to-day operation of politics. It also suggests why "business as usual" returned so quickly, and why that quick return is important.

[12] For a more general statement of the relationship between commitment and democratic stability, see Gabriel A. Almond and Sidney Verba, *The Civic Culture: Political Attitudes and Democracy in Five Nations* (Princeton, 1963), chap. 15.

Bradley S. Greenberg and Edwin B. Parker

Social Research on the Kennedy Assassination

Most of the studies in this volume were conducted by psychologists, sociologists, political scientists, communication researchers, and other social scientists, but they do not use the behavioral scientists' usual strategy for seeking generalizations; they are concerned here with a unique event. Nevertheless, an accurate description of social communication processes and of people's reactions to such a historically significant event is valuable in its own right. It is valuable both to those concerned with the assassination and its aftermath as a unique sequence of events and to those concerned with abstracting from such unique sequences a more general understanding of certain social processes.

No previous single event has generated as much empirical social science research. The only comparable body of data about any one event came from studies of the televised debates between Kennedy and Nixon, for which a similar claim was made three years ago.[1] It is ironic that Kennedy was a central figure in both these research efforts, which may have ushered in a new era in the use of behavioral science research methods to study significant contemporary events.

The purpose of this summary is three-fold: (1) to pull together in as meaningful a configuration as possible the major modes of public response to the assassination as they have been isolated in this volume's

[1] Elihu Katz and Jacob J. Feldman, "The Debates in the Light of Research: A Survey of Surveys," in *The Great Debates*, ed., Sidney Kraus (Bloomington, Indiana, 1962), pp. 173–223.

TABLE 1

Immediate Reactions to News of the Assassination

Reaction	Respondents who said this was their "very deepest feeling."	
	National sample (n = 1,384)	Dallas sample (n = 212)
Felt so sorry for his wife and children	92%	90%
Felt sorry that a strong young man had been killed at the height of his powers	88	83
Felt ashamed that this could happen in our country	83	86
Felt the loss of someone very close and dear	79	72
Felt angry that anyone should do such a terrible deed	73	68
Worried about how his death would affect the political situation in this country	47	41
Worried about how his death would affect our relations with other countries	44	42
Worried about how the United States would carry on without its leader	41	33
Was so confused and upset, didn't know what to feel	38	40
Thought it was done by some Communist or other radical to get rid of the President	24	28
Wondered if anybody could really be safe in this country these days when the President himself can get shot	21	20
Worried how this might affect my own life, job, and future . .	20	24
Thought it was done by a segregationist or extreme right-winger	18	15
Hoped the man who killed him would be shot down or lynched	11	9
Worried whether person who did it would be a member of my race or religion and bring on persecution	6	7
Felt that in many ways the President had brought it on himself	4	3

papers, (2) to point to major inconsistencies in data or interpretations, and to indicate if and how they may be accommodated, and (3) to determine whether broader theoretic generalizations or hypotheses may reasonably be inferred from these specific data.

Schramm has done part of this in his introductory chapter. He has summarized the responses of the media to the assassination as a news event, the responses of persons to first hearing about the assassination, and the responses in the immediate aftermath of the assassination. He has discussed how communication media influenced the flow of information and the formation of beliefs and feelings. We do not wish to duplicate his efforts. Instead we wish to point out the remarkable similarity of the results obtained by different researchers using samples from different parts of the country. In all the research, there are very few contradictions.

Table 1 compares the immediate reactions found by the NORC national sample and those found by the Dallas sample. One might well expect to find regional differences in such data, but it is the similarity between the two samples that is striking. In no case is the discrepancy more than eight percentage points, and the average discrepancy is only three percentage points. Dallas respondents were less likely (by eight percentage points) to "feel quite deeply worried about how the United States would carry on without its leader," and less likely (by seven percentage points) to "feel deeply the loss of someone very close and dear."

Similarly, the physical or emotional symptoms found by the studies are alike. Table 2 compares the national sample with the Dallas sample. On all such measures but one, "felt like getting drunk," Dallas respondents reported a higher incidence of symptoms, but the average difference was still only five percentage points. The greatest difference was fourteen percentage points between the NORC and Dallas samples in "feeling very nervous and tense." By the next week, the average difference in the incidence of the symptoms was down to two and a half percentage points.

The major finding of Sigel's comparison of adults' and children's responses is their similarity. Ninety-two per cent of the adults and 93 per cent of the children "felt so sorry for his wife and children"; 83 per

TABLE 2

Physical and Emotional Symptoms

Symptom	Felt during four days		Felt at time of interview	
	National	Dallas	National	Dallas
Didn't feel like eating	43%	52%	12%	15%
Smoked much more than usual	29	34	10	8
Had headaches	25	26	9	7
Had an upset stomach	22	26	5	6
Cried	53	56	20	20
Had trouble getting to sleep	48	53	18	17
Felt very nervous and tense	68	82	24	36
Felt like getting drunk	4	3	1	1
Felt more tired than usual	42	50	15	18
Felt dizzy at times	12	14	4	7
Lost temper more than usual	19	21	4	3
Hands sweated and felt damp and clammy . .	17	19	4	4
Had rapid heart beats	26	32	6	6
Felt sort of dazed and numb	57	69	20	14
Kept forgetting things	34	35	12	8
Felt none of these	11	a	50	a

a Not reported in this study.

cent of both children and adults "felt ashamed that this could happen in our country."

Effects of the Assassination

Some researchers were able not only to describe responses to the assassination but also to provide some evidence about how the responses differed from what they would have been had the assassination not taken place. Bradburn and Feldman compared the incidence of grief and anxiety symptoms among the same people before and after the assassination, and showed that there was an increase in grief symptoms but not in anxiety symptoms. Using data from an experiment in progress at the time of the assassination, Sears demonstrated that the assassination reduced political partisanship among Republicans.

Another standard behavioral science approach to the measurement of effects was used by Hurn and Messer in their analysis of the relationship between the experience of grief and a subsequent rededication to basic social values. By demonstrating the existence of the basic relationship and then presenting evidence that progressively ruled out at least the most plausible of the alternative explanations, they strengthened their hypothesis that there is a causal connection between grief and rededication.

These measures of the assassination's effects obviously cannot adequately separate the effects of any one of its complex facets from those of any other facet. There was no way to determine how the response might have differed if Kennedy had died of a heart attack instead of an assassin's bullet, or if the assassin had espoused right-wing extremist views, or if he had been a member of a conspiracy. There was no way to reliably measure the effects of the one kind of television coverage we had. Speculative comparisons with Europe, which lacked our pervasive coverage, might suggest that the extensive television exposure during the weekend enable people to achieve "cognitive closure." Such closure apparently was not achieved in Europe; uncertainties and suspicions about possible conspiracies, doubts about Oswald's guilt, lingered much longer than in the United States. However, relevant data were not systematically collected in Europe. In any case, we still would not know which differences between the United States and Europe to attribute this difference to.

Most social scientists focus their interest not on the unique event, however significant, but on generalizations about human behavior. For example, the Spitzers examined the diffusion of news, not about the one event, but about two. They then compared these findings with a dozen previously reported studies of news diffusion, and were able to make broader generalizations. Greenberg showed that the diffusion pattern of assassination news supported the general hypothesis that person-to-person communication is the first source of news primarily for events that receive maximum or minimum attention from the public.[2] Such uses of the data are beyond the scope of this volume, but we hope that they will provide base lines for many other comparisons.

The data in this volume generally indicate that the responses of different groups of Americans differed not so much in content as in degree. However, closer examination of who was affected in what manner shows that people varied more than was immediately apparent in both the content and the degree of their responses. This was so whether the responses dealt with attention to the event, attitudes and beliefs about it, physical and emotional symptoms, or the rate and manner of recovery.

Comparisons of the responses of Republicans and Democrats, middle-class and working-class respondents, Negroes and whites, for example, can tell us much in general about our society and the behavior of groups in it. If meaningful generalizations are to be extracted from these event-bound data, this is the most likely way. However, this approach is limited by the available data. In one sense the data are amenable to it and in two others they are not. On the positive side, most investigators provide data on the differential responses of subgroups determined by a rather small set of characteristics, principally race, sex, age, political preference, and social class. On the negative side, these studies deal with different populations, and use different measures for the background variables and somewhat different measures for the response variables. The other limitation is that most of the studies lack any multivariate analysis. Rarely have we found more than one background variable in a table of responses. It is therefore necessary to consider one by one the correlations of each background variable with the response characteristics. Given the data in their present form, we cannot isolate intervening or mediating variables, or specify combined effects. For example, we cannot compare the response of a Democratic Negro with that of a Democrat or a Negro, or even a Republican white. Many study directors have subsequently begun such analysis, where their sample size permitted. Some

[2] Bradley S. Greenberg, "Person-to-Person Communication in the Diffusion of News Events," *Journalism Quarterly* (1964), *41*, 489–94.

delayed those analyses in order to prepare their findings for this volume.

We could also lament those background variables that appear in none or few of the reported studies. Religion, for example, is strangely absent. Surely religion was for many a critical component of their identification with Kennedy. But such lament could be endless; no study measures every variable someone might want.

Let us now see what relationships there may be between the response classes and the background variables of sex, race, age, social class, and political preference. The data focus on three aspects of response to the assassination: attention and exposure to the news, physical and emotional symptoms immediately and some time after the event, and attitudes toward the assassination and related events.

Sex differences in responses to the assassination

Men and women differed both in how they first heard the news and in their subsequent use of mass media and interpersonal communication. These differences appear to be a function of the different social roles of men and women.

At the time of the shooting, women were more likely to be at home and men were more likely to be at work (Bonjean, Hill, and Martin). Women had more access to mass media, and so tended to hear about the events sooner, and either to hear about them on television or to turn to television after first hearing about them (Bonjean, Hill, and Martin; Greenberg). Men depended more on other persons, principally co-workers, for the first news of the assassination. For confirmation, the men typically turned to radio, which was the more accessible medium for them (Greenberg). Women tended to pass the first news of the assassination on to others more frequently than men. The importance of that role was minimized, however, by the speed of the diffusion. If there had not been so many communication channels providing the same assassination news, the earlier awareness of women and their subsequent interpersonal actions might have been more important. As things were, they had little opportunity to influence perceptions of the day's events. They concentrated their interpersonal activity in the first moments after the assassination was announced. As the weekend continued, men asserted themselves in interpersonal channels. By the time the data were gathered, men had discussed the assassination with more people on more occasions in more settings than women (Greenberg). Women had six to eight hours more television exposure than men, or an additional full day before the set, during the three and a half days of broadcasting. Only among teen-agers and young children does this viewing difference vanish.[3]

Women were more upset than men on first hearing of the President's assassination. More women stopped what they were doing (Bonjean, Hill, and Martin). Being at home rather than at work made this easier for them. Beyond this, however, women consistently displayed deeper, more emotional reactions. They reacted with greater sorrow and with a more intense sense of personal loss (Bradburn and Feldman; Bonjean, Hill, and Martin; Coleman and Hollander). They were more shocked and more upset not only by Kennedy's death but also by Oswald's mur-der (Feshbach and Feshbach). Women grieved more than men; they cried, prayed, and generally engaged in more grief-stricken than cogni-tive or evaluative activities (Hurn and Messer). Interestingly, men were more likely to exhibit grief symptoms if they were at work or with others than if they were alone (Hurn and Messer). This suggests that overt grief may be not only facilitated by social reinforcement, but ac-tually stimulated by it. One may feel obligated to display expected emotions, whether one feels these emotions or not. In contrast, if we con-sider symptoms of grief, such as nervousness, difficulty in sleeping, or loss of energy and appetite, the sex difference in these symptoms at the time of the Kennedy assassination was no greater than it was some weeks earlier (Bradburn and Feldman). That is, both men and women showed marked increases in grief symptoms but since they were at different levels to begin with, their increases were equivalent in magnitude.

Women responded to the news of the assassination more vividly and dramatically than men, as they might for most major social disruptions. The responses of men were typically more tempered, or at least were more typically masculine. They drank and smoked more, for example (Bonjean, Hill, and Martin; Coleman and Hollander).

As attitudes and beliefs about the assassination developed, the more intense emotions of the women continued. They turned to religion and prayer more than men did (Bonjean, Hill, and Martin). Their suspicions were more prevalent and extensive; they were more likely to see a Com-munist conspiracy, to see the events as caused by prejudice, to feel less safe and more restless (Coleman and Hollander). Women were more likely to assume collective responsibility for the events, to say "We are

[3] A. C. Nielsen Co., *TV Response to the Death of the President* (issued January 29, 1964).

all responsible." They were more likely than men to say that such occur-
rences are inevitable, and to say that too much lawlessness exists in our
society (Friedman and Pierce-Jones). They were less certain that Oswald was guilty (Friedman and Pierce-Jones), and preferred execution
for Ruby rather than any lighter punishment (Feshbach and Feshbach).

By and large, however, there was little sex difference in beliefs about
the political consequences of the assassination (Bradburn and Feldman;
Coleman and Hollander), despite the generally greater interest among
men in those political consequences (Bonjean, Hill, and Martin).

Age differences in responses to the assassination

Younger persons used personal channels somewhat more than older
persons to diffuse information about the assassination. Those in their
40's or younger were more likely than older persons to hear the news
first from other persons. Differences in use of interpersonal channels
during the rest of the weekend are more marked for different age groups:
37 per cent of those in their 20's, 24 per cent of those in their 30's, 22
per cent of those in their 40's, and 15 per cent of those over 50 had
twenty or more separate conversations with as many different persons
(Greenberg).

Nielsen reports that both younger heads of households (under 54)
and younger housewives (under 50) averaged about four more hours
of viewing over the weekend than older people. But when one looks at
the whole public rather than at heads of households, the correlation between age and viewing is positive. Both men and women from 18 to 34
watched television about eight to ten hours *less* than those over 34. Viewing time apparently reduced conversation time. Adults over 34 watched
television for an average of 26 hours in the three and a half days, those
from 18 to 34 watched for 16 hours, children from 12 to 17 watched for
18 hours, those from 6 to 11 watched for 15 hours, and the smallest
children, from 2 to 5 years old, watched for an average of 8 hours.

The reactions of different age groups to the assassination were not
compared in these studies. Yet Kennedy was widely considered to be the
focus for many young adults' political energies. If he was, those young
adults could be expected to respond more intensely and to be more concerned about the future. However, there is very little to distinguish the
emotions, feelings, and behavior of young adults from those of older

adults. The responses of college undergraduates (Greenstein) corresponded quite closely with those of older people in various occupational groups (Barber). Greenstein's students required immediate media confirmation when they first heard of the shooting. Their responses included disbelief, shock, and intense emotion. They compared his death with deaths of persons close to them. They responded to Kennedy as President, to his personality, to his policies, to his family. All these responses were also found by Barber and were quite apparent in the reactions of the national sample (Sheatsley and Feldman). The major activity of Greenstein's subjects was communication. They turned to both mass media and interpersonal channels, as did older citizens (Sheatsley and Feldman; Bonjean, Hill, and Martin). Some of the researchers contend that this very commitment to communication made possible the rapid social recovery from the assassination (Schramm; Mindak and Hursh; Barber). Coleman and Hollander believe communication was critical in forming the remarkable consensus of beliefs and attitudes about most aspects of the assassination.

What were the reactions of children and young adolescents? Two studies asked parents to estimate how much their children between the ages of 4 and 12 were upset by the assassination. In one, 23 per cent said their children were very upset, 45 per cent said they were somewhat upset, and 30 per cent said they were not upset at all (Sheatsley and Feldman). In another survey, 21 per cent said their children were very upset, and 33 per cent said their children were not upset (Bonjean, Hill, and Martin). Each study found that two-thirds of the parents attempted to explain to the children what had happened, most frequently by merely passing on factual information without any guided interpretation. Neither of these studies asked about the responses of children in their early teens. Sheatsley and Feldman assumed such responses would correspond closely to parental reactions. The findings of these two studies suggest that young children were considerably less upset than their parents. However, Sigel's data, obtained from children in the fourth through twelfth grades, contradict that conclusion. Parents thought their children were not upset; the children themselves indicated they were at least as upset as their parents, if not more.

Sheatsley and Feldman found that a majority of adults felt very deep sorrow for Kennedy's wife and children (92 per cent), shame that this

could happen in our country (83 per cent), the loss of someone close
(79 per cent), and anger about the deed (73 per cent). No other item
received this response from a majority of adults. Sigel found that children's responses to the same four items were equally intense (93, 83,
71, and 82 per cent, respectively). In addition, she found that a majority
of children were worried about what would happen to our country, what
would happen to our relations with other countries, and how the U.S.
would carry on without its leader.

The incidence of physical symptoms reported by children was quite
similar to that reported by adults, except for the tendency to cry (or at
least willingness to report crying). Over half the adults reported crying
(Sheatsley and Feldman), but only 39 per cent of the children did
(Sigel). Loss of appetite, headaches, upset stomachs, and difficulty in
sleeping were reported equally for adults and children. Crying, of course,
is generally frowned upon as a social response. Some children may have
denied crying because of parental and peer-group pressure not to be
demonstrative in that manner. As Sigel says, "If we are to believe the
children, 81 per cent of all the crying was done by girls." This kind of
inhibition appears in another fashion among college students. They frequently attributed to others desires that they personally denied, for example, wanting to call home and wanting to see Oswald killed (Greenstein). The greatest discrepancy between adults and children was in the
expression of punitive feelings toward Oswald. Forty per cent of the
children wanted him shot or beat-up, whereas only 11 per cent of the
adults felt this way. The younger the child was, the more aggression he
showed. Further, the children were at a distinct disadvantage in trying
to understand why Oswald did it; 38 per cent of the children, compared
with 15 per cent of the adults, could not cite a reason. Children were also
less able to entertain any conspiracy notions; more of them said he
acted alone. In general, these data indicate that elementary school children from the fourth grade on were at least as emotionally involved in
the weekend's events as their parents.

Social-class differences in responses to the assassination

Some investigators stratified their respondents by income levels;
others by education, occupation, or a composite measure of social class.
All these measures will be considered here.

Nielsen reported that as many lower- as higher-income families had their television sets turned on on each of the four days, but that they watched for a total of two to three fewer hours during the four days. The reduced time was on Sunday and Monday, presumably as some tedium set in. Maximum viewing (three more hours) was done by those who had had some or all of high school rather than by the best or least educated. With a different measure of social class, Bonjean, Hill, and Martin also found that middle-class persons (small businessmen and salaried administrative or clerical employees) had more exposure to both radio and television each day. Children of white-collar fathers increased their habitual amount of television viewing more than children of blue-collar fathers (Sigel).

Persons from the higher classes were more likely to use interpersonal channels, both for the first news and for subsequent social intercourse. More high-occupation persons heard that the President had been shot or assassinated from personal sources than from the mass media (Greenberg). Occupational level was positively related to the frequency and diversity of conversations about the assassination (Bonjean, Hill, and Martin; Greenberg). Those in higher-status occupations have a greater variety of social outlets in which person-to-person communication may be used.

In Dallas, middle-class respondents heard about the shooting earlier than upper-class respondents because more of them heard the early radio and television announcements. They were more likely to be alone when they heard about it (Bonjean, Hill, and Martin). Interpersonal contacts were thus inhibited. This finding is probably due to sex differences; the middle-class group in the Dallas sample was mostly women, who were more likely to be at home.

All the studies consistently found an *inverse* relationship between social status and the intensity of feelings and beliefs about the assassination. Working-class and, to some extent, middle-class respondents expressed more intense sadness and sorrow and more extreme opinions than those with upper-class educations, incomes, or occupations. This relationship held for both the immediate responses and the responses a few weeks later, when most passions had somewhat subsided. What those of higher status did was resort to cognitive rather than affective behavior. In a sample of white citizens, the less-educated exhibited more sorrow and a greater sense of personal loss than the more-educated. Educational differences were absent in a comparable Negro sample, but the investigators attribute this to the restricted educational range of that sample (Bradburn and Feldman). Working-class, semiskilled, and un- skilled respondents in Dallas were described as considerably more upset than upper-class respondents on several response categories. They also felt more like being left alone, whereas upper-class respondents went to church and prayed (Bonjean, Hill, and Martin). On a set of questions designed to examine consensus in beliefs, the more-educated uniformly were less likely to see any particular cause of the assassination, were less likely to give extreme responses, shifted less away from their previous attitudes, and revealed the least passion. Coleman and Hollander attrib- ute these differences to the "civilizing effect" of education.

Another aspect of this class distinction may be inferred from Barber's study. Of his eight groups, only one—the group of service-club mem- bers—consisted of high-status or high-occupation persons. The others were laundrywomen, cooks, firemen, truck drivers, and so on. The serv- ice-club members were the major deviant group in his analysis of the stages of recovery from the assassination. They consistently exhibited fewer emotional responses. Barber thought this tendency was partly the result of guilt feelings about having opposed many Kennedy programs.

Differences in social class apparently did not cause the same differ- ences in physical reactions to the assassination that they did in cognitive ones. Better- and less-educated cried in almost equal numbers, were as nervous as each other, showed equal loss of appetite, etc. (Bradburn and Feldman; Bonjean, Hill, and Martin; Hurn and Messer).

Class differences were related to opinions about the long-range im- pact of the assassination, and to the incidence of conspiratorial notions about the assassination. Working-class respondents felt no good would come from any of these misfortunes; upper-class respondents spoke of the assassination's uniting the country. The former spoke of the nega- tive impact on their own lives and jobs; the latter spoke of the blame and collective responsibility that belonged to everyone (Bonjean, Hill, and Martin). In another study, high-status persons gave more rededicatory responses. They spoke of improving their lives, promoting brotherhood, and becoming better citizens. Those with lower status asked for tighter security measures or recommended more restrictions on extremist ac- tivity (Hurn and Messer).

The major contradiction we have found in these studies is in the re- lationships between the respondents' class and the punishments they recommended for Ruby. In Thread City, blue-collar workers (33 per cent) and the less-educated (28 per cent) favored capital punishment for Ruby more than white-collar workers (13 per cent) and the college-educated (6 per cent). These data also show that the lower-status persons preferred more repressive actions in the conduct of public affairs (Lipsitz and Colfax). More children of blue-collar families preferred to see Oswald shot or beat-up than children of white-collar families (Sigel). The contradiction is that the Dallas investigators report that 30 per cent of their upper-class, 17 per cent of their middle-class, and 10 per cent of their working-class group demanded Ruby's execution (Bonjean, Hill, and Martin). There may be a regional basis for this difference, although the Dallas data closely resemble those from the national sample on all major findings, as Tables 1 and 2 show. Lower-status respondents in Dallas may have identified with Ruby as a vicarious outlet for their punitive feelings toward Oswald. Higher-status respondents, perhaps more concerned about Dallas's image, may have resented Ruby's damaging their city's reputation more. Another study found that college students from Texas felt no more sympathy for Ruby than college students from other parts of the country (Friedman and Pierce-Jones).

A special analysis of NORC data by Bradburn shows that there is the same inverse relationship between class and recommendation of punishment for Oswald also. This appears in the national sample, separately for white and Negro subsamples. Generally, those with lower status were more prone to extreme beliefs and opinions. Those with higher status offered more tempered, less primitive responses, and were less likely to harbor suspicions about a conspiracy.

Political differences in responses to the assassination

Nine of the studies in this volume emphasized the role of political preferences in the responses to the assassination. Although the evidence relating mass media exposure and diffusion of information to political classifications is meager, there is consistent evidence that opponents of Kennedy, whether Republicans or Southern Democrats, watched less television during the four days than Kennedy supporters (Feshbach and Feshbach; Sheatsley and Feldman). In fact, children who would have voted Democratic had they been old enough also watched more television than their Republican counterparts (Sigel). Adult Republicans watched about six hours a day, adult Democrats about eight to ten hours a day (Sheatsley and Feldman).

Anderson and Moran investigated the effects of party preference and of political opinions on perception of bias in the media coverage. Although fully 66 per cent of the respondents said no bias existed (which compares well with the 60 per cent of the Mindak and Hursh sample who said TV did nothing poorly), the bias perceived by the rest was highly correlated with their political predispositions. Nearly half described the perceived bias as pro-Kennedy; another 11 per cent said it was generally manipulative in nature. Perception of bias was related to party preference; 35 per cent of the Republicans and 28 per cent of the Democrats said the media were slanted. It was also related to the intensity of the preference; among the stronger party supporters, the proportions were 42 per cent and 23 per cent, respectively. A person's opinion of Kennedy was more significant than his party loyalty. Of those who thought favorably of Kennedy, regardless of party preference, only 25 per cent criticized the media; 67 per cent of those who thought poorly of Kennedy criticized the media. Those who generally supported the administration in political arguments saw less bias, as did those who had seen Kennedy in person and were more impressed than they had expected to be.

The immediate emotional and physical effects of the news were far greater on Kennedy partisans. They reported more crying, difficulty in sleeping, nervousness, enervation, and numbness (Sheatsley and Feldman; Bonjean, Hill, and Martin). Each of these symptoms was reported by half or more of all Democrats, and by 5 to 25 per cent fewer Republicans. Of the fifteen symptoms examined, the Republicans exceeded the Democrats only in the desire to get drunk (Bonjean, Hill, and Martin). Democratic children also did more crying, were more upset, and were generally more "mixed up" (Sigel).

Republicans were less upset not only over the Kennedy assassination, but also over the Oswald slaying. Kennedy supporters were more upset at first, and were upset for a longer time (Sheatsley and Feldman). Seven of Barber's eight informal groups were probably Democratic. It was the eighth that appeared to be less emotional and more inhibited.

Political preferences were similarly related to immediate beliefs and attitudes about the assassination events. In a study of changes in belief immediately and during several weeks after the assassination, Coleman and Hollander found that people who had voted for Nixon formed less extreme beliefs, and subsequently changed them less, than those who had voted for Kennedy. In other studies, Democrats responded to Kennedy's death more as to that of a family member than as to that of a national figure—the loss was more personal, the sorrow was greater (Bonjean, Hill, and Martin; Sheatsley and Feldman). Democratic children also expressed more thoughts about losing someone close to them (Sigel). Democrats worried more about their own jobs and lives as well as about the country's future and its relations with other countries (Bonjean, Hill, and Martin).

Democrats were more likely than Republicans to ascribe general blame, to say "We are all responsible." They were less likely to doubt that Oswald was guilty, and more likely to perceive lawlessness in contemporary society, and to believe that tragedies of this order were to be expected and that the lawless South created public disrespect for the law (Friedman and Pierce-Jones). These same attitudes were cross-classified in terms of conservative and liberal beliefs about politics, race relations, and economics. The results corresponded very closely to those obtained for political preference. Liberals in all three areas were more aware of collective responsibility and attributed more responsibility to social lawlessness than conservatives. The political and economic liberals were more fatalistic about the events. Economic and race-relations liberals not only gave even more weight to the idea of collective responsibility, but also blamed the South in general more than conservatives (Friedman and Pierce-Jones). A similar pattern emerges from the study of grief and rededication to social values (Hurn and Messer). Those who thought Kennedy was doing a good job exhibited significantly more grief. When asked what should be done to prevent any repetition of this kind of event, they also talked about the promotion of brotherhood and better citizenship.

In Sears's study of the influence of the assassination on political partisanship, party positions on hypothetical bills were experimentally manipulated. The assassination reduced the partisanship of both strong and weak Republicans, but more for the weaker. The influence of their own party decreased, and that of the Democratic party increased. There was more general acceptance of previously objectionable political leaders; their influence also was enhanced by the President's death. Interestingly enough, Republicans unanimously thought there should be a moratorium on politics or partisan issues; only a third of the Democrats thought this was necessary.

What is most apparent about these relationships between political preferences and responses to the assassination is that political predispositions functioned almost as they function in less dramatic circumstances. Exposure to information followed partisan lines. Evaluation of that information followed partisan lines. Intensity of response was greater among those partisans for whom the stimulus was most salient. Selective attention, selective perception, and selective retention were all functioning.

Racial differences in responses to the assassination

Many studies in this volume found differences between the reactions of Negro and white Americans. The differences supported the general hypothesis that Negroes would be particularly affected by the murder of a man who advocated civil rights progress and acted accordingly. It was known that many Negroes identified very strongly with Kennedy, as well as that eight out of every ten of them had voted for him in 1960. Yet, the overwhelming reaction by the vast majority of Americans, Negro and white alike, also suggests that it was not race that produced differential reactions as much as political preference or personal preference for Kennedy. That is, given the nearly unanimous liking of Kennedy by Negroes, their responses could be shown to be not particularly dissimilar to those of white Democrats who favored Kennedy. It appears that if race were held constant, the differences caused by political predispositions would remain unchanged; on the other hand, if political predispositions were held constant, racial differences would be minimal. Negro responses were more like those of white pro-Kennedy Northerners than those of any other regional or political group (Sheatsley and Feldman).

White respondents in Dallas watched more television than Dallas Negroes (Bonjean, Hill, and Martin). This may not have been a matter of choice however. Whereas 15 per cent of the general public said it was not able to watch as much television as it wanted to, twice that percentage of Negroes said this (Sheatsley and Feldman). More Negroes probably had to work that weekend. In fact, the one segment of the Negro population that did have available time—Negro children—watched significantly more television than their white counterparts (Sigel).

White respondents also talked to more people about the assassination (Bonjean, Hill, and Martin; Sheatsley and Feldman). It is likely that their occupations and their social positions facilitated such contacts. They also heard the news sooner (Bonjean, Hill, and Martin). Negroes tended to be alone at the time they heard the news, were more likely to get it first from mass media channels, and expressed greater desire to remain alone or with their immediate families than to seek any broader social outlets (Bonjean, Hill, and Martin; Sheatsley and Feldman).

Negroes showed more sorrow, a greater sense of personal loss, and more physical symptoms than white respondents (Bradburn and Feldman; Bonjean, Hill, and Martin; Coleman and Hollander; Miller and Zimmerman; Sheatsley and Feldman). For example, on the grief index developed by Bradburn and Feldman (a summary measure of changes in sleep, appetite, smoking, crying, etc.), the Negro increase was much greater than that of whites, although both increases were significant.

Negro children were affected in a similar manner. Comparing Negro and white children, Sigel found that the Negro children felt less like eating, had more trouble sleeping, felt they had lost someone close to them, and had most of the other symptoms of their parents.

Many Negroes said they were so upset they did not know what to do. They were more concerned than whites about their own lives, jobs, and futures. Many wondered whether anyone was really safe anymore (Sheatsley and Feldman).

The Negroes' more vivid immediate reactions persisted longer than the reactions of white respondents (Bradburn and Feldman; Coleman and Hollander; Miller and Zimmerman). The intensity of most reactions subsided with time for both Negroes and whites, but Negroes persisted in contending that not too much had been made of the assassination. They continued to be more shocked by it. They saw it more as a disgrace in the eyes of the world (Coleman and Hollander). Bradburn and Feldman speculate that the greater grief of Negroes, who have traditionally been apathetic about politics, means either that this particular event drew out a unique response set or that Negroes are generally emerging from their apathy because of the civil rights movement.

Negroes perceived more than whites the impact of the assassination on civil rights, U.S. prestige, and the general international situation. When the same questions were repeated some weeks later, the decline in remembered impact was less for Negroes (Miller and Zimmerman). Negroes blamed segregationists or Communists for the deed more than they blamed right-wingers (Sheatsley and Feldman), but generally did not know whom to blame (Bonjean, Hill, and Martin). Whites' responses focused more on right-wingers than those of Negroes (Bonjean, Hill, and Martin).

Fear was common among Negroes, but not among whites. One study reports a significant decrease in anxiety responses for white respondents, but not for Negroes. Indeed, Negroes exhibited a slight, though not significant, increase in anxiety symptoms (Bradburn and Feldman). Another study, whose interviews were spaced at longer intervals, stated that those feelings that persisted among Negroes centered on fear or anxiety. Negroes continued to feel unsafe, to perceive considerable political unrest, to see prejudice and hatred around them, and to be more concerned about lack of leadership (Coleman and Hollander). That President Johnson was elected with the nearly unanimous support of American Negroes has probably ameliorated such feelings. But for some time after the assassination Negroes were the only segment of the population that continued to be afraid.

Implications for future research

The articles in this volume have demonstrated some of the advantages of behavioral science research on contemporary historical events. Obviously, we can learn much about ourselves and our society by studying public responses to such events. The usefulness of such research will undoubtedly increase as its techniques are improved. One major disadvantage of collecting data hurriedly after a significant event is that not enough attention can be paid to developing reliable measures of critical variables. Researchers must use measures previously developed or hastily improvised. Given the current state of the art, the measurement of such variables as grief, anxiety, rededication, and political commitment leaves room for considerable improvement. Looking at the data on affective responses to the assassination, one has a nagging suspicion that some of the differences between men and women, or between working-class and middle-class respondents, may be due in part to differences in their tendencies to acquiesce in the statements presented in questionnaires irrespective of the content, or to use more extreme statements habitually rather than as an indication of deeper feeling. As our research techniques become more sophisticated, we can expect more precise measurement in future studies.

Most of the analyses were concerned with demographic variables. Such variables seldom explain the discovered relationships satisfactorily without further analysis. How much do the responses of men and women reflect basic emotional differences, whose origin might be sought in the sexually differentiated socialization of children? How much do they reflect correlation of physical location with social role, for example, with women's being at home and thus being more likely to use mass media than interpersonal communication channels? How much are social-class differences functions of differences in cognitive style, political affiliation, sense of social efficacy, language facility, and so on? Both for their explaining of such demographic differences and for their own sake, we would have liked more use of psychological variables. Although they are harder to measure than demographic variables, the Feshbachs, among others, have demonstrated their utility.

We also would have liked more multivariate analyses. This would have tested various explanations of observed relationships by using control variables that could permit examination of alternative explanations. Differences between whites and Negroes are not explained by mere description. Such differences must be due to characteristics such as education, income, sense of political efficacy, or political preference. Description of differences should be followed by developing and testing general explanations of those differences.

The substantive findings in this volume contain many leads. Which ones are pointed out depend in part on the interests of the pointers. Here we shall draw attention to a few that seem promising to us as communication researchers.

One major aspect of communication to which not enough attention has been paid is the process by which the mass media make decisions about selecting and handling news. Americans get very little of their information by direct observation; they get most of it at second hand from mass communication personnel. What criteria do newsmen use in selecting material to report? Often professional communicators are also not direct observers of what they report; they must depend in turn on information that originates with others. Since little research had been done on the processes that intervene between events and the media reports about them, we included in the first section of this volume descriptions of information processing by the processors themselves. A striking feature of these descriptions is the use, when more direct exposure is lacking, of other newsmen and, in some cases, of other media as reliable sources (for example, Wicker's use of radio and television reports). Studies of the sources newsmen consider to be credible, trustworthy, or expert would help us understand their use of sources. The obvious competitive pressure to report as facts certain statements whose accuracy has not been checked, as in the reports about the make of the rifle Oswald used, could also stand some study. What kinds of statements, given by what kinds of people in what kinds of situations, do newsmen consider newsworthy in themselves, regardless of their validity? Cohen sheds some light on the questions in his study of foreign-policy reporters, but much more research is needed.[4]

How accurate are newsmen's perceptions of their audience? What information do the media have about the amount of information their intended audience has and needs? How much is the intended audience kept in mind during the construction of the messages? In what ways are perceptions of the audience distorted? How much do reporters report for their colleagues and editors rather than for the public? The social pressures that influence the performance of mass media personnel also merits further investigation. A start on this was made in an early study by Breed.[5]

The selection processes themselves make it impossible for any medium to report the "whole truth." This fact is perhaps less obvious for television than for print media. In many ways live television coverage involves much less mediation than printed coverage. On the other hand, television often provides less useful kinds of mediation. It may present a direct picture of the confusion in a police headquarters as a rifle and a can of paraffin are carried aloft down a busy hallway. But, as Pettit pointed out, television is ill-equipped for the interpretive reporting that could find out exactly what these things meant as evidence that might link Oswald to the assassination. One study that compared the perceptions of persons who were at a parade with those of persons who saw it on television showed that the two audiences had quite different pictures of the event.[6] Much more research could be done on the process of selecting content and presenting it on television, and on how the same process differs for print and broadcast journalism. Audience perceptions of the mediation process should also be studied. There is already some evidence that television gives such a sense of direct observation that it misleads segments of the audience about how much mediation there is in both what is shown and how it is shown.[7]

[4] Bernard C. Cohen, *The Press and Foreign Policy* (Princeton, 1963).
[5] Warren Breed, "The Newspaperman, News, and Society" (Ph.D. dissertation, Columbia University, 1952).
[6] Kurt Lang and Gladys Lang, "The Unique Perspective of Television and its Effects: A Pilot Study," in Wilbur Schramm, *Mass Communications* (Urbana, Illinois, 1960).
[7] Richard F. Carter and Bradley S. Greenberg, "Newspapers or Television: Which Do You Believe?" *Journalism Quarterly* (1965), 42, 29–34.

How much are events shaped by the media themselves? The pressures of the mass media had considerable influence on decisions made by the Dallas police department, as it has on many situations in our society. It would certainly be useful to know how public officials are influenced by the media in making decisions, and to examine the social and psychological mechanisms such pressures use.

The growing literature on the diffusion of news, represented by four papers in this volume, has rarely examined the content of the messages that are received. Nor do we know about possible changes in content as messages are passed from person to person. The speed with which the news of the assassination and of Oswald's slaying was diffused did not allow much distortion or interpersonal influence. Usually values are imposed on and transmitted with the information. Studies of the diffusion of news, here and elsewhere, focus on unexpected events rather than anticipated events. Future research should examine such additional aspects of the news diffusion process.

Data on children's responses to the assassination indicate that even very young children were aware of the events and of their implications. The children's responses were surprisingly similar to those of adults, more similar than their parents believed. For children, the event was perceived as a tragedy because of their previous political socialization (all but the youngest were aware who Kennedy was). The assassination coverage taught children more about the political process and how it works. Even without the assassination, children growing up with television undoubtedly know much more than children did a generation ago about political organization and political processes. There has been little empirical research into how children learn about the political system and acquire political beliefs, or into the role of the mass media as a major supplement to parental influence in this process.[8] Children's learning and attitude formation during elections, for example, warrant serious investigation.

Our understanding of both adults and children's responses to the assassination and to other social events would be deepened by an improved understanding of how human beings process information. A man confronted with a change in some element of his environment codes that information in a way that influences his response. His reactions are

[8] For one such study, see Fred I. Greenstein, "Children's Political Perspectives" (Ph.D. dissertation, Yale University, 1959).

shaped in part by his knowledge of how others are reacting (or will probably react) and of how others are expecting him to react. The news of the assassination was highly disruptive. Behavior during the weekend was dominated by exposure to both mass media and interpersonal communication about the event and its implications. Communication channels may have had their "magnetic" attraction during the weekend because people were trying to reestablish some kind of cognitive balance. Those who had better information sources, including wider interpersonal contacts, probably would have had more information about how various people were reacting and restructuring their cognitions. Hence, they would have been better able to arrive at satisfactory cognitive solutions for themselves. The extensive use of communication channels to share responses rapidly may have made possible a general social reorientation.

The communication channels reassured people that the functions of government were being carried on smoothly, that there was no conspiracy, and that there was no further threat. If the content of the consequent communication had not been so reassuring, fear and anxiety might have been magnified to the point of hysteria. We need to know much more about how people process information, about how their attitudes form or change, before we can confidently predict under what circumstances the public response would have been different, or under what circumstances it will be the same for some other event.

Indexes

Subject Index

Name Index